The Cry for Help

Norman L. Farberow, Ph.D., is Co-director of the Suicide Prevention Center at Los Angeles, California; and Investigator at the Central Research Unit, Veterans Administration Center, Los Angeles. Dr. Farberow is also Clinical Associate Professor of Psychiatry (Psychology), School of Medicine, University of Southern California.

Edwin S. Shneidman, Ph.D., is Co-director of the Suicide Prevention Center, Los Angeles, California; Investigator, Central Research Unit, Veterans Administration Hospital, Los Angeles; and also Clinical Associate Professor of Psychiatry (Psychology), School of Medicine, University of Southern California.

THE CRY Edvard Munch

The Cry for Help

edited by
Norman L. Farberow, Ph. D.
Edwin S. Shneidman, Ph. D.

Foreword by Robert H. Felix, M. D.

McGraw-Hill Book Company
New York London Sydney Toronto

First McGraw-Hill Paperback Edition, 1965
5678910 MUMU 7654321
ISBN 07-019943-4

Library of Congress Catalog Card Number: 59-7311

McGraw-Hill Paperbacks

Contributors

HEINZ L. ANSBACHER, PH.D.

THEODORE J. CURPHEY, M.D.

LOUIS E. DE ROSIS, M.D.

SOLOMON DIAMOND, PH.D.

NORMAN L. FARBEROW, PH.D.

SAMUEL FUTTERMAN, M.D.

MAURICE R. GREEN, M.D.

HERBERT HENDIN, M.D.

GEORGE A. KELLY, PH.D.

BRUNO KLOPFER, PH.D.

CALISTA V. LEONARD, M.A.

ROBERT E. LITMAN, M.D.

EDWIN S. SHNEIDMAN, PH.D.

NORMAN D. TABACHNICK, M.D.

To

RUTH S. TOLMAN

whose wisdom and devotion were an inspiration
to all who were privileged to know her

Foreword

Each year approximately eighteen thousand persons in the United States commit suicide. Each year one person in every ten thousand of our population carries out an irrevocable and awful decision to cease to live. Suicide is a major mental health problem in our country, as it is in most of the civilized nations of the world. It is an affliction that robs us of some of the most productive members of our community. It is a form of mental illness that is most disturbing to contemplate, a mental illness in which the anguish and terror of the victim lead him to prefer death to his suffering.

The most promising approach to the problem of suicide, in fact the only practical approach, is prevention. As we learn to recognize the danger signals of impending suicide, and as we marshal our medical and social resources to help the potential suicide, we can begin to make substantial progress in coping with this distressing problem. The work of the Suicide Prevention Center in Los Angeles has been most promising in this respect. In cooperation with mental health and other agencies in the community, the Center has had signal success in treating the suicidal patient. It has also carried out important basic research which hopefully will improve our ability to deal with the problem of suicide.

The title of this volume, *The Cry for Help,* symbolizes the work of the interdisciplinary team of therapists and researchers at the Suicide Prevention Center. They have listened to the cry for help, and they have searched for new ways to provide the needed help. The results of their clinical and research activities, as reported in this volume, will, I hope, stimulate other communities to establish suicide prevention facilities and encourage further basic work in this most important mental health problem area.

Robert H. Felix, M.D.
President, American Psychiatric Association
Director, National Institute of Mental Health
U.S. Public Health Service

Preface

The phenomenon of suicide presents problems in many areas—legal, ethical, philosophical, and moral. As a matter of considerable concern for public health, suicide continues to rank high in the list of "killers," as evidenced by the fact that it is among the first ten causes of death in almost half our states and that it continues officially (and conservatively) to claim from fifteen to twenty thousand lives each year in the United States. Society's attitudes and feelings toward the considerable waste of life and potential human resources have been manifested with considerable variability from early recorded history to the present, ranging from severe condemnation (as in stern Catholic prohibitions and old English laws against *felo de se*) to acceptance and incorporation as a way of life (as in the Japanese samurai code of seppuku and the Indian custom of suttee). The phenomenon of suicide has received much less attention than it has merited, although there seems to be a trend currently discernible that may well be a reflection of a growing psychological orientation in our culture to view such activities as the behavior of persons under psychosocial duress and to seek to understand the motivations underlying these behaviors within the milieu in which they occur.

But as a complex psychologic, psychiatric, and sociologic phenomenon, suicide has been accorded surprisingly little investigation and analysis. In our previous book, *Clues to Suicide,* attention was focused on the varied complexities of the whole gamut of suicidal behavior and ideation. This present book represents part of our continuing activities in the area of suicide research but focuses particularly on the responses by the community and by individual theoretician-practitioners to the suicidal cry for help, attempting to understand suicide in terms of the communication of inter- and intrapersonal factors.

The communication aspects of suicide help to unify the contents of this volume. The title, *The Cry for Help,* is meant to convey our feelings (from our work with suicidally disturbed persons) about the messages of suffering and anguish and the pleas for response that are expressed by and contained within suicidal behaviors. Yet society, perhaps because of the very nature of the phenomenon and the kinds of feelings evoked by suicidal activity, has tended to deny its very existence. Some examples of the responses society has made are presented in Part I, "The Community Response to the Cry for Help." This part describes agencies that have been established in the community of Los Angeles and in other communities throughout the world specifically to respond to the suicidal cry, elaborates some of the emergency techniques for evaluating and treating suicidal persons that have been developed by the Suicide Prevention Center in Los Angeles, and indicates some of the special problems and procedures that have been initiated in the Los Angeles County Coroner's office in the handling of equivocal suicidal cases.

Individual practitioners have been, of course, responding to the suicidal cry for help for some time. Part II, "The Therapeutic Response to the Cry for Help," reflects the approaches of several theorist-clinicians, in terms both of theoretical formulations about the personality in which suicidal processes occur and of therapeutic techniques that may be employed. The basic interests of these contributors are personality theory and the implications for treatment of suicidal behavior. Part III contains a bibliography on suicide which covers the years from 1897 through 1957. These are, of course, the communications about suicide which represent the thought, effort, understanding, creativity, and imagination expended on the topic for the past sixty years. The bibliography should serve the purpose of providing the reader with the references to all these writings in one readily available place.

The diversity in the nature of the material in the first two parts expresses what we feel to be a desirable cross-disciplinary multifaceted approach to the problem of suicide. Some will see in this diversity the old argument of pure science versus applied science, of theory versus practice, etc.

We are reminded of the wise words of Ruth Tolman, to whom this volume is dedicated, who, in her presidental address to the Western Psychological Association (*American Psychologist,* 8:721–733, 1953), discussing the virtues and vices of contemporary psychology, said:

> Now "amity" is represented by two fine, upstanding fellows moving their plows evenly together across a fertile field, leaving behind them two long, neat rows of black, rich, upturned earth. It is this amity, which might also be called harmony or friendly cooperation, that I should like to discuss. The two men with the plows in our little game will be in psychology the "pure" scientist and the "applied"; or the theoretician and the professional practitioner. I am going to contend that psychology cannot afford to separate these two right now.

Some of the chapters in this volume were originally presented in a symposium (Symposium on Theory and Therapy in Suicide) at the American Psychological Association convention in New York, September, 1957. In this symposium (in which the original members were Drs. Ansbacher, Farberow, Hendin, and Klopfer), the same case, of an attempted suicide, was analyzed from the point of view of different theoretical orientations. Once publication had been decided upon, five additional contributors (Drs. De Rosis, Diamond, Futterman, Green, and Kelly) were invited to add their specific points of view. The orientation and background of each contributor is described in a short biography preceding his chapter. The complex phenomenon of suicide lends itself, of course, to many interpretations and formulations and to varied techniques in the handling and treatment of suicidal persons. These have not heretofore been collected in one place for the practitioner, theoretician, or interested lay person. Part II attempts to fill this need.

It is hoped that the contents of this volume will be of value to persons of varied interests: psychiatrists, psychologists, sociologists, coroners, social workers, ministers, etc.; in short, theoreticians and practitioners in the broad range of human psychopathology.

As before, we wish to express our sincere appreciation to the several organizations who have been actively cooperative and helpful to us in our work on suicide: the Veterans Administration, which by fostering an intellectual climate of free inquiry and research has given direct stimulus to our efforts; the U.S. Public Health Service, which has continued to support our efforts through research and project grants; the Los Angeles County Coroner's office, and specifically Coroner Theodore J. Curphey, M.D., who has been actively cooperative in every way possible; the Los Angeles County General Hospital, where our interest in this field has been nurtured by the hospital's assistance. In addition, sincere appreciation is acknowledged to Eunice H. Pierce, who, as our secretary, made the thousand and one detailed problems inevitable in the undertaking of a book disappear by her efficiency and devotion; to Erma Bley, Jacqueline Bailey, Sabina Poole, and Inez Tweed, for their aid in typing; and to Alcon Devries, for his considerable assistance in statistical procedures and computations.

A word about the frontispiece: The engraving "The Cry" is by Edvard Munch (1863–1944), eminent Norwegian artist, who was the subject of a book by Frederick B. Deknatel (New York: Chanticleer Press, 1950). Appreciation is extended to the Chanticleer Press for permission to reproduce this illustration and to Drs. Stanley Steinberg and Joseph Weiss, who provided us with the engraving, which they reproduced in their article "The Art of Edvard Munch and Its Function in his Mental Life" (*Psychoanalytic Quarterly*, 23:409–423, 1954). The original work is in the Lessing J. Rosenwald Collection, Gallery of Art, Washington, D.C.

Norman L. Farberow
Edwin S. Shneidman

Contents

PART III BIBLIOGRAPHY

PART I

The Community Response to the Cry for Help

I

Introduction

NORMAN L. FARBEROW AND EDWIN S. SHNEIDMAN

Society has, for many thousands of years now, taken various positions in relation to the subject of suicide, particularly about society's responsibilities toward suicidal behavior. Today in societies throughout the world, attitudes toward suicide range from complete condemnation through mild disapproval to acceptance and incorporation as one of the mores of communal life. Just as there are differences between societies, there are also differences of attitude toward suicide within a society over a period of time. The history of attitudes toward suicide makes fascinating reading and provides the sociologist, cultural anthropologist, and professional mental health worker with a useful background against which to view the suicidal phenomena of today.[1]

Nevertheless, in spite of the variety, there is no question but that the predominant attitude of civilized society toward suicide today is one of condemnation. Perhaps one of the best proferred explanations of why this is so is contained in Fedden's *Suicide* (London, 1938), in which he states that suicide is condemned mainly because it is a form of *lèse-majesté*. Fedden indicates (p. 42):

> Suicide shows a contempt for society. It is rude. As Kant says, it is an insult to humanity in oneself. This most individualistic of all actions disturbs society profoundly. Seeing a man who appears not to care for the things which it prizes, society is compelled to question all it has thought desirable. The things which makes its own life worth living, the suicide boldly jettisons. Society is

[1] The reader is referred to such books as Dublin and Bunzel's *To Be or Not to Be;* Williams' *The Sanctity of Life and the Criminal Law;* and Shneidman and Farberow's *Clues to Suicide,* for reviews of the literature and legal (societal) points of view regarding suicide. (See Bibliography, Part III, for complete references.)

troubled, and its natural and nervous reaction is to condemn the suicide. Thus it bolsters up again its own values.

There are different suicide rates from various national groups (as reported by, for example, the World Health Organization). We agree with the often-stated assertion that the statistics on committed suicides are on the conservative side and that the figures are undoubtedly made low because of the pervasive social pressures against the certification of a death as suicidal in most parts of the world. Statistics for attempted suicides are even less available because, contrary to deaths, which usually have to be reported in some category, they often do not become part of any official record. There have been many comparative estimates of the number of attempted suicides, the usual estimate being that attempted suicide is around six times as frequent as committed suicide. Our own work has shown that the rate of attempted suicide for Los Angeles County for 1957 was 111.4 per 100,000 population, about eight times the rate of committed suicide, which was 14.5 per 100,000 population. (The national U.S. suicide rate for 1957 was 9.8 per 100,000 population.)

All suicide, whether committed or attempted, involves tremendous disruption of life, emotional turmoil, social discord, etc. Yet, as Dr. Menninger stated in the foreword to our previous book, *Clues to Suicide* (p. *v*):

> To the normal person, suicide seems too dreadful and senseless to be conceivable. There almost seems to be a taboo on the serious discussion of it. There has never been a wide campaign against it, as there has been against less easily preventable forms of death. There is no organized public interest in it. . . . In many instances [it] could have been prevented by some of the rest of us.

Many other investigators have pointed out the presence of communication elements in suicidal behavior, so it appears that in many cases the opportunity exists for elements within the community to respond to the plea for assistance. In general, the number of responses remains distressingly low. It is a sincere hope of the editors and contributors to this book that their efforts will stimulate further organized response on the part of many persons in numerous communities.

Part I describes some of the responses by communities to the suicidal cry for help. The chapters are divided into three groups, with Chapters 2 through 6 reporting some phases of our research and demonstration projects. Chapter 2 describes the Suicide Prevention Center, its procedures, its operations, its functions, and its goals. This is a project that has been set up in Los Angeles with the support of a U.S. Public Health Service project grant to help persons who have attempted suicide. Chapter 3 reports a survey of Los Angeles County that was conducted in order to determine the number and characteristics of the population of attempted suicides, a group for whom accurate statistics had heretofore not been available. Chapters 4 and 5 describe in detail some clinical procedures that have evolved in the operation of the Suicide Prevention Center relative to the assessment and evaluation of self-destructive potentialities. Chapter 6 presents information that will be useful to mental hospital staffs in the identification of the suicidal patient. These data were obtained from analyses of records of schizophrenic patients who committed suicide as compared systematically with similar records of schizophrenic patients who did not kill themselves.

Chapters 7 through 9 refer to the activities of the Suicide Prevention Center staff in its unique liaison with the coroner's office in Los Angeles County. In Chapter 7, Dr. Theodore J. Curphey, Los Angeles County Coroner, describes the operations and responsibilities of the coroner's office and indicates how the social scientist can play a significant role in obtaining data relevant to the certification of suicide. Chapter 8 gives some sample investigations made by the Suicide Team, focusing on the motivational aspects of deaths that are equivocal as to mode. Chapter 9 presents some of the reflections about the current taxonomy of death that coroners are required to use in their certifications and presents a psychologically oriented taxonomy for consideration.

Chapter 10, rather than describing activities being carried out in the Los Angeles community, describes the activities of several agencies that are now (or had been) functioning in various parts of the world whose main focus is to respond to the suicidal cry for help.

2

The Suicide Prevention Center

EDWIN S. SHNEIDMAN, NORMAN L. FARBEROW,
AND ROBERT E. LITMAN

The number of active suicide prevention agencies in the United States might be counted on the fingers of two hands, and within many communities the number of facilities available for ongoing suicide prevention activities is nil. The basic question in any community is whether or not there are adequate facilities for dealing with the important other-than-purely-medical aspects of individual suicide attempts. It was in an effort to give at least a partial positive answer to this question in one specific metropolitan area that the Suicide Prevention Center (hereinafter referred to as the SPC) was initiated. The need for community organizations established specifically to explore new avenues leading to more effective suicide prevention programs would seem to be evident. In 1958, under the purview of a five-year U.S. Public Health Service project grant (administered through the University of Southern California), the SPC was established in the Los Angeles community. The purposes of this chapter are to indicate the goals of the SPC and how it attempts to achieve these aims and to describe SPC operations and functions.

Considering the magnitude and seriousness of suicide as a public health problem, it is remarkable how little organized work has been done to further the basic understanding and prevention of suicide. The primary aims of the SPC have to do, of course, with both long-range and immediate prevention of suicide. The three main goals of the SPC are as follows: (A) The primary goal of SPC activities is to save lives. The selection, diagnostic, referral, and therapeutic activities of the SPC are conducted with this goal in mind. We shall refer to this activity as the *clinical aspect* of the SPC. (B) Another aspect of SPC activities is to establish the SPC as one of the public health agencies in the Los Angeles area. These activities focus on the integration and liaison of the SPC with such other agencies in the community as the city health department, the county health department, the police department, the Welfare Planning Council, and the coroner's office. We shall refer to these activities as the *community aspect* of the SPC. (C) A concomitant SPC goal is to utilize its psychiatric, psychological, and social work data, obtained from a variety of suicidal types, to test various hypotheses concerning suicidal phenomena. We shall refer to these activities as the *research aspect* of the SPC.

The remainder of this chapter will describe in detail each of the three major functions indicated above: to save lives, to integrate with other agencies within the community, and to obtain important, systematically organized data that can be employed in research designs.

CLINICAL ASPECT

Obviously, suicide prevention efforts must be directed toward living persons before they kill themselves. The question arises whether or not there is, usually, a preliminary prodromal phase during which the suicide victim reveals his self-destructive intention. On the basis of recent studies by Robins et al. [6], Dorpat et al. [1, 2], Stengel and Cook [8], Jensen and Petty [4], and the SPC [5, 7], it is possible to conclude that the great majority of suicides do display a recognizable presuicidal phase. The concept is proposed that there exists in the community, at any given period, a population of persons who can be designated as potentially suicidal or presuicidal because they have threatened verbally to commit suicide, or have made recent suicide attempts, or have shown certain specific behavior changes (e.g., the depressive syndrome or sudden increase in barbiturate and alcohol intake) that are prodromal for suicide. Cases for direct anti-suicide efforts would come from this group of presuicidal persons on the presumption that it would include within it, as a smaller subgroup, a good proportion of those who will actually commit suicide.

Relatively little is now known about the total number, range, and characteristics of the population of presuicidal persons. At what rate do individuals leave this population and new persons enter? What happens eventually to most presuicidal persons? Do presuicidal persons tend to repeat suicidal behavior from time to time over the years? Do they usually seek help from physicians? What proportion see psychiatrists? If suicide attempts and suicide threats were made reportable conditions, some major gaps in our knowledge could be filled, but, unfortunately, according to Los Angeles city and county public health authorities, it is impossible at this time to make these conditions reportable. Meaningful statistics on self-destructiveness can be derived from hospital records only with maximal research effort, for there is no code number in the standard nomenclature of medical diseases for suicide, suicide attempts, or suicide threats. Relatively few hospitals use a special code number for suicide or suicide attempts, whereas others do not designate suicidal behavior in any way on the charts but code only the nature of the injury.

At present, at least three methods are being employed by the SPC to obtain needed data on presuicidal persons. These are (A) surveying the physicians in the community, using questionnaire and interview techniques; (B) abstracting large numbers of charts from emergency hospitals, general hospitals, and psychiatric hospitals; and (C) accumulating detailed case materials at the SPC. In addition, information about persons who have committed suicide has been collected through interviews with surviving relatives, friends, physicians, and other informants. Eventually, it should be possible to compare data from four main groups: committed suicides, suicide attempts, suicide threats, and nonsuicidal persons.

Conservatively, as many as six thousand persons make serious attempts at suicide in Los Angeles County each year (see Chapter 3). The SPC is limited for very practical reasons in the number of persons whom it can effectively treat. At present, the primary type of person seen by the SPC, although other types are also seen, is a person who has made a serious suicide attempt *and* who is hospitalized on the wards of the Los Angeles County General Hospital (LACGH) for medical or surgical treatment as a result of the suicidal behavior.[1] Any typical Monday morning, thirty to forty persons who have cut their wrists or throats, shot themselves, taken poison, ingested barbiturates, etc., in more or less lethal suicide attempts may be found on these wards. By and large, persons who have attempted suicide are selected by the SPC for help and for study on the basis of duplicating proportionately the characteristics (as to sex, age, race, religion, socioeconomic distribution, etc.) of the total group of suicide *attempters* in Los Angeles County. The base line for their representative sample was ascertained in our inquiry of physicians and our survey of hospital records (see Chapter 3). The actual selection of a subject for SPC processing is made after an examination of the records by members of the SPC staff, usually including one psychiatrist, one psychologist, and one psychiatric social worker.[2] Once a tentative selection has occurred,

[1] The SPC is presently located on the grounds of the Los Angeles County General Hospital, although it has a separate mailing address: P.O. Box 31398, Los Angeles 31, Calif.

[2] At present the staff of the SPC consists of the following members: two co-project

the patient is interviewed (usually at bedside), and if deemed suitable, processing by the SPC staff is begun. The SPC processing of a subject usually consists of several steps: (A) work-up, (B) contact with collaterals, (C) staffing, (D) referral, and (E) follow-up. The work-up typically consists of two or three hours of psychiatric interviewing, in which the psychiatrist develops at least a partial anamnesis and obtains something of the circumstances of the suicide attempt and some inferences of the psychodynamics of the patient.

Psychological testing is done with a battery that includes the Thematic Apperception Test (TAT), the Make A Picture Story (MAPS) Test, the Sentence Completion Test, the Minnesota Multiphasic Personality Inventory (MMPI), and some special tests in which the patient is asked to write a personality self-description and either to write a duplicate of his suicide note or to compose the suicide note that would have been written. At the same time the social worker may be interviewing important relatives, which may be the spouse, the parents, or the grown children, focusing his attention on interpersonal dynamics, potential psychological and financial resources within the family, and so on. He is also thinking of appropriate agencies or persons to whom to refer the patient (and perhaps the relative also) for treatment. Each patient processed by the SPC is discussed at length (although not presented in person) at a staff meeting in which an attempt is made to comprehend the meaning of the suicidal behavior for that patient, to understand the intrapsychic and interpersonal context within which the suicide attempt occurred, and then to make a realistic referral for treatment. These referrals vary in nature. They may include referral for hospitalization (to the LACGH Psychiatric Unit, a state hospital, a Veterans Administration hospital, or a private hospital); referral to a social agency for family and casework; referral to a clinic or to an individual therapist for group or private psychotherapy; and, on occasion, referral to the SPC itself for either individual psychotherapy or dyadic psychotherapy, in which both husband and wife are taken into individual treatment at the same time. When referrals are made, an attempt is also made to obtain follow-up data so that information can be funneled back to the SPC from the treatment resources, thus permitting the SPC to continue to evaluate the relative effectiveness of various methods of treatments for suicide attempts.

As word of the SPC spread (through advertent and inadvertent publicity), telephone calls, referrals, and consultations concerning persons who have *threatened* suicide have resulted. These calls have come from various

---

directors, a psychiatrist-director, two clinical psychologists, two psychiatric social workers, a biometrician, and a psychological technician.

sources in the community, such as other agencies, physicians, friends, or relatives of the patient, and from the patients themselves. Sometimes these calls could be handled on the telephone simply by sympathetic listening or referral to an appropriate resource, such as agency, physician, minister, friend, or relative. At other times, however, when the situation has seemed to warrant, the caller has been asked to come in and/or bring the patient in for an interview. When the suicidal conflict was such that it was judged to require professional help, appropriate referral was made. When the suicide danger was evaluated as high (see Chapters 4 and 5), no substitute has been found for the safety and other therapeutic advantages of a psychiatric ward. Experience has shown that the recommendation for hospitalization usually meets with some resistance. Even if the resistance is minor and the patient accepts the idea of voluntary hospitalization, he nearly always has some business to transact before he feels he can enter a hospital. At such times one of the social workers has actually accompanied the patient on these errands to make sure that he did get to the hospital.

Generally, in working with patients who had attempted suicide, it became immediately apparent that the individual's interpersonal relationships were very important in precipitating the suicide attempts and that the nature of these continuing relationships was significant in determining the prognosis. Thus a number of cases involving marital and parental relationships could be seen as family neuroses and, as such, could be treated by social work agencies, with the agencies using the SPC as a consultation service in relation to the suicide potentiality.

Further, it was found that dangerous suicidal situations were often denied and repressed by patients and their families and they would reject offers of assistance from the SPC. (Some of the same processes have been found even among members of hospital staffs, with the effect that, on occasion, a patient is discharged prematurely from the hospital.) The SPC has had to develop timesaving techniques for rapid and intensive evaluations of suicidal risk and for prompt and decisive action, when deemed necessary. When the suicidal danger is evaluated as high, the SPC has maintained continued contact through active intervention, including telephone calls and home visits, in order to keep the "bonds" intact between the SPC and the suicide-prone person during the days of crisis.

COMMUNITY ASPECT

One of the goals of the SPC is to fill a gap in the health and service needs of the community. In order to operate with any degree of efficiency within the community, it was found desirable to devote a great deal of attention (especially during the early phases of operation) to integrating the SPC with other health and welfare agencies in the community. With this in mind, exploratory conferences and consultations were held with a number of agencies in the Los Angeles area, including the following: city health department; county health department; police department; fire (rescue) department; Welfare Planning Council; State (of California) Department of Mental Health; county general hospital; city emergency hospitals; county coroner's office; county medical association; Southern California Psychiatric Association; University of Southern California and University of California at Los Angeles medical schools; several of the local hospitals. There was unanimous encouragement and offers of general cooperation. Another result was that LACGH, to whom the SPC owes special thanks, provided office space. As it turned out, these conferences were wise precautions for still another reason. In the course of early SPC activities a number of calls came to these community authorities, inquiring, sometimes suspiciously, about the SPC and what it was doing. Once again we were impressed with the fact that suicide is a taboo and sensitive subject. During the first year of activity, the SPC was in touch with more than fifty community agencies and resources in its efforts to help patients. Once they had checked and discovered that the SPC was reputable, every one of these agencies was cordial and cooperative and helpful to the best of its ability. Several social agencies reversed a policy of the past of not dealing with suicidal persons and worked with the patients that we referred to them. Subsequently, the SPC has received numerous requests for information and brief consultation and acted as a referral service for many cases. The SPC has been asked for consultation opinions on such issues as the following: What should a telephone operator or intake social worker say to persons who threaten suicide over the phone? How should a suicide occurring on a psychiatric ward be handled with the other patients and medical personnel? How can we predict when recovering suicidal patients are ready for discharge? Representatives of the police and fire departments have requested further guidance in their activities with suicidal persons, and there have been numerous questions about emergency 24-hour service. We have considered methods for establishing a 24-hour emergency psychiatric service for suicidal persons but are not at this point able to manage it financially.

In the workaday activities of the SPC, it has become increasingly clear that when any organization attempts to deal with the problems of suicide in a metropolitan community, it does well to have secure relationships with health, welfare, and governmental agencies within that community.

One aspect of the SPC's work with community agencies is unique enough to merit separate description; namely, the relationship with the county coroner's office, and especially with the coroner himself, Theodore J. Curphey, M.D. (see Chapter 7). As background data, it might be mentioned that equivocal cases of "accident-suicide" constitute an important problem area in the coroner's case load. These are cases in which the *cause* of death, as supplied by the coroner's toxicologist or biochemist or microscopist, may be completely clear (as, for example, a lethal dose of pentobarbital), but the *mode* of death, whether accident or suicide, for example, may not be clear at all. The *sine qua non* for suicide is, of course, the intention to destroy oneself, and intention is primarily in the *psychological* domain. Coroner Curphey felt that the social sciences (psychiatry, psychology, and social work) could add a new dimension to the diagnosis of intention, even in a person already dead. He designated the SPC staff members as his Suicide Team. The team's task is to clarify each of the questionable suicide cases. This they do by obtaining a great deal of information from a number of persons (spouse, friends, etc.) who knew the victim, and then reconstructing the *life style* of the deceased and extrapolating over the last days of his life. The empirical data obtained by the SPC staff are reviewed with the coroner at sessions that have been labeled "psychological autopsies," and they do indeed clarify the mode of death in a number of cases. Use of the skills of the psychologically oriented social scientist in the coroner's office has exciting professional significance and far-reaching community mental health implications; it has already demonstrated its use in furthering the mental health of the survivors of the deceased. This development is discussed by Dr. Curphey in Chapter 7, and some cases illustrative of the work of the SPC with the coroner's office are presented in Chapter 8.

An important aspect of community relations has been the dissemination of information about the SPC. Members of the SPC staff have given lectures within the community, have conducted workshops for professional personnel, and have participated in radio and television programs concerning suicide prevention. In addition, the SPC has been publicized in several newspaper and magazine reports. All this has resulted in not only an increased case load but, more importantly, strengthened relations in the community. In appearances before lay groups and in popular presentations in mass media, members of the SPC staff have often taken the occasion to correct commonly believed "facts" about suicide, each one of which is, in reality, false. Taken together, these misconceptions constitute the folklore or mythology of suicide, and it is especially important to dispel these because erroneous beliefs about suicide can have extremely serious consequences. This list of mistaken notions includes the following:

1. *People who talk about suicide won't commit suicide.* Our own studies have shown that, in one group of persons who had committed suicide, fully three-fourths, or around 75 per cent, had previously either attempted or threatened suicide or both. This means that, whether the suicidal act is an attempt or a threat, statistically it must be taken seriously.

2. *Suicide happens without any warning.* One of the most important results of our own studies and of others (like that of Dr. Eli Robins and his associates, in St. Louis) is that the suicidal act generally does not occur suddenly without warning beforehand, but rather that the suicidal person has given many clues, warnings, and indications of his intentions. Alertness and sensitization to these clues will help prevent suicidal behavior.

3. *Improvement after a suicidal crisis means that the suicide risk is over.* Our investigations have shown that almost half the persons who were in a suicidal crisis and subsequently committed suicide did so within 90 days of having passed the emotional crisis and after they had seemed to be on the way to recovery. This is a critical period during which physicians, relatives, and others must be especially cautious and watchful. Improvement is often confused with this (dangerous) increase in psychomotor energy.

4. *Suicide and depression are synonymous.* The statement "I can't understand his doing this, he didn't act like he was unhappy" points to the commonly mistaken belief that suicide occurs only when depression is present. Many suicides show agitation or anxiety, psychosis, organic impairment, or other symptoms. There are other roads to suicide than the avenue of depression. Depression, however, does remain the best single indication of potential suicide.

5. *All suicidal persons are insane.* Our study of over 700 genuine suicide notes indicates that, although the feelings expressed are often intense, disturbed, and varied at the time of the suicidal act, just as frequently the quality of reasoning, judgment, and logic expressed is sound, provided the basic premises are accepted. A large minority of suicides, usually older persons in physical pain, are logical and rational and not psychotic. The majority of persons who commit suicide are tormented and ambivalent; i.e., they are neurotic or have a character disorder, but are not insane. It is circular reasoning to say that suicide is an insane act, and therefore all suicidal persons are insane.

6. *Suicide is a single disease.* It becomes almost immediately apparent that suicide is expressed in various forms and shapes. It appears in all ages,

in both sexes, and in all economic levels. If we view suicide as the ultimate self-destruction, it becomes possible to see this can occur in many degrees, with different meanings, with multitudinous motivations, with various degrees of lethal intent. The first major task in any thoroughgoing scientific study of suicide is the development of a taxonomy or classification of types of suicides.

7. *Suicide is immoral.* Dublin and Bunzel in their book *To Be or Not to Be* [3] and Glanville Williams in his book *The Sanctity of Life and the Criminal Law* [9] give extensive accounts of the ways in which the attitudes toward suicide have changed over the ages culturally, morally, ethically, and religiously. The Greek Stoics approved of suicide, Oriental cultures have sanctioned it, and in some South Sea Islands it is often looked upon as an honorable act. It becomes immediately apparent that whether or not one thinks of suicide as immoral depends on the time and place in which one happens to live. Apparently behavior and customs are neither eternal nor universal.

8. *Suicide can be controlled by legislation.* Authorities point out that legislation against suicide may have two opposite effects: a person may make a more serious attempt so that he will really kill himself and not fall within the clutches of the law; or persons who have made unsuccessful suicide attempts may be discouraged from seeking proper advice and treatment, with the result that there is again an increase in actual number of suicides. There is an interesting comparison on this point between England and Scotland: in the former there are laws against suicide; in the latter there are not; the suicide rate in England is almost twice that of Scotland. On the other hand, legislation concerning specific aspects of suicide prevention (such as those relating to barbiturate prescription) might be well advised.

9. *The tendency to suicide is inherited.* There is no clear evidence that suicide is inherited. The fact that a father and his child have both committed suicide is no more evidence that it runs in families than is the fact that both spoke French, and few would maintain that ability to speak French is inherited. There are some "anniversary suicides," but these are special cases and not the general rule.

10. *Suicide is "the curse of the poor" or "the disease of the rich."* Some social and economic writers have seemed to indicate that suicide covaries almost exclusively with socioeconomic status, some relating suicide to the struggle of the poor and some to the ennui of the rich. Neither argument is borne out by controlled studies, which indicate that almost all strata contribute their prorata share to the over-all suicide rate.

RESEARCH ASPECT

It is a manifest truth that there is a fundamental relationship between clinical practice and research; clinical practice is improved largely through the findings of research efforts. A total program on suicide must therefore not only save lives today but investigate why persons take their lives, so that suicidal behavior can be prevented in the future by increased knowledge concerning its causes. In line with this reasoning, the SPC (while primarily a lifesaving agent) has built within its operations carefully designed research procedures. With this in mind, a specific proportion of staff time is devoted to basic research activities. The data for these studies consist of suicide notes, details of the psychiatric case histories, psychological tests, social service data, information from the coroner's office, ecological and sociological data from the community, etc. (Names of subjects are, of course, never used.) We have been able to formulate a number of specific hypotheses to be tested, and to date the general results of this procedure seem to be promising.

As indicated above, case histories and anamneses are obtained from patients and significant relatives and friends by the professional staff members, and a battery of psychological tests is administered by a clinical psychologist. Much of the information obtained is coded and punched on IBM cards for statistical analysis. In addition, the primary staff member involved in each case completes a standard 100-item true-false form of personality inventory for every case processed. We have been particularly interested in evaluating the degree of suicide danger through such indicators as the psychiatric diagnosis, the effects the patient's communication has on others, the meaning to the patient of his self-destructive behavior, the actual lethality of his behavior, the prominent dynamics, and the self-image (see Chapter 5). Possibly, with the aid of computing machines, we will be able to construct formulas or evolve regression equations for reducing these diverse and complex data to a relatively few comprehensive indices of suicidal danger.

There are also some control data. Persons who have attempted suicide and who are hospitalized in the LACGH but cannot be seen by the SPC staff automatically become the nonseen (control) cases in the over-all activity of the SPC. These cases make it possible to evaluate the effectiveness of this activity. It should be pointed out that the treatment given by the SPC at the LACGH is, of course, in addition to any treatment proferred by the hospital.

The SPC is in the pivotal position of being painfully aware of the many needs within the community in relation to suicide prevention. There are many techniques of active suicide prevention that cannot be employed at present because of limitations of staff time, and there are many obvious research leads that cannot be followed for the same reason. One way to expand our activities would be to obtain additional sources of financial support. Recently, a separate organization, Suicide Prevention Center, Incorporated, was established specifically as a nonprofit organization eligible to receive tax-exempt donations.

After a few years' operation, we believe that some general benefits of a suicide prevention center can be listed. These include the following:

1. Some presuicidal persons receive lifesaving treatment and/or referral who might not otherwise get treatment.

2. Much needed data, especially longitudinal studies of the lives of presuicidal persons, are collected and analyzed.

3. The functioning of a number of different agencies and community resources, where they are concerned with suicide, is facilitated, leading to smoother handling of presuicidal persons.

4. Educational information for police, physicians, judges, and others in a position to recognize presuicidal persons is provided.

5. Proper publicity to help overcome the popular prejudice against psychiatric hospitalization is disseminated.

6. An opportunity for experimental activities, such as a psychiatric emergency call service and the use of supervised volunteers in emergency situations, is provided.

7. Finally, it should be said that such a center demonstrates that there is more to suicide than mental illness. In a sense, self-destruction reflects the relationship of the individual to his community and his civilization. It may be that a certain minimal level or rate of suicide is built into our competitive culture, part of the price we pay for our prized individual freedom to dispose of our lives as we wish. As the SPC develops its operations, we hope to increase our knowledge of suicide, sharpen our diagnostic accuracy, and contribute answers to some of the questions we have raised, but as far as we can see into the future, suicide and suicide prevention will continue to present new problems.

Members of the staff, recognizing the important research function of disseminating information as part of the total SPC activity, have tried to be active in presenting and publishing professional papers. A list of the publications to date of the SPC staff includes the following:

Farberow, N. L. Personality patterns of suicidal mental hospital patients, *Genetic Psychology Monographs,* 42: 3–79, 1950.

Farberow, N. L., and E. S. Shneidman: A study of attempted, threatened, and completed suicide, *Journal of Abnormal and Social Psychology,* 50: 230, 1955.

Farberow, N. L., and E. S. Shneidman: Suicide and the police officer, *Police,* 2: 51–55, 1958.

Farberow, N. L., and E. S. Shneidman: A Nisei woman attacks by suicide, in Georgene Seward (Ed.), *Clinical Studies in Culture Conflict.* New York: The Ronald Press Company, 1958.

Litman, R. E.: Some aspects of the treatment of the potentially suicidal patient, in *Clues to Suicide,* New York: McGraw-Hill Book Company, Inc., Blakiston Division, 1957.

Litman, R. E.: A dream predicting suicide. (Unpublished paper, 1960.)

Litman, R. E., E. S. Shneidman, and N. L. Farberow: A suicide prevention center, *American Journal of Psychiatry* (to be published).

Shneidman, E. S., and N. L. Farberow: Clues to suicide, *Public Health Reports,* 71: 109–114, 1956.

Shneidman, E. S., and N. L. Farberow: Some comparisons between genuine and simulated suicide notes, *Journal of General Psychology,* 56: 251–256, 1957.

Shneidman, E. S., and N. L. Farberow (Eds.): *Clues to Suicide,* New York: McGraw-Hill Book Company, Inc., Blakiston Division, 1957.

Shneidman, E. S., and N. L. Farberow: TAT heroes of suicidal and non-suicidal subjects, *Journal of Projective Techniques,* 22: 211–289, 1958.

Shneidman, E. S., and N. L. Farberow: Suicide and death, in Herman Feifel (Ed.), *The Meaning of Death,* New York: McGraw-Hill Book Company, Inc., Blakiston Division, 1959.

Shneidman, E. S., and N. L. Farberow: A sociopsychological investigation of suicide, in Henry P. David and J. C. Brengelmann (Eds.), *Perspectives in Personality Research,* New York: Springer Publishing Company, 1960.

Shneidman, E. S.: Some logical, psychological and ecological environments of suicide, *California's Health,* 17: 193–196, 1960.

Shneidman, E. S., and N. L. Farberow: Suicide and the aged, *Hearings before the Subcommittee on Problems of the Aged and Aging, Committee on Labor and Public Welfare, United States Senate,* 86th Cong., 1960, part 4, pp. 970–980.

Suicide Prevention Center, Los Angeles: University of Southern California Press, 1960.

Tabachnick, N. D.: Observations on attempted suicide, in E. S. Shneidman and N. L. Farberow (Eds.), *Clues to Suicide,* New York: McGraw-Hill Book Company, Inc., Blakiston Division, 1957.

Tabachnick, N. D.: Interpersonal relations in suicide attempts: A psychodynamic formulation and some indications for treatment, Archives of General Psychiatry, 4: 16–21, 1961.

Tabachnick, N. D.: Some observations on countertransference crises in suicidal attempts, Archives of General Psychiatry (to be published).

References

1. Dorpat, T. L., and J. W. Boswell: Evaluation of suicide intent. (Unpublished paper, 1959.)
2. Dorpat, T. L., H. S. Ripley, and R. Leidig: A study of suicide in Seattle. (Unpublished paper, 1959.)

3. Dublin, L. I., and Bessie Bunzel: *To Be or Not to Be: A Study of Suicide,* New York: Random House, 1933.
4. Jensen, V. S., and T. A. Petty: The fantasy of being rescued in suicide, *Psychoanalytic Quarterly,* 3: 327–339, 1958.
5. Litman, R. E.: A dream predicting suicide. (Unpublished paper, 1960.)
6. Robins, E., J. Gassner, J. Kayes, R. H. Wilkinson, Jr., and G. E. Murphy: The communication of suicidal intent: A study of 134 consecutive cases of successful (completed) suicide, *American Journal of Psychiatry,* 115: 724–733, 1959.
7. Shneidman, E. S., and N. L. Farberow (Eds.): *Clues to Suicide,* New York: McGraw-Hill Book Company, Inc., 1957.
8. Stengel, E., and Nancy Cook: *Attempted Suicide: Its Social Significance and Effects,* Maudsley Monographs no. 4, London: Chapman & Hall, Ltd., 1958.
9. Williams, G. L.: The prohibition of suicide, in G. L. Williams, *The Sanctity of Life and the Criminal Law,* New York: Alfred A. Knopf, Inc., 1957.

3

Statistical Comparisons between Attempted and Committed Suicides

EDWIN S. SHNEIDMAN AND NORMAN L. FARBEROW

The purpose of this chapter is to present the comparative results of a survey of persons who attempted suicide and persons who committed suicide, specifically during the year 1957 in Los Angeles County. Because the data on attempted suicides for a large-scale metropolitan community have been heretofore relatively unavailable (most of the data on this group has been obtained from selected and unavoidably biased sample populations), the characteristics of suicide attempters have generally had to be inferred or extrapolated. This survey, however, presents some empirically derived data about attempted suicide and, in addition, by virtue of obtaining similar data on the person who committed suicide in Los Angeles County during the same period, permits a number of comparisons between the two groups.

In the scientific literature, the terms *suicide* and *suicidal* are often found to have varied and ambiguous meanings. The greatest confusion seems to exist between two specific implications of the term, namely, suicide meaning (A) killing oneself (i.e., committing suicide) and (B) injuring oneself in a suicidelike way with more or less lethal intention (i.e., attempting suicide). Many examples of scientific studies can be given in which nonsuicidal subjects are contrasted with suicidal subjects, the latter consisting of both attempted and committed cases. In these instances, the implicit assumption is that there are no important differences between the attempted and committed groups, the two somehow being rendered similar by the semantic blanket of the word *suicide*. On the other hand, some writers [5, 9] have pointed out that it is dangerous to make assumptions about the relationships between attempted and committed suicide, in that one cannot a priori assume either that they are the same or that they are different. Although there are several noteworthy surveys of committed suicide, the data on attempted suicides are much more sparse. This is probably so because fairly accurate data for attempted suicides are relatively difficult to come by, whereas statistics for committed suicides are relatively easy, often misleadingly easy, to obtain.

The sociological approach to the explication of data on *committed* suicide is, by now, a time-honored tradition. It includes what is probably the best known single work on the topic of suicide, Durkheim's *Le Suicide* [4], which, when it was published in France, in 1897, established a model for sociological research generally. There have been many subsequent studies of this genre. Some of the best known of these are the monographs or books on committed suicide by Cavan [1], Schmid [11, 12, 13], Sainsbury [10], Yap [24], Henry and Short [6], and the compilations of Dublin and Bunzel [3]. All these fall within the ecological tradition of taking a plot of ground—a city or a country—and figuratively or literally reproducing its map several times to show its socially shady (and topographically shaded) areas and their many relationships to suicide rates. We believe that it might be a fundamental methodological error simply to assume that the characteristics of the population that commits suicide are the same as those of the population that attempts suicide. Stengel and Cook, in their (1958) studies of attempted suicide in London (based on subjects admitted to five hospitals), have raised this same question [18]. The matter is definitely one for empirical investigation. The difficulties in obtaining reliable data concerning attempted suicides probably result in large part because persons who do not lose their lives either cover up their own attempts or have their attempts covered up for them by others. Perhaps the best sources of such information would be physicians and hospitals in a large metropolitan community. This is the task to which we, in the study being reported in this chapter, addressed ourselves. Our own motivation in making this study of attempted suicides was to obtain a base line for our operations at the SPC so that our sample of subjects at the SPC would represent pro rata the population of *attempted* suicides in the Los Angeles community.

Data were collected for both completed suicides and attempted suicides for Los Angeles County [1] for the calendar year 1957. For the *completed* suicides, the data were obtained from the Los Angeles coroner's office. By county law, all persons who die by suicide, homicide, or accident or unat-

[1] Los Angeles County has an area of 4,083 square miles and a fairly heterogeneous population of over five million persons. A comprehensive overview of the characteristics of the Los Angeles County population is presented in *Background for Planning* [20].

tended by a physician for 90 days must be certified by the coroner's office. Equivocal cases of suicide (as in deaths by marginal doses of barbiturates in an apparently nonsuicidal person) are currently investigated by the Suicide Team of the SPC, as described in Chapters 2 and 7. In 1957, the certification of suicide was made solely by the coroner and his deputies and may contain unknown errors. Nonetheless, our procedure was to search the coroner's records, make a note of each person indicated as having committed suicide in 1957, and then examine each folder, abstract each case, and translate the data onto our forms. For each case, information was obtained in the following categories: sex, age, race, nativity, marital status, occupation, time in the Los Angeles community, method of suicide, presence or absence of suicide note, serology (especially ethanol), with whom the victim had been living, the type of dwelling (house, apartment, hotel, etc.), and the address.

For the *attempted* suicides, the sources of our data were three: (A) the physicians in the Los Angeles area, (B) the total records for 1957 of the Los Angeles County General Hospital, and (C) the 16 Los Angeles municipal emergency hospitals. We shall describe the data obtained from the physicians first. This type of study, we believe, had never been done before. The greatest untapped source of information about attempted suicides, we thought, was the physicians in the community. It was thought that probably the majority of persons who attempted suicide were seen by their personal or family physicians, were treated medically, and were returned to their routine functioning in the community without any information being recorded in any official document in the community. Our experience in the investigation of committed suicides at the SPC supported this notion. Other investigators too have pointed out that large numbers of suicidal persons had been treated by their family physicians (Dorpat et al. [2], Motto and Greene [7], Robins et al. [8], and Vail [20]).

Working closely with the two medical associations in Los Angeles County, we contacted each of the 6,602 Doctor of Medicine (M.D.) members of the Los Angeles County Medical Association and each of the 1,534 Doctor of Osteopathy (D.O.) members of the Los Angeles County Osteopathic Society. Our letter, describing the project and asking their cooperation, was accompanied by a cover letter from the president of the respective organization which, in the case of the LACMA, stated as follows: "The purpose of this letter is to endorse the enclosed project, which is concerned with the problem of suicide prevention in Los Angeles County. The plan for this project was presented to the Council of the Los Angeles County

Medical Association and has received its unqualified approval. You are urged to cooperate with this project, the results of which will be extremely important to the community and to all physicians." We enclosed a card, asking each physician to report "the total number of individuals seen professionally because of an actual suicide attempt," from Jan. 1, 1957, to Apr. 30, 1958.[2] In the cover letter, suicide attempt was defined as an actual act (such as cutting wrists or ingesting barbiturates) and was not to include either suicide threats or any cases in which the subject did not survive the attempt, so as to avoid any duplication with the coroner's data. Further, if the number of such cases seen in 1957 was zero, it was requested that the card be returned (with the number zero on it) so that a complete tabulation might be made. All this mail material was sent out by Addressograph, and addressed, stamped envelopes were provided for the return mail.

The percentage of returns can be commented upon. Of the 6,602 letters to M.D.s, we received over 5,000 responses (77 per cent), and of the 1,534 letters to D.O.s, we received over 1,000 responses (66 per cent). This kind of response to a mail survey from physicians is in itself noteworthy and reflects the interest in this topic. The exact breakdown of number of responses and number of patients reported is given in Table 3-1.

TABLE 3-1

SURVEY RETURNS FROM PHYSICIANS AND ATTEMPTED SUICIDE CASES REPORTED, LOS ANGELES COUNTY, 1957

Group	*Letters Sent Out*	*Cards Returned*	*Zero Attempted Suicides Reported*	*One or More Attempted Suicides Reported*	*Average Number of Attempted Suicides Seen by Physicians*	*Estimate of Attempted Suicides Treated* *
D.O.	1,534	1,004 (66%)	679	325	2.22	826
M.D.	6,602	5,048 (77%)	3,665	1,383	2.26	3,061
Total	8,136	6,052 (71%)	4,344	1,708	2.24	3,887

* The figures in this column have been corrected for two factors by subtracting proportionately for the 4 extra months (January through April, 1958) for which the physicians reported and by adding proportionately for the percentages of M.D.s and D.O.s (23 and 34%, respectively) who did not report at all.

[2] The letter was sent out to physicians in May, 1958. The numbers and percentages of attempted suicide reported in this paper are proportionate (twelve-sixteenths) to estimate the data for the 12 months of 1957 in order to compare them with other data.

As these cards were returned to us, we followed the response by sending each physician who had reported one or more suicide attempts one questionnaire for each attempted suicide that he had reported. The questions to be answered for each patient were sex, age, race, religion, date of suicide attempt, marital status, previous contacts with physician, previous suicide attempts, method of suicide attempt, whether other physicians were involved, whether the patient was hospitalized for the attempt, what reasons the patient gave for the attempt, the disposition by the physician, medication, how the patient was saved, the physician's rating of the seriousness of the attempt, the patient's occupation and estimated income, the patient's approximate address, and the nature of the physician's own practice; the patient's name was not asked. The number of returns from these questionnaires is indicated in Table 3-2.

TABLE 3-2
NUMBER OF QUESTIONNAIRES RETURNED BY PHYSICIANS ON ATTEMPTED SUICIDES, LOS ANGELES COUNTY, 1957

Group	*Number of Questionnaires Sent Out*	*Number of Physicians Replying*	*Number of Patients Reported*	*Number of Questionnaires Used* *
D.O.	302	178	263	163
M.D.	1,287	461	714	470
Total	1,589	639	977	633

* This column represents the total number of usable questionnaires on the basis of the completeness of information contained within them.

As indicated above, other than physicians, our sources of information about suicide attempts in Los Angeles were the county and city hospitals. Los Angeles County General Hospital is an approximately 3,000-bed general, medical, surgical, and neuropsychiatric hospital. A large number of patients who attempt suicide are taken, usually by emergency ambulance, to LACGH. The files of all patients discharged from this hospital in 1957 with the diagnosis of attempted suicide were examined, and the necessary data were abstracted. The names of patients who were identified as having come from the emergency hospitals were eliminated from the tabulation in order to eliminate duplication. In all, 494 cases of attempted suicide (210 men and 284 women) were obtained.

The Los Angeles city emergency hospital system has a large central receiving unit and 15 branch hospitals scattered throughout strategic areas of the city to treat the many and varied emergency cases that occur in a large metropolitan community. Over 200,000 records for 1957 were individually examined for all cases marked either suicide attempt or possible suicide attempt and all cases where the injury seemed to indicate a suicidal attempt (such as wrist cutting or ingestion of lye in an adult), and the pertinent available data were abstracted. Since these hospitals are emergency in nature, the amount of data available from their records was necessarily brief, but information for 1,525 suicide attempts for 1957 (498 males and 1,027 females) was obtained. Thus the total number of attempted suicides found for 1957 was 5,906; 3,887 reported by physicians and 2,019 obtained from the records of the county and city hospitals.

How thoroughly do these figures represent Los Angeles County for 1957? There are two main sources of error to be kept in mind. First, there are those persons who attempt suicide and who never reach a physician or a hospital, either because their wounds or their illness are not severe enough to bring them to the attention of a physician or because they somehow obtain family care or self-care; second, there are a number of small private emergency hospitals scattered throughout the city that are not represented in this report. To have gone to their files would have entailed inordinate expenditure of time and effort. Over and above this, it was felt that the number treated in them were, for the most part, obtained in response to the letter to the physicians who staff these hospitals. So far as number is concerned, it is felt that relatively few additional cases would have been obtained. The number obtained, 5,906, represents, we believe, a fair but undoubtedly conservative figure for the number of attempted suicides in Los Angeles County in 1957.

In 1957, there were, according to the official records of the coroner's office, 768 persons who *committed* suicide. (This represented a slight increase in number from previous years within the last decade but a slight decrease in rate in relation to the growing total population.) During this same calendar year, the number of *attempted* suicides reported to us by physicians and obtained from hospital records was 5,906. The ratio of attempted suicides to committed suicides was 7.69:1 (5,906:768), or approximately 8:1.

The results, presented in Tables 3-3 and 3-5, are discussed in three sections: Sociological Data, Suicidal Data, and Ecological Data. These tables report only those attempted suicides for which it was possible to obtain data and not the total number of attempted suicides known to have occurred.

TABLE 3-3
PERCENTAGE DISTRIBUTION BY SEX OF SOCIOLOGICAL FACTORS FOR COMMITTED AND ATTEMPTED SUICIDES IN LOS ANGELES COUNTY, 1957

Sociological Factors	*Committed Suicide, %* *			*Attempted Suicide, %* *		
	Male (n = 540)	*Female* (n = 228)	*Total* (n = 768)	*Male* (n = 828)	*Female* (n = 1,824)	*Total* (n = 2,652)
Sex	70	30	100	31	69	100
Race						
Caucasian	94	98	95	89	88	89
Negro	3	1	3	8	7	8
Oriental	2	...	1	1	1	1
Other and don't know	1	1	1	3	3	2
Age						
10–19	2	1	1	6	8	8
20–29	10	9	9	27	29	28
30–39	19	21	20	27	28	28
40–49	21	25	23	17	18	17
50–59	20	19	20	12	8	9
60–69	14	18	15	5	4	4
70–79	9	7	9	2	2	2
80–89	4	1	3	1	0	0
90 and over	0	0	0	0	0	0
Don't know	0	0	0	2	3	3
Marital Status						
Single	15	9	13	32	21	25
Married	53	48	52	46	58	54
Divorced	13	14	13	7	7	7
Widowed	6	20	11	3	4	4
Separated	8	7	8	6	5	5
Other and don't know	4	2	4	7	5	5
Occupation						
Professional	7	8	7	4	3	4
Semiprofessional	3	0	2	3	1	2

* See page 27 for footnote.

TABLE 3-3
PERCENTAGE DISTRIBUTION BY SEX OF SOCIOLOGICAL FACTORS FOR COMMITTED AND ATTEMPTED SUICIDES IN LOS ANGELES COUNTY, 1957 (*Continued*)

Sociological Factors	*Committed Suicide, %* *			*Attempted Suicide, %* *		
	Male ($n = 540$)	*Female* ($n = 228$)	*Total* ($n = 768$)	*Male* ($n = 828$)	*Female* ($n = 1,824$)	*Total* ($n = 2,652$)
Artisan	10	4	7	6	2	3
White-collar	14	3	11	7	1	3
Clerical	4	13	6	3	9	7
Skilled	17	3	13	19	4	9
Semiskilled	12	2	9	12	7	8
Unskilled	25	10	20	15	6	9
Student	2	0	2	2	3	3
Housewife	0	50	16	1	45	31
Don't know	6	7	6	28	19	22
Religion						
Protestant	1	1	1			
Catholic	2	1	1			
Jewish	1	1	1			
Other	1	1	0			
Don't know	95	97	96			
Nativity						
North America	82	84	83			
Mexico	1	1	1			
Scandinavia	1	1	1			
Italy and Spain	1	0	1			
Europe (outside Scandinavia, Italy, and Spain)	11	10	10			
Orient	1	0	1			
Other	1	2	1			
Don't know	2	2	2			
Subject living with						
Spouse	44	42	44			

* See page 27 for footnote.

TABLE 3-3
PERCENTAGE DISTRIBUTION BY SEX OF SOCIOLOGICAL FACTORS FOR COMMITTED AND ATTEMPTED SUICIDES IN LOS ANGELES COUNTY, 1957 (*Continued*)

Sociological Factors	*Committed Suicide, %* *			*Attempted Suicide, %* *		
	Male (n = 540)	*Female (n = 228)*	*Total (n = 768)*	*Male (n = 828)*	*Female (n = 1,824)*	*Total (n = 2,652)*
Parents	5	3	4			
Siblings	1	2	2			
Progeny	1	7	3			
Friends	2	2	2			
Self	22	20	21			
Other	4	7	5			
Don't know	21	17	19			
Was subject referred for subsequent treatment?						
Yes				44	63	53
No				1	3	2
Don't know				55	35	44
To whom was subject referred?						
Psychiatrist				45	20	25
Psychologist					2	1
Social services				1	3	3
Medical services				3	2	2
Other				4	4	4
Don't know				32	28	29
Hospital				15	41	36

* All figures add up to 100% (approximately) within each subcategory.

SOCIOLOGICAL DATA

The sociological data will be discussed in separate categories, as presented in Table 3-3, and will include sex, race, age, marital status, occupation, religion, and nativity.

Sex

The difference in the percentage distribution between the two sexes is a most striking one: for committed suicides the percentage of males and females are 70 and 30, respectively, whereas for attempted suicides the percentages for males and females are 31 and 69—an almost exact reversal. These proportions of male to female (approximately 2⅓:1 for committed suicide and 1:2⅓ for attempted suicide) are somewhat lower than many of the estimated proportions suggested by other investigators (4:1 and 1:5 for "commits" and "attempts," respectively). These figures also contain interesting implications, especially in regard to the percentage of attempts who go on to commit suicide (and, conversely, the percentage of commits who have previously attempted suicide). From our previous work with male veterans (hospitalized in Veterans Administration neuropsychiatric hospitals) we have found that almost 80 per cent of persons who committed suicide had previously attempted or threatened it. It would appear that the percentage of males who attempt and subsequently commit suicide is different than the percentage of females and that individual instances of attempted suicide must be evaluated, by and large, quite differently in males than in females.

Race

Among the committed suicides, over 9 out of every 10 persons were white (95 per cent), whereas Negroes committed about 3 per cent of the suicides. These percentages compare with the national statistics for 1957, which show the same proportion of races. The attempted suicides also show a high proportion of whites, though the percentage (89 per cent) is not quite so high as for the commits (95 per cent). There are proportionately more Negroes who attempt suicide than commit it (8 versus 3 per cent).

Unfortunately, the percentages of racial distribution in Los Angeles County for 1957 were not available, and no comments can be made about the relative racial proportions of committed and attempted suicides within the county.

Age

Except for a small percentage of attempted suicides (3 per cent), chronological age was known for practically every case. The committed suicides and attempted suicides showed marked variation in age distribution. Both male and female commits show a modal age of forty-two, whereas among the attempted suicides the peak occurs at age thirty-two for males and twenty-seven for females. For both sexes, attempts in the sixties and above are relatively rare compared with commits (6 versus 27 per cent). There are more attempts among both sexes in their twenties and thirties than there are commits (56 versus 29 per cent). Indeed, more than three times as many females in their twenties attempt suicide rather than commit it (29 versus 9 per cent). In general, the older the person, the more likely that suicidal behavior will have lethal consequences. (It is well known that suicide *rate*, especially in males, goes up with each decade after age fifty.)

Some additional specific details about age can be given. The *number* of males (as contrasted with females) who kill themselves remains relatively high as one goes into the upper age bracket, even in the eighties. This, of course, would indicate that the rate for males goes up in Los Angeles County, as it does in the national statistics. At the other extreme it is of some sad interest to note that 11 of the 768 committed suicides (1 per cent) were age nineteen or younger, the youngest being eleven. However, among the attempted suicides, as much as 8 per cent of the attempts occurred below age twenty, and of these, about 1 per cent occurred below age fifteen. At around age forty there are about three times as many attempts by females as by males, but this ratio decreases until the numbers are about the same at age seventy and over. Among the committed suicides only 10 per cent occur below age thirty, whereas 36 per cent of the attempted suicides occur below this age; further, less than one-third of the committed suicides (30 per cent) have occurred before age forty, whereas two-thirds of the attempted suicides (64 per cent) have occurred before this age. Conversely, one-fourth (27 per cent) of the committed suicides occur after age sixty, whereas only 6 per cent of the attempts occur after this age.

Marital Status

Even discounting the percentages of both attempts and commits who are in their teens and twenties, it is still surprising to see the relatively large percentage of both attempts (54 per cent) and commits (52 per cent) of both sexes who are married. However, in Los Angeles County, 64 per cent of persons of all ages are married, so this category contributes proportionately less than its share. Proportionately fewer single persons (13 per cent) commit suicide (there are 19 per cent single persons in Los Angeles County), but proportionately more single persons attempt suicide (25 per cent). The divorced and separated groups contribute disproportionately to the committed suicides (13 and 8 per cent, respectively) as compared with these categories in the population of Los Angeles County (5 and 4 per cent, respectively). The divorced and separated groups among the attempted suicides are approximately the same as the Los Angeles County population (7 and 5 per cent, respectively). Widowed persons accounted for 11 per cent of the committed suicides and 4 per cent of the attempted suicides, as compared with 9 per cent in the county population, indicating that the widowed generally are more lethal in their suicidal activity. It is of further interest to note that about five times as many widows commit suicide as attempt suicide (20 versus 4 per cent), whereas about twice as many widowers commit suicide as attempt suicide (6 versus 3 per cent).

When the attempts are compared further with the commits, we see that, although about the same percentage of each are married, about twice as many single persons attempt as commit suicide (25 versus 13 per cent). The divorced, separated, and widowed groups commit suicide twice as often as they attempt it (32 versus 16 per cent). It seems probable that the losses and disturbances in dyadic relationships occurring among the older groups, where more divorced, separated, and widowed appear, are also more likely to result in more lethal suicidal behavior.

Occupation

The commits and attempts seem essentially similar in occupation; i.e., if the percentages of males and females in each occupational group of attempts and commits are compared, it is seen that the percentages tend to be the same. This statement is based on the assumption that the obtained percentage of "don't knows" (6 per cent of the commits and 22 per cent of the attempts) would distribute itself proportionately among the various categories. The main differences seem to be that more white-collar males commit suicide than attempt it (14 versus 7 per cent); more unskilled males commit suicide than attempt it (25 versus 15 per cent); more professional women commit suicide than attempt it (8 versus 3 per cent); and more semiskilled women attempt suicide than commit it (7 versus 2 per cent). The largest single category for both female "commits" and female "attempts" is housewife (50 and 45 per cent, respectively). In general, among the committed suicides, the unskilled, semiskilled, and skilled laboring groups make up 42 per cent, and white-collar and clerical workers contribute 17 per cent of the total committed suicides. Among the attempted suicides, these groups contribute 26 and 10 per cent, respectively.

Attempts were made to compare these figures with the occupational distribution in Los Angeles County generally (see Table 3-4). In Los Angeles County 25 per cent of the population are in occupations labeled professional, technical, managerial, proprietor, and kindred occupations. If the professional and semiprofessional are combined in our listings, we

TABLE 3-4
PERCENTAGE DISTRIBUTION BY SEX IN OCCUPATIONS IN
LOS ANGELES COUNTY (1950 CENSUS)

Occupation	*Male, %*	*Female, %*	*Total, %*
Professional, technical, etc.	12	14	12
Farmers, farm managers	1	...	1
Managers, proprietors	15	6	12
Clerical	7	32	15
Sales workers	10	9	9
Craftsmen, foremen, etc.	22	2	16
Operators, etc.	18	16	17
Private household workers	1	7	2
Service workers, except household	7	12	9
Farm laborers, unpaid family workers	0	0	0
Farm laborers, except unpaid laborers and foremen	1	...	1
Laborers, except farm and mining	6	...	5
Not reported *	1	1	1

* Nonlabor force is not included above. Percentages do include housewives, students, and retired persons.

find only 9 per cent of the commits in these groups, so in Los Angeles it appears that the higher status groups do not provide a higher proportion of committed suicides, as has been stated elsewhere [3]. As the data from the various socioeconomic areas in Los Angeles County (as shown in Table 3-7) also indicate, the commission of suicide is neither the rich man's curse nor the poor man's disease.

Religion

The death certificate (and other data in the coroner's office) in California does not indicate religion. Sometimes one can make a rather astute guess from the name of the cemetery or mortuary, but this is not always so. Our data on religion for the committed suicides are predominately in the "don't know" category, and thus no comparisons between commits and attempts are possible. This (we rationalize) may be just as well, inasmuch as the question of religious affiliation is by no means so simple as some writers seem to have assumed it to be. Take, for example, the deceivingly simple question: Is the person a Catholic? Does one mean: Were his parents Catholic? Was he baptized a Catholic? Is he currently attending mass and confession? Does he himself have questions and doubts about his belief? Especially in this area, simple tabulations along a single dimension can mask a great deal of meaningful data.

Nativity

The place of birth of those who attempted suicide was not indicated in sufficient number, so comparisons with committed suicides cannot be made. Among the commit group, over 80 per cent were born in the United States, and the next highest single percentage, around 10 per cent, were born in European countries other than Italy, Spain, or Scandinavia.

With Whom Was the Subject Living?

In this table there is information for committed suicides only. The information indicates that 44 per cent of the men and 42 per cent of the women were living with their spouse and that 22 per cent of the men and 20 per cent of the women were living by themselves. Thirteen per cent of the males and twenty-one per cent of the females were living with others (parents, siblings, progeny, etc.). These data do not lend support to the common assertion that suicide is primarily an isolated event. Rather they tend to show suicidal behavior as a dyadic, interpersonal event and indicate that many persons who committed suicide (whether male or female) were living with their spouses, generally in an apartment setting. These figures are all the more striking when one remembers that approximately 15 per cent of this group are single.

Was the Subject Referred for Treatment and to Whom?

These data refer, of course, to the attempted suicides. The information indicates that at least 44 per cent of the men and 84 per cent of the women were referred for subsequent treatment. Of these percentages, 45 per cent of the men and 20 per cent of the women were referred specifically to a psychiatrist for treatment. It is surprising to see the small percentages referred to social service agencies. Most women were referred to a hospital for treatment, which may reflect the need for treatment (such as gastric lavage) of their most frequent suicide attempt method, barbiturate ingestion.

SUICIDE DATA

The suicide data will be discussed in the categories presented in Table 3-5 and will include month of suicide, day of suicide, time (hour) of suicide, serology, method of suicide, presence of suicide note, seriousness of suicidal action, and "reason" for suicidal behavior. For the last two rubrics, the information for the attempted suicides is for only those cases reported by the physicians, inasmuch as these data were not available from municipal and county hospital records.

Month of Suicide

The data do not show any significant temporal variations in suicidal phenomena by month. February is the lowest month (5 per cent), and most other months vary between 8 and 9 per cent. Although December and January have the highest percentages (11 and 10 per cent, respectively), the variation is not significant. Among the attempted suicides, the lowest month is April (5 per cent); most other months again vary between 8 and 9 per cent.

Day and Hour of Suicide

There does not seem to be any significant variation for either committed or attempted suicides in terms of the day selected for the suicidal behavior. Our data do not bear out the notion of "blue Monday" or any other single day as being a peak period for suicidal behavior. (Although it is one of the greater frequency days for attempts, it is one of the lower frequency days for committed.) As for the hour when suicides are committed or attempted, there are not sufficient data to warrant any conclusions.

Method of Suicide

On an a priori basis, one would expect differences in the methods used by persons who die and persons who do not, and these differences are found empirically. By and large, suicidal methods can be divided into two groups: those in which the point of no return is reached precipitously, and those in which the point of no return is reached gradually. The former, which include gunshot wounds, hanging, and jumping, are identified almost exclusively with committed suicide, whereas wrist cutting and throat cutting are identified almost entirely with attempted suicide. There are some exceptions: carbon monoxide poisoning, although not precipitously effective, is, for males, the third cause of suicidal deaths after gunshot wounds and hanging. A second major exception is barbiturates, which occupies an important role as a method in both attempted and committed suicides. For women it is clearly the first method for both attempted and committed suicides; for men it is the first-ranking method for attempted suicides and the fourth-ranking method for committed suicides. As indicated above, there are marked sex differences in method for committing suicide. Males

TABLE 3-5
PERCENTAGE DISTRIBUTION BY SEX OF SUICIDE DATA FOR COMMITTED AND ATTEMPTED SUICIDES IN LOS ANGELES COUNTY, 1957

Suicidal Factors	*Committed Suicide, % **			*Attempted Suicide, % **		
	Male ($n = 540$)	*Female* ($n = 228$)	*Total* ($n = 768$)	*Male* ($n = 828$)	*Female* ($n = 1,824$)	*Total* ($n = 2,652$)
Month of suicide						
January	10	8	10	7	10	9
February	5	5	5	10	9	9
March	8	6	8	9	8	8
April	8	10	8	6	5	5
May	9	9	9	8	8	8
June	8	10	8	7	10	9
July	7	6	7	7	9	8
August	9	10	9	10	9	10
September	8	7	8	10	9	9
October	8	10	8	9	7	8
November	9	8	8	7	9	8
December	10	11	11	9	8	8
Day of suicide						
Monday	12	13	12	15	14	15
Tuesday	13	12	13	15	13	14
Wednesday	13	10	12	15	13	13
Thursday	16	16	16	10	11	11
Friday	13	16	14	12	12	12
Saturday	12	13	12	14	12	12
Sunday	14	14	14	13	12	13
Don't know	6	7	7	7	13	11
Time of suicide						
6 A.M.–12 noon	12	11	12			
12 noon–6 P.M	18	11	16			
6 P.M.–Midnight	11	11	11			

* See page 36 for footnote.

TABLE 3-5

PERCENTAGE DISTRIBUTION BY SEX OF SUICIDE DATA FOR COMMITTED AND ATTEMPTED SUICIDES IN LOS ANGELES COUNTY, 1957 (*Continued*)

Suicidal Factors	*Committed Suicide, %* *			*Attempted Suicide, %* *		
	Male (*n* = 540)	*Female* (*n* = 228)	*Total* (*n* = 768)	*Male* (*n* = 828)	*Female* (*n* = 1,824)	*Total* (*n* = 2,652)
Midnight–6 P.M.	8	7	8			
Don't know	51	60	53			
Method of suicide						
Cut wrist	1	0	1	20	12	15
Cut throat	1	3	2	6	2	3
Gunshot, head	35	14	29	2	...	1
Gunshot, other	6	4	6	3	1	2
Barbiturates	13	46	23	34	54	48
Poisoning	4	6	4	9	9	9
Hanging	16	7	13	2	1	1
Jumping	3	4	3	1	1	1
Drowning	1	4	2	0	0	0
Carbon monoxide, auto	14	6	11	2	...	1
Illuminating gas	2	2	2	4	3	3
Stabbing	1	1	1	1	1	1
Other and don't know	3	2	3	15	17	16
Suicide note						
Yes	35	39	36	2	1	1
No	65	61	64	98	99	99
Serology at death						
Ethanol absent	28	23	25			
Less than 1.5 ethanol	11	4	9			
More than 1.5 ethanol	13	7	9			
Don't know, ethanol	2	1	2			
Barbiturate present	9	33	20			
Poison present	2	2	2			

* See page 36 for footnote.

TABLE 3-5
PERCENTAGE DISTRIBUTION BY SEX OF SUICIDE DATA FOR COMMITTED AND ATTEMPTED SUICIDES IN LOS ANGELES COUNTY, 1957 (*Continued*)

Suicidal Factors	*Committed Suicide, %* *			*Attempted Suicide, %* *		
	Male (*n* = 540)	*Female* (*n* = 228)	*Total* (*n* = 768)	*Male* (*n* = 828)	*Female* (*n* = 1,824)	*Total* (*n* = 2,652)
Carbon monoxide present	9	3	7			
Combinations (of above)	5	9	6			
Don't know	21	18	20			
Seriousness of suicidal action						
Really wanted to die				36	27	29
Undecided; left survival up to chance				23	19	20
Expected to be saved, did not intend to die				25	40	37
Don't know or not indicated				16	14	14
"Reasons" indicated for suicidal action						
Ill physical health	26	20	24	8	4	5
Ill mental health	9	18	12	4	3	3
Love affair	2	1	2	2	3	4
Jealousy, anger, rage	1	3	1	1	1	1
Death of other	2	5	3	2	1	1
Loneliness	1	1	1	1	2	2
Marital difficulties	15	9	13	11	29	24
Business, employment, finances	8	1	6	10	1	3
Psychological depression	13	16	14	9	20	18
Guilt over sexuality	0	0	0	1	1	1
Other and don't know	23	26	24	51	35	38
How subject was saved						
Subject asked someone for help or came for help				18	26	24
Someone stopped subject				9	10	10
Someone found subject				72	64	65

* All figures add up to 100% (approximately) in each subcategory.

use guns 41 per cent of the time, whereas women use them only 18 per cent of the time. Women use barbiturates 46 per cent of the time to kill themselves, whereas men use them 13 per cent of the time. Men also use hanging and carbon monoxide poisoning more often than women. Among the attempts, males use cutting (26 versus 15 per cent) and guns more often (5 versus 1 per cent) than females. Women use barbiturates more often than men (59 versus 34 per cent).

Two points seem to stand out from these data: the sex differences, with greater lethality for males from use of methods in which the point of no return is reached quickly; and the ubiquitous and significant role of barbiturates in suicidal behavior, emphasizing the need for careful precautions in prescribing these drugs.

Compared with national figures for rates by method of committing suicide, as supplied by the National Office of Vital Statistics, U.S. Department of Health, Education, and Welfare, the Los Angeles County rates by method of committed suicide do not differ significantly. There are, of course, no national rates for attempted suicide. There does tend to be a somewhat greater rate for deaths by carbon monoxide poisoning in Los Angeles (1.6 Los Angeles versus 0.8 U.S.), which may reflect the greater concentration of automobiles in the Los Angeles area. Generally, the rates by method for committed and attempted suicide found in Los Angeles County would probably apply in most large metropolitan areas. It is of interest to note that methods for committing and attempting suicide change over the years, so problems of control that were predominant two or three decades ago (especially caustics and poisons) have now changed to the problem of controlling barbiturates.

Suicide Note

It is of interest that 35 per cent of the males and 39 per cent of the females left suicide notes. This figure is somewhat more than what has been reported by other investigators [18]. The percentages may differ for several reasons: official attitude toward the notes as public documents, varying standards for certification of suicide by coroners, etc. The small percentage of attempt notes is a result of the fact that notes from this group are not public property in Los Angeles County but remain in the possession of the attempter or the rescuer.[3] It may be sufficient to mention in passing that suicide notes offer an unusual opportunity for the investigator to obtain some important insights into the thoughts and feelings of suicidal persons, written as they are within the context of suicidal be-

[3] In our SPC, we make an effort to obtain such data by asking the person we are working with to duplicate his note or to write the note he would have written.

havior. In other publications we have analyzed the content of suicide notes from various points of view [16, 17].

Serology

Serology is, of course, pertinent only to the cases of committed suicide. It is of interest to note that 24 per cent of the "commit" males had some ethanol content, and 11 per cent of the females had some ethanol content. The presence of other chemicals, such as barbiturates, poisons, and carbon monoxide, simply reflected the method of committed suicide.

Seriousness of Suicidal Action

In the questionnaire to the physicians, we asked the doctors to check the seriousness of the specific suicide attempt. Although we are well aware that the reliability of these ratings is open to much question, there are some very interesting tendencies to be commented upon. Of the males who made suicide attempts 36 per cent were adjudged as really wanting to die, with 23 per cent leaving survival up to chance. Only 25 per cent of the male attempters were adjudged as expecting to be saved. Among the females the physicians thought that only 27 per cent really wanted to die, 19 per cent left survival up to chance, and 40 per cent definitely expected to be saved. This points up the seriousness of the phenomenon of attempted suicide and also the important role of the rescuer in the actual saving of lives.

"Reasons" for Suicidal Behavior

Although it is believed that the reasons for suicide cited in this section are not reliable scientific data, they are nevertheless presented for their general interest value. The sources of the reasons for the commits were the police reports and deputy coroner reports (as obtained from witnesses) on file at the coroner's office; the source for the reasons for the attempts was the questionnaire filled out by physicians. An additional, and much better source, for reasons are the suicide notes themselves, as indicated in another publication [17]. We believe that the reasons for suicide derived in this manner at best reflect only the more superficial, precipitating causes for suicidal behavior and leave untold the more important sustaining causes, primary causes, etc. With these preliminary comments out of the way, we can see that, among men who commit suicide, ill health, marital difficulties, and psychological depression, the latter of which might well cut across the first two, are given as the three main reasons. Among women who commit suicide, physical ill health, mental ill health, and depression are given.

What the police and the coroner have told is almost a tautology; namely, that persons who hurt (are in pain) and who are depressed are suicidal. Among attempted suicides ill health does not rank high (except for males), but rather such causes as marital difficulties and depression are given most often for both sexes and financial and employment difficulties are added for men.

How the Subject Was Saved

The information given by the physicians indicates that the largest percentage (72 per cent of the men and 64 per cent of the women) were found by someone, usually the spouse. Twenty-four per cent of those who attempted suicide actually asked for help.

ECOLOGICAL DATA

We wished to plot the distributions of attempted and committed suicides within the socioeconomic geographic areas of Los Angeles County. First, of course, we needed to obtain each subject's address. For committed suicides we obtained the address from the death certificate, and for attempted suicides we obtained the address either from hospital records or from the physicians' questionnaires. In the questionnaires, in which we did not ask for the patient's name, we obtained the address by asking the following: "Do not indicate the patient's exact address. Instead, indicate the street number within the same 100 block, the correct postal zone, and the subsection. Address is important so that a careful ecological distribution of suicide attempts can be made and used for planning purposes, etc." The procedure was then (A) to translate each address into the correct census tract, (B) to translate the census tract into 1 of 100 study areas, and (C) to translate each study area into 1 of 9 area types.[4] These terms merit some explanation. Los Angeles County consists of several hundred census tracts, which shift with different census activities. In order to give some

[4] In another publication [17], we compared for 1957 (A) the sociological data for each of these same nine area types with (B) suicidal information, i.e., number of suicides, sex distribution, race, marital status, etc., for the area type and with (C) psychological information, or data concerning the emotions, quality of interpersonal relationships, etc., of persons who committed suicide in each of the area types as obtained from an analysis of 948 *suicide notes* for the 3-year period, 1956–1958. The major finding of that study was that both sociological and psychological factors were important and necessary in understanding suicidal phenomena. In other words, *both* Durkheim and Freud were right; suicidal incidents can be understood best as events neither exclusively of the psyche nor exclusively of society but as an admixture of both, as sociopsychological phenomena.

stability to the changing patterns (for research and planning purposes), the Los Angeles Welfare Planning Council made an extensive study of the census data of Los Angeles County and then, on the basis of the analyses, divided the county into 100 relatively stable, relatively homogeneous study areas (based on such factors as average economic income, average educational level, percentage of home ownership, and occupational levels). It then distributed these 100 study areas (on the basis of an intensive investigation of urbanization and social rank) among nine general area types. The names and descriptions of these nine Area Types are given by the council as follows [*22*]:

Area Type I, Most Advantaged Suburbs (Four Areas)

Familiarity with the neighborhoods in this area confirms the fact that it has many social advantages: fine schools, effective churches, plenty of play space for the many children in large backyards with many swimming pools, safe street play areas, riding stables, and a high percentage of college-trained persons who provide a reservoir of potential volunteer leadership for activities such as scouting. The area is definitely suburban and will remain so indefinitely, for most of the persons living there earn their living by commuting 15 miles or more to the cities of Los Angeles, Pasadena, Burbank, and Glendale. Single-family detached dwellings predominate.

Area Type II, Most Advantaged Residential Communities (Fourteen Areas)

Fine houses, spacious yards, many recreational facilities, churches, and good schools are found. The community is somewhat older. There is a tremendous reservoir of city-wide leadership owing to the presence of the University of California at Los Angeles. Some commercial establishments may be found here, such as exclusive restaurants, shops, and nightclubs.

Area Type III, Most Advantaged Apartment House Areas (Five Areas)

This area is well built up, with a fairly high population density owing to the apartment house pattern. Few children but many professional persons are found here. There is a city-wide shopping center.

Area Type IV, Moderately Advantaged Suburbs (Thirteen Areas)

Some older estates are found in the area, but recent subdivision into tract housing is most common. Spacious yards and play space prevail. An abundance of volunteer leadership, many churches of the neighborhood variety, and good though crowded schools are found. Commuting imposes special problems on families who live there. Young veteran families and white-collar and skilled workers predominate.

Area Type V, Moderately Advantaged Natural Communities (Thirty-four Areas)

This type includes more than one-third of all the areas in Los Angeles County. Housing is moderately new and of the single-family type, with small yards and restricted play space. The area is fully built up. There are a variety of churches and schools in the area. Leadership is fairly abundant, community organization is well developed. There is little industry. The distance to Los Angeles city center is 10 miles. There is a wide range of occupations represented.

Area Type VI, Moderately Advantaged Multiple-dwelling Areas (Eight Areas)

Population density is greater in this area because of the multiple-family dwellings. Space is limited for recreational facilities. There are many older persons, many on smaller incomes, and fewer children. This area shows port-of-entry characteristics, and converted dwellings are seen.

Area Type VII, Least Advantaged Rural Area (One Area)

Only one area, an unincorporated part of Los Angeles County, was included in this group. It is still the center of the dairy industry. There are pockets of older, substandard Mexican-American housing surrounded by much open space still devoted to agriculture or lying waste. Low-cost tract housing is filling up some of the open spaces. Community organization is weak. Leadership is somewhat limited because of the lower educational attainments of the residents. Churches tend to be of the evangelical variety.

Area Type VIII, Least Advantaged Industrial Communities (Fourteen Areas)

Area 17 (San Pedro), part of the harbor of Los Angeles, is typical of this area type. Population density is moderate, with few yards and many multiple dwellings. Shipping and industry are associated with blighted neighborhoods, skid row districts, etc. There is need for outside help to solve problems. Housing projects, nationality and minority groups in distinctive numbers, settlement houses, boys' clubs, and missions are found.

TABLE 3-6

DISTRIBUTION OF TOTAL POPULATION AND ATTEMPTED AND COMMITTED SUICIDES AMONG AREA TYPES, LOS ANGELES COUNTY, 1957

Area Type	*Population* *	*% of Total Population*	*No. of Committed Suicides*	*% of Total Committed Suicides*	*Ratio of Committed Suicide to Area Population* (per 100,000)	*No. of Attempted Suicides*	*% of Total Attempted Suicides*	*Ratio of Attempted Suicide to Area Population* (per 100,000) †
I	265,180	5	31	4	.00012	129	5	.00049
II	828,884	16	132	17	.00016	452	17	.00055
III	200,279	4	44	6	.00022	118	4	.00059
IV	1,097,822	21	93	12	.00008	327	12	.00030
V	1,673,977	31	236	31	.00014	538	20	.00032
VI	392,863	7	84	11	.00021	379	14	.00100
VII	119,000	2	4	1	.00003	20	1	.00017
VIII	529,354	10	68	9	.00013	255	10	.00048
IX	192,989	4	37	5	.00019	193	7	.00100
Area Unknown			39	5		241	9	
Total	5,300,348	100	768	100	(av. = .00014)	2,652	100	(av. = .00054)

* Population based on 1957 figures from a special census of Los Angeles County.

† Rates presented in this column are approximately 45% of their true value, inasmuch as 2,652 of the total population of 5,906 attempted suicides are represented (assuming proportionate distribution among the nine area types of the uncharted attempted suicides).

Area Type IX, Least Advantaged Rooming House and Apartment Areas (Seven Areas)

Older houses have been converted to rooming houses or apartments. There are buildings in the rear, and apartment houses are run-down. There is no play space, and much blight is found where industry and business have encroached on housing areas. Minority groups (Negroes, Mexican-Americans, Chinese, Japanese) predominate here. The population is declining, and community consciousness is weak. There are churches of many sects. Leadership is limited and needs to be supplemented from the outside by professional agencies, settlements, etc.

The distribution of attempted and committed suicides among these nine socioeconomic area types is indicated in Table 3-6. Also in Table 3-6 are the percentage of total population within each area type and the ratios of committed and attempted suicides (per 100,000 population) for each area type. For attempted suicides, the total again is for that part (2,652) of the total population of attempters in Los Angeles County (5,906) on which information was available. The columns of numbers of attempted suicides and per cent of total attempted suicides in Table 3-6 therefore do not give exact attempted suicide population figures but do provide proportionate results, which allow the areas to be compared with one another. The percentage distribution of both attempted and committed suicides among the nine area types is for the most part consistent with the percentage distribution of population within Los Angeles County. There are some notable exceptions, specifically in Area IV (moderately advantaged suburbs), which contains 21 per cent of the population but only 12 per cent of the committed and attempted suicides. Area V (moderately advantaged natural communities) contributes less than its share of attempted suicides, 20 per cent out of 31 per cent of the population. Area VI (moderately advantaged apartment areas), which contains 7 per cent of the population, contributes somewhat more than its share of committed suicides, 11 per cent, and a still higher share of the attempted suicides, 14 per cent.

Another way to view these data is to note the *rates* of committed and attempted suicide for each area type (number per 100,000 total Los Angeles County population). Among the committed suicides, we find the rate in Area III (most advantaged apartment house areas) and Area VI (moderately advantaged apartment house areas) is fairly high (22 and 21 per cent, respectively). Both Area III and Area VI have relatively high proportions of females and of widowed and divorced persons. The lowest

TABLE 3-7
SOME SALIENT CHARACTERISTICS OF COMMITTED AND ATTEMPTED SUICIDES, LOS ANGELES COUNTY, 1957

Characteristic	*Committed Suicide*	*Attempted Suicide*
Sex	More males	More females
Race	For both sexes, almost entirely Caucasian	For both sexes, predominantly Caucasian
Age	For both sexes, greatest number in forties; for males, continues proportionately high in sixties and over	For both sexes, greatest number in twenties and thirties
Marital status	For both sexes, large percentage married (though low proportionately), more divorced, separated, and widowed; for females, high proportion of widowed	For both sexes, large percentage married (though low proportionately), high proportion single
Occupation	For females, high proportion of housewives; for males, high proportion skilled and unskilled	For females, high proportion of housewives; for males, high proportion skilled, semiskilled, and unskilled
Nativity	For both sexes, predominantly native-born	For both sexes, predominantly native-born
Method of suicide	For males, mostly gunshot wounds, hanging, carbon monoxide; for females, mostly barbiturates and gunshot wounds	For both sexes, mostly barbiturates, some wrist cutting
"Reason" for suicide	For both sexes, ill health, depression; for males, marital difficulties	For both sexes, marital difficulties, depression; for males, financial and employment difficulties
Socioeconomic areas	For both sexes, highest in apartment areas of all types (most, moderately, and least advantaged)	For both sexes, highest in apartment areas, particularly least and moderately advantaged

rates, 3 and 8 per cent, appear in Areas VII and IV (least advantaged rural areas and moderately advantaged suburbs, respectively). Both of these areas have high well-knit family concentrations.

In relation to attempted suicides, Areas VII (least advantaged rural area), IV (moderately advantaged suburbs), and V (moderately advantaged natural communities) are relatively low in their rates. Again, all these areas contain a relatively high percentage of married persons with family-type dwellings and well-developed community organization. On the other hand, Area IX (least advantaged apartment areas) and Area VI (moderately advantaged apartment areas), which have relatively higher percentages of single persons, have proportionately higher rates of suicidal attempts. It thus appears that there is some tendency for a high rate of both committed and attempted suicides to be associated with apartment living, especially among widowed and separated females. Even Area III, a luxury apartment house area, has a higher rate of attempts. Apparently this factor cuts across social class factors and applies to lower, middle, and, to some extent, upper socioeconomic strata. These figures raise some interesting questions for city planners, especially in Los Angeles, where there is a noticeable trend toward building large apartment communities. One would have to investigate what is cause and what is effect: Does apartment living exacerbate suicidal impulses, or do suicidal persons gravitate to apartments? Nonetheless a thought might be given to enhancing the community features in any large apartment edifice.

What general sociological comparisons can be made between attempted suicides and committed suicides (for Los Angeles County for 1957)? Table 3-7 summarizes most of the preceding material by presenting some of the salient features of the data presented in this chapter. From this table, it is possible to delineate *modal* (or *typical*) portraits of the suicide committer and the suicide attempter, if the reader will keep in mind the important cautions that these are oversimplified; they refer only to statistically outstanding features, and in a clinical or emergency setting each case must be decided from its own idiosyncracies. With these temporizing comments in mind, we may say the following:

The *modal suicide attempter* is likely to be (A) female, (B) Caucasian, (C) in her twenties or thirties, probably the former, (D) most likely married or single, (E) a housewife, and (F) native-born, and to (G) attempt suicide by barbiturates, (H) give as a "reason" marital difficulties or depression, and (I) live in an apartment in an apartment house area.

By way of contrast, the *modal suicide committer* is likely to be (A) male, (B) Caucasian, (C) in his forties or older, (D) married, (E) a skilled or unskilled worker, and (F) native-born, and to (G) commit suicide by gunshot wounds, hanging, or carbon monoxide poisoning, (H) give as a reason ill health, depression, or marital difficulties, and (I) live in an apartment in an apartment house area.

One point now seems evident: on the basis of the statistical study of sociological factors presented in this chapter, it appears that one cannot combine attempted suicides and committed suicides (and call them both suicidal) without masking a good number of differences, which can, in themselves, be extremely important. A corollary is that studies investigating selected samples of attempted suicides should not, in seeking other sources of information, match their data from committed suicides on the assumption that the two are essentially the same.

References

1. Cavan, R. S.: *Suicide,* Chicago: University of Chicago Press, 1926.
2. Dorpat, T. L., H. S. Ripley, and R. Leidig: A study of suicide in Seattle. (Unpublished paper, 1959.)
3. Dublin, L. I., and Bessie Bunzel, *To Be or Not to Be,* New York: Random House, 1933.
4. Durkheim, E.: *Le Suicide,* Paris: Libraire Felix Alcan, 1897; *Suicide,* Glencoe, Ill.: Free Press, 1951.
5. Farberow, N. L.: Personality patterns of suicidal mental hospital patients, *Genetic Psychology Monographs,* 42: 3–79, 1950.
6. Henry, A. F., and J. F. Short, Jr.: *Suicide and Homicide,* Glencoe, Ill.: Free Press, 1954.
7. Motto, J. A., and Clara Greene: Suicide and the medical community, *A.M.A. Archives of Neurology and Psychiatry,* 80: 776–781, 1958.
8. Robins, E., J. Gassner, J. Kayes, R. H. Wilkinson, Jr., and G. E. Murphy: The communication of suicidal intent: A study of 134 consecutive cases of successful (completed) suicides, *American Journal of Psychiatry,* 115: 724–733, 1959.
9. Rosen, A.: Detection of suicidal patients: An example of some limitations in the prediction of infrequent events, *Journal of Consulting Psychology,* 18: 397–403, 1954.
10. Sainsbury, P.: *Suicide in London: An Ecological Study,* New York: Basic Books, Inc., 1955.
11. Schmid, C. F.: Suicide in Seattle, 1914–1925: An ecological and behavioristic study, *University of Washington Publications in the Social Sciences,* Seattle: University of Washington Press, 1928.
12. Schmid, C. F.: Suicide in Seattle, Washington, and Pittsburgh, Pennsylvania: A comparative study, *University of Pittsburgh Bulletin,* 27: 149–157, 1930.
13. Schmid, C. F.: Suicide in Minneapolis, Minnesota: 1928–1932, *American Journal of Sociology,* 39: 30–48, 1933.
14. Schmid, C. F., and M. D. Van Arsdol, Jr.: Completed and attempted suicides: A comparative analysis, *American Sociological Review,* 20: 273–283, 1955.

15. Shneidman, E. S., and N. L. Farberow (Eds.): *Clues to Suicide,* New York: McGraw-Hill Book Company, Inc., Blakiston Division, 1957.
16. Shneidman, E. S., and N. L. Farberow: Some comparisons between genuine and simulated suicide notes, *Journal of General Psychology,* 56: 251–256, 1957.
17. Shneidman, E. S., and N. L. Farberow: A sociopsychological investigation of suicide, in Henry P. David and J. C. Brengelmann (Eds.), *Perspectives in Personality Research,* New York: Springer Publishing Company, 1960.
18. Stengel, E., and Nancy Cook: *Attempted Suicide: Its Social Significance and Effects,* Maudsley Monograph no. 4, London: Chapman & Hall, Ltd., 1958.
19. Tuckman, J., R. J. Kleiner, and M. Lavell: Emotional content of suicide notes, *American Journal of Psychiatry,* 116: 59–63, 1959.
20. Vail, D. J.: Suicide and medical responsibility, *American Journal of Psychiatry,* 15: 1005–1010, 1959.
21. Welfare Planning Council: *Background for Planning,* Los Angeles: Welfare Planning Council, 1955, no. 15.
22. Welfare Planning Council: *Differentiating Communities in Los Angeles County,* Los Angeles: Welfare Planning Council, 1957.
23. Welfare Planning Council: *Fact Sheets on 100 Study Areas, Los Angeles County, 1957,* Los Angeles: Welfare Planning Council, 1957.
24. Yap, P. M.: *Suicide in Hong Kong,* London: Oxford University Press, 1958.

4

Emergency Evaluation of Self-destructive Potentiality

ROBERT E. LITMAN AND NORMAN L. FARBEROW

At times, professional persons in the mental health field (psychiatrists, psychologists, social workers, etc.) are asked to make a rapid assessment of someone's self-destructive potential. This is illustrated most dramatically by telephone requests for immediate consultation and advice. These calls may come from a variety of sources, such as persons engaged in medical, legal, educational, or social welfare activities, who request an evaluation of suicidal clues in a patient or client; they may come from a concerned spouse, relative, or friend; or they may come directly from the self-destructive persons themselves.

The professional person's role in answering such emergency consultation requests can be divided into three phases. First he obtains necessary information, then he forms an evaluative judgment of the situation, and finally he recommends appropriate action. He may, for example, recommend immediate hospitalization for a case; or he may interpret the suicidal communication as having low lethal potentiality and recommend outpatient treatment. Frequently he makes arrangements for additional evaluative interviews with the aim of developing a more definitive treatment plan.

As a method of assembling information, the telephone interview under emergency pressures has definite shortcomings. There is a tendency for the most dramatic and emotionally disturbing aspects of the picture to obscure other equally relevant elements. Several important questions may remain unanswered. The consultant may recommend a course of action based on incomplete data when actually more complete information was potentially available.

A systematic approach to the problem of obtaining the most pertinent indicators of self-destructive danger (or safety) within a limited amount of time is provided by a schedule of areas that should be explored during the interview. The following short schedule, derived from the experience of the staff of the Suicide Prevention Center, focuses on matters the evaluator wants to know about immediately. The first group of questions is factual and can be answered in one or two words with occasional brief amplification (e.g., age, sex, recent illnesses, loss of spouse). The second group of questions is evaluative and requires special training and skill in interviewing and diagnosis (e.g., is there depression, psychosis, ability to communicate).

The main items in the schedule are outlined below. This is followed by a discussion of their relevance to the problem of evaluating self-destructive potentiality. Some case illustrations are then provided as examples of the application of the schedule. (For a more extensive and complete schedule, for cases where time is no problem and all the information desired is available, see Chapter 5.)

SHORT SCHEDULE FOR ASSESSMENT OF SELF-DESTRUCTIVE POTENTIALITY

I Case history: factual

- *A*. Age and sex
- *B*. Onset of self-destructive behavior: chronic, repetitive pattern, or recent behavior change? Any prior suicide attempts or threats?
- *C*. Method of possible self-injury: availability, lethality?
- *D*. Recent loss of loved person: death, separation, divorce?
- *E*. Medical symptoms: history of recent illness or surgery?
- *F*. Resources: available relatives or friends, financial status?

II Judgmental-evaluative

- *A*. Status of communication with patient
- *B*. Kinds of feeling expressed
- *C*. Reactions of referring person
- *D*. Personality status and diagnostic impression

CASE HISTORY: FACTUAL

Age and Sex

The age and sex of the patient are generally the first items of information to be considered. These two facts provide a framework within which the emergency classification and appraisal of self-destructive persons can proceed. At all ages, suicidal communications from males arouse more concern than similar communications from females, and, in general, the older the person, the more serious is the self-destructive potentiality. Moreover, the danger increases with age much more for males than for females. We have rarely encountered a nonlethally intended suicidal action in a man over fifty. Thus, a self-destructive communication from or about a person in this age and sex group immediately raises suspicion of a high-risk situation, and the burden of proof that this is not an emergency rests upon the other data that can be obtained.

By contrast, the group of young females, aged fifteen to thirty-five, provides the largest number of self-destructive nonlethal communications and suicidal attempts, i.e., the least number of completed suicides. In this group, the goal of influencing another person's behavior, with little or no intention to die, is more often prominent. Other factors involved in the lower emergency danger rating for women are their choice of less violent methods of self-injury (pills rather than guns) and their greater willingness to communicate (ask for help and accept it). In the middle-aged and older female group, suicidal threats and attempts tend to become more serious (see below).

Onset of Self-destructive Behavior

As a general rule, the more acute and precipitous the onset of the self-destructive behavior, the better the ultimate prognosis and, paradoxically, the greater the need for active intervention. Thus, a history of recent personality change combined with a history of recent actual suicidal attempts is a major danger signal for the immediate future. If there has been a pattern of repetitive self-destructive behavior over a long period of time, the eventual outlook may be extremely pessimistic, especially as the potential victim grows older and the condition gradually grows worse. However, in such chronic cases, although emergency intervention may be necessary for the immediate situation, it usually has no lasting effect, and a more gradual long-term rehabilitation plan must be formulated in addition. A crucial point in the evaluation is whether the person with a chronic, repetitive self-destructive pattern has completely exhausted his emotional resources (see section on Resources).

Method of Possible Self-injury

The method of self-injury proposed by the patient sometimes reflects the degree of emergency. In general, a specific choice of time, place, and method for the proposed suicide is a serious indication, but if the method is aspirin ingestion or cold pills, the emergency is dissipated. By contrast, the person who owns a gun and proposes to use it against himself should be the object of immediate emergency efforts, if not toward him, at least toward removing the gun. Similarly, ideas of jumping from a high place should be taken more seriously and may call for questions as to where the person is, etc. Nearly all pills used to produce sleep can be lethal in large amounts, but the rapid-acting barbiturates, such as pentobarbital and secobarbital, are by far the most effective for suicide.

Recent Loss of Loved Person

Many suicide attempts, especially in young persons, occur after the separation from a spouse or a loved one. In these circumstances, self-destructive behavior is often undertaken with ambivalent feelings. The wish to die is balanced by a wish to live and to be rescued and reunited with the loved person. Frequently, these suicide attempts are successful as a form of adaptational behavior in that they do serve to bring the loved person back. On the other hand, in many of these gambles with death, death wins. When there has been a definite loss of a loved person, such as a spouse, parent, child, lover, or mistress, within the previous year (by death, divorce, or separation), the potentiality for self-destruction is increased. Certain persons, such as some widows of ages forty to sixty who have been extremely dependent on their husbands, display exaggerated mourning and grief reactions associated with strong self-destructive urges.

Medical Symptoms

A history of recent hospitalization or medical consultation may indicate increased self-destructiveness, especially in older persons. Medical conditions most often associated with suicidal reactions are psychosomatic diseases, polysurgery, malignant tumors, and various symptoms associated with depression. Some indicators of depression are anorexia, weight loss, sleeplessness, fatigue, impotence, loss of sexual desire, and hypochondriacal preoccupation, especially cancerophobia. When a chronic debilitating disease such as cancer actually exists, suicidal reactions tend to be precipitated by incidents that the patient interprets as rejection from family and physician.

Resources

Often the attitudes of spouse, relative, or friend may mean the difference between life or death for persons involved in symbiotic relationships. A consultant wants to know who brings the patient to the attention of helping authorities and why? Are there relatives in the picture? Is there a history of solidarity with spouse, relatives, or friends? Or, contrariwise, is there a history of instability, constant ambivalent relationships, desertion, and distrust? Financial resources need to be included in the evaluation, as these determine to some extent what types of treatment are available. A recent loss of job or sudden drop in financial status may constitute a traumatic loss to certain persons, especially middle-aged men and career women. Persons who have a lifelong history of direct self-destructiveness, as illustrated by unstable interpersonal relationships, alcoholism, impulsivity, and hostile dependency, often reach a crisis in the fourth or fifth decade when they find that they have exhausted themselves financially and interpersonally; they are, so to speak, emotionally bankrupt. After a long pattern of suicidal gestures, this may be the point when such persons actually do commit suicide.

JUDGMENTAL-EVALUATIVE

Status of Communication with Patient

For a person struggling with strong currents of self-destructiveness, the life line is one of unbroken communication with other persons. When a patient is able to express his troubled feelings and cry for help, the self-destructive danger may be high, but it is never so extreme as when the patient has given up and withdrawn and is no longer communicating. A warm, receptive, hopeful, encouraging, responsive attitude by the consultant will help to keep the communication line intact. Repeated telephone connections with the patient can help to weather a short period of crisis. Usually, an emergency self-destructive situation is ominously foreshadowed by a break in the communication, cancelled appointments, unanswered telephone calls, and silence.

The most perplexing problem is presented by those self-destructive persons who reject offers of consultation, assistance, or therapy. With a life at stake, how can we help someone against his own will? This represents a most complicated medical, legal, and ethical problem, and this is not the place to examine the issue in detail. However, in a limited number of experiences with this situation the SPC staff has found that often the hostile attitudes, objections, and resistances of the potentially self-destructive person were relatively superficial and would melt away when exposed to sympathetic, firm, consistent, and coordinated helping efforts.

Kinds of Feelings Expressed

Typical presuicidal communications include verbal statements such as "I am tired of life," "I mean to end it all," "my family would be better off without me," or "soon I won't be around." On a behavior level, efforts to put business and social affairs in order, the making out of a will, and unusual preparations as if for an absence may have a similar significance. Suicidal threats designed primarily to taunt or punish the recipient or to gain a distinct goal or advantageous objective (for example, to force a marriage or obtain a therapeutic abortion) carry a relatively low emergency lethal valence. The affective state associated with these communications should be evaluated. The most serious suicidal potential is associated with feelings of helplessness and hopelessness, exhaustion and failure, and the feeling "I just want out." A combination of agitation and confusion, however, particularly in a person who has had a previous psychotic episode, may constitute an emergency. When the predominant feeling is one of frustration, anger, or rage, without overwhelming confusion, the lethal danger is generally somewhat less.

Reactions of Referring Person

If the referring person is a spouse, relative, friend, or other lay person, a number of possible reactions require evaluation. First, are there indications of a close and ambivalent symbiotic relationship and, if so, is it possible that the referring person is actually also disturbed? Does the referring person's attitude reflect a need to have a sick, dependent partner leaning upon him? Is there an attitude of rejection and a desire to get rid of the potentially suicidal person? A defensive, paranoid, rigid, punishing, moralistic, or hopelessly dependent attitude on the part of the referring person indicates that little help can be expected from that source, although attempts should be made nevertheless to secure as much cooperation as possible. It is generally encouraging when the referring person expresses sympathy and concern for the patient, together with an admission of his own sense of helplessness in the situation and need for assistance. Often the referring person, with guidance and advice, can be a source of strength and support in the emergency situation.

Professional persons sometimes express an exaggerated or disproportionate degree of anxiety over a relatively mild self-destructive communication from a patient or client. Reassurance from a consultant will often encourage such persons or agencies to proceed with their own appropriate techniques. On the other hand, some emotional reaction is expected from the referring person, no matter what their professional training and experience, because emotions activated by suicide go very deep in human psychology, well beyond the usual concept of countertransference. This also applies to calls from professional psychotherapists, whose requests for consultation bring up special problems. When a referring psychotherapist indicates no feelings of personal concern about his potentially self-destructive patient, one wonders whether the therapist's judgment and insight can be relied upon for purposes of evaluation. If the therapist recognizes feelings of annoyance or irritation with the patient in himself and can discuss them with the consultant, this in itself reduces one's feeling about the immediate suicidal potentiality of the patient. If the psychotherapist reports honest feelings of helplessness in himself and a breaking off of communication between himself and the patient, then it would appear that an emergency situation has developed and it is time for some sort of active intervention. In these situations, the source of the difficulty may be some specific countertransference problem in the therapist, which can be resolved by a supervisory consultation. Often the SPC has provided, in addition to such consultations, needed practical information about community resources, available clinics, methods of hospitalization, commitment procedures, etc.

Personality Status and Diagnostic Impression

Much of the information that might be subsumed under this heading has already been discussed above. What should be re-emphasized is the importance of evaluating the possible presence of psychotic thinking and severe depressive affect. If either of these indicators is present, and especially if combined with alcoholism, the question of emergency hospitalization must be seriously considered. One asks about previous hospitalization for mental illness and looks for the various symptoms of disordered thinking (confusion, disorientation, delusions, disturbed body image, etc.). One wants to know, in addition, about past periods of elation or depression and the extent of the depression. The course and outcome of previous psychotherapy efforts should be ascertained. A previous pattern of failure in therapy is a danger signal.

ILLUSTRATIVE CASES

The above schedule includes the most important immediate emergency indicators for evaluation of suicidal danger. However, patterns of suicidal behavior vary. The following examples illustrate how different items of the schedule carry different weights, depending on the total context.

Case 1

A supervisor of nurses called the SPC. A 23-year-old female staff nurse, Mrs. F., had been on sick leave for a week and had returned to work obviously depressed. The supervisor asked a few questions, and Mrs. F. revealed that she had made a serious suicide attempt with barbiturate capsules because her husband had left her to go to Las Vegas with another woman. Because of the suicide attempt her husband had stayed with her to help her. However, Mrs. F. was afraid he might still leave her. The nursing supervisor was told that this was not an emergency, and an appointment was made to see this nurse the next day. She was interviewed and accepted at the SPC for psychotherapy.

Comment. Completed suicide occurs infrequently in young married women, even though this group contributes most heavily to the number of suicide threats and suicide attempts. In 90 per cent of the cases, rejection by a man is the source of the self-destructive behavior, although occasionally the rejection is from a parent. This patient's pattern of self-destructive behavior indicates that she needs serious evaluation and eventual treatment, although the method of threatened self-injury (sleeping pills) is of low lethality in this age group. We judged that this was not an acute emergency case because (A) the lost love object, the husband, had returned, (B) the patient was able to communicate her feelings to her supervisor, and (C) her usual personality was described as compliant, conscientious, and obsessive rather than alcoholic and impulsive; she was described as nonpsychotic. The prognosis for immediate and long-range treatment was deemed to be excellent. In general, most suicide threats made by young women are because of rejection in love and are of low lethality. The exceptions to this rule are persons with schizoid and schizophrenic personalities.

Case 2

A social worker called from the Bureau of Public Assistance about a 19-year-old girl, who was recently discharged from a state hospital with the diagnosis of schizophrenia, improved. Although she was working part time and making a better adjustment than before, this girl expressed to the worker her feelings that life was not worth living. She had previously made a suicide attempt by cutting her wrist with a razor blade. The girl led a very lonely life. Her foster mother was often hostile toward her and threatened to have her sent back to the hospital. The social worker was told that, although this was not an emergency situation, nevertheless the suicidal danger was high and considerable care, effort, and activity were called for in this case.

Comment. Concern was expressed about this patient because this type of case carries with it a chronic risk of suicide. However, the main problem is schizophrenia and not suicide. The diagnosis of chronic schizophrenic reaction is extremely important because the proportion of suicides is high from this category and the prediction of suicide in this group is difficult.

The previous self-destructiveness together with the recent communication of a wish to die indicates a serious chronic suicidal danger. Nevertheless, the girl should not be considered a permanent candidate for hospitalization. The patient's best chance for improvement in the underlying schizophrenic process is through working at a job, living in the community, and having a supportive relationship with the social worker. We recommended that the social worker continue casework with the girl, looking forward to a long-term relationship in which she would give the girl someone to talk to and some psychological and practical support in organizing her life. Continuing consultation with the SPC was offered. The rejecting attitudes of the foster mother might be changed by some guidance and counseling.

Case 3

Mrs. V. called the SPC as a self-referral from a family service agency. She had called the agency about her husband, Mr. V., an engineer in an aircraft plant. According to his wife, he was a compulsive gambler who lived in a dream world of his own and refused to recognize the damage he was doing by his gambling and to accept psychiatric help. She had threatened to divorce him many times, and now she was desperate. The previous day her husband told her he had worked out a plan whereby he would commit suicide so that Mrs. V. could collect the insurance and pay off their debts, which, however, were more than the insurance would cover. Mrs. V. suspected that her husband's real plan was to gamble his pay check in the hope of getting enough money to keep the house. They had one child, and she was pregnant with another. Her plan was to have him committed so she could collect his pay check and use the money to straighten out their financial situation.

Comment. Suicidal communication in men should be taken a great deal more seriously than similar communications in women. In this case more information was needed about the husband and quickly. The actual facts gathered indicated that he was working in a responsible position, which contradicted the wife's implication that he was in a dream world or nearly psychotic. Possibly the main disturbance in the family centered in the wife rather than in the husband. The pattern of gambling, unaccompanied by severe alcoholism or acute depression, does not usually lead to suicide in young men. The husband was called and was told that his wife was worried about him and had asked us to call. The impression gained while talking to him was that he was not depressed, not psychotic, and not suicidal. He did feel that he and his wife needed some sort of help and accepted an appointment to come to the office for an evaluation interview and possible referral for marriage counseling.

Case 4

Sometimes one particular element of the schedule stands out and overshadows all the others. An example is the immediate danger when a lethal weapon is not only at hand but is presented as the threatened suicidal method. A certified clinical psychologist, who practices in an outlying community, called to report this problem. The previous night he had been asked to see a 19-year-old man whose mother and father had recently separated as a prelude to divorce. The young man had become moody and depressed. The preceding afternoon he had locked himself in his room with a .22 rifle and threatened to kill himself. The psychologist was called; he was able to talk to the young man through the locked door and thought he had established a relationship. He made an appointment for the young man to come to his office the next day. When the patient did not show up, the psychologist called the home and learned that the young man was again locked in his room with the gun. According to the psychologist, this man had made no previous destructive actions, had made regular progress in school, and displayed no schizophrenic disturbance in thinking.

Comment. This was evaluated as an emergency situation that carried an excellent prognosis for the long run, provided the short-term danger was negotiated successfully. The psychologist was advised to secure the cooperation of the father, the mother, all members of the family, friends, clergyman, indeed everyone who might be able to communicate with the young man, and return with them to the house. The primary immediate aim was to persuade him to give up the gun and to remove it from the house. This done, efforts toward establishing a therapeutic relationship could be renewed. This was accomplished, with the SPC continuing to act as consultant to the therapist as needed.

Case 5

Key indicators of suicidal danger in persons who have made suicidal communications are the presence of alcoholism or clinical depression in someone over age 40. A physician in general practice called because a 50-year-old woman in his office seemed quite depressed. She had been an alcoholic for 15 or 20 years, had been three times divorced, had been taking large amounts of barbiturates for more than a year, and was now asking for a large prescription. In answer to our questions, the physician reported a history of several surgical operations in the last few years and said that she was out of money and out of friends. She said that she didn't care whether she lived or died. In fact, she wished she was dead. He added that he was worried about her and he didn't know what he could do to help her.

Comment. Dependent persons who have led unstable lives and who tend to collect frustrations and disappointments and soothe them with alcohol and barbiturates generally make unsuccessful suicidal attempts when they are younger, but these attempts become more serious in the later stages of life and should be taken seriously. This case was deemed an emergency, and we suggested to the physician that he send the woman to our office immediately, which he did. She was seen by us on a supportive basis and responded well for several weeks to a good deal of encouragement along with energizing drugs and mild sedation. However, she lapsed into depression again when it became clear to her that her current boy friend had no intention of marrying her. At this point she was willing to accept hospitalization at a state hospital.

Case 6

On the referral of the mental hygiene counselor of the superior court, two sisters called for help about their father, a 52-year-old construction foreman, who was periodically an alcoholic and was threatening to commit suicide by shooting himself on his birthday (the next day).

Comment. This situation was regarded as an emergency. Age and sex were in the high suicide range, and the recent onset of self-destructive behavior, highly lethal method, and repetitive pattern of alcoholism further indicated an emergency. In addition, one got the impression of a man who was agitatedly depressed. On the positive side, the resources were not exhausted, there was still communication by the patient, and it seemed that with quick action a tragedy might be forestalled and the outcome might be good. A physician in the neighborhood was called and informed about the circumstances. On our recommendation, the physician together with the daughters and the man's two brothers went to the house, and there was a series of consultations back and forth between the family and the physician and the SPC. With this intervention, the patient's mood improved considerably. He expressed the feeling that he had thought everybody had deserted him and hated him. He was touched by the display of family affection and concern. Hospitalization was not necessary, but continued observation was recommended.

Case 7

The wife of a 51-year-old photographer, who had made a recent mild suicide attempt and was treated at the county hospital, sent a letter to the hospital at his suggestion, stating that her husband had become depressed again. She begged for advice and help, and the letter was referred to the SPC. We called the husband, who reacted with great gratitude and appreciation to the idea that we were concerned about him. He talked for almost an hour on the phone to the social worker.

Comment. Although the patient was depressed, it was not felt that this was an emergency because of his willingness to communicate and his desire for help. Most persons who call the SPC for help for themselves seldom represent emergencies. We have found that such persons can be given an appointment for the next day, or often several days in advance, and they will keep it. Usually we make a series of telephone calls to keep in communication with the patient until they are able to come to see us. It is only when communication is broken off that we become alarmed and feel that an emergency situation may have developed. The patient appeared the next day for psychiatric interview and psychological testing and was found to be extremely depressed. Hospitalization was recommended and accepted.

SUMMARY

In responding to a request for emergency consultation regarding a problem of potential self-destruction, the consultant must obtain the most pertinent information, evaluate the situation, and recommend a course of action, all within a limited time. The use of a short schedule, specifying the questions to ask and the areas of information to explore, facilitates the consultation process. Use of the schedule tends to correct distortions induced by the limitation of time, the pressures of anxiety and other emotions, and certain technical restrictions inherent in such consultations. Several typical problem situations involving self-destructive potentiality are discussed in terms of the emergency evaluation procedure and the recommended plans of action.

5

The Assessment of Self-destructive Potentiality

NORMAN D. TABACHNICK AND NORMAN L. FARBEROW

This chapter represents an attempt to synthesize material currently available regarding the evaluation of self-destructive potentiality in persons who are emotionally disturbed. The synthesis stems from attempts to integrate the theoretical material that has appeared regarding suicide and self-destruction within the last 25 years with our clinical experience, which daily encompasses the evaluation and treatment of self-destructive persons, most of whom have been treated at the Suicide Prevention Center, in Los Angeles.

In developing the notions that will be discussed below, it has seemed useful to formulate a schedule of the rating factors to be considered in the investigation of self-destructive potentiality.[1] Self-destruction, perhaps because it is part of that great tabooed category, death, is a phenomenon of

[1] The need for a more definitive, evaluative scale emerged from the experience of the staff at the SPC. A preliminary scale of lethality had been constructed when the center was first established to aid in selecting and evaluating the patient. The scale set up a six-step continuum from 0 to 5 along which lethality could be rated. Zero indicated no lethality (e.g., ingesting colored water), and 5 represented most lethal (e.g., gunshot in the head). This scale was applied only to persons who made an attempt, with the primary consideration in the estimation being the nature of the method. Occasionally other factors would be considered to modify the rating, such as the provisions for rescue. In testing the reliability of the scale, Neuringer [7] presented interview materials on 15 patients to five members of the staff and obtained independent ratings on each. The scores were then correlated with each other. The results indicated that, although all but one of the coefficients were significant at or beyond the .05 level of confidence, the values were far too low (ranging from .44 to .60) to serve as adequate indices of reliability.

existence that is often avoided by both lay person and professional worker. A number of reasons for this powerful taboo have been discussed in other places and will not be repeated here. What we, as clinicians interested in the welfare of our self-destructive patients, must face is that many of these reasons may be operative in ourselves and that these can influence us in the appraisal of such situations, e.g., the ability to assess appropriately the intensity and the lethality of self-destructive behavior. A check list of pertinent factors regarding the evaluation of self-destructive potentiality becomes a helpful guide and provides one method of dealing with this turning-away tendency.

The purpose of such a check list should be distinguished from those lists which have been proposed for use in the *identification* of the self-destructive patient. This is a task to which many investigators have turned their attention, and the literature is filled with symptoms, syndromes, prodromal clues, etc., which have been proposed for such a purpose. Farberow [3] summarizes a number of the prodromal aspects advanced by various investigators; Menninger [6] provides many insights into early identification of self-destructive tendencies in his extensive discussion of the continua of life patterns in which these tendencies may emerge; Pokorny [9], Motto and Greene [8], Dorpat et al. [1], Robins et al. [10], and many others have discussed this area. Though many clues have thus far been elicited, it is not felt that all, or even necessarily the most significant ones, have as yet been described. This is one aspect of the continuing task of investigation by the staff of the SPC.

In general, what is attempted here is a synthesis of significant information. The schedule is not intended to be applied to self-destructive persons in the hope that one can come out with a figure pinpointing the percentage of self-destructive energy. Rather it should be considered as a comprehensive check list dealing with pertinent areas of information regarding self-destructive potentiality. There are, of course, situations that would call for modifications of a general theoretical schedule, such as, for example, emergency suicidal consultations (see Chapter 4). In other types of situations, such as psychotic reactions or grief reactions, still another schedule might be more pertinent. It is certain that there would be much overlap and that many of the items listed in an emergency schedule would be found in the list of factors in this chapter. Essentially, the schedule presented in this chapter assumes that all the desired information, the kind one has usually only after long familiarity with the patient, is available.

The specific items enumerated in our schedule are meant as a tentative list. Some items may turn out to be not the most meaningful ones and may eventually be eliminated, whereas other factors may gain in importance as research continues. However, it is felt that there might be some value in setting down the ideas at this point so that they can now be subjected to more public consideration and discussion.

The reader will note that in this chapter the term *self-destruction* is used in place of the term *suicide*.[2] Considerable confusion has arisen around the word *suicide,* inasmuch as it has been applied to such a variety of activities, feelings, tendencies, and behavior that it has lost its meaning as a definite and specific concept. For example, suicide, in its most common context, is a quasi-medicolegal term, referring particularly to the specific certification that must be placed upon a death certificate as an indication of the mode of death. *Self-destruction* is a specific psychological construct and is thus more useful for theoretical purposes in its assumption of conscious and unconscious psychodynamics and implications of inhibiting or facilitating ego characteristics, etc.

The theoretical framework within which the schedule has been developed may be commented upon. This framework is one in which the emphasis has derived from two interrelated viewpoints, adaptation theory and communication theory. Dynamic, topographic, economic, and sociological theories are neither ignored nor discarded. Concepts from all these interrelated approaches can be seen in the factors used within the schedule.

Human beings have, as do other organisms, a number of adaptive mechanisms, which have been developed in order to provide for the gratification of certain instinctual needs within the setting of their milieu. When these adaptive mechanisms become inadequate to secure the desired gratification, one possible result is the utilization of self-defeating and self-destructive acts. Such actions may represent an exhaustion of pleasure-gratifying attempts on the part of the organism and a resort to developmentally earlier modes of dealing with its needs and impulses. The disparity between the earlier modes of behavior and the more advanced expectations along with the actions of the milieu on the individual may result in a self-destructive state. Thus, it becomes important to know about a person's intentions in regard to dying. Is he really intending to do away with himself, or does he hope to wrest some gain from his environment or to alert someone to his desperate plight? These, in general, are the considerations dealt with in Part I of the schedule, which concerns mainly intrapersonal aspects of self-destructive behavior.

[2] We are convinced that such an alternative term is sorely needed, but the substitution is carried out consistently only in this chapter. It is difficult to break old habits and customary usage.

Part II, interpersonal aspects, is based on the consideration of self-destructive behavior as a means of communicating to others various feelings and demands or pleas. The self-destructive behavior thus becomes, in part, a communication with a particular purpose and content directed toward a specific audience. This approach emphasizes such factors as the content, audience, degree of directness, and purpose of the communication. In addition, it is important to know what the relationship between the individual and his environment has usually been. How does he relate to his environment, and how does his environment relate to him?

The third part examines implementation in self-destructive behavior. This section adds an objective scale of lethality of method for persons who have already made self-destructive attempts. It does not contradict the dynamic implications of the first two parts of the schedule but adds a further measure for evaluation of potentiality. It, of course, can be used only in situations where an actual self-destructive attempt has occurred.

Below are listed in outline form the main items and the subsidiary elements that make up our schedule. These are followed by an explication of the categories and a discussion of their relevance to the problem of self-destruction.

SCHEDULE FOR ASSESSMENT OF SELF-DESTRUCTIVE POTENTIALITY

I. Intrapersonal aspects

  A. Intention

    1. Conscious intention

      a. Awareness of the effect of his threats and/or attempts on others

      b. Awareness by the person of the results of his own self-destructive behavior

      c. Patient's knowledge about the method contemplated or used

      d. Conscious provisions for rescue (has made or is making)

    2. Unconscious intention

      a. Constellation of dynamics (important in self-destruction): anxiety, tension, guilt, depression, hostility, and dependency

      b. Kinds of fantasies: death, rescue, hurting, killing self or others, failure, impotence, loss of hope

      c. Unconscious manipulation of others through threats or attempts

      d. Life pattern of person: dangerous activities or occupations

      e. Unconscious provisions for rescue (had made or is making)

B. Ego organization
1. Impulsivity versus efficacy of controls
2. Rigidity versus flexibility
3. Isolation versus relatedness

II. Interpersonal aspects

A. Communicative aspects
1. Degree of directness of the communication (is it specific and its implication unavoidable, or is it a tenuous communication?)
2. What is being communicated? Desperation, at end of rope, anger, desire for help, irritation, disdain
3. To whom is the communication addressed? To specific persons or to world at large; if to specific persons, what kind; are they living or dead?
4. Purpose of the communication: to cause guilt, prepare others for death, manipulate them

B. Environmental aspects: who are the significant others in the environment?
1. Patient's attitude toward environment and/or significant others, facilitating or inhibiting positive communication
2. Attitude of significant others toward the patient, facilitating or inhibiting positive communication
3. Cultural and religious attitudes toward death

III. Implementation (in attempts)

A. Objective scale of lethality: (*a*) gunshot wound and explosives; (*b*) jumping from high places; (*c*) cutting and piercing of vital organs; (*d*) hanging; (*e*) drowning; (*f*) poisoning; (*g*) cutting and piercing of nonvital organs; (*h*) drowning (can swim); (*i*) gas poisoning; (*j*) analgesic and soporific substances
1. Point of no return: length of time between initiation of act and occurrence of death
2. Feasibility of intervention or rescue for interruption or reversal of self-destructive action

INTRAPERSONAL ASPECTS

This section focuses on the evaluation of the internal psychological mechanisms that can result in or affect the question of self-destruction in an individual. The two main subcategories in this section concern intention, that is, the strength of the intention to do away with oneself, and ego organization, especially the character structures that tend to inhibit or facilitate the carrying out of self-destructive intention.

Intention

Intention, as used in this schedule, involves the concept of motivation. This includes both conscious and unconscious motivation, each of which can contribute significantly to a person's self-destructive tendencies.

Conscious Intention. This includes the aspects of purpose, meaning, and awareness of the self-destructive behavior that are available to the conscious mind of the subject.

Awareness of the effect of his threats and/or attempts on others. When a patient is very much aware of the effect of his threats and/or attempts on others, the manipulative element in his behavior assumes great significance. This will vary, to some extent, with age; it is especially true in younger persons, in their twenties and thirties. However, this is not so true for older persons, sixty and above, where the nature of the suicidal behavior assumes other significance. In general, however, the more consciously aware the patient is of the effect of his activity upon other persons, the more likely it is that his behavior represents a nonlethal kind of self-destructive activity.

Awareness by the person of the results of his own self-destructive behavior. Under certain conditions there may be little awareness of the realistic significance of death. These conditions may be the result of little experience with death, or lack of depth in the development of feelings, or extremely strong processes of denial and repression. In general, the more aware of and the more sensitive the person is to the realistic implications of his self-destructive behavior, the more serious is the self-destructive potentiality.

Patient's knowledge about the method contemplated or used. It is obvious that not all persons are equally informed about the lethality of different self-destructive methods. Aspirin to an uninformed person who has had neither experience nor information about it might seem a quite lethal mode of self-destructive activity, whereas other cases may show that some powerful caustic had not been recognized as a tissue poison by the person taking it. Information about this category is important in assessing the conscious intention to do away with oneself.

Conscious provisions for rescue. The amount of planning, the timing, the place selected, and the arrangements of details for discovery that the person has consciously provided are significant here. There is obviously a difference in the lethal potentiality between the person who arranges the details of his act of self-destruction so that he could not possibly be interrupted or rescued and the person who does just the opposite. Sometimes the question whether or not provisions for rescue have been made on a conscious or unconscious basis is difficult to determine. In general, the more provisions made for rescue, the less lethal is the potentiality for self-destruction.

Unconscious Intention. These are probably the most difficult aspects of intention to evaluate inasmuch as they all must be inferred. Since they must frequently depend on second-, third-, and even higher-order inferences, the certainty of the inference must, of course, vary considerably. However, it is the evaluation of just these aspects of the person's functioning that will be most important. Drives, impulses, needs, etc., operate primarily from deep unconscious levels, which are only relatively slightly modified by various controlling aspects of the personality. Therefore, what one can learn about the motivation that exists at these deep levels is most significant.

Constellation of dynamics. All the dynamics present in self-destructive persons are present to some degree in normal persons. However, when the dynamics felt to be most significant for self-destruction exist with great strength in the subject under consideration, and particularly when two or more of them are very strong, the lethal potentiality increases. The important dynamics are as follows: depression, particularly when accompanied by anxiety; tension and agitation; hostility and guilt (these seem to lead to acting out motor impulses that may be directed upon the self); and dependency needs, particularly if they have been frustrated or threatened to any considerable degree.

Kinds of fantasies. One of the windows through which the professional person may look at the patient's motivations are the fantasies he produces. Such fantasies may be tapped in a number of ways, such as dreams, daydreams, and psychological test productions. When these fantasies contain ideas of self-destruction, destruction of others, self-injury or injury, failure, worthlessness, hopelessness, rescue, rejuvenation, nirvana, paradise, and reincarnation, a higher degree of potentiality for self-destruction is present. It is true that these fantasies are found to some degree in every person, but when they begin to occupy and fill a large portion of the total content of the person's productions, they lend strong support to the growing strength of self-destructive tendency.

Unconscious manipulation of others through threats or attempts. When the patient engages in self-destructive behavior yet indicates a complete lack of conscious awareness of any of the implications of his behavior, he will also be unaware of the effects of that behavior on others. However, unconscious manipulation of significant others can be observed in a patient's behavior by a professional person. To the degree that a subject must express his needs through unconscious manipulation of others the potentiality for self-destruction is greater.

Life pattern of person. Examination of a person's life pattern may yield information about his self-destructive tendencies operating on an unconscious level. Many occupations and activities contain disproportionate elements of dangers. These include motorcycle racing, sand hogging, and many forms of construction work. One could similarly list a number of hobbies (e.g., mountain climbing or skin diving) that have self-destructive possibilities. Preference for these activities or constant seeking for the extra thrill the danger seems to have may indicate the presence of significant drives toward self-destruction within a person. Menninger [6] lists in detail the wide variety of activities that by inference contain unconscious tendencies toward self-destruction.

Unconscious provisions for rescue. Sometimes the person will make provisions of which he is not aware for rescue from his self-destructive behavior. He may unconsciously provide opportunities for the self-destructive attempt to fail, or he may communicate his disturbance to others, who will be alerted to his need for help and will respond to it. In general, the more provisions for rescue both conscious and unconscious that can be detected, the lower the potentiality for self-destruction.

Ego Organization

Having evaluated the motivational or intentional aspects of self-destructive tendencies within the personality, there remains to be considered the structure and the framework of the personality in which these self-destructive intentions operate. A person may have relatively weak or slight tendencies in the direction of self-destruction, but if his ego organization is such that controls or checks upon his behavior do not exist, he might be a high self-destructive risk in contrast with someone in whom ego controls are such that he is able to continue to function despite a high degree of self-destructive pressure and strain. Obviously, many of the factors that ordinarily go into ego formation have some significance in controlling self-destructive tendencies. However, the attention of this part of the schedule is directed mainly at those continua of character traits that have been found to be most significant in determining lethality in self-destructive persons.

Impulsivity versus Efficacy of Controls. This continuum ranges from the poorest adjustment, where impulsivity is high (no direction and/or control of impulses), to the optimal adjustment, where the efficacy of the controls is high and the handling and disposition of impulses is personally and intrapersonally effective. In general, the more impulsive a person, the greater the possibility of self-destruction. It should be recognized that in certain kinds of situations persons may be more impulsive than at other times; a person under the influence of alcohol or in the end stages of an exhaustive emotional situation is more likely to act impulsively than the same person operating in a different milieu.

Rigidity versus Flexibility. Another significant continuum in evaluating the organization of ego defenses is rigidity versus flexibility. In terms of adaptation, a rigid person is one who has relatively few modes of reacting to an environmental situation available to him. If these become exhausted or are found to be wanting and nongratifying, the person's pattern of defenses generally begins to deteriorate. It is at this time that the possibility of self-destructive actions increases. On the other hand, a flexible person has a relatively large number of instinctually gratifying methods by which to adapt to various situations. Such a person is less likely to utilize regressive methods, which may include self-destructive ones.

Isolation versus Relatedness. In general, it is felt that the closer a person is to the isolation end of this continuum, the more likely it is that self-destructive potentiality exists. This refers, in part, to the fact that the person has relatively few resources in his environment from which support may be drawn, but, in addition, a feeling of loneliness is frequently found among persons with high self-destructive potentiality. Loneliness, hopelessness, and despair seem to be related qualities. On the other hand, a person with a high degree of relatedness has many paths to follow in his efforts to seek some feeling of identification and has more sources of support from his environment.

Some comments should be made in the present discussion about the immaturely dependent person. Although he seems to relate closely to others, his relationship is such that, should his needs be even slightly frustrated, he may react with anger, which often will be turned inward and result in self-destructive activity. However, the original formulation would still hold under normal circumstances; that is, overdependence functions as a defense against feelings of aloneness and is thus helpful in avoiding self-destructive activity.

INTERPERSONAL ASPECTS

Man is continually in relationship with others around him upon whom he exerts considerable influence and who, in turn, exert much influence upon him. Self-destructive acts, contrary to widely held opinion, are rarely solitary incidents. Rather, they are acts which, if they can be understood as communications with meaning for the significant other person or persons involved, lend themselves more readily to the evaluation of the self-destructive potentiality present.

Communicative Aspects

This part of the schedule discusses in detail what can be learned from an analysis of the communicative aspects of the situation involving the self-destructive person. The communication can be verbal or behavioral (nonverbal). Verbal communication can be threats, ideation, or fantasies. Suicide notes and other written communications would be included here. Nonverbal, or behavioral, communications range from actual attempts to destroy the self to less immediate, less direct self-injurious behavior. All communications can be examined for degree of directness, content, audience, and purpose for clues to the potential lethality of self-destructive behavior.

Degree of Directness of the Communication. The directness of a communication in a self-destructive situation may range from no communication to quite direct communication. Actually, it would be very unusual for a person to give no indication of his intention to kill himself. More often, there are clues in the form of subtle and indirect allusions, or there may be direct statements indicating the state of mind and the exact intention of the person.

What Is Being Communicated? The content of the communication in self-destructive activity may suggest many of the meanings and dynamics underlying the act. At times, intense feelings of conflict or desperation may be expressed, and the behavior serves as a plea for help. At other times, feelings of hopelessness and helplessness may appear. Sometimes suicide notes will attempt to explain the action or will include instructions and admonitions about various details to be taken care of. Sometimes the content simply includes reflections of the state of the world and philosophic ideas in general. It can be seen that the judgment of the lethality of the attempt will be affected depending upon the meaning attributed to the behavior.

To Whom Is the Communication Addressed? The main significance of the audience to whom the communication is directed is what their anticipated reaction to the communication will be. In general, the audience can be divided into two main groups: those who are likely to react with lifesaving responses to the communication, and those who are likely to react with indifferent or even hostile responses. If the communication is directed toward the first group, the self-destructive potentiality is considered to be much less than if it is directed toward the second group.

Purpose of the Communication. Sometimes the purpose of the communication is very explicit; sometimes it is more subtle. Some possible purposes are to manipulate, control, and direct others, evoking particular actions and feelings in others so that situational details can be changed more to meet the patient's own need; to place the blame, cast shame, or arouse guilt in others; to blame oneself and absolve others, to prepare others for the possibility of self-destruction so that the shock when it does occur will not be quite so great; to enter a plea for consideration and a cry for help. It is not easy to specify the lethal potentiality subsumed in each purpose, as defined in this section. However, one can say that for certain purposes, such as manipulating someone else to secure desired changes in the environment, there is a lower correlation. However, if the purpose is realistically to prepare others for death, then the lethal potentiality is greater.

Environmental Aspects

Our theoretical approach assumes that the development of impulses, tendencies, and ideations toward self-destructive activity do not occur only as a result of factors within the individual. A person lives and functions within a social milieu, usually in close, intimate relationship with a small group, with a less intense relationship with members of his class within society. The development of motivations and needs will stem from the quality of the interrelated significant others within the environment. It becomes apparent that, in order to evaluate self-destructive potentiality properly, attention must be turned to the environment and to the facilitating or inhibiting factors that it contributes to the situation. The first step must be to identify the individuals and groups within the environment who are significant to the patient.

Patient's Attitude toward Environment and/or Significant Others. If the patient's attitude toward the significant others in his environment has been based on procedures facilitating communication, the potentiality of lethality in self-destructive acts is decreased. If the communication is used in the service of gratification of instinctual and interpersonal needs, support for the above is added. If, however, relations with the significant others in the environment has inhibited communications and decreased gratification, the lethal potentiality is greater.

Attitude of Significant Others toward the Patient. The principles advanced in the preceding paragraph are, of course, equally applicable in the reverse situation, that is, the attitude of significant others to the self-destructive person. Thus, if the significant others are accepting and tend to facilitate communication with the patient, the lethal potentiality is decreased; if they are rejecting, angry, and desirous of breaking off relationships with the patient, the lethal potentiality is increased.

Cultural and Religious Attitudes toward Death. Many cultures and subcultures contain attitudes regarding self-destruction that are of significance in evaluating the lethal potentiality in persons within those cultures. By rewarding or punishing self-destructive activity in various ways, they influence the possibility that such activity will occur. Examples are the Japanese culture, whose warrior code includes self-destruction as an honorable act, and the Catholic Church which considers suicide one of the worst possible sins.

IMPLEMENTATION

This part of the scale evaluates the lethality of the method employed for self-destruction and is utilized only if an attempt has actually been made. It departs from the general theoretical approach used in constructing the first two parts of the schedule, by offering a more or less objective means of appraisal of one particular aspect of the self-destructive activity, the attempt. This was done by constructing an objective scale ranking the lethality of the various self-destructive modes.

Objective Scale of Lethality

The objective scale was constructed in the following manner: A list of the methods used in self-destruction was obtained from the publications of the National Office of Vital Statistics, Department of Health, Education and Welfare. These are the standard classifications of methods in self-inflicted death used throughout the United States. They were listed in random order and presented to persons from the medical, psychiatric, and psychological professions with instructions to rank them in terms of lethality. Agreement between the groups was generally high. The ranking obtained listed the methods from the most lethal to the least lethal as follows: (*a*) firearms and explosives, (*b*) jumping from high places, (*c*) cutting and piercing of vital organs, (*d*) hanging, (*e*) drowning (can't swim), (*f*) poisoning (solids and liquids), (*g*) cutting and piercing of nonvital organs, (*h*) drowning (can swim), (*i*) poisoning (gases), and (*j*) analgesic and soporific substances. Two other integrally related elements offer further information about the lethality of the methods. These are discussed below.

Point of No Return. This refers to the speed with which the point is reached, after the initiation of the first step in the act, at which the chain of events becomes irreversible and death ensues. In general, a gunshot wound through a vital organ has an almost immediate point of no return; that is, it is practically zero once the trigger is pulled. To take an example from the opposite end of the scale, the ingestion of a soporific substance such as twelve 1½-gr barbiturate capsules has a point of no return of at least several hours (from the time the tablets are ingested).

Feasibility of Intervention for Rescue. This factor is closely related to the point of no return, since one important consideration in rescue is the time available to carry out the lifesaving activity. However, time is not the only consideration in the feasibility of rescue. The method used for self-destruction is also of importance. For example, some self-destructive modes allow the victim several hours before death, and yet the possibility of the damage being reversed may not be proportionately great. This occurs with some poisons, such as mercuric chloride, which can impair the kidney to such an extent that no effective treatment is possible, and the person may die several weeks later.

ILLUSTRATIVE CASE

Below is presented the description of a patient who was seen by the SPC and who was evaluated on the above schedule. The relevant details of the psychiatric examination and history will be reported as they pertain to each section of the schedule.

The patient was a 54-year-old, single, male Caucasian who had been brought into the hospital because of severe self-inflicted lacerations of the throat, which had been nearly fatal.

INTRAPERSONAL ASPECTS

Intention

Conscious Intention. *Awareness of the effect of his threats and/or attempts on others.* The patient was judged to have been in a state of psychotic dissociation at the time of his self-destructive attempt. This was the result of alcoholic excesses imposed on a long-standing schizoid character. The patient was a chronic alcoholic. Because of the state of dissociation we judged that the patient had little conscious awareness of the effect of his threats or attempts on others at the time of the attempt.

Awareness by the person of the results of his own self-destructive behavior. Again as a result of the dissociation and the other disintegrative aspects of psychosis, which were present, we judged that the patient had little integrated awareness of the results of his own self-destructive behavior.

Patient's knowledge about the method contemplated or used. This patient was a high-school graduate. It could be safely assumed that his general knowledge would enable him to know that the method he had used was a potentially lethal one.

Conscious provisions for rescue. Since we felt that the patient had had little integrated conscious awareness of his intention to make a self-destructive attempt, we judged that there were no conscious provisions for rescue.

Unconscious Intention. *Constellation of dynamics.* These were the events immediately preceding the self-destructive attempt. The patient was an extremely dependent person who was also a chronic alcoholic. Shortly before he made the self-destructive attempt he had decided to end an alcoholic binge of several days. This was probably because of lack of funds. He was extremely anxious as a result of the withdrawal of the alcohol gratification (and probably also because of the onset of an alcoholic psychosis). He went to the police, begging them to send him to a hospital for treatment. However, because of some difficulty in making himself understood or because of the reluctance of the police to accede to his request, he was not sent to the hospital. As a result of this he became extremely angry at the police and at the same time his anxiety mounted to new heights. In this patient, therefore, two of the important dynamic indicators for self-destructive activity were present, anxiety and hostility.

Kinds of fantasies. The patient's history pointed to a large number of rescue fantasies. He was constantly seeking to be taken care of and had actually carried out this desire on many occasions. In addition, there were strong fantasies of being hurt, which were revealed in hostile, paranoid descriptions of some of the events leading up to the self-destructive attempt.

Unconscious manipulation of others through threats or attempts. There was apparently a strong drive unconsciously to manipulate others, as his attempt was made in a fairly exhibitionistic way in an area where he could not fail to be noticed. In addition to this, before he made the attempt by cutting his throat, he tried to throw himself before some slow-moving vehicles. We might also infer that there was some attempt to manipulate the police through several overt threats of suicide when he was with them.

Life pattern of person. Certain self-destructive trends manifested themselves in the life pattern of this patient. He had a serious chronic illness (tuberculosis), the treatment of which he frequently interrupted against medical advice. He also followed a not unusual alcoholic pattern of not providing sufficient food, clothing, and lodging for himself.

Unconscious provisions for rescue. The patient had made fairly marked unconscious provisions for rescue. This was evident by his making the attempt in an area where he was certain to be detected. As a matter of fact, it was this feature of the patient's activity which led to quick treatment, which saved his life.

Ego Organization

Impulsivity versus Efficacy of Controls. Both the self-destructive attempt and various episodes in the patient's past history reveal that he was an impulsive person.

Rigidity versus Flexibility. The patient was a rigid person. He had gratified his needs most of his life by appealing to some stronger person or authority for satisfaction. Failing this, he would become quite anxious. The self-destructive attempt that brought him to our attention was only one of a long list of examples of this type of functioning.

Isolation versus Relatedness. The patient lived a quite isolated life. He was cut off from his family, and there were no friends with whom he was very deeply involved at the present time. There was evidence of few such relationships having existed in the past. The type of relationship that characterized his life was a dependent one. In this type of relationship he would receive from others but would not otherwise become deeply involved with them.

INTERPERSONAL ASPECTS

Communicative Aspects

Degree of Directness of the Communication. The patient's communication was a very direct one. He had communicated directly to the police, and this failing, he communicated (through his attempt) to the world at large by making his attempt on a busy street. Thus, an audience to respond to the communication was immediately available.

What Is Being Communicated? We can judge that there was a good deal of anger being communicated in this patient's self-destructive attempt. However, this would not have been obvious to the particular audience who received his communication. What they did see, eventually, was the desperation, a message that was received and acted upon.

To Whom Is the Communication Addressed? This communication was apparently addressed to the world at large. The patient, apparently, universalized his feelings and felt that what was going on was the result of the cruelty of the world and that the world would have to be responsible for the results of its treatment of him.

Purpose of the Communication. The purpose of the patient's communication was to achieve some respite from his anxiety and, specifically, to get into the hospital. The purpose was achieved by his activity.

In the discussion of the communicative aspects for this patient only the communicative elements of the suicidal attempt were discussed. Not a great deal was learned of the patient's other communicative functioning except the entreaties to the police already mentioned.

Environmental Aspects

Patient's Attitude toward Environment and/or Significant Others. The patient had a chronically dependent, resentful, and paranoid attitude toward his environment. He made frequent attempts to secure dependent gratification from the environment, but particularly when his anxiety was high, he tended to go about this in a resentful way, which often provoked rejection.

Attitude of Significant Others toward the Patient. As far as we could determine, the patient was not, at the time of his self-destructive attempt, relating to persons who were interested in facilitating any positive communication with him, nor were they familiar enough and sympathetic enough with his life picture to be able to understand him well.

Cultural and Religious Attitudes toward Death. The patient came from an American Indian background, which possibly had stoic and masochistic traits culturally associated with it.

IMPLEMENTATION

Objective Scale of Lethality

The patient used method *g*, cutting and piercing of nonvital organs (slashing of throat), which is approximately halfway down the list of self-destructive methods. As to the point of no return, there was time before exsanguination could occur, and the feasibility of rescue and reversal of self-destructive action was good in this particular case.

DISCUSSION

The degree of lethality inferred from the patient's self-destructive implementation alone differs from the evaluation when all parts of the schedule are taken into account. The patient used the method of throat cutting in such a way and place that he was quite likely to be rescued. Intrapersonally, we see that consciously the patient had little awareness of his behavior and its implications. This is a somewhat ominous sign, for, in general, if patients are aware of their intentions in their self-destructive activity, the lethality tends to decrease. When the factors under unconscious intention are evaluated, the picture grows worse. The patient had exhibited in high degree at least two of the dynamics found in lethal attempts: hostility and anxiety. His fantasies were significant in their preoccupation with hurt and hurting and being rescued and being taken care of. His life pattern indicated neglect of himself to such an extent that strong underlying patterns of a self-destructive nature are implied. All these were negative signs. The one positive sign was that he was still making unconscious provisions for his rescue, implying that the wish to die was not yet paramount. The patient's ego organization was such that the potentiality for lethality was increased, for in every one of the significant continua the patient fell on the negative side. He was impulsive, he was rigid, and he was isolated.

Part II of the schedule, dealing with interpersonal aspects, helped fill out the picture. It was a poor sign that the patient had difficulty in communicating positively with his environment, in which there were practically no significant others with whom he had a favorable relationship, and also faced an environment that was unsympathetic to him. In addition, certain cultural attitudes from his American Indian background tended to enhance self-destructive activity.

The communicative aspects indicated some positive prognostic signs. The patient was making a relatively direct communication of his feelings of desperation to the world at large. Moreover, he was doing this in a dramatic way and in a way likely to ensure that the communication would be responded to. The purpose of his communication seemed to be aimed at achieving some respite from his anxiety. This was a relatively favorable purpose as opposed to, for example, the desire to make others feel bad by seeing him dead.

In summary, this was a person whose conscious and unconscious intentions of self-destruction were ominous. The analysis of his ego organization added to the feeling of lethal potentiality. However, these negative factors were somewhat ameliorated by a rather direct (almost primitive) and effective type of communication. It was as if there were two important trends in this patient's personality, which had not been integrated with each other. The lethal potentiality was judged to be high for this patient but on a relatively long-term chronic basis. The short-term, immediate lethal potentiality was considered to have abated with the gratification of his immediate demands. The SPC was active in having the patient admitted to the psychiatric unit of the hospital for a recuperative stay and in establishing a liaison with a community social agency, which took over treatment and handling of the case, using the SPC as consultant.

SUMMARY

This chapter has presented a plan for the evaluation of self-destructive potentiality. It includes both an objective evaluation of the lethality of self-destructive attempts and certain theoretical considerations, which involve both interpersonal and intrapersonal considerations. It is our premise that applying a schedule that attempts to evaluate all or most of the factors that are significant in self-destructive personalities helps to ensure consideration of all necessary areas and to compensate for any difficulties resulting from the unconscious tendency to avoid the area and topic of death.

References

1. Dorpat, T. L., H. S. Ripley, and R. Leidig: A study of suicide in Seattle. (Unpublished paper, 1959.)
2. Eissler, K. R.: *The Psychiatrist and the Dying Patient,* New York: International Universities Press, Inc., 1955.
3. Farberow, N. L.: Personality patterns of suicidal mental hospital patients, *Genetic Psychology Monographs,* 42: 3–79, 1950.
4. Feifel, H. (Ed.): *The Meaning of Death,* New York: McGraw-Hill Book Company, Inc., Blakiston Division, 1959.
5. Freud, S.: *Beyond the Pleasure Principle,* London: Hogarth Press, Ltd., 1948.
6. Menninger, K. A.: *Man Against Himself,* New York: Harcourt, Brace and Company, Inc., 1938.
7. Neuringer, C.: An Exploratory Study of Suicidal Thinking, unpublished doctoral dissertation, University of Kansas, 1960.
8. Motto, J. A., and Clara Greene: Suicide and the medical community, *A.M.A. Archives of Neurology and Psychiatry,* 80: 776–781, 1958.
9. Pokorny, A. D.: Characteristics of forty-four patients who subsequently committed suicide, *A.M.A. Archives of General Psychiatry,* 2: 314–323, 1960.
10. Robins, E., J. Gassner, J. Kayes, R. H. Wilkinson, Jr., and G. E. Murphy: The communication of suicidal intent: A study of 134 consecutive cases of successful (completed) suicides, *American Journal of Psychiatry,* 115: 724–733, 1959.

6

Suicide among Schizophrenic Mental Hospital Patients

NORMAN L. FARBEROW, EDWIN S. SHNEIDMAN, AND
CALISTA V. LEONARD

Within the community, the mental hospital is frequently seen as the final treatment resource for the person who has become so emotionally disturbed that he can no longer exercise appropriate judgment or control in relation to harming himself. Hospitalization, of course, is for the hospital staff merely the beginning of the problem of management and treatment, inasmuch as the hospital, as a minimum, assumes responsibility for the physical safety and welfare of a suicidal patient. In addition, one of the major problems that faces any mental hospital staff is the assessment of possible suicidal behavior in *any* patient. Predicting suicidal potentiality is particularly difficult, not only because of the complexity of human behavior, but also because relatively little research has been done on this topic. Thus, whether with patients who enter the hospital labeled as suicidal or with all other patients, a mental hospital staff is faced with the need for careful assessment of suicidal potentiality, not only when the patient is actually within the hospital, but also when the time approaches for him to leave, whether on pass, extended leave, or discharge.

As part of a larger research project on suicide a detailed study has been made of persons who committed suicide while patients in a mental hospital. A survey made among such hospitals revealed that the largest number (and a disproportionately high percentage) of the committed suicides in these hospitals was accounted for by those patients diagnosed as schizophrenic [1];

[1] Patients diagnosed as schizophrenic contributed about 70 per cent of the total number of suicides and also made up around 68 per cent of the general mental hospital patient population studied.

indeed, many persons who committed suicide in mental hospitals were admitted by virtue of their schizophrenic symptoms in the absence of indication of any suicidal potential. This chapter reports the results of a systematic comparison of a group of hospitalized schizophrenic patients who committed suicide with a matched group of hospitalized schizophrenic patients (controls) who did not commit suicide. The intention of this study is to focus on the differences between these two groups to find clues relevant to the prediction and prevention of suicidal behavior in the mental hospital setting, as well as to obtain additional information about suicidal behavior in mentally disturbed patients in general.

SUBJECTS

The detailed clinical records of 60 schizophrenic patients hospitalized in 37 mental hospitals throughout the United States in the 1955–1958 interval were examined intensively. Thirty of these persons had committed suicide while they were under hospital jurisdiction (in or out of the hospital), and thirty were mental hospital patients who did not commit suicide and who had been discharged from the hospital rolls during this same period. All 60 subjects were male and Caucasian with a primary diagnosis of schizophrenia (no attempt was made to select for subtypes among the schizophrenic disorder, but these data were recorded). The 30 suicide cases were randomly selected from a larger group of suicide cases, and the 30 controls were then selected to match the 30 suicide cases as closely as possible on a man-to-man basis in terms of age, religious affiliation. marital status, and year of suicide or discharge.

PROCEDURE

An intensive analysis of all the records available for each of the 30 suicide and 30 control cases was undertaken in a three-step procedure outlined below:

1. A detailed and comprehensive abstract was prepared of each patient's history, his course in the hospital, and all other available information about him. This abstract was obtained from records such as doctors' notes and orders, nurses' notes, social service reports, psychological test reports, psychiatric and medical summaries, and therapy reports. In addition, the patient's behavior, symptoms, and feelings in his day-by-day stay in the hospital were noted, and all his medications and treatments were recorded and plotted on a time-line graph so these could be correlated with any changes in his status. All orders for the granting of privileges, passes, leaves of absences, and trial visits were noted, as well as any visits to the

patient and by whom. The final disposition of each case was noted; i.e., the place, method, and circumstances of death were added for the suicide cases, and the type of discharge and procedures involved were recorded for each control case. Special attention was paid to patterns that emerged, i.e., to the relationships found between the patient's behavior, his medications, the hospital actions and reactions, and the behavior on the part of the patient's relatives and other potential resource persons (see sample abstract sheet at end of this chapter).

2. The second step in the analysis was to conduct an intensive *psychological autopsy* for each individual case. A team of psychologists and psychiatrists were given an oral presentation of all the pertinent information concerning the case except for the last one or two entries in the abstract. Thus, they were given a complete case history up to, but not including, the identification of the case as either a suicide or a control.

Summary sheets were filled out by each participant in the psychological autopsy, recording the salient features under the headings listed above, the psychodynamics of the patient, and clues that might have been indicators of possible suicide or lack of potential suicidal behavior. After each consultant had predicted the outcome of the case, i.e., whether it was a suicide or control, the identity of the case was revealed and the clues that had been elicited were discussed further in light of the known outcome, and the lesson to be learned from the case was recorded (see sample summary sheet at end of this chapter).

3. The third step was to extract and synthesize the basic similarities and differences between suicide and control cases on the basis of the information compiled during the 60 case abstractions and psychological autopsies. Both quantitative and qualitative aspects of the cases were examined, and the differences that appeared to distinguish the suicide from the control cases were noted.

OVERVIEW OF RESULTS

An overview of the findings may be given. The results of the analyses seem to indicate that, in general, the following characteristics distinguished the suicide cases from the control cases among the schizophrenic mental hospital patients[2]:

Schizophrenic patients who were in mental hospitals and who committed suicide were, by and large, persons who felt under stress. A majority (over

[2] The measure used for significance of differences between the groups was the χ^2, with the level of confidence at .05 or better.

70 per cent) had a history of previous suicidal attempts or suicidal ideation. Under stress these persons were extremely tense, restless, and impulsive. They made many requests or demands that something be done to relieve their tensions, although what they wanted and the way they demanded or asked for it varied, depending upon their individual characteristics, as outlined below. They appeared driven to find some kind of relief, including doing something themselves, if their tensions continued unabated.[3]

The above characteristics constitute a general description of almost all the members of the suicidal group. Among the total group of schizophrenic mental hospital patients who committed suicide,[4] three subtypes could be distinguished:

The Unaccepting Patient

Typically, the unaccepting patient resisted or rejected the hospitalization and did not believe, or did not admit, that he was mentally ill (in spite of the fact that he was often grossly disturbed and delusional on admission to the hospital). The unaccepting patients were frequently grandiose in their delusions, insisting that there was nothing wrong with

[3] Stress must be defined not only in terms of the *reality* of a stressful situation (i.e., a situation that would be stressful to most of us) but also in terms of the patient's own attitudes and feelings. For this reason the assessment of stress depends upon variables apparent only after careful study of each patient's background. As an example, a patient leaving the hospital where he had felt secure and returning to what was deemed by the staff to be a loyal wife and an understanding employer might find the situation unbearably stressful because of deep-seated homosexual conflict and overwhelming feelings of inadequacy concerning his male role.

[4] A comment about the word *schizophrenic* is in order. Ordinarily, the words *schizophrenic suicide* conjure up the image of a psychotic person who might kill himself in response to a hallucinated command, delusional impulse, or a dereistic thought. One of the several findings to emerge from this study was that, among the schizophrenic suicide group, suicide occurred in almost all cases where there was some evidence of *improved* organization and control in the patient. This is contrary to the notion that suicide in schizophrenic patients represents the depth of psychotic-like behavior. The data from the present research indicate that in almost all the 30 schizophrenic suicides studied, the suicide was a somewhat organized and planned action by the patient in an apparent effort to extricate himself from his intolerable life situation, from which he could see no other way out. They appeared to have good "reasons" for self destruction, even though they were still clinically schizophrenic at the time (see E. S. Shneidman and N. L. Farberow, *Clues to Suicide,* New York: McGraw-Hill Book Company, Inc., 1957, Chap. 4). This finding has encouraging implications from the standpoint of identifying prodromal clues to suicide and for the control of suicidal behavior of the schizophrenic patient.

them and demanding to be released from the hospital. They were exceedingly restless, hyperactive, impulsive, and occasionally assaultive. In general, they did not express feelings of guilt or inadequacy, seldom had somatic complaints, and did not manifest any overt signs of depression. A previous history of suicidal activity or ideation was present in approximately 60 per cent of these patients. Most of them received tranquilizing medications, which quieted their symptoms so passes or leaves could be given. Suicide on pass or leave occurred in 60 per cent of these patients.

The Dependent Satisfied Patient

In general, the dependent satisfied patient was dependent on hospitalization, usually realized he was ill, and counted on the hospital to help him. Under stress the behavior of such patients showed some of the following characteristics: They were restless and impulsive but almost never assaultive. They were overtly depressed and filled with anxiety and tension, and they expressed many feelings of guilt or inadequacy. Somatic complaints were frequent, as were requests for treatment of various sorts (sedation, restraint, seclusion, psychotherapy, etc.). They sought much attention and reassurance. A previous history of suicidal activity or ideation was present in 75 per cent of the group. Regardless of the admission symptoms, the dependent satisfied suicidal patient improved and became somewhat deceptively nonsuicidal in the hospital. It was only when release from the hospital was considered or implemented that there was a return to the previous disturbed behavior. Suicide on pass or trial visit occurred in 83 per cent of these patients.

The Dependent Dissatisfied Patient

This type was very similar to the dependent satisfied patient in realizing he was ill and depending on the hospital for help. The dependent dissatisfied patient also generally showed much restlessness, depression, and tension, made many requests or demands for treatment of various kinds, and developed frequent somatic complaints. A history of suicidal activity or ideation was present in 87 per cent of this group. This patient depended upon the hospital for help but, in contrast with the dependent satisfied patient, apparently came to feel after a while that the hospital was not giving him what he needed. Thus, instead of becoming quiet and nonsuicidal in the hospital, these patients became increasingly tense, depressed, demanding, and attention getting. Expressions of feelings of self-deprecation and suicidal ideation increased, and constant attention and reassurance was sought. Suicide in the hospital occurred in 75 per cent of these patients. The above three subtypes of suicidal patients are described more fully below.

The Control Patients

By way of contrast, the schizophrenic hospital patients who did not commit suicide (the control cases) generally showed the following characteristics, which distinguished them from the suicide cases. They almost never asked for or demanded any sort of treatment; they were seldom assaultive, impulsive, or restless and seldom manifested somatic complaints or expressed feelings of guilt or inadequacy. A previous history of suicidal activity or ideation was present in approximately 40 per cent of the control cases, indicating that simply knowing this fact is not an accurate indicator of suicide in a schizophrenic group. The schizophrenic control cases were often quite delusional, hallucinatory, preoccupied, or withdrawn but seemed able to make a somewhat passive adjustment to their own disordered mental processes and thus showed fewer indications of stress or acute discomfort. They often seemed indifferent to hospitalization and unaware of their own illness. By and large, control cases did not do a number of things that characterized many of the suicide cases. They did not demand to leave the hospital, pace the corridors, strike their fists against walls, need constant attention or reassurance, request various types of treatment, or continually ask to see the doctor, nurse, or chaplain. Among the control cases there was one subgroup, labeled the marginal nonsuicidal schizophrenic group, which was characterized particularly by the fact that these patients seemed able to function outside the hospital in a marginal way. Hospitalization, when it did occur, often was precipitated by some unusual incident or stress in the employment situation, or by a chance arrest for vagrancy, or after an alcoholic episode. Upon release from the hospital, they appeared able to resume the same marginal adjustment that had characterized them before hospitalization.

PATTERNS OF BEHAVIOR IN SUICIDE AND CONTROL CASES

This section presents detailed information about the suicide and control schizophrenic mental hospital patients.

The Unaccepting Patient

Ten of the suicide cases were unaccepting patients. These patients were usually brought into the hospital grossly psychotic, out of contact with reality, very disturbed, restless, hyperactive, and often assaultive. If these patients were able to realize that they were actually in a hospital, they demanded their release, claiming there was nothing wrong and insisting upon their religious and civil rights. These patients frequently had delusions of omnipotence and showed a remarkable absence of the feelings of self-deprecation, somatic complaints, and physical discomfort that were so conspicuously present in other types of suicide patients.[5] The unaccepting patients appeared to have little insight into their illnesses; yet the severity of illness on admission tended to be high, with an obvious and urgent need for hospitalization. The distinguishing features about these patients appeared to be not only an agitated, acting-out behavior pattern under stress (usually requiring the use of sedation, wet packs, or restraints) but also a complete resistance to the hospital and to the idea that there was anything wrong with them.

During the course of hospitalization, tranquilizing drugs[6] were used for nine of these patients and appeared to have a calming effect on all but one patient (who did not respond to shock treatment either). Shock treatment had been used at some time for seven of these patients. Eight of these patients improved with the administration of tranquilizing drugs, and six were considered for passes and leaves fairly rapidly. Although this is a difficult feature to assess, it appeared that, although these patients improved in the hospital in that they became somewhat more cooperative, they never lost their basic resistance to hospitalization. Insight into their illness was limited, and their cooperation seemed actually to be a better organized effort at getting *out* of the hospital.

During the psychological autopsies, it became increasingly evident that tranquilizing drugs were most helpful in calming these disturbed unaccepting patients but that this calming apparently did not reduce their suicidal potential. In the eight unaccepting patients who improved with tranquilizing medications, tranquilizers were still being administered at the time of the suicide or shortly before. There was no doubt that these patients had improved with tranquilizing drugs so they were no longer so highly disturbed as they had been on admission and were in fairly good contact with reality. The question was frequently raised, however, whether the quieting action of the drugs made the patient *appear* better than he actually was

[5] Although many of these patients were diagnosed paranoid schizophrenic, this diagnosis alone did not seem to distinguish the unaccepting patient. There were also many control cases diagnosed paranoid schizophrenic who did not show this reaction pattern, and there were many dependent patients as well who were diagnosed paranoid schizophrenic and yet did not show the reaction pattern described above.

[6] In both suicide and control cases in this study, the most commonly given tranquilizing drug was chlorpromazine, with dosages usually ranging from 150–600 mg per day.

and permitted passes and leaves to be prematurely given. A question also raised was the possibility that the calming effect of the drugs might allow the patient to have painful insights before he was prepared to cope with them.

When passes and leaves were considered, these patients seemed to be in a particularly difficult "double bind" position. They could not accept hospitalization, and if, in addition, their home environment was unbearably stressful, it was apparent that they would face an intolerable situation either way. With the restless, impulsive, acting-out type of behavior these patients had shown under stress, they were not able passively to accept a difficult home situation and self-destruction became the escape chosen. Suicide was committed by eight of these patients at a time when there was a remission of their illness and under circumstances indicating that there had been considerable planning and organization in bringing about their own deaths. Six of the suicides occurred while the patients were on pass or leave.

The Dependent Satisfied Patient

Twelve of the suicide cases were patients characterized by a high degree of dependency on the hospital and were patients who seemed fairly satisfied with their hospitalization. Their behavior whenever they were under stress, however, was generally tense, anxious, and restless; they had many somatic complaints and made many requests for treatment of various kinds; they were overtly depressed and often expressed feelings of guilt and/or inadequacy. They usually realized they were ill (many were voluntary admissions) and were depending on the hospital for help. A past history of suicidal activity or ideation was present in nine of them.

Tranquilizing drugs were given to all these patients during the course of their hospitalization and seemed to be very helpful in calming most of them; however, that tranquilizing drugs did not eliminate suicidal potentiality in these patients is evidenced by the fact that eight were receiving such drugs at the time of suicide. Shock therapy was received by six of these patients, and one had just finished a course of shock treatment at the time of suicide. Group or individual psychotherapy had been part of the treatment of six of these patients.

Most of the dependent satisfied patients seemed to improve in the hospital, and as they did, their behavior became deceptively nonsuicidal. It was only when passes or leaves were considered or given that there was a return of the tension and anxiety previously shown under stress. Many of these patients were released on pass or trial visit to what appeared to be a fairly optimal environment (a supportive wife or parents, a job held open for the patient during his hospitalization, and so forth). However, on close investigation it was evident that the patient felt a great deal of conflict and ambivalence about his home environment and that it was *to him* a most stressful situation. All these patients showed tension or anxiety as passes and leaves were considered or given, and ten committed suicide on pass or trial visit. Eleven of these patients were not considered delusional or hallucinatory but were felt to be in good contact at the time of their suicide.

Assessment of suicidal potentiality in these patients was particularly difficult during the psychological autopsies; however, it became increasingly apparent that suicidal risk was based on the extreme importance of hospitalization to these patients. They simply could not be separated safely from the hospital until they had found another sanctuary that was acceptable to them or until they had learned new means of coping with outside stresses.

The Dependent Dissatisfied Patient

The eight dependent dissatisfied patients, like the dependent satisfied patients, showed a high degree of dependency on the hospital and a realization that they were ill (with somatic complaints, requests for treatment, etc.). Seven of the eight patients had a history of previous suicidal activity or ideation. Although this type of patient usually showed great dependency in his original hospitalization and appeared hopeful of help, this attitude changed radically when he felt the help was not forthcoming. As the patient began to feel that the hospital could not or would not help him, he showed a dissatisfaction with his hospitalization along with increasingly disturbed behavior. With the patient's dissatisfaction came a sharp increase in restlessness, further demands for attention, depression, suicidal ideation, somatic complaints, criticism, hostility, and threats to elope or leave the hospital against medical advice. In many cases these patients made excessively self-centered demands for attention that were simply impossible to satisfy. Frequently there would be an oscillation, with shifts from this disturbed activity to an opposite reaction of docile, hopeful, oversubmissive behavior as the patient tried desperately to find a way to meet his needs, followed by a return of the agitated, disturbed behavior. Statements such as "nothing is being done for me," "other people don't like me," "I should end it all," and "there's no place for me anywhere" were frequent and were further indications of desperate dissatisfaction.

The demanding, time-consuming, attention-getting behavior was often irritating and disturbing to the hospital staff and to other patients as well.

Any manifestation of annoyance or hostility on the part of the hospital staff or other patients seemed only to intensify the plight of the dissatisfied patient. He had clearly indicated his inability to handle his tensions outside the hospital, and yet he had been unable to find the help he needed in the hospital. He literally had no place to go, as he could neither leave the hospital nor tolerate his anxieties and unsatisfied needs within it. Six of the eight dependent dissatisfied patients committed suicide within the hospital, and all six were on tranquilizing drugs at the time of the suicide. (Obviously no causality is implied, but masking effects might legitimately be inferred.) These patients were generally considered in good contact, and two left suicide notes.

By and large, the dependent dissatisfied patient appeared to be a person who couldn't leave the hospital and yet seemed to have lost faith in the therapeutic potential of his hospitalization. Often these patients felt (with some justification) that they were not liked by others ("nobody likes me," "the doctors think I'm making this up," "this is the only way out").

The Nonsuicidal (Control) Patient

An important characteristic that generally distinguished the typical nonsuicidal (control) patient from the suicide case was his passive, accepting, somewhat indifferent attitude toward hospitalization and toward his environment in general. There were 16 of the 30 nonsuicide schizophrenic patients who were designated marginal. This type of patient accepted his hospitalization without complaint or demand and without asking for treatment or objecting to what he got. He did not seem dependent on the hospital, nor did he seem to reject or resist. He didn't ask to leave the hospital or leave without permission nor did he seem to need to stay in the hospital; he often seemed somewhat indifferent to being discharged from the hospital. Although frequently quite delusional, hallucinatory, isolated, or preoccupied, this type of patient nevertheless had seemed able to make a passive adjustment to his illness. He could live with it. His degree of illness therefore did not appear quite so severe as in the disturbed, restless, hyperactive patient, who seemed unable to make much of an adjustment to the stresses that beset him. If it can be said of the suicide cases that suicide resulted when they found themselves in a stressful situation from which they saw no other means of escape, it might also be said of the marginal nonsuicidal (control) patient that he had no need to escape anywhere. He was almost never demanding, impulsive, or assaultive. He rarely eloped and rarely expressed feelings of guilt and/or inadequacy. He was usually not depressed or restless and did not usually have somatic complaints. He tended to be an older, single man, often alcoholic, whose degree of illness did not seem quite so severe as in other schizophrenic patients. He was often able to function outside the hospital in a marginal way, and many times hospitalization was precipitated only by unusual situational stresses or perhaps after a prolonged alcoholic episode.

Viewing the course of hospitalization for these patients, it was seen that in a few cases where situational stresses had precipitated hospitalization, the patient improved rapidly with custodial care and tranquilizing drugs and was released within 2 or 3 months. Hospitalization seemed to be primarily a temporary period of observation. In other cases, however, hospitalization was necessary for a year or more, and in some cases there was a history of hospitalization for many years.

Nine of these sixteen patients had had shock treatment at some time in the past, in some cases without improvement and in other cases with a temporary improvement that could not be maintained. Only three patients had received individual or group therapy, apparently because it was not usually felt that this type of schizophrenic patient would benefit particularly from this kind of therapy.

All 16 patients had been given tranquilizing drugs, with considerable apparent improvement in all but three cases (a mildly calming effect appeared in these three cases). Tranquilizing drugs appeared to benefit some of these patients remarkably, in some cases completely ending periods of mute withdrawal that long hospitalization and shock treatment had been unable to modify. Eleven patients were on tranquilizing drugs at the time of discharge. Tension or apprehension at being given passes or discharge was rarely shown.

There was a great deal of variation among the 14 remaining control cases; they are grouped together for descriptive convenience and not because they were particularly similar in characteristics. The group ranged from those patients who seemed most to resemble the marginal control group to a few who closely resembled the suicide cases. In the case of the few controls who seemed potentially suicidal, an unusually supportive environment seemed primarily responsible for their nonsuicidal outcome.

DISCUSSION AND CONCLUSIONS

An Evaluation of the Treatment Methods Used for the Schizophrenic Suicide Cases

The clinical folders of the suicide patients indicated that a number of different methods of treatment were applied. These are described below along with some impressions about them.

Symptomatic Treatment. Symptomatic treatment, such as sedation, tubs, packs, or restraints, was frequently used for the disturbed patient who later committed suicide. These temporary measures seemed helpful in quieting patients and were frequently asked for by many of them. Tranquilizing drugs (usually chlorpromazine) were used for all but one of these patients and appeared to have a calming effect in almost all cases and to be very beneficial in a great many cases. There is no doubt that the use of tranquilizing drugs was most helpful to these patients and to the hospital staff in quieting patient disturbance and alleviating tension and distress. However, there appeared to be a danger involved in the use of tranquilizing drugs, which stemmed from the apparent assumption by the hospital staff (and probably the patient and his family as well) that, because the patient was calmer and appeared improved, he was well enough for passes and leaves. This appeared to be a confusion of symptomatic treatment with fundamental treatment. The use of tranquilizing drugs is presumed to render a patient more amenable to treatment, but he must still learn a better adjustment to environmental stresses before he may be safely released on passes or leaves.

Psychotherapeutic Treatment. Group therapy and individual psychotherapy. Not enough patients had received this type of treatment to make a meaningful evaluation. Such therapy was tried and discontinued for a few patients who could not apparently benefit from it. Some suicide cases and some control cases had had extensive therapy. One patient who had received individual psychotherapy for the six weeks of his hospitalization committed suicide on his first pass home.

Milieu therapy. Milieu therapy was apparently a standard hospital treatment method used in almost all cases and appeared to be enjoyed by most patients. It seemed to have considerable value in helping with improvement *in the hospital;* there was, however, a lack of evidence that this therapy left these suicide patients better equipped to face the stresses of life outside the hospital. Therapy of this sort most frequently consisted of leatherworking classes, woodshop, metal shop, swimming, basketball, calisthenics, and so forth.

Notes in the patient's folder from therapists who conducted these various groups were often highly revealing in their reports of variations in the patient's behavior. Such reports by therapists about increased tension, restlessness, and suicidal ideation in a patient appear to be a valuable source of additional information for the staff in assessing suicide potentiality.

Electrical, chemical, and surgical treatment. Shock treatment (electrical, chemical, or both) had been given to 18 of the 30 suicide cases. Such treatment seemed to give only temporary relief and did not appear to do even that in some cases. As a symptomatic treatment it seemed far less effective than tranquilizing drugs. Fear of shock treatment was expressed by some patients, and two suicides occurred in which there was some indication that one of the precipitating factors was fear that shock treatment would be instituted.

One patient had received a lobotomy and one a leukotomy; yet both subsequently committed suicide. The patient who received the lobotomy had also had many courses of shock treatment over a period of several years but had continued highly disturbed and actively suicidal, repeatedly attempting suicide by hanging. Even after the lobotomy had been performed, he had remained suicidal, although he was somewhat calmer. He finally succeeded in hanging himself in spite of the vigilance of the hospital staff, who were alert to the suicidal danger in this patient. He had not been given tranquilizing drugs inasmuch as his death occurred before they were being widely used.

Other Forms of Treatment. It is apparent from the preceding paragraphs that, although symptomatic treatment seemed effective in most suicide cases, no basic treatment methods appeared to improve these patients' ability to adjust more satisfactorily. During the psychological autopsies held on the individual cases, it was frequently suggested that they most needed a treatment primarily of continuing support and protection. This meant not only supportive hospitalization but also that a very supportive home environment seemed essential to the patients' welfare, and release from the hospital into an *un*supportive home environment seemed to be most hazardous. It was suggested that perhaps, in some cases, these patients were simply not able to assume the responsibilities expected in our society and that to force these responsibilities upon them was suicidogenic. These patients appeared to need a place to go, a sanctuary where they would be protected from their own tensions, impulses, and anxieties. If the home environment could not provide this sanctuary, it seemed apparent that the hospital (or some other resource) was needed for this purpose until such patients could develop new adaptive mechanisms for facing stressful life situations.

Psychodynamic Implications

Suicidal Potential and Psychosis. It is known that the suicidal rate among schizophrenics (compared with everyone else) is disproportionately high. One question frequently asked about suicide in the mental hospital setting is: Are most schizophrenics potentially suicidal? On the basis of the present study, there appeared to be one large group of schizophrenic (control) cases who did not seem potentially suicidal. The schizophrenic suicide patients in this study seemed suicidal not necessarily because they were schizophrenic per se, but because there were other suicidogenic forces disturbing them. These forces seemed to be (A) a driving necessity for relief from tension; that is, a restless, demanding, solution-seeking behavior under stress; (B) a life situation that was too difficult and stressful for the patient to endure without relief; and (C) an inability to find a better way out of their difficulties. There was surprising (and fairly strong) evidence in the present study that suicide did not usually occur in schizophrenics in response to impulsive delusional thoughts or hallucinations but rather that self-destruction occurred in a somewhat planned and organized attempt at extrication from intolerably stressful life situations. That these patients could see no other means of escape except through suicide might well be one manifestation of their illness, as a constriction of focus and lack of flexibility seem generally to be accepted as characteristic of schizophrenia.

The evidence in this study that most of the suicides did not occur as a result of delusional actions gives rise immediately to an interesting speculation: if these patients' illnesses were in remission, could psychosis then be thought of as a protection against suicidal impulses in schizophrenic patients? Is it possible that the partial lifting of a psychotic state without substituting adequate new defenses leaves these tension-ridden, solution-seeking patients at the mercy of their tensions? If psychosis is for these patients an escape from intolerable stresses of reality, perhaps the partial easing of the psychotic state through medication or tranquilizing drugs brings these patients to a state of painful insight before they are able to cope with new insights. It has been suggested that perhaps one effect of tranquilizing medications is to render a return to the former protective psychosis difficult or impossible. Certainly these questions warrant further investigation.

Suicidal Behavior and the Drive for Relief of Tension. One of the best single clues that appeared to distinguish suicidal schizophrenics from control schizophrenics was the presence of behavior under stress that indicated the patient was undergoing a tremendous drive for relief of tension. Not only were symptoms such as restlessness, tension, and anxiety present, but the patient usually made other active attempts to change his situation through demanding, insistent behavior. In discussing the drive for relief of tension, the immediate (circular) question arises: Is the degree of tension greater in the suicidal schizophrenics, or are they simply less able to bear tension than the more passive control cases? The nonsuicidal (control) schizophrenic patients, in general, appeared to be just as hallucinated, delusional, mute, isolated, withdrawn, and preoccupied as did the suicidal schizophrenic patients. However, the control cases seemed to lack the restlessness, activity, and demand for relief of tension displayed by the schizophrenic suicides. Although many suicide cases were subject to unusually severe and realistic stresses, this was also true of some control cases. In many suicide cases, the stress felt by the patient seemed to be due primarily to his own idiosyncratic feelings and attitudes rather than to a realistically stressful outside environment. Although this difficult question of stress tolerance in the suicidal schizophrenic presents formidable methodological problems for investigation, one intriguing point in the approach to the problem is the possibility that muteness, isolation, and withdrawal may be safer defenses (against the stress that is prodromal to suicide) than the restless striving of the suicidal patient.

Suicidal Behavior and Extremes of Emotional Behavior. Another highly interesting characteristic shown by the suicide cases almost without exception, and absent in the majority of control cases, was the presence of highly charged feelings and attitudes about their illness and about their hospitalization. The controls appeared to lack this depth or intensity of emotional involvement. However, among the suicide cases it was present, and in quite different forms. On the one hand, there were those suicide patients who were highly involved in a dependent relationship with the hospital, knew they were ill, and depended on the hospital for protection. At the opposite extreme, there were suicide patients who not only completely resisted help from the hospital but did not seem to realize they were ill or were at least unwilling to admit their illness (in spite of the fact that most had been admitted to the hospital in a severe psychotic state). These differences among the suicide cases suggests some intriguing possibilities. It could be that these extremes of attitude toward their illness and hospitalization represented different defenses against the same underlying psychodynamic disturbances, such as severe feelings of inadequacy, lack of personal worth, or guilt. Another possibility is merely that extremes of behavior are a general characteristic of those patients who resort to such an extreme final act as self-destruction.

The coexistence of extremes of behavior appeared more generally both among all suicide cases and within a single suicide case than in control cases. For example, many individual suicide cases alternated between quiet, cooperative behavior and periods of loud, aggressive, and hostile actions. As just noted, many suicide cases rejected any need for assistance by the hospital, whereas others were highly dependent on the hospital to help them in their illness. These extremes of behavior may represent basic differences in lifelong behavior patterns between the suicide cases and the control cases, or they may merely represent desperate attempts on the part of the suicide case to handle the inner turmoil besetting him. Further study of the presence of extremes of behavior in the suicide cases seems indicated.

Suggestions for the Management of Suicidal Behavior

In spite of the best care that a mental hospital can provide, an occasional suicide by a patient does occur. This is due in large part to the difficulties inherent in the problem: the confusion of psychosis and suicidal tendencies and the uncertainties of assessing suicidal potentiality because of lack of knowledge and limited research findings on the problem. Many of the following suggestions are standard procedure in mental hospitals. Some have emerged as a result of this study and are now in the process of being put to empirical test. The suggestions for prevention of suicide presented below are made in relation to the three types of suicide cases: the unaccepting, dependent satisfied, and dependent dissatisfied patients.

The Unaccepting Patient. Inasmuch as the unaccepting patient resists hospitalization and often has little insight into his illness, control of suicidal behavior appears particularly difficult. Because he is often quieted rapidly with tranquilizing medications and is anxious to leave, the problem of when to give passes or leaves is crucial and his *home environment* becomes of vital importance. Some suggestions follow.

1. Considerable social service investigation and careful evaluation of the patient's home environment is particularly indicated *before* release of patient on pass or leave.

2. Orientation of family members to the patient's illness is necessary. Many family members seem to lack understanding and seem to place undue pressure on the patient upon his release from the hospital because he may seem improved.

3. Although ideally this type of patient should be provided with the opportunity to learn new ways of coping with outside stresses, this may prove difficult because he has little recognition of his illness. The necessity for providing a supportive home environment for him is apparent.

4. Both the hospital staff and the patient's family members should be aware of the suicidal risk in releasing this patient on pass or leave, should his home environment prove too stressful.

5. For the unaccepting patient who must remain in the hospital, it ap-

pears of primary importance to give him some hope of an eventual release into an outside environment that he will look forward to.

In summary, the following can be said about the management of the unaccepting patient: if he must remain in the hospital, he must be given the *hope* of eventual release into an environment he will look forward to. There is suicidal risk as he improves. If he seems well enough for passes or leaves away from the hospital, he must *not* be released into a stressful environment. He will want to leave because he is now improved, but this doesn't mean he can handle outside stresses. A careful evaluation of his home situation must be made *before* giving passes or leaves, and a substitute environment must be found if his home environment is not satisfactory.

It should be re-emphasized that not only is the unaccepting patient resistive of hospitalization, but his past behavior pattern under stress has been restless, demanding, and impulsively acting out. If he is returned to a stressful environment, this dangerous reaction pattern may reappear.

The Dependent Satisfied Patient.

1. The extreme importance of hospitalization to this patient needs to be recognized. This patient is often deceptively nonsuicidal as he improves in the hospital, but his basic dependence on the hospital and lack of ability to control his impulses away from the hospital has not changed.

2. Hospital protection for the dependent satisfied patient is needed for protection against his own impulses until he has another sanctuary that is acceptable to him or until he has learned new methods of coping with stress. In many suicide cases, early passes or leaves were often given in spite of direct statements by the patient that he feared he would be unable to control his impulses away from the hospital and in spite of anxiety and tension that would occur with the giving of passes.

3. Recognition must be given to the danger in the assumption that, because a suicidal patient has improved *in the hospital,* he is therefore well enough to be released into the same stressful environment from which he had been hospitalized. Symptomatic treatment, primarily tranquilizing drugs, which reduced the disturbance, anxiety, and depression in the hospital did not necessarily provide the patient with better means to cope with the stresses of life away from the hospital.

4. Psychological testing might be done before giving passes or leaves in order to determine whether the improvement shown in the patient represents genuine improvement or whether the underlying conflicts are still

present with the possibility that stress would cause his suicidal tendencies to flare up again when he left the hospital.

5. There is a need for a long and close protective association with the hospital and a gradual release of this patient into a new environment that he will accept as a sanctuary. Some control subjects who seemed potentially suicidal were fortunate in having this close protective association with the hospital. Unlike the unaccepting patient, who resisted being held in the hospital, the dependent satisfied patient seemed quite willing to stay; the problem was how to get him safely out of the hospital once he had shown improvement.

6. Before even a gradual release of this patient from the hospital, a careful evaluation of the home environment needed to be made from two standpoints: (A) there must be a realistic evaluation through social service investigation to determine the supportiveness of the home environment; (B) *most importantly,* there must be an evaluation of the stressfulness of the home environment from the standpoint of the patient's own feelings and attitudes. Regardless of the reality of the situation from the standpoint of others, if the patient felt the home situation to be unbearably stressful, then it *was* nonsupportive. Anxiety and tension about leaving the hospital was shown by all dependent satisfied suicide cases. If there is any question, it is safest to allow the dependent satisfied patient to remain in the hospital.

To recapitulate, the management of the dependent satisfied patient can be described as follows: This patient does not seem suicidal so long as he stays *in the hospital,* but if there is any tension or anxiety about passes or leaves away from the hospital, there is suicidal risk. This patient is often deceptively nonsuicidal as he improves *in the hospital* under tranquilizing drugs, but he cannot be released safely on pass or leave; he needs hospital protection against his own impulses (and usually asks for this protection) until he can be gradually released into another sanctuary that he can accept or until he has learned new defenses against stress *outside the hospital.* It should be emphasized that no matter how supportive the home environment seems, if the patient shows tension or anxiety at the thought of leaving, it is *not* safe to separate him from the hospital and release him into a stressful environment.

The Dependent Dissatisfied Patient. The problem of control of suicidal behavior in this patient rests on the recognition of the extreme importance of the hospital to him and of his inability to leave it. The first steps in the control of suicidal behavior depend upon giving him the emotional support he needs *in the hospital.* If this can be accomplished, the problem of releasing him safely from the hospital is the same as that outlined in the preceding paragraphs for the dependent satisfied patient.

Suggestions for the immediate control of suicidal behavior in the dependent dissatisfied patient while in the hospital are the following:

1. The establishment of a "buddy system," in which carefully selected volunteers might act as "big brothers" for the patient. This might be a valuable adjunct to other hospital and therapeutic procedures, and the purpose of this relationship would be to convey to the patient a sense of interest, a feeling of belief in his own worth and his own integrity, and meanwhile to protect him from his own self-destructive impulses. This might help to satisfy, at least temporarily, some of the excessive needs for attention and reassurance in this type of patient.

2. Often the institution of *any* new treatment or medication gives this patient *temporary* relief and improvement.

3. Sympathetic recognition on the part of the hospital staff that the excessively complaining, demanding, depressed behavior of the dissatisfied patient is an expression of desperate, although excessive, need for care and support.

4. Hospital staffs should be alerted to the fact that repeated suicidal threats or mild suicide attempts that are attention-getting devices ***must be taken seriously.*** The fact that this behavior is a demand for attention does *not* mean that the patient will not kill himself. Just such attention-getting behavior preceded many actual suicides, and suicide almost always occurred in the hospital with the dependent dissatisfied patient.

In summary, the management of the dependent dissatisfied patient should take the following into account: the complaining, depressed, restless, attention-seeking behavior of this overly dependent patient is a desperate plea for emotional reassurance and attention. Even though this may have been going on for some time, if he does not get the help he is demanding, he may indeed eventually commit suicide and this will probably occur in the hospital. Suicide threats may be attention-getting devices, but this *does not mean* that the patient will not go on to commit suicide if his plight continues unrelieved. If he is not satisfied in the hospital or out of the hospital, he really has no place to go. Suicidal ideation or threats must be taken seriously; suicidal precautions should be observed. Temporary measures to reduce suicidal potential are the following: beginning any *new* treatment or medication; assigning a "buddy" to him; giving him as much as possible the extra attention he demands; above all, providing sympathy and understanding, *even though* his behavior may make this most difficult for those around him.

The long-range control of suicidal behavior seems to rest on securing a satisfactory adjustment in the hospital and then applying the suggestions for control of suicidal behavior listed in the preceding section for the dependent satisfied patient.

This chapter is concluded by presenting the salient characteristics that appeared generally to distinguish the three types of suicide cases from the majority of the control cases. These characteristics have been arranged as a check list to provide a convenient brief method for assessing suicidal potentiality in a hospitalized schizophrenic patient, based on the empirical data developed in this chapter.[7, 8]

In addition, there are reproduced some of the forms used in the evaluations of patients in this study. The data are for one of the schizophrenic patients in the study, an unaccepting patient who committed suicide by gunshot wounds while at home on pass. These forms include (A) an abstract sheet (in which a brief abstract is made of the patient's records), (B) a summary sheet (filled out at time of the psychological autopsy), and (C) a sample score sheet for this patient based on the check list of suicidal potential for hospitalized schizophrenic patients.

[7] This check list must be filled out by someone familiar with the patient's present behavior and past history as well. It may be filled out at any time, of course, but is particularly designed to be used when a schizophrenic patient is well enough to be considered for passes and the question of possible suicidal behavior becomes particularly urgent.

[8] The check list has been scored for the illustrative case of John Doe which follows.

CHECK LIST OF SUICIDAL POTENTIAL FOR HOSPITALIZED SCHIZOPHRENIC PATIENTS *

Patient's Name Doe, John Ward ________ Date ________ Initials ________

Instructions: For each horizontal row, put an **X** before the phrase that best describes the patient. If there are duplicate phrases or if more than one phrase seems to describe the patient, check both. If none seems applicable, omit that row.

Control	Unaccepting	Dependent Satisfied	Dependent Dissatisfied
Part A—Attitudes toward hospitalization and illness			
Patient has never demanded to leave hospital.	**x** Patient has on occasion demanded to be released from hospital.	Patient seems to feel safer in hospital.	Patient does not want to leave hospital.
x Doesn't seem to realize he is really ill.	**x** Doesn't seem to realize he is really ill.	Realizes he is ill.	Realizes he is ill and expects hospital to help him.
Never asks for anything.	**x** Will ask for something on occasion.	**x** Will ask for something on occasion.	Constantly asking for or wanting something.
Doesn't seem to need attention or reassurance.	**x** Has been loud and demanding on occasion.	Likes attention and reassurance.	Needs constant attention and reassurance.
x Indifferent to hospital staff.	**x** Has on occasion been assaultive toward a staff member.	Very attached to some staff member (doctor, nurse, therapist, etc.)	Frequently asking to see doctor, nurse, chaplain, therapist, etc.
Has seldom asked for any kind of treatment or medication.	Has seldom asked for any kind of treatment or medication.	**x** On occasion has asked for some type of treatment (sedation, seclusion, medication, etc.)	Frequently asks for some type of treatment (medication, therapy, sedation, etc.)
Total 2	Total 5	Total 2	Total 0

(Indicate the total number of phrases checked in each column in Part A)

* Check list has been scored for illustrative case of John Doe, abstracted on pp. 102–106.

Control	Unaccepting	Dependent Satisfied	Dependent Dissatisfied
Part B—Behavior pattern under stress (both present and past behavior)			
Not restless.	**x** Has been extremely restless on occasion.	**x** Has become restless on occasion when under stress.	Is frequently restless, pacing.
Not impulsive.	**x** On occasion has impulsively assaulted others, struck fists against walls, etc.	**x** Has in the past on some occasions impulsively struck things, overturned tables, etc.	**x** Can be very impulsive on occasion.
x Seldom has somatic complaints.	**x** Seldom has somatic complaints.	Has somatic complaints when things aren't going so well for him.	Has frequent somatic complaints.
x Seldom expresses any feelings of inadequacy, inferiority.	**x** Seldom expresses any feelings of inadequacy, inferiority.	Has on occasion expressed feelings of lack of personal worth, inadequacy.	Has frequently expressed feelings of lack of personal worth, inadequacy.
Is usually isolated and withdrawn.	**x** On occasion has been antagonistic or interfering with others.	Varies between periods of isolation and sociability.	Tends to be a nuisance and bothersome to staff and to other patients.
x May have history of past suicidal activity, but not suicidal in hospital.	**x** May have history of past suicidal activity, but not suicidal in hospital.	Has previous history of suicidal activity and has been suicidal in hospital on occasion.	Has previous history of suicidal activity and has threatened suicide in hospital or has made mild attempts.
Total 3	Total 6	Total 2	Total 1

(Indicate the total number of phrases checked in each column in Part B)

CHECK LIST OF SUICIDAL POTENTIAL FOR HOSPITALIZED SCHIZOPHRENIC PATIENTS (*Continued*)

Part C—Stressfulness of patient's life situation (supportiveness of home environment, patient's attitude toward home environment and toward release from hospital)

Control	Unaccepting	Dependent Satisfied	Dependent Dissatisfied
x Shows no particular tension or anxiety with passes or leaves away from hospital.	**x** Shows no particular tension or anxiety with passes or leaves away from hospital.	Shows some tension and anxiety with passes or leaves away from hospital.	Resists passes and leaves away from hospital; shows tension and anxiety with them.
Indifferent to whether or not he can get along away from the hospital.	**x** Feels he can do all right away from the hospital.	Has on occasion said he was afraid he couldn't control his impulses away from the hospital.	Feels that no one is interested in him or trying to help him.
Somewhat indifferent to home environment.	**x** Has mixed feelings toward home environment.	Home environment seems all right, but patient has mixed feelings about it.	Patient ambivalent toward home; home environment is also ambivalent toward him.
x Patient has never tried to elope.	**x** Patient has eloped or has demanded to leave the hospital.	Patient has seldom made any attempt to elope; fairly satisfied in the hospital.	Patient has threatened to elope but doesn't really want to leave the hospital.
Much improved with tranquilizing drugs; patient has never shown a pattern of great disturbance.	**x** Although quieter with tranquilizing drugs, patient does not seem to have learned new methods of coping with home environment.	**x** Although quieter with tranquilizing drugs, patient's basic problems haven't changed.	Tranquilizing drugs don't seem to do much for him; still unhappy most of the time.
Patient seems able to endure unhappiness somewhat passively.	**x** Patient being released into same environment from which he was originally hospitalized.	Patient is much happier in the hospital than out.	Patient is unhappy in the hospital and out of the hospital.
Total 2	Total 6	Total 1	Total 0

(Indicate the total number of phrases checked in each column in Part C)

Assessment of suicidal potential *

If there is an absence of many phrases checked in the other three columns and if there is a score of 4 or more in *each* of the parts (A, B, and C), there is reassurance that the patient is probably not suicidal at this time. Note particularly that there is a similarity between the control (nonsuicidal) patient and the unaccepting suicidal patient. The unaccepting patient has, however, an apparent potentiality for acting out.	A score of 3 or more in *each* of the parts (A, B, and C) indicates a possible suicide in or out of the hospital.	A score of 3 or more in *each* of the parts (A, B, and C) indicates a possible suicide on pass or leave.	A score of 3 or more in *each* of the parts (A, B, and C) indicates a possible suicide in the hospital.

* If patient appears potentially suicidal, refer to suggestions for management.

ABSTRACT SHEET

Doe, John (suicide case)		
Anytown, U.S.A. (hospital)	Date of suicide	Suicide on trial visit
Diagnosis:	———, 1958	Method of suicide:
schizophrenia, undifferentiated		gunshot wound

10/15/59 (case reviewed)

Presummary: 41-year-old white male, Protestant. Married. Parents died when he was 5, and he was raised by aunt, Miss Doe, to whom he was very attached. Graduated from high school and began working at an early age. In Army 1940–1943. Married girl overseas, had one child, was later divorced. Upon discharge, he was in hospital 35 days; diagnosis, schizophrenia. Released on trial visit and discharged 1944. Worked as mechanic 8 years. Married again, has two children (and one stepchild). Living in substandard home. Wife exceedingly obese (200 lb). Wife jealous of patient's continued attachment to his aunt. Patient described as quiet, gentle, goodhearted. Illness began again in spring, 1957, but patient not hospitalized until 1958. Developed delusions of persecution. Thought somebody had it in for him. Fearful, worried about his job. Felt he was being crowded in by women ever since he was born. Felt guilty about his divorced wife. Was committed when, in a delusional state, he tried to take small daughter and take plane to join his divorced wife overseas. Admitted to hospital, April, 1958.

Date	Hospital Course	Passes	Medication
April, 1958	Brought in by police. Very aggressive, disoriented. Upset about being in locked room. Thinks it is a gas chamber and the overhead light is an X ray, Believes he is going to be killed. Reading Bible most of P.M.		
4/19/58	Ate fairly well. Appears oriented but apprehensive. Became disturbed about 3 P.M. but manageable. Moved mattress and bed covers around room. Read Bible by night light. Refused to have ceiling light on. Hammered on doors and walls with pitcher. About 9 P.M. asked to see a police psychiatrist or any doctor. Wouldn't		

ABSTRACT SHEET (*Continued*)

Date	Hospital Course	Passes	Medication
	take sedative. Before doctor arrived, patient had removed ceiling light and wiring, broken bulbs on floor; room strewn with wreckage, covers, reading materials. Patient bleeding from cuts. At 10 P.M. doctor came, and patient was removed to another room with only a mattress. Patient was given Bible. Special aide present.		
4/20/58	Patient crawled inside mattress cover and turned over so he was covered by mattress; shouted "air raid." Wrist restraints applied. Refused food. Attendant present. Still moves bed around room. Reads Bible, tears pages out and stuffs them in toilet. Has broken ceiling light. Wrist restraints again.		Chlorpromazine, 150 mg/day
4/21/58	Patient refuses medication because of religious beliefs. Talks constantly, rambling. Demands cigarettes frequently. Vomited oral dose of chlorpromazine. Patient is tense, suspicious. Takes Bible in shower and refuses to let anyone hold it for him.		Chlorpromazine, 300 mg (orally)
4/22/58	Tense but cooperative. In good contact. Routine laboratory and x-ray examination ordered.		Chlorpromazine, 200 mg
5/1/58	Patient has had occasional disturbed spells. In between these he is cooperative, talks well with ward personnel. When disturbed, he has jerked wall light from wall, torn lock off window sash, and ripped open mattress, removing a small part of spring.		
5/7/58	Behavior continues variable; at times pleasant, then confused and disturbed.		

ABSTRACT SHEET (*Continued*)

Date	Hospital Course	Passes	Medication
5/12/58	To dental clinic for treatment. Five teeth extracted.		
5/18/58	Sarcastic, negativistic. Assaulted aide when approached. Hyperactive, pacing, calling out, complaining of pain from recent dental extraction.		
5/21/58	Hyperactive, yelling, demanding release, complaining of pain in jaw after visit to dental clinic yesterday, restless, stealing anything he can from other patients. Pulled fire alarm.		
5/24/58	Hyperactive. Disturbing other patients.		Chlorpromazine, 600 mg
5/26/58	Preaching to ward. Giving orders to aides.		
5/31/58	When aides opened door of patient's room at bedtime, they found he had made a 14-ft rope of sheets. His belt was attached to it also. Patient had been talking about leaving here at first chance. Patient to be observed closely.		Chlorpromazine, 900 mg
6/1/58	Hyperactive. Demanding medicine for pain in jaw. Became hostile when his request to go to church was refused.		
6/2/58	Assigned to corrective therapy, manual arts therapy, and educational therapy.		Chlorpromazine, 300 mg; Equanil, 400 mg
6/8/58	. . .		Equanil discontinued
6/22/58	Gate pass for card party.	Gate pass	Chlorpromazine, 400 mg
7/1/58	Partial privileges granted.		Chlorpromazine, 200 mg
7/9/59	Patient apparently very much improved physically and mentally. Has adjusted well to ward routine. Interested in everything. Transferred to open ward.		

ABSTRACT SHEET (*Continued*)

Date	Hospital Course	Passes	Medication
7/11/58	On pass with wife. Took along supply of medicine.	On pass	
7/18/58	Patient states he enjoyed his leave very much and seems in good contact.		

Social Service, Manual Arts Therapy, Educational Therapy reports:

Date	Hospital Course	Passes	Medication
July–August, 1958	Social service: Wife has been living on relief. Children in need of dental care. Relationship of wife and patient was cool and distant during recent years, but they were beginning to reach a better understanding. Patient is quiet, mild, dependent. Will need considerable support in making adjustment to home. Patient and wife encouraged to call upon social service. Wife's letter to hospital indicates she didn't want patient released from hospital "before he was cured because I wouldn't want him to break down on us. It was awfully hard on us." Wife wrote that July visit home was very successful and that patient had "stood up" to his aunt and told her he was busy with his family (wife resented patient's close attachment to his aunt). Manual arts therapy report: Patient very quiet. Talks in low moderate voice. Attitude toward work and family excellent. Plans to build own boat and trailer when he goes home. Educational therapy report: Patient was very depressed when he entered ET in June but was in good contact and did well in studies. He talked freely with therapist about his family, work, home, hob-		

ABSTRACT SHEET (*Continued*)

Date	Hospital Course	Passes	Medication
	bies. Seems in much better spirits now. Changes seemed to come after he visited home.		
8/4/58	Letter from patient's old employer indicates his job is waiting for him.		Chlorpromazine, 100 mg
8/7/58	Patient presented to special staff with Dr. A. who felt patient was looking for a close dependent relationship and had difficulty separating from his aunt. Dr. A. recommended fairly early discharge, feeling it would be helpful.		
8/11–19/58	On pass with wife. Returned in cheerful spirits. Cooperative.	On 3-day pass	
8/22/58	Pretrial visit report indicates need to go slowly. Patient is attending group therapy.		
8/27/58	Trial visit approved for patient, in custody of wife, as soon as his dentures are completed and fitted. He may travel unaccompanied.		
9/4/58	Patient cleared for trial visit beginning 9/9/58.		
9/9/58	Patient left hospital for trial visit. Given 3 weeks' medication. Request for trial visit follow-up and continued psychotherapy for both patient and wife sent to district clinic.	On trial visit	Chlorpromazine, 100 mg, continued
(Stop here for psychological autopsy)			
9/10/58	Patient shot himself at home. When patient returned home on 9/9/58, he seemed quiet and preoccupied with his thinking. He asked his wife to take the children and go off; gave no reason why. Kept repeating "it's good to be home." When wife went to store next day, he sent children out of the house and shot himself.		

SUMMARY SHEET

Patient's Name: Doe, John Hospital: Anytown, U.S.A.

1. *Diagnosis: summarize main behavior symptoms:* Schizophrenia, undifferentiated. 41-year-old white male. On admission: fearful, assaultive, disoriented, delusions of persecution.

2. *What medications were prescribed for this patient, tranquilizers, and others? Was patient receiving tranquilizers separately or in combination, etc.?* Chlorpromazine primarily. Equanil given with chlorpromazine for 4 days only.

3. *Describe the course of the medications for the patient, particularly relating the increases, decreases, and introduction of new ones, dropping of old ones, etc., to the course of the illness:* (See abstract sheet.)

4. *If suicide, at what stage of the dosage did it occur?* After patient was stabilized for several months on maintenance dosage of 100 mg chlorpromazine.

5. *What seemed to be the pattern of passes and leaves for this patient? Did the use of tranquilizers relate in any way to this pattern?* Passes begun after acute period. Passes were given within 3 months after entry. Passes with wife for 1 whole week and no indication of any special safeguards.

6. *What seemed to be the physicians' attitudes toward the patient, in terms of ward management, interest, etc.?* Given passes rather quickly after rather severe breakdown (2 months later). Not allowed to vegetate. Hospital interests evidenced by prescription changes, assignment to therapy, social service investigation.

7. *What facts or speculations are there about the cause of the suicide?* The wife (who was recommended for therapy) was not the best family-situation resource for him to go to on trial visit. He was actually worse than everyone thought. He was *out* of the hospital and had no place to turn.

8. *If suicide, could this suicide have been predicted? In what way?*

Clues *for* suicide	Clues *against* suicide
(*a*) Unlikely that psychosis was remitted sufficiently to permit him to live through a 90-day period without disturbance.	(*a*) Was making plans to build boat, trailer.
(*b*) Strong guilt feelings (patient is seen as essentially guilt-laden and	(*b*) No prior suicidal indications noted except on admission note.

SUMMARY SHEET

Clues *for* suicide	Clues *against* suicide
driven to find a lost love object rather than depressed).	
(*c*) Possibility that the tranquilizing effect of medication masked patient's inner turmoil and made him appear better than he was.	(*c*) Had had passes with wife and returned apparently undisturbed, in good spirits.
(*d*) Unsupportive home environment.	

Guestimate:
Dr. X: Control case, 25 per cent confidence level.
Dr. Y: Suicide case, 45 per cent confidence level.
Dr. Z: Suicide case, 40 per cent confidence level.

[At this point, the members of the psychological autopsy were told that this was a suicide case.]

9. *Lesson to be learned from this case:* (*a*) Need for exit psychiatric interview and exit psychological testing to determine patient's genuine feelings about trial visit, etc., and the extent of actual remission of illness. (*b*) Need for intensive social service to assess home environment. (*c*) Some psychotics, although overtly well, will commit suicide. The inner turmoil that they are aware of when in remission may be greater than is suspected. Although tranquilizers quiet the patient's disturbance, they may have permitted him to have disturbing insights that could not be reflected in his overt behavior. (*d*) Danger of releasing patient into the same environment from which he was originally hospitalized before he is actually able to cope with its stressfulness.

10. *Summarize:* Patient adjusted well in the hospital with medication that appeared to control symptomatic disturbance. Had the medicine been discontinued, his symptoms might have returned. The tranquilizing effects of the medication may have suppressed overt indications of his illness and made him appear more improved than he actually was.

SAMPLE SCORE SHEET FOR PATIENT JOHN DOE *

	Control	Unaccepting	Dependent Satisfied	Dependent Dissatisfied
Part A	Total score 2	5	2	0
Part B	Total score 3	6	2	1
Part C	Total score 2	6	1	0

It is apparent that John Doe may be classified as an unaccepting patient. It can be seen that, even allowing for some difference of opinion about scoring this patient, his high scores of 3 or more in each of Parts A, B, and C in unaccepting category indicate that he was essentially an unaccepting patient with rejecting attitudes towards his hospitalization and denial of his illness, an agitated behavior pattern under stress, and a stressful life situation (for an unaccepting patient).

As noted in the general suggestions, a more thorough evaluation of the home environment might have been helpful. Certainly it is apparent from hindsight that, although the patient was improved in that he was much quieter and was apparently enjoying his passes, he had been released to an outside home environment that was for him suicidogenic.

* Based on his scores on Check List of Suicidal Potential for Hospitalized Schizophrenic Patients.

7

The Role of the Social Scientist in the Medicolegal Certification of Death from Suicide[1]

THEODORE J. CURPHEY

One might account for a pathologist's fraternizing with a group of psychologists and psychiatrists on the basis of the gregarious tendencies for which pathologists are noted, or, perhaps more accurately, it might be attributed to my own penchant for wandering. It is of interest to note that Whitehead, in his *Science and the Modern World,* has a few words to say about wandering: "Modern science has imposed on humanity the necessity for wandering. Its progressive thought and its progressive technology make the transition through time from generation to generation a true migration into unchartered seas of adventure. The very benefit of wandering is that it is dangerous and needs skill to avert evils." My wandering has brought me into contact with the members of the Suicide Prevention Center, with the fortunate results that are set down in this chapter. Since October, 1958, I have had the singular experience of collaborating with a group of social scientists—psychologists, psychiatrists, and social workers—who, for the last several years, have been actively engaged in the establishment of a suicide prevention center in Los Angeles County, which, incidentally, is the only one of its type in the nation at this time. An amendment voted to the Los Angeles County Charter, in 1956, made it mandatory that the coroner be a doctor of medicine and a certified pathologist. As part of the reorganization of the coroner's office, the aid of various scientific, profes-

[1] Portions of this chapter were first presented at the Symposium on Death, Western Psychological Association, San Diego, Calif., April, 1959.

sional, and medical groups in the county has been elicited on a consultative basis. Further, as part of this policy, the SPC group was requested to assist us in evaluating certain cases that require special knowledge in the fields of psychology and psychiatry and in which suicide was one of the possible *modes* of death. By virtue of their unique experience with suicide, it has been possible to obtain considerable assistance in those cases where the accumulation of information from routine case investigation still left doubt as to the mode of death. The greatest area of such difficulty lay in distinguishing accidental from suicidal deaths. The staff members of the SPC investigate these areas for the coroner's office, having been appointed deputy coroners so that they can represent themselves as identified with our office. The data they gather are then examined and interpreted in procedures they have designated as psychological autopsies. Their conclusions are then considered along with the results from the medical autopsy and other correlated laboratory studies in deciding the final certification.

To have a pathologist head up a medicolegal office in a metropolitan area represents something more than the progress of science into the field of forensic medicine. Although, according to current evaluations, we have the best of everything in the special fields of psychiatry, psychology, cardiac surgery, industrial health, and public health, a statement was made as far back as 1945 at a joint committee of doctors and lawyers meeting under the auspices of the American Medical Association, indicating that of all the countries in the world, medicine in the United States had contributed least to the administration of justice. Accepting this statement as a challenge makes it almost mandatory to introduce the scientific spirit of investigation into the study of death. Some of us in forensic pathology have become acutely conscious of the gaps and blank spots in many of our investigations of death. This may be because the present status of forensic medicine in this country is essentially in the stage of development that general medicine was about 75 years ago, when the general practitioner was charged with the full responsibility of treating the entire spectrum of diseases with the limited scientific knowledge at his disposal at that time. We have made remarkable progress by dividing medical problems among various specialists, but there has been correspondingly little progress in the application of current medical knowledge and techniques to the scientific investigation of death. The hard fact we find in this country in most jurisdictions, except perhaps a few large metropolitan areas, is that the medical components of the medicolegal spectrum utilize largely the same body of knowledge that has existed in medicine for the past 50 or 75 years. In Los Angeles, as a result of the nationally known work of the members of the SPC, it seemed logical to me to invite them to associate themselves with the coroner's office to lend their special skills in evaluating motivation and intention, especially in those cases where the mode of death was equivocal.

The medicolegal certification of death from suicide carries with it a number of important implications within our present social pattern and hence deserves more attention on the part of those of us charged with the responsibility of certification.

In the Los Angeles County Coroner's office in the fiscal year 1957–1958, for example, there were 818 cases listed as suicide from a total of 9,959 cases studied by the office, roughly 8 per cent of the caseload. Suicide ranked third in Los Angeles County as a certified mode of death, accounting for roughly three times the number of deaths from homicide and exceeded in number only by deaths from natural causes and deaths from accidental means. It was inevitable that a number of cases would raise questions as to the appropriate mode of death. It was these equivocal cases, where there was a *possibility* of suicidal certification, that were referred to the Suicide Team for further investigation.

The average medicolegal agency, whether organized around a medical examiner or a coroner, is likely, by virtue of knowledge and experience with natural and accidental death, to feel greater confidence in the accuracy of certification with those two modes than with deaths certified as suicidal. A major reason for this, of course, is that both the pathologist and the lay investigator lack sufficient training in the field of *human behavior* to be able to estimate with any fair degree of accuracy, the mental processes of the victim likely to lead to suicidal death. It is here that the social scientists, with their special skills in human behavior, can offer us much valuable assistance.

We know that the specialists upon whom the coroner traditionally calls, the pathologist, the toxicologist, the biochemist, etc., can fairly accurately tell the *cause* of death, but the social scientist is in a pivotal position in cases of equivocal suicidal deaths to render the most significant information as the difference between suicidal death and death by some other mode is primarily a matter of the victim's *intention* to kill himself. Intention and motivation are neither chemical nor tissue matters; they are psychological in nature. This is where the social scientists can assist the coroner's office.

The members of the Suicide Team, when asked what techniques they use, have stated that essentially what they do is interview persons who knew the deceased, the spouse, grown children, neighbors, employers, physicians, etc., and attempt to reconstruct the life style of the deceased. As part of this, they obtain information about any psychiatric idiosyncrasies or the presence (to their especially attuned ears) of any prodromal clues to suicide that the victim may have dropped into the matrix of communication and then they make a scientific extrapolation of the victim's behavior over the days preceding his death, using all the information they have obtained.

The types of information gathered by the Suicide Team may be described under the following categories: (A) anamnestic or life history details (such as the history of previous suicide attempts); (B) psychiatric-psychological data (such as indices of depression and agitation; for example, recent loss of appetite, loss of interest, or changes in habit patterns); (C) communication information, i.e., indications of morbid content of thought as exemplified in such statements as "I can't go on," "life isn't worth much," or "I'm a worthless person"; and (D) detective-type information, which may not be primarily psychological in nature but which nevertheless frequently appears in the course of intensive investigations and which throws additional light on the mode of death, e.g., discovery of a small mophead stuffed in the bathtub over the drain, indicating that the victim had made careful preparation for death by ensuring sufficient water in the bathtub in which to drown.

If we regard as one of the coroner's major functions an interest in the health and welfare of the public, it follows that the coroner has a very definite responsibility to evaluate properly deaths that might be considered suicidal. Those interested in the history of public health recognize that in the last decade or so public health specialists have expanded the definition and scope of their efforts. These used to be limited to prevention of disease and inquiry into cause of death, what one might call the negative approach to death. Nowadays, a proper definition of public health activities includes the positive side, i.e., developing a sense of well-being and health in the individual, the community, the state, the nation, and the world. The enhancement of healthy social and mental well-being is now considered an integral part of the responsibility of public health authorities. Thus, the accurate certification of suicide is definitely in the interests of the public health of the community. I have been personally impressed by the paradox that pathologists, who perforce are material-minded in their approach, must evaluate many of these suicidal deaths, where a knowledge of the psyche is so important. One needs only to be faced with the problem of making such diagnoses to recognize the need for special skills to aid the forensic pathologist in evaluating these deaths. We already have specialists in toxicology, microscopy, tissue investigation, etc.; what could be more logical than to add specialists to investigate the psyche in its social setting?

Does it make any difference what mode of death one puts on a death certificate? It does. Apart from its significance in the statistical sense, there are any number of other very important matters. For example, there is the impact of an incorrect certification of death, e.g., calling an accident or a natural death a suicide, on the emotions and the subsequent adjustment of the family concerned. This may be particularly important in communities of small size or in large communities of small subdivisions, such as we face in Los Angeles, where a strong social stigma may exist in the minds of many persons against the children of adversity and against the family generally. The statement, "your father committed suicide," made to a child may cause genuine anguish and even severe trauma for years to come. Public health authorities are responsible for the most accurate certification possible. Another significant ramification of correct certification lies in the economic area. The majority of insurance policies carry cancellation clauses for suicide, two years being the average limit beyond which the policy is payable and below which it is cancellable. It is surprising in our jurisdiction to find how often cases occur that fall just about on that line. If death is inaccurately judged to be suicidal, the victim's family may stand to lose a considerable amount of insurance. The members of the Suicide Team do their investigations, of course, without knowing whether or not there is any insurance policy, but not too infrequently, as a result of their thorough investigations, we have been able to certify as accidental a death that initially looked like suicide. The converse, of course, may occur as often, but even in these cases we feel that accurate reports, based on *all* the facts, are ultimately in the best interests of the over-all mental health of the community.

Some general impressions and practical implications from the investigations by the Suicide Team of equivocal deaths have emerged.

1. Some cases illustrate the limitations faced by the coroner when problems of certification are resolved on superficial or incomplete evidence or on impressions and preconceived opinions rather than on the objective accumulation of all the possible facts, including histological, toxicological, and *psychological* data. The medicolegal authority must avoid fictitious accuracy, if it expects to enjoy the confidence of various agencies and interests in the community. Altogether too many certificates of death fall

within this category of fictitious accuracy, more especially in those jurisdictions where there is no semblance of the scientific method in studying the case material. In fact, it may be that one good criterion by which to evaluate the scientific accuracy of a medicolegal office is, paradoxically, the percentage of equivocal deaths annually certified as of *undetermined* cause or mode. It might be added that, even after their intensive investigations, the Suicide Team will not infrequently recommend an "accident-suicide, undetermined" certification, indicating that the equivocal nature of the matter was not resolved. One practical result of such realistic certifications is the increased *validity* of statistics for modes of death, so that statistical comparisons and evaluations for different parts of the country can be made with a greater feeling of security that the figures used actually pertained to similar phenomena.

2. One must not underestimate the taboo nature of the suicide label (and the heavy responsibility one has in its accurate application). A recent case brought this especially to mind. A forty-seven-year-old Caucasian female was discovered comatose late one night, and she died in the hospital a few days later. Chemical tests performed at the hospital indicated 9.6 mg pentobarbital per 100 cc of blood, which is compatible with a lethal dose. On the basis of this routine evidence, the case was closed as suicide and a death certificate issued accordingly. Subsequently the coroner's office received a petition, signed by several of the victim's neighbors as well as by her husband and her attorney, indicating that she had been a good citizen and a dutiful wife and mother. The petition asked explicitly that the certification of suicide not be applied to this person because of the impression it would create in the community. In light of this, the case was reopened and turned over to the Suicide Team for further investigation. Their efforts brought forth a number of very interesting facts, chiefly that, although everything in the petition was true, it was also true that the deceased had been a member of Alcoholics Anonymous (because of what had been a chronic drinking problem) and that she had received psychiatric care for anxiety and depression. Also, in the few weeks before her death, she had taken a leave of absence from her job and had been to several physicians, from whom she had received a variety of prescribed medication. It was also discovered that two days before her death she had been to see a psychiatrist, who had written a report that he deemed the victim to be acutely depressed and in need of hospitalization. In general, the results of the investigation of the Suicide Team strongly substantiated the certification of death by suicide. It is surmised that much of the information found by the Suicide Team was also known by the relatives,

neighbors, and friends and that their petition was addressed not so much to the accuracy of the diagnosis as to the taboo attached to the label.

3. It might be mentioned that, so far as interprofessional relationships are concerned, it is noteworthy that the introduction of the social scientists of the Suicide Team into the Los Angeles County Coroner's office has elicited positive reactions from the other professional members of the office.

4. One further function of the Suicide Team merits mention: the therapeutic secondary benefits that often occur as the result of team members' contacts with the bereaved survivors of the deceased. They report that on several occasions the surviving widow or surviving grown child has indicated to them, at the conclusion of their interviews, that the sessions had been a helpful and therapeutic experience for them. The members of the Suicide Team, because of their special skills, are alert, in their interviews with survivors of persons who have committed suicide, to evidence of extreme guilt, serious depression, and the need for special help on formulating plans for solving specific problems, such as caring for children whose parent has committed suicide. Since we noted this phenomenon, the coroner's office has, in some few cases, referred distraught survivors of suicide victims to members of the Suicide Team specifically for supportive interviews, even when the suicidal mode of death was not in doubt.

The purpose of this chapter is to emphasize changing concepts in the field of forensic medicine and to point out the opportunities offered to those working in this field to help shape the pattern of future development of this specialty. With the increasing infusion of scientific methods into this field in the last half century, we are now at the stage where the investigation of sudden or unexpected deaths calls for the same approach, using several specialties, that medicine currently uses in the diagnosis and treatment of the live patient.

Our aim must be to bring more and more special knowledge to the investigation of death. We are justly critical of the lay coroner, who certifies deaths frequently with no medical facts to work with or who depends on the gathering of the medical facts by a physician who has had no training in forensic medicine. We must recognize, however, that many of us with training in the field are unwittingly falling into somewhat the same error when we allow ourselves to express opinions in areas of forensic medicine where we have no special training or competence. The forensic pathologist has recognized the importance of special knowledge in the field of toxicology, and this specialty is now part and parcel of any well-organized medicolegal office. He is also recognizing that in complex fields like virology and immunohematology he must seek assistance from specially trained persons. It seems time to give thought to attracting specialists in human motivation—psychologists, psychiatrists, and social workers—to help in investigating those cases in which suicide is in question. That this effort is well worthwhile is attested by the experiences of the Los Angeles County Coroner's office in the recent past years.

8

Sample Investigations of Equivocal Suicidal Deaths

EDWIN S. SHNEIDMAN AND NORMAN L. FARBEROW

This chapter is meant as a companion piece to the previous chapter and is intended to illustrate various types of investigations, conducted by the Suicide Prevention Center, of equivocal cases in which suicide is a possible mode of death in the process of certification by the Los Angeles County Coroner's office. It is intended to present an abbreviated casebook of actual investigations by the SPC, which might serve as guidelines for persons who must decide certification as to mode of death.

To recapitulate briefly, Los Angeles County Coroner Theodore J. Curphey, M.D., invited members of the SPC to assist him in equivocal cases of possible suicidal deaths by conducting psychological autopsies focused primarily on the *personality* elements associated with suicide, such as suicidal intention, subtle communications relating to suicidal intent, reactive or psychotic depression, and schizophrenia. The coroner named this group, when they worked in connection with his office, the Suicide Team. The approach of the team was to reconstruct the life style and personality of the deceased, mainly by interviewing the spouse, grown children, parents, physician, and others who knew him well. On the basis of these psychological data, and any other physical evidence of suicide, accident, homicide, or natural death that might be found, the Suicide Team attempted to make informed extrapolations over the last days of the victim's life and then to report these conclusions and recommendations to the coroner for final integration with his other findings.

The activities of the Suicide Team have raised some interesting questions concerning suicide statistics in general.[1] Whereas mortality rates are probably extremely reliable (the operational definition of *dead* is fairly clear-cut and unambiguous) the instances of suicide, within any geographic area and for any given temporal interval, are not so reliably reported and are, in no small part, squarely dependent on the certifications as to mode of death made from case to case. These certifications are often influenced by social, religious, and sentimental factors. While the activities of the Suicide Team in the Los Angeles County Coroner's office may result in raising or lowering the apparent suicide rate in Los Angeles County (either would be an artifact); at least, the veridical value of the statistics for "suicide" from that area should be increased.

It is not implied that every death should be certified as suicide, homicide, accident, *or* natural, even if one accepts this somewhat archaic classification (see Chapter 9). Dr. Curphey has stated that, so far as he is concerned, one of the characteristics of a scientifically operated coroner's office is its willingness to certify deaths as probable or undetermined (as, for example, suicide or accident, undetermined) in those cases where the facts neither warrant nor justify straightforward certification by one of the four usual modes. This concept is introduced to indicate that a legitimate outcome of an investigation by the Suicide Team is a firm recommendation, based on clearly inconclusive evidence, for an undetermined certification.

With these comments as preamble, some sample cases will be presented. These cases have been selected to illustrate each of the following general circumstances[2]: (A) a death recommended for certification as *suicide;* (B) a death that initially appeared suicidal but was recommended for certification as *accidental;* (C) a death recommended for certification as *probable suicide,* in which some psychic homicide played a role; (D) a death recommended for certification as *suicide or accident, undetermined.* (E) a death finally recommended for police investigation for *homicide;* (F) a death recommended for certification as a *natural death;* (G) a case

[1] It may be of interest to note that "the word 'statistic' is derived from the Latin *status,* which, in the Middle Ages, had come to mean a state in the political sense. 'Statistic,' therefore originally denoted inquiries into the condition of the state." Until the eighteenth century, this discipline was called *political arithmetic;* later writers termed it *vital statistics.* In these early labors, much attention was given to tables of mortality for the state, so that a discussion of statistics on suicide is, in the original sense of the word, particularly appropriate. (From Wynnard Hooper, "Statistics," *Encyclopoedia Britannica,* (11th Edition, 1910), vol. 25, pp. 806–811.

[2] All names, dates, and places have, of course, been changed to protect the anonymity of the persons involved.

of unequivocal suicide in which *therapeutic functions* for the bereaved were served.

The following case was recommended for certification as *suicide*.

A 33-year-old male of German descent, working as a butler for a well-to-do investment broker, was found dead in his bathtub with his head under water. The bathtub was filled to the brim. The police report stated that he had been in ill health for the preceding two months and that the day prior to his death he had told the cook where he worked that he did not feel well. A glass containing a yellow crystalline substance was found on top of the water closet next to the bathtub. Autopsy revealed a large quantity of water in his stomach and proximal small bowel, associated with marked pulmonary edema. The heart and aorta were essentially normal. Toxicological examination showed the absence of alcohol and the presence of 1.4 mg per 100 cc barbiturates in the blood. The residue in the glass was found to be pentobarbital.

With these facts, the preponderant opinion was that this was a suicide, but in light of the realistic possibility that this could have been an accident, it was felt that an investigation by the Suicide Team was indicated. Their study revealed many interesting facts. It was ascertained that the victim had been depressed for some time previous and had made a serious sucide attempt just two months before in the home of a nurse, where he had been staying. As a result of that attempt, he had been taken to a local hospital, where he had been comatose over 24 hours and where he had then spent 8 days. On recovery he told his nurse friend that he had taken 24 Nembutal tablets.

His life history, as reconstructed from the informants, was most interesting. At the age of 15 he had entered a military academy in Germany; Hitler was then in power. He was trained as a fighter pilot and engaged in heavy fighting. While he was on a mission, his best friend had been killed. Upon his return, he requested his superior officer to send him again so that he could either avenge or join his friend. Upon denial, he threatened suicide and actually attempted it by shooting himself through the left chest. He survived this attempt and was hospitalized. Later, he was taken prisoner by the British and sent to Egypt in 1945. In 1946, he returned to Germany and fell in love with an airline stewardess, who was later killed in an airline crash. He then left Germany and went to Argentina, where he flew for Peron until the dictator was ousted. From there he went to Brazil and later to Venezuela, where he worked until the revolution occurred and he lost everything he had. He finally made his way to the United States in 1956, and came to Los Angeles, where he worked until the time of his death.

In the course of gathering the foregoing information, members of the Suicide Team investigated the actual scene some days after his death. Because of the feelings of his employer, the victim's quarters had been left undisturbed during this time. The investigators, on checking the bathtub, found a wad of cloth stuffed in the safety, or overflow, drain, thus allowing the tub to be filled to the very top. Mindful of the victim's prior experience with barbiturates, we reconstructed that he had taken this precaution to make certain of his death by drowning, if the barbiturates failed to kill him.

The most striking general principles to emerge from these investigations are (A) the importance of obtaining as complete a history of the past life of the victim as possible, as a basis for making judgments about the victim's personality, and (B) the importance of examining, if possible, the actual site of death, inasmuch as such an examination may well yield significant evidence necessary for the proper decision.

The following case initially appeared suicidal but was recommended for certification as an *accident*.

In practically any coroner's office, a death that results from playing Russian roulette would automatically be certified as suicide. Indeed, there is now legal precedent for such certifications. Because of a special interest on the part of the Suicide Team in this type of death, this case was turned over to them by the coroner for investigation, with, as it turned out, extremely surprising results. On the basis of interviews it was ascertained that the victim, a 28-year-old male, was an Army veteran who had a collection of revolvers, which he kept in perfect operating condition. It was determined from his best friend that the victim's favorite activity at parties was to play Russian roulette (following the usual rules of the game by having one chamber of the cylinder loaded) and that he had done this literally dozens of times in the preceding few years. At this point, the Suicide Team wondered about the psychology of a man who would behave in such a fashion: was he psychotic or was he intent on killing himself? Interviews with the widow clarified the situation: the victim had told her that there was no possibility of his hurting himself, as he always glanced at the gun to ascertain that the bullet was in a nonlethal position before he pulled the trigger. If the bullet was one notch to the left of the barrel, he would spin the cylinder again. There had been no suicidal ideation and no evidence of depression, psychosis, or morbid content of thought. What had happened? The Suicide Team knew that the death had occurred in someone else's home. Interviews developed the information that he shot himself with a revolver that was not his own but belonged to his host of the evening. What seemed most important was the fact that, whereas his collection consisted entirely of Smith & Wesson revolvers, he had killed himself with a Colt revolver. The actions of the two guns are different; i.e., the cylinder of the Smith & Wesson revolves counterclockwise, while the cylinder of the Colt revolves clockwise. It was believed that the victim, checking and seeing the bullet one space to the right of the barrel, thought that he could not possibly kill himself, whereas in reality pulling the trigger put the bullet in the lethal position and he died immediately.

In the absence of any indication of suicidal affect or any indications of suicidal ideation, and with the additional information about the two types of revolvers, the Suicide Team recommended that this death be considered as accidental. One member of the Suicide Team labeled this case as one of Soviet Roulette, that is, Russian roulette wherein one cheats.

The following case was recommended for certification as *probable suicide,* in which some psychic homicide played a role.

The autopsy report concerning a 57-year-old female who was found dead in her home indicated that the cause of death was acute barbiturate poisoning. On the face of it, the mode of death appeared equivocal, and the case was referred by the coroner to the Suicide Team for investigation.

The victim's physician was contacted and he reported that she had been emotionally upset for several years. She felt her husband's personality had changed and that he was moody and was not spending time or doing things with her. On two occasions she had been severely depressed but seemed to have come out of these moods fairly quickly. Prescriptions from her physician made it possible for her to have refills for tranquilizers and barbiturates whenever she wished. The physician did not know how long before the victim's death she had had the prescription refilled nor how many pills she actually had. It was his impression that she was not a heavy drinker or an alcoholic.

An appointment was made with the victim's husband. He exhibited many feelings of remorse and guilt, with much crying at times. He had a number of questions concerning the coroner's decision as to the cause of his wife's death and how available this information would be to the public and, particularly, to his neighbors. He felt suicide was a stigma and hoped his wife's death would be certified as the result of a heart attack, although it was fairly clear that there was little rational cause for him to entertain this hope.

The husband stated they had been married for 25 years; there were no children. From the beginning the marriage had many elements of discomfort in it as a result of his wife's hysterical, excessive demands and lack of consideration of their economic situation. After about 10 years of marraige, there was a period of separation by divorce, but they came together again and eventually remarried. He at first stated there had never been any prior suicidal attempts or threats, but it later became known there actually had been many. These were described of minimum lethality and had had a dramatic quality to them. For example, she would put a little iodine around her lips and say that she had swallowed some, but when he took her to the hospital iodine was not found in the stomach contents. On a number of such occasions, he had responded with a good deal of anger to his wife's suicidal attempts. Once she had threatened to kill herself with a knife and he had given her a hunting knife, telling her to use that since it was sharper.

The husband stated that during the previous 6 to 8 months he had made up his mind that his marriage would never be successful. He had not communicated this to his wife, because he did not intend to divorce her.

It was felt that the husband was a man who had very marked dependency needs which were not being met by his wife, and that he had reacted to these with a good deal of anger and rejection of her. The wife apparently needed the marriage very much, and she made the suicidal threats and attempts in an effort to bring her husband closer to her. On most occasions, such suicidal attempts or threats brought about a reconciliation. However, at this particular time, the possibility of reconciliation had lessened considerably because of the husband's decision. Whether this decision was based on something specific, such as an attraction to another woman, was impossible to tell. He denied this specifically, however, even without being asked.

At the time of the suicide, the husband, a salesman, had gone to a neighboring city to conduct some business. His usual practice was to call his wife and tell her the time he would be home for dinner. He tried but was unable to reach her until late. She was very angry when he arrived home and threatened to leave him. He told her to go ahead, and then he went out to a restaurant. Later he returned home and found his wife sleeping on the floor in the hall, "breathing heavy." Her clothing was not disarranged in any way, so he had given no thought to anything like violence being involved, and he supposed she had simply gone to sleep on the floor. He apparently made no attempt to arouse her except to place a pillow under her head to allow her to sleep more comfortably. He then left the house and went to a hotel. One significant fact the husband related was that the night before her death his wife had called her sister and brother-in-law and had made a will, leaving all her possessions to the sister.

The impression by the investigator was that this was a chronically depressed woman of hysterical type, anxious about the separation from her husband, and that the husband, for reasons unknown, had decided not to continue the marriage on an effective basis. What was considered pivotal was the denial by the husband to himself of his wife's desperate situation, which was probably symptomatic of their destructive symbiotic relationship. While unconscious death wishes on the part of the spouse might be inferred, what seemed clear was that the dyadic relationship was onc that permitted the rejection of the victim by the potential rescuer. Thus, the victim's gamble with death was lost because the person who could have saved her did not permit himself to receive the intended communication.

The following case was recommended for certification as *suicide or accident, undetermined.*

The case is the death of a 45-year-old male, operating a small business involving the use and storage of lacquer thinner. At 3:30 A.M., witnesses saw the place of business on fire. The police and fire department reports noted that an explosion had taken place, the front windows of the shop having been blown out. The victim was found face down and showed extensive burns. A sample of blood showed 45 per cent carbon monoxide and was negative for alcohol. The victim was in the habit of returning to his shop to work after hours. On this particular occasion he left for the shop around 2:00 A.M. His wife called a neighbor after he left, expressing concern about him, upon which the neighbor volunteered to drive to the place of business. When he did so, he found it on fire. Later information revealed that the victim was careless about smoking in the shop around the cans of explosive or inflammable material used in the course of his work. The arson experts who studied the scene and the evidence were unable to decide whether it was a set fire or an accidental explosion. Interestingly, the police officers of the Arson Squad were of the opinion that it was set with suicidal intent, and the captain from the Los Angeles Fire Department who was commanding officer at the scene disagreed that a flash explosion of this type could have been induced with suicidal intent.

This case with its voluminous records was turned over to the Suicide Team for investigation and opinion. A large array of friends and neighbors were interviewed about the victim's mental state and his work habits. The final report stated: "There are no indications of a previous life pattern consistent with suicide. However, it should be noted that the informants most likely to give information indicative of such a pattern were (as usual) defensive because in this case the widow informed us that an insurance settlement hinges to some extent on the type of death certificate.... The reconstruction of the psychodynamics in this case appears to offer no sound basis for an opinion as to the mode of death."

In view of the general disagreement, therefore, the certification of the mode of death was recommended as accident or suicide, undetermined.

The coroner's comments to the SPC on this investigation touched on a special point:

The insurance economics of this case are most interesting. The victim had fire insurance on his store. If his death were accidental, the insurance was collectible; if suicidal, it would be voided on the basis of the perpetration of a felony. His life insurance was even more interesting. He had taken out a policy 3 weeks before his death and had not yet paid the first premium. Because of the 1-month grace period in premium payment, if his death was accidental, there was a question as to whether his survivors would recover from the insurance company without his having invested a penny of his own. This case illustrates the limitations at times faced in arriving at final certification, if such certification is to be based on the objective gathering of facts and not on impressions and preconceived opinions, as is often true when these problems are handled on the basis of superficial or incomplete evidence.

The following is an ambiguous case in which the final recommendation was that the police investigate for *homicide*.

It is an unfortunate fact that in the public mind the coroner's function is largely to ferret out undiscovered homicides (this misconception is fostered by mystery stories and TV programs). It is also true that oftentimes police personnel, in making an investigation of a death, will lose interest precipitously if it appears that the case cannot possibly involve homicide. So far as the coroner's office is concerned, cases of homicide actually make up the smallest percentage of his caseload but receive the greatest percentage of publicity.

The following case is one of the rare instances in which the certification lay between suicide and accident and was discussed with the coroner with the recommendation that it be returned to the police department for further investigation as a homicide.

The deceased, a 55-year-old male who was found drowned in the bathtub of a downtown hotel, was fully clothed except for his shoes. Autopsy and postmortem analyses revealed he died by drowning and that there was neither ethanol nor barbiturate nor any other poison in his system. The story, as pieced together from his widow, two of his brothers-in-law, his attorney, a government employee who had been a friend of the victim, and an individual who had loaned the victim a considerable sum of money, was a complicated and confusing picture.

On the morning of his death the victim had been at a hearing at which he had been accused of having obtained over $200,000 from wealthy persons under false pretenses. His wife, who was his third wife, felt he was a wonderful, God-fearing and religious man who would never do any wrong, even though she knew he had been in penitentiaries twice before. One brother-in-law, a professional man, thought that the victim was the world's worst scoundrel and in a 2-hour interview openly expressed a great deal of hostility toward him, feeling he was capable of any kind of culpable behavior. The second brother-in-law, an equally eminent professional person, thought the victim was a pathological liar but was not angry at him and had been rather bemused by his behavior. The fourth informant, the victim's attorney, indicated that he thought the victim had a good chance of winning his case and that he had been in much tougher situations before, that the evidence had really disappeared, and the victim was never the kind of person, considering his character structure, who would ever think of suicide. The informant from the Corporate Commissioners Office said that office had been following the victim for many months and knew a great deal about him. He had indeed been in prison, had married other women, had swindled other persons, had pretended to be wealthy but was not, and had put on such a wonderful front that very responsible persons would trust him with great sums of money, never thinking to ask him for a receipt. The sixth person contacted was an individual who had lost a considerable sum of money to the victim and characterized him as an extremely clever man. None of the informants, his widow included, felt that he was ever suicidal or depressed. All but the widow felt that he was a "cool customer" who could ride out any storm, especially when his chances of acquittal seemed quite good. The widow reported that he was to have met some persons from Kansas City in the hotel room to get back money that he claimed he had loaned them, in order to repay the local persons from whom he had taken money. The attorney also believed that he had met some persons in the hotel room. When the victim checked into the hotel, he had rented a safe-deposit box, which he might do in anticipation of receiving some money. In addition, it seemed difficult to understand his drowning himself, sober and undrugged, in a bathtub.

In the absence of any clear psychological or psychiatric features pointing to suicide, and in the presence of psychopathy, extremely large sums of money, mysterious goings-on, etc., it was deemed a logical possibility that foul play might have been involved. The case was recommended for further police action.

The following case was recommended for certification as a *natural death.*

A 55-year-old female died in the hospital as a result of severe bromide intoxication. The investigator reported that he interviewed the husband, who described his wife's illnesses, which had been considerable for the previous 10 years. She had had, among other things, kidney stones and surgery for a kidney suspension, osteoporosis, stomach ulcers, and a sympathectomy. Reading backward chronologically from the time of her death, she had spent 4 days in a general hospital and 11 days immediately preceding in a sanitarium. She had been home for a month before that and, preceding that, had been in still another sanitarium for 1 month. In the 3 years preceding this, she had been hospitalized twelve separate times for her various medical and psychiatric illnesses. She had lost weight from 120 to 95 lb, and she had begun to exhibit blackouts, which would occur at unpredictable intervals. In the last several months she had lost control of bladder and bowels and suffered continuously from severe pain. During the last month of her life she drank Bromo Seltzer and gulped aspirin in excessive amounts. The husband could not say how much she had taken, but she apparently would frequently reorder bottles of Bromo Seltzer from the pharmacy as well as have him bring supplementary supplies from the grocery store. She was taken to a sanitarium with a tentative diagnosis of toxic (bromide) poisoning and, after 11 days, was transferred to a general hospital for more intensive medical care. She died after 4 days in the hospital.

It was learned that 3 years previously the victim had consumed an overdose of Seconal, estimated around 10 or 12. This is the only report of a prior attempt on her own life by the victim. She worked as a registered nurse, and the last place of employment was a sanitarium for alcoholics. The marriage of the couple occurred 10 years previously and was the first marriage for both. There were no children. Much of their married life was filled with the illness of the victim. She was practically incapacitated much of the time, unable to keep house or to prepare meals.

The files of the local general hospital revealed that the victim had been a patient twice in the previous 5 years, the most recent admission being for a possible hyperparathyroidism and gastrointestinal bleeding. In addition, when she was discharged, the diagnoses of chronic brain syndrome and reactive depression were added. The history described inappropriate behavior, disorientation for time and place, confusion, and memory impairment. It also stated that she took many Seconal tablets when she could get hold of them. The previous hospitalization 5 years before was for similar complaints, with reports of delusional and hallucinatory experiences. An additional diagnosis of narcolepsy was noted at that time.

In summary, the victim was seen as someone who suffered primarily from severe bromide intoxication. Prior to this she had had a great variety of illnesses which had required at least 14 known hospitalizations within the preceding 2 years. Mentally and psychologically, from a pleasant, hard-working person she had developed into a person unable to care for herself, to think logically or appropriately, or to judge and direct her own actions adequately. There were symptoms of blackouts, confusion, delusions, and hallucinations, indicating that mental control and judgment were rather seriously affected. The victim had attempted to control severe pain with almost uninhibited ingestion of analgesics. There may have been some inkling in the victim's mind that her use of medications was approaching excess, but it was impossible to evaluate the extent of the intention finally to terminate her troubles. Conversation with her physician indicated that she was barely rational and was a severe management problem during her last 2 weeks of life. In the light of the mental status of the victim and the lack of any substantial evidence of intention to end her own life, the certification of natural death was recommended.

The following is an unequivocal suicide case in which *therapeutic* functions for the bereaved were served.

The coroner serves several functions. Not only does he keep his fingers on the health pulse of the community (by knowing what persons are dying of), and not only is he in the position of upholding medical standards (for example, through his investigation of deaths under anesthetics), but among his other functions he also can act for the best mental health of survivors of deceased persons.

Since the Suicide Team began to work with the coroner's office, there have been a few instances where the coroner has asked members of the Suicide Team to see a bereaved person (where there was literally no question of the mode of death) with the advertent purpose of helping the emotional orientation of the surviving person.

The victim in this case was a 40-year-old female who was found dead in her automobile in her garage with the door closed, the automobile engine having apparently operated until it ran out of gasoline. She was dead from carbon monoxide poisoning. It seemed to be a clear case of suicide. The husband, who appeared to be an intelligent and generally sophisticated man, came to the coroner's office not so much to urge a change in the certificate of the mode of death as apparently to ventilate his general distress and somehow to obtain some reassurance. At this point the coroner suggested that he be seen by a member of the Suicide Team. An appointment was made to interview him at the SPC.

The husband was a 47-year-old, outgoing advertising executive, bluff, hearty, and gregarious. He had become successful by his own wit and effort. He now found himself in the position of not only having to integrate the loss of his wife, but in addition, to be solely responsible for his four young children. The greatest block, however, to his emotional well-being was the terrible sense of shame that his wife had committed suicide.

During the interview he expressed a great number of feelings: guilt, dependence, and even resentment and hostility toward his late wife. He seemed to imply, but did not directly state, that she had been emotionally distraught, if not mentally ill. It was an hour filled with a great amount of ventilation for him, in which he gained a few insights. At the end of the meeting he expressed the opinion that, in spite of the content of the discussion, the interview had been a rewarding experience for him. He expressed his gratitude and felt that it had been therapeutic to talk about some of his feelings.

During the interview he had casually mentioned the name of a physician. This physician was subsequently contacted by telephone and asked about the deceased. It was learned that the dead woman had been emotionally disturbed, in fact, acutely schizophrenic. In fact, the physician had administered electroshock treatment to her some months before because she had been hallucinatory and had had bizarre religious delusions. Further, she had not been making an entirely satisfactory adjustment after the shock treatment. The physican felt that the husband was blind to the wife's disturbances because of his affection for her. The doctor said that he had no doubt in his mind that the victim was psychotic at the time of her death. He also had no question that the death was a suicide not only because of the manner in which she had died but also because she had been psychotic and depressed.

Thus, in this case, which unequivocally was suicide, the Suicide Team still performed an important function by assuaging some of the feelings of distress in the surviving spouse. It needs only to be added that this same function has been served in several other cases.

9

A Taxonomy of Death—a Psychological Point of View

EDWIN S. SHNEIDMAN, NORMAN L. FARBEROW, AND ROBERT E. LITMAN

At the outset some explanation for the inclusion of this chapter in a book on suicide may be in order. It would be platitudinous to say that suicide inextricably involves death. But it may be more meaningful to indicate that a thoughtful consideration of a definition and classification of suicide involves one, willy-nilly, in a consideration of all manners of death. Our reflections with the Los Angeles County Coroner, especially on the role of psychological variables in suicide, have led us to some consideration of the role of these factors in death in general.

There are many *causes* of death: the International Classification of the Causes of Death lists 137 different causes, such as pneumonia, meningitis, malignant neoplasms, and myocardial infarctions; but in general practice there is a much smaller number of usually recognized *modes* of death. In practice there are four common modes of death: accident, suicide, homicide, and natural. In some cases, cause of death is used synonymously to indicate the natural cause of death. Thus, the standard U.S. Public Health Service Certificate of Death has an entry for cause of death (implying the mode as natural) and in addition, provides opportunity to indicate accident, suicide, or homicide. These four modes of death constitute the final ordering into which each of us must be classified. That some of us do not fit easily into one of these four crypts is the fact that provided the essential impetus for this chapter.

The purpose of this chapter is to explicate a suggested revision to the current taxonomy of the *modes* of death, specifically one incorporating some thoughts from the *psychological* point of view. The subject matter of this chapter is therefore of interest not only to psychologists or psychologically oriented personnel but also to coroners, attorneys, judges, public health officials, and others who need to concern themselves with the medicolegal aspects of death. A complex phenomenon such as death is, of course, amenable to various taxonomic approaches. The optimal taxonomy depends in large part on the purposes for which it is employed. Our purpose is to present a classification of death of greatest usefulness for accurate certifications of the mode of death.

The accurate certification of death is by no means a perfunctory or unimportant mortality tabulation. The accuracy of this certification has at least two far-reaching consequences.

First, the usefulness of any set of statistics ultimately depends on the initial veridical status of those figures. Inaccurate statistics, so far as they mislead, may be worse than no statistics at all. For example, the apparent differences in suicidal rates among various countries may very well turn out to hinge, in part, on different definitions for suicide and on the general accuracy of reporting. An apocryphal story is told about a certain county in a specific state that had a remarkably low suicide rate and an even more remarkably high percentage of suicidal persons who left suicide notes. The enigma became clear when it was ascertained that the coroner almost never certified a case as suicide unless a suicide note had been found. Pressures of a religious or cultural nature have also been known to influence the accuracy of certifications of suicide. The taboo nature of suicide in certain countries and among certain subcultural groups contrasts sharply with the acceptance and even approval in them. *In other words, suicidal statistics as they are presently reported must be interpreted cautiously in light of the known variability of such certifications.*

The second important consequence of accurate certification of suicide is related to the first and has to do with the mental health of the surviving spouse, parents, and children; thus it indirectly affects the general mental health of the entire community. Attitudes of neighbors, feelings within the community, status, and position are influenced by the mode of death listed on the death certificate. The implication is not that suicide should never be certified but rather that maximum accuracy of such certification should be sought. The community can feel confident in the scientific methods and procedures applied in arriving at impartial conclusions. The facts, based on all the available evidence, are in the best services of good community prophylactic mental hygiene.

We have indicated that the traditional certifications of death are the four modes of natural, accident, suicide, and homicide. The shortcoming of this straightforward conceptualization is that, in its oversimplification and failure to take into account certain necessary dimensions, it often presents serious problems in classifying deaths. What are some of the basic ambiguities among the four rubrics? These might be seen best by focusing on the distinctions between natural and accidental death. The distinction between natural (intrasomatic) and accidental (extrasomatic) is essentially oversimplified. On the face of it, the argument can be advanced that most deaths are antinatural. Perhaps only in the cases of degenerative catabolic death of old age might the termination of life legitimately be called natural. One does not ask to have his body invaded by a lethal virus (natural death) any more than one asks to have it invaded by a lethal steering wheel (accidental death) or a lethal bullet (homicidal death). Conversely, diseases are accidents, in that few men want to catch diseases or to have strokes. Medicine does not speak of "cerebral vascular naturals" but rather calls them "cerebral vascular accidents." What has been confusing in the traditional approach to the classification of death is that the modes of death are divided in an artificial way. An essential component has been left out, namely, the person himself, or, more specifically, the role of the individual in his own death.

Our view of the individual is that he is more than just a biological organism; that he is rather a psychological-social-biological organism. The obvious implication of this is that a person's manner of dying (and his reactions to his consciousness of dying) are probably very much characteristic of his ways of living. This approach stresses what has been left out of previous classifications of death, i.e., the all-important motivational or psychological components. Our proposed classification attempts to deal with the inexorable fact that motivation *is* present in *some* deaths and that a comprehensive taxonomy of death must therefore include components that reflect the role of the individual in his own death.

A threefold classification of death, defined from the pragmatic point of view and focused essentially around a psychological dimension, is proposed. The three general classes of death are labeled unmeditated death, premeditated death, and submeditated death and are defined as follows:

UNMEDITATED DEATH

If death has not been brought about primarily from any conscious or unconscious act of the individual, then it has been brought about by accident, disease, illness, act of God, homicide, etc. In this type of death, the role of the individual in his own death is essentially nil, and he is a victim of elements, or forces, or happenstances that as far as he is concerned, take his life. The subcategories of this class of death are (A) death from unanticipated trauma, such as having been hit by an external agent (an automobile, a bullet, or a chandelier); (B) death from uninvited acute or chronic disease, physiological assault, or the disequilibrium of a natural somatic process, such as cancer or pneumonia; (C) death from unanticipated consequences of ordinary or innocent acts, which may be due to a combination of the potent nature of the stimulus and/or the idiosyncratic physiologic reaction of the victim; examples are a child ingesting alcohol or an allergic reaction to antibiotic drugs.

PREMEDITATED DEATH

If death occurred primarily as a result of the victim's behavior directed against his own life, then death has been brought about by the individual himself (*mortus de se*). The essential feature is that the individual has played a direct, conscious role in his own death. In these deaths it should be noted that *meditated* does not necessarily imply *deliberation;* such a death might also be the result of impulsive behavior. *Meditated* is thus roughly synonymous with the presence of psychological or motivational factors as an important component in the etiology of death. The subclasses of this category are (A) death from self-imposed injury, ordinarily called suicide (most, but not all, suicides are premeditated deaths; as we know, suicidal deaths themselves constitute a complicated array of phenomena, but these are dealt with separately in Chapters 4 and 5); (B) death from unreasonably dangerous activity, which occurs when a person takes a calculated risk to lose his life or an advertent gamble with death in which he has stacked the cards against his survival. This would be so even where there has been no voiced suicidal intention, but where death is an obvious common-sense logical possibility within the entire situation that precedes death.

SUBMEDITATED DEATH

If death appears to have been largely motivated by subconscious or latent wishes to die (or to be killed), then death will have been critically exacerbated by the victim's carelessness, disregard, imprudence, foolhardiness, amnesia, or other psychological mechanisms. In each case the person's unconscious role in his own death can be reliably inferred. In this type of death, the role the victim plays in his own death is *indirect*. Another way of conceptualizing submeditated deaths is to think of them as unconsciously meditated deaths.

Submeditated deaths include the following classes: (A) psychosomatic deaths, in which the cause of death is a physical disease that seems definitely to have been exacerbated by psychic factors within the victim that hastened or precipitated death; (B) death precipitated by negligence and carelessness, especially subsequent to warnings, such as a diabetic who disregards his diet; (C) death from exposure to dangers of known possible lethal potential, as by doing dangerous or daredevil feats for which a person lacks adequate training or safety precautions. A skilled pilot does not perform a dangerous task, but when a completely untrained person attempts to pilot an airplane and is unsuccessful, he dies in either a premeditated or submeditated way. A person who is not a professional circus performer and who, without conscious suicidal intentions, walks along the railing on a bridge and slips and falls to his death might well be certified as submeditated death.

The rubric of submeditated deaths provides a logical place for those deaths in which psychological factors seem to play an effective but not voluntary (premeditated) role. Such varied examples as the following illustrate this category: A person with tuberculosis, when the disease is in remission, leaves the sanitarium and follows the pattern of getting drunk, sleeping in vacant lots or in the gutter, etc., and suffers an exacerbation of the tuberculosis [3]. Many addicts and chronic barbiturate users live for years on the brink of death. Alcoholism, in the face of repeated warnings by a physician pointing out the danger of death from cirrhosis of the liver, in a person who continues to drink is a kind of chronic suicide, which, after death, might well be classified as submeditated death. Indeed, the phrase "he drank himself to death" comes immediately to mind. When such deaths occur, they are often, from the coroner's point of view, equivocal between accident and suicide. Labeling such deaths as submeditated cuts across the problem of suicide or accident and appropriately points up the subtle role of unconscious death motivation in such cases. Another interesting example in the borderline area is the person who behaves in such a way as to provoke a homicidal attack on himself. Indeed, there is a series of studies on the role of the individual in what are called victim-precipitated homicides [4]. An even more speculative example has to do with the role of psychological factors in such a time-honored disease as cancer, in which it has been suggested that psychological factors may play an important role in some cancer patients in terms of the *rate* of neoplastic growth [1]. Thus one sees that this classification points to what might be called the psychosomatics of death.

If it should be protested that the coroner cannot make the kinds of psychological judgments required for the proposed classification, the answer is that coroners throughout the country are making judgments of this nature every day of the week. The coroner in the situation of evaluating a possible suicidal death, for example, often acts (perhaps without knowing it) as psychiatrist and psychologist and as both judge and jury in a quasi-judicial way. This is because the certification of death as suicide implies some judgment or reconstruction of the victim's motivation or intention. Coroners do make these judgments (perhaps more coroners ought to use the category of undetermined), and the making of judgments is inexorably part of the coroner's function. A judgment is in most cases an inductive leap from the facts at hand. What this chapter says is that the facts relative to labeling the mode of death include not only the traditional biochemical, histological, and toxicological facts but also the psychological facts. We hope that discussion here of the role of psychological facts will make them more explicit in the judgments of the mode of death. Further, we point out that the coroner (as well as practically everyone else in life) is, in making judgments, caught between the poles of usability, on the one hand, and complexity, on the other. For persons interested in accurate certification of death, this is a particularly difficult dilemma. One wants a usable classification of modes of death but not with loss of accuracy. On the other hand, a highly accurate classification may become so complex that it would be unusable. To put it another way, the dilemma is to choose between a taxonomy that is usable but oversimplified (and may thus mask important differences) and a taxonomy that is meaningful but also more complex, which may pose formidable practical difficulties in putting it into useful operation. In this chapter we cannot attempt to resolve this dilemma but can only hope to make the problem more explicit.

Relatively speaking, the unmeditated deaths and the premeditated deaths are fairly easy to identify. In the former the victim plays no essential voluntary role in his own death (whether it is an accidental, natural, or homicidal death), whereas in the latter he plays a direct voluntary role in his own death; indeed, he kills himself. It is in the area of submeditated deaths that the difficulties of delineation are most pronounced. What does it mean to say that a person plays *some* role in his own death, an *indirect* or *unconscious* or *covert* or *subtle* role? Some clarification of this concept can be obtained by comparing it with the well-known ideas of Karl Menninger in *Man Against Himself* [2], in which he introduces the concepts of *chronic* suicide (under which he includes asceticism and martyrdom, neurotic invalidism, alcoholic addiction, antisocial behavior and psychoses), *focal* suicide (under which he includes self-mutilation, malingering, polysurgery, purposive accidents, and impotence and frigidity), and *organic* suicide (under which he discusses the psychological factors in organic disease). These provocative notions of suicide, which are concerned with partial self-destruction as brought about by general personality constriction and self-attacks upon the body, are similar to the present concept of submeditated suicides.

SUMMARY

There are many possible taxonomies of death. The particular classification suggested in this chapter is intended primarily for persons concerned with the medicolegal aspects of death. The distinguishing feature of the proposed taxonomy is that it is psychological in nature and proposes that some deaths must be classified in terms of the dying person's motivations. The position is taken that in some cases the manner of dying is part and parcel of the manner of living; man is seen as a psychosocial-biological organism reacting dynamically with his changing environment, so it is an artifact in the direction of oversimplification to view many deaths solely as a biological event. Further, the position is taken that almost no deaths (except the catabolic degenerations of old age) are natural and that practically all deaths (whether from a lethal virus, a lethal bullet, or a cerebral vascular accident) can be seen as accidental. Thus the distinction between natural and accidental becomes blurred and meaningless, and the suggestion is made that this classification be voided. A threefold classification is suggested in which the motivational aspects pertaining to the *role of the individual* in his own death are emphasized. The three categories are unmeditated, premeditated, and submeditated death. Some examples illustrating these types of death are presented, and some difficulties in classifying death are discussed.

References

1. Gengerelli, J. A., and F. J. Kirkner (Eds.): *Psychological Factors in Human Cancer,* Berkeley and Los Angeles: University of California Press, 1953.
2. Menninger, K. A.: *Man Against Himself,* New York: Harcourt, Brace and Company, Inc., 1938.
3. Shneidman, E. S., et al.: The case of Jay, *Journal of Projective Techniques,* 16: 471–475, 1952.
4. Wolfgang, M. E.: Suicide by means of victim-precipitated homicide, *Journal of Clinical and Experimental Psychopathology and Quarterly Review of Psychiatry and Neurology,* 20: 335–349, 1959.

10

A Survey of Agencies for the Prevention of Suicide

NORMAN L. FARBEROW AND EDWIN S. SHNEIDMAN

This chapter presents information on some of the organizations established in various parts of the world to deal primarily with the problem of suicide. It cannot, of course, hope to be complete, neither in listing all the agencies which are or have been in existence, nor in describing any one agency as it now functions. The reader will note that the organizations are all located in the United States or in Europe. Although there are other centers engaged in study and research in the problem of suicide, we have not come across any actual agency established specifically for the purpose of the prevention of suicide in continents such as Asia, Africa, or South America. The information presented herein on each organization described below has been obtained by direct contact, by personal letter, and from published materials, such as books, journals, newspapers and magazine articles, and brochures of the agency. For each agency described, a footnote indicates the source and the approximate date of the information. Although the description of some agencies will be less than complete, it is hoped that the reader will find these data useful as a beginning in the collation of important and practical information from a widely scattered variety of sources.

FORMER SUICIDE PREVENTION AGENCIES

Reference to organized efforts of suicide prevention go back to the beginning of this century. We know of some centers that were established primarily for the purpose of the prevention of suicide, or at least included it as one of their major functions, but now either no longer exist or have shifted their focus. In some instances, this change has come about through an evolutionary process within the agency, in the course of which its activities may have expanded or shifted so that its focus was on other problems. In other cases, they seem simply to have passed out of existence, or their function has been taken over by a larger bureau with many other interests into which the purpose of suicide prevention was merged.

A report by J. Fels, published in 1906 in a weekly newspaper,[1] presents the tabulated statistics on 720 suicide and suicide attempt cases to which the Lemberger Freiwilligen Rettungsgesellschaft (the Lemberg Volunteer Rescue Society) had been called in the thirteen years of its existence (1893 to 1906). Further details of the organization of the agency itself are not given, so it is not clear how the agency was organized and how it functioned. It is clear, however, that the agency served as a volunteer emergency service, not only for suicide and suicide attempts, but for emergencies of other kinds as well. The report also refers to a similar agency with the same name that existed in Budapest at about the same time, so that it may be that there was an association or federation of such agencies in selected cities in Europe at about this time. These agencies do not seem to exist as separate independent organizations any longer and have either been discontinued or have been absorbed into other services.

From an article by Rudolf Dreikurs,[2] we learn of several agencies established for the prevention of suicide in Vienna in the earlier part of this century. Recent communication from the Vienna Police Department indicates that these are no longer functioning. The first was an agency started by the Welfare Department of the Vienna Police Department, under the directorship of Hofrat Walkhoff. All persons whose suicide attempts came to the attention of the police were reported to the Welfare Department. A written summons was sent out which, if not heeded, was followed by a second one. If this too received no response, a social worker would make a home call. Home calls were often necessary, even after a consultation. Dreikurs reports that, in 1928, 2,373 cases of suicide attempts were reported to the Welfare Department, of which 1,035 were hospitalized, 100 of them in the mental institution of Am Steinhof as mentally ill. Of those summoned more than 80 per cent appeared. Only 544

[1] J. Fels, Siebenhunderdundzwanzig Selbstmord und Selbstmordversuche zusammengestellt aus der Lemberger freiwilligen Rettungsgessellschaft (Seven hundred and twenty suicides and suicide attempts collected by the Lemberg Volunteer Rescue Society). *Deutsche klinische-therapeutische Wochenschrift,* 1906, pp. 33, 34, 35, 805, 833, 863.

[2] R. Dreikurs, Zur Frage der Selbstmord prophylaxe (On the question of suicide prevention). *Zeitschrift für Psychiatrie,* 93: 98–114, 1930; also personal communication.

cases did not require care beyond consultation or home call, whereas 1,422 required more intensive care, such as financial assistance, the procurement of employment, or the alleviation of housing problems. Among the 2,373 attempted suicides in 1928, 8 were attempts by children under fourteen years of age and 158 were by juveniles.

Another organization was the Lebensmüdenstelle der Ethischen Gemeinde (Ethical Society Agency for Suicidal Persons) in Vienna, an organization that tried to reach suicidal persons before they attempted suicide. The agency was established by Wilhelm Borner, Walter Loewit, and Rudolf Dreikurs (the last also served as psychiatric consultant) with about forty volunteer counselors and social workers. The public was informed of the existence of the agency through releases in the press. In the first year of their operation, 1,506 persons were seen, of which 10 per cent were considered seriously suicidal and another 50 per cent probably suicidal. Environment difficulties played a large part, and help in alleviating these difficulties, as well as psychological counseling, was offered. In 10 per cent of the cases, neuropsychiatric conditions were found, including alcoholism, epilepsy, postencephalitis, hysteria, neurotic and psychotic depression, and schizophrenia. The number of paranoid conditions was felt to be disproportionately high.

The Jugendberatung (Youth Counseling Service), an organization for the prevention of suicide in juveniles was organized by Viktor Frankl in Vienna, in 1928, following the example of Hugo Sauers in Berlin. About thirty private counselors, physicians, lawyers, teachers, social workers, and priests made themselves available to give counseling in their own homes at certain regular times. Their names were made known to the youths by announcements in the press. In the two years reported on, 1,500 juveniles had availed themselves of the service. It was felt that the agency was often successful in intervening at a time when irreparable damage to the lives of these persons was still avoidable.

Aside from these three main agencies, Dreikurs also mentions smaller ones that were established for the same purpose by private organizations. He refers to the Bund für Lebensreform, the counseling agency of the Society for the Reform of Life, which was founded by Richard Schwartz. Dreikurs indicates that it was Schwartz who first publicized and propagandized the idea of caring for suicides and, as a disciple of Feinsilber, from Budapest, attempted to provide personal help to suicidal persons. He also mentions the Caritas' Lebensmüdenfürsorgestelle, which will be described in more detail below, inasmuch as it continues to function as one of the most active centers for suicide prevention in Europe today.

SUICIDE PREVENTION AGENCIES CURRENTLY IN OPERATION

The agencies described below are presently functioning with the primary purpose of preventing suicide and aiding the suicidal person. A rough outline form has been followed in presenting information about the various agencies so that, in general, similar data would be provided for each agency. In order to make the information as practical as possible, where available, addresses and telephone numbers have been included.

Anti-Suicide Department, Salvation Army [3]

Established around 1906.

Location. Social Work Department, Middlesex House, 110–112 Middlesex Street, London E.1, England.

Sponsor. Salvation Army, supported by voluntary contributions. The Salvation Army was one of the earliest agencies to establish a specific department aimed at preventing suicide and offering aid to those who had attempted it. Apparently, efforts were made to establish similar departments in other branches in different parts of the world. However, these departments tended to lose their identity as a special suicide prevention bureau and to spread their services into other problem areas, such as homeless men and unmarried mothers.

Method of Contacting the Agency. In general, the department has been responsible for persons who have attempted suicide and for whom responsibility had been disclaimed by their relatives. The referrals to the department are generally made by the London Metropolitan Relief and the Surrey County police.

Procedures and techniques. The patients are interviewed, and those patients in whom mental disorders are found are advised to accept treatment in a mental hospital. Sometimes these cases are dealt with by certification. Once the man has entered the hospital, the department rarely has any further contact with him. The department also interviews many persons who come to them for advice on varied problems, in the course of which they reveal that their thoughts have turned to suicide. The treatment itself may consist of advice or assistance, as needed, with the offer of the general evangelical teachings of the Salvation Army, if desired.

Experience. The results over a seven-year period (1949–1955) indicate that the department saw a total of 227 men. Of these, 22 per cent were in their twenties, 20 per cent were in their thirties, and 19 per cent were in their forties. Of the group, 35 per cent had been sent to the mental hos-

[3] Personal communication, 1956.

pital for treatment, 5 per cent had been sent to the general hospital, 20 per cent were listed as uncooperative, and 40 per cent were listed as "other reasons." Included among these other reasons were primarily that there was a police charge on the person or that other arrangements had been made. One person was listed as having died. The department has tabulated the results as 55 per cent successes, 45 per cent not accepted; 14 per cent of the total obtained employment.

National Save-a-Life League, Inc.[4]

Established in 1906, by Rev. Harry M. Warren, a Baptist preacher.

Location. The headquarters are at 505 Fifth Avenue, New York 17, N.Y. Telephone number is MUrray Hill 7-2142. Representatives can now be found in various cities throughout the United States. They can be located by referring to the local telephone directory or by writing to the headquarters office in New York.

Sponsor. The organization is supported entirely by voluntary contributions. It is nonprofit and nondenominational in its operation, and no fees are charged. The annual budget is approximately $55,000, entirely from donations. The board of directors is headed by Harry M. Warren, Jr., president, the son of the founder. The board of directors consists of a number of persons from the ministry, from psychiatry, and from the law.

Staff. The staff consists of seven full-time employees, four of whom are counselors, nonreligious in orientation. Psychiatrists are available for consultations and are used when the occasion makes it necessary. Social workers are used in the same way. At one time their advisory committee included Dr. A. A. Brill; later Dr. Hamlin Starks served with their committee.

Method of Contacting the Agency. Contacts are made by interested persons as a result of the many printed articles, TV programs, radio talks, and word of mouth from doctors, clergymen, and friends. People contact the agency either by phone or by letter. The agency conducts a 24-hour phone service. Most of the persons seen by the league are self-referrals; the rest of the contacts are referred by a great many sources, such as friends, neighbors, clergymen, and physicians.

Procedures and Techniques. When a disturbed person contacts the agency, he is asked to come in to see a counselor. If in the course of the interview he does not respond to spiritual and practical suggestions, or if he gives a history of having at one time been confined in a mental institution, he is referred to a psychiatrist for further information. If a legal matter is

[4] Brochure, newspaper and magazine articles, and personal communication, 1957.

involved, the agency legal advisor is available and offers such consultation without charge. There is no formal inpatient or outpatient treatment. All confidences are strictly guarded, and the patient is assured that no interference will occur without his consent.

In other instances, where a suicide attempt has been made, workers will visit the home or the hospital and make contact there. The services offered then may include helping the family and offering advice and practical environmental manipulation for the family where possible. In some cases this includes sending the children of a suicide to a camp or to a rest home as early as possible. Since 1932, the league has handled many children in this way.

Experience. The league estimates that it sees approximately 1,000 people each year in the more than half century since it was first established.

Follow-up Procedures. The league maintains the policy of corresponding with many persons whom it has treated. Cards are sent at holiday seasons, and persons are encouraged to write back to the league to tell how they have been doing.

Rescue, Incorporated [5]

Established March 1, 1959, by Rev. Kenneth B. Murphy.

Location. The agency is located in the Boston City Hospital, Room 25 BD South Department, 745 Massachusetts Ave., Boston, Mass. The telephone number, which is listed as a 24-hour service, is HAncock 6-6600. A branch of the agency has been established in Worcester, Mass., where the telephone number is PLeasant 6-1100.

Sponsor. The agency is sponsored by the Catholic Church and is supported by contributions from the church, from the Boston City Hospital, and by private donations. The agency lists Richard Cardinal Cushing as honorary president, and has a board of directors that includes the names of 18 persons prominent in religious, secular, medical, and legal circles of the community.

Staff. There are no salaried positions. The staff consists of 70 members, headed by Rev. Kenneth B. Murphy, president, and includes psychiatrists, psychologists, physicians, ministers, rabbis, nurses, and social workers, all of whom contribute their time.

Method of Contacting the Agency. Most patients contact the agency by use of the emergency medical phone service which is conducted on a 24-hour basis. In addition, the local and state police and fire department

[5] Brochure, newspaper and magazine articles, and personal communication, 1959.

cooperate by referring persons to the agency when these persons need such help.

Techniques and Procedures. The procedures are described as those in which psychological support, clarification, and environmental modification are used. Spiritual guidance is offered to the patient if he desires it. Psychiatric counseling is offered at the Boston City Hospital Psychiatric Department when necessary. Research is included in the procedures of the agency. At times some group therapy is offered, primarily by Father Murphy and a social worker, on a Suicides Anonymous basis. The Psychiatric Department at Boston City Hospital is used for cases where psychiatric treatment is necessary. Dr. John F. Sullivan, Chief Psychiatrist at Boston City Hospital, and members of his staff arrange for the necessary psychiatric treatment. Drs. John P. Conlin and James Saccotti, Superintendent and Assistant Superintendent at Boston City Hospital, respectively, coordinate the medical needs where necessary.

Experience. The agency handled over 800 cases from March, 1959, to March, 1960, with the loss of only 1 case because the agency had been called too late. Their statistics showed their referrals to be men in their mid-twenties and late thirties, and women in their late thirties and mid-forties. Most calls came between midnight and 4:00 A.M.; barbiturates were used most often, followed closely by slashing of the wrist, gas inhalation, jumping, hanging, and drowning.

Lebensmüdenfürsorgestelle (Suicide Prevention Agency)[6]

Location. Währinger Gürtel 104, Wien IX, Austria.

Sponsor. Caritas, Catholic Welfare Organization, Erzdiözese, Wien.

Staff. The director is Erwin Ringel, M.D. Some social workers are paid by Caritas; others are volunteers. Others on the staff include psychiatrists (from the University of Vienna Psychiatric-Neurologic Clinic), psychologists, and ministers. Most members work on a volunteer basis.

Method of Contacting the Agency. The police department and individual hospitals report all cases of suicide attempts to the agency. The University of Vienna Psychiatric-Neurologic Clinic receives many of these cases and refers them to the agency. Close professional liaison is maintained with the clinic. In addition, the agency actively propagandizes in newspapers and other publications in order to call public attention to the organization. The agency feels that it thus contacts almost all those persons who attempt

[6] Personal communication, and book: E. Ringel, *Der Selbstmord* (Suicide), Wien-Düsseldorf: Wilhelm Maudrich, 1953.

suicide. In 1948, the official number of suicide attempt cases registered in Vienna was 1,063, and the agency had contact with 1,050. In 1949, the official number was 975, and the agency contacted 929.

Techniques and Procedures. The organization started originally as a social agency and, in 1948, became more specifically directed to the problem of suicide. The agency makes earnest attempts to meet the psychic needs of its patients. To this extent all the disciplines on the professional staff may be involved. In general, the social worker makes the contacts, the psychiatrists work with the patient in self-understanding, the psychologists work with tests and in therapy. Clergymen are used, but the services are optional and independent of the individual's persuasion. Persons are never pushed to expose themselves. In more detail, the social worker establishes the relationship and goes out to meet the patient, thus seeking him out and making the contact. The first contact is frequently in the hospital. The social worker attempts to explore and understand the patient's personal situation and investigates the home environment. Attempts are made to improve the environment as much as possible, not necessarily by money, but as best as possible. It has been found that the best time to contact the patient is while he is in the hospital and before he is released and goes home to the influence of his relatives and the environment again. One of the primary tasks of the social worker is to bring the patient into contact with the psychiatrists of the agency. The psychiatrist examines the patient, determines the kind of therapy and the therapeutic plan best suited, and carries out ambulatory psychotherapy for nonhospitalized patients. The principles of individual psychology are followed, the aim being to uncover the basic causes of the personality difficulty. Catharsis, active encouragement, and affirmation of life are pertinent aspects and procedures in the therapy. The relationship between the therapist and the patient has been found to be especially critical in the first hours. A good relationship established then bodes well for the future. The psychologist does psychodiagnostic work, using psychological tests, particularly the Szondi, and participates in the psychotherapeutic procedures. The minister does spiritual work and counseling and not psychotherapy. "The physician heals, the minister hallows." He offers absolution of sin. Both inpatient and outpatient therapy is used. The depressives and the psychotics have been found to be best off in the hospital. Several times a year the agency calls all the patients together, renews contact, and thus continues to follow the patients' progress.

Experience. In the years 1948 through 1950, the agency reports a total of 2,879 patients contacted. Through August, 1951, only 42 had repeated their attempts, only 1 successfully. The completed suicide was known as a schizophrenic; the other 41 repeat attempters were those with whom contact had been established but whose cases were hampered by alcoholism, psychosis, hospitalization, and distance. There were no repeat attempts or completed suicides among those who had come to the agency voluntarily.

Follow-up Procedures. Aftercare and continued contact is felt to be important. The gathering held in the agency at least once a year for all patients has been felt to be very useful in maintaining contact.

The Samaritans [7]

Established November, 1955, by Rev. Chad Varah.

Location. St. Stephens Church, Walbrook, London E. C. 4, England. Telephone numbers are Mansion 9000, Mansion 2277. In addition, a number of branches of the Samaritans have been started, or are to be started, in other parts of England and in some other countries. The following cities now have branches functioning: Edinburgh, Liverpool, Stanmore, Glasgow, and Aberdeen. The following cities are scheduled to have branches initiated before the end of 1960; Hampstead (London N.W.), Derby, Sheffield, and Istanbul, Turkey. The telephone numbers of these agencies may be obtained from the local directories.

Staff. The agency has one paid person, the director, Rev. Chad Varah. The rest of the paid staff includes two curates, one psychiatric social worker, one social worker and one secretary. About 150 volunteers contribute their time with about 100 of them very active and most useful because of their training. The volunteer helpers include one psychiatrist, who is available for consultation and who gives one evening a week to patients who are referred to her. Carefully selected lay psychotherapists are also used. For the past 3 years a grant (3,000 pounds per year) has aided in the operation of the agency. Donations make up other sources of support.

Method of Contacting the Agency. Most clients are self-referred and have heard about the agency from the publicity given to it by the press. In addition, good relationships with the police have resulted in a number of direct referrals.

Procedures and Techniques. The procedures are described as a combination of religion and psychotherapy; "defending"; and helping with practical problems. The client calling the agency is strongly urged to come

[7] Personal communication, magazine, and newspaper articles, 1957.

immediately to the office to be interviewed. If the call is at night, the person is directed to come to the agency the next morning. If immediate action is required, a staff member may go to the person to give whatever assistance necessary. Patients are rarely put into a mental hospital, since it is felt that the primary aim is to keep them out. Interviews are conducted, and psychotherapy is provided through the psychiatrist and the lay psychotherapists.

The medical profession has been cooperative and helpful with their activities, so contact with the family doctor is routinely made when permission is sought to call in relatives, whom they ask both for information and cooperation in manipulating the milieu. The police have been very helpful, particularly in making referrals and in making it a point not to pay attention to persons seen entering the church. This is particularly important because in England, an attempt at suicide is still a legal offense.

Problems. In reporting problems met in working with patients of this nature, reference was made to the shortage of qualified paid staff and to the shortage of funds. There was a great need for environmental manipulation for many of the clients, particularly the arrangement of a supervised environment for many persons after the pattern used for epileptics. In an attempt to meet this problem, the agency now operates a 6-bed hostel in a home (donated to them) for use by persons in need. The senior curate is in charge.

Experience. As of August, 1960, the total number of patients treated was over 3,207. These were divided roughly equally into psychological problems, spiritual and moral problems, and sexual and marital problems, with much overlapping. Clients were primarily between the ages of twenty and fifty, and about equally divided between both sexes. A survey of the first 2,000 cases dealt with by the Samaritans showed that 12 per cent had problems which were primarily spiritual, for whom some form of Christian therapy was felt to be the only hope. Psychological cases formed 27 per cent of the total, and of these, 5 per cent required psychiatric treatment, 5 per cent clinical psychotherapy, and 17 per cent only counseling and befriending by someone with psychological insight. Of the total, 26 per cent had sexual and emotional problems, and of these 14 per cent were marital, 8 per cent were cases of frustration and loneliness, 2 per cent were homosexual, and 2 per cent had other perversions. Of the remainder, 2 per cent were long-term chronic cases and 2 per cent psychopaths, while 30 per cent were not readily classifiable under previous headings and were regarded as needing general rehabilitation. The feeling was that spiritual and religious philosophical problems hit men harder than women, while emotional problems hit women harder. One important lesson that had been learned was to treat both parties if the suicidal person was married.

Lebensmüdenbetreuung [8]

This agency, an organization for the care of suicidal persons, is one branch of an international organization within the Episcopal Church; the Order of St. Luke, the Physician. This order has representatives in many parts of the world whose churches provide healing services. Some suicide prevention work, as part of the wide number of problems handled by the organization, occurs regularly. However, it is not the primary problem focused upon. The Lebensmüdenbetreuung in Berlin, formerly under the leadership of Dr. Klaus Thomas and now headed by Dr. Weissinger, although it treats many other problems, concentrates its efforts on recognition, care, treatment, and prevention of suicide.

Location. Berlin-Steglitz, Bismarckstrasse 66 Ruf (Telephone): 32 01 55.

Sponsor. Order of St. Luke, the Physician, Episcopal Church.

Staff. The staff is headed by Dr. Weissinger, in West Berlin. There are 25 volunteer assistants, drawn from various professions, some of them specially trained.

Method of Contacting the Agency. The names of those who attempted suicide the previous day (generally anywhere from 3 to 10 daily) are obtained from the police and the hospitals, and these persons are then either visited or invited to come in for an interview.

Procedures and Techniques. Patients are treated according to their need from the psychological, psychiatric, and pastoral approaches. Psychotherapy includes hypnosis and group therapy, sometimes psychoanalysis when feasible, and chemotherapy, particularly the tranquilizers. Pastoral care and counseling, according to the ministrations of the Order of St. Luke and consisting of special services, bible classes, intercession-hours, etc., are offered to those who desire them.

Experience. In their first two years, the agency received more than 800 outpatients, of whom 500 were suicidal. As of the beginning of 1959, the number of persons seen by the agency was over 6,000, with the average number of counseling sessions around four. Of these, it is estimated that about 2,000 have been suicidal.

Addendum. The Order of St. Luke, the Physician, of which the Lebensmüdenbetreuung is a part, was founded by the Rev. Dr. John Gayner Banks. The warden, Rev. Alfred W. Price, is in Philadelphia, Pa., while

[8] Personal communication, newspaper articles, 1957.

the associate wardens are located in San Diego, Calif.; Natal, South Africa; and London, England. Clergy chaplains and lay workers are listed in England, Canada, Australia, South Africa, Scotland, Wales, Ireland, Switzerland, Germany, Holland, Brazil, France, and Ceylon. Headquarters are at 2243 Front Street, San Diego, Calif.; Mrs. Ethel Tulloch Banks, secretary. The organization publishes a monthly journal called *Sharing,* which indicates a list of churches providing healing services.

The Suicide Prevention Center.

This center, founded in 1958 and located in Los Angeles, is discussed in detail in Chapter 2.

Other Agencies

There are now available in a number of large cities published telephone numbers which persons can call for assistance and guidance.

In Zurich, Switzerland, there is an agency called Die Dargebotene Hand (The Outstretched Hand); the telephone number is TEL 5-40660. The agency is headed by Pfarrer Kurt Scheitlin, now at the Freie Gymnasium. The agency reports having had 2,137 telephone calls in the first 7½ months of its existence, with 60 per cent of these calls coming from males and 40 per cent from females. The reasons listed were depression, 42 per cent; illness, 18 per cent; family and financial difficulties, 10 per cent; chronic alcoholism, 6 per cent; and miscellaneous, 24 per cent.

A similar agency exists in Geneva, Switzerland. The name is La Main Tendue (The Outstretched Hand), the address is Case Postale 62, Genève 7 (Servette), Switzerland, and the telephone number is 33 81 33. The organization is headed by Rev. Raynald Martin, and is now planning to form an information service, including the publication of a directory of all organizations throughout the world dealing with the problems of suicide.

An agency called Das Diakonische Werk (The Deacon's Work) is in operation as a telephone agency in Kassel, Germany, under the leadership of Dr. Stange. A group of approximately 40 volunteer workers (pastors, M.D.s, lawyers, social workers, housewives, etc.) assist in the work. Branches are reported in Düsseldorf, West Berlin, and Frankfurt.

Rev. Eric Bernspang, a Lutheran minister, has become known as the "suicide minister" in Sweden. His mail address is Torpsdal, Sweden, and his telephone number is Boras 7-0340. He has been concentrating on the problem of suicide prevention for the past four and a half years. Clients contact him through telephone calls, letters, and personal visits. Occasional referrals are made to psychiatrists and mental hospitals, but most of the cases can be helped with counseling and supportive techniques. Rev. Bernspang indicates that in a number of cities in Sweden, such as Stockholm, Orebro, Malmo, Sundsvall, etc., a Castastrophe Number has been set up and is made available to the general public for use in suicidal emergencies. Volunteers respond to these calls. Rev. Berndt Backlund has been active in effecting these arrangements. In addition, in Malmo, Sweden, an organization calling itself Ankaret (Anchor) has been formed under Mr. Hermanson which addresses itself to the suicidal problem. Thirty-five persons, all volunteers, such as ministers, public officials, business men, and nurses operate as the staff. They have been functioning without any outside source of support since the inception of the organization 1 year ago.

Two churches in Chicago have also arranged a telephone service for disturbed persons, which includes suicidal persons. The Peoples Church of Chicago, a Methodist church, under Rev. Virgil A. Kraft, associate pastor, has set up a system called Emergency Call.[9] This consists of a 24-hour telephone-answering service, which refers calls to one of about twenty-two clergymen or psychiatrists who are prepared to talk to disturbed people on the telephone. The girls who answer are instructed to show a friendly manner and to obtain the name, address, and telephone number of each person who calls. If one prefers to remain anonymous, the girls will give the caller the telephone number of a minister or, if the case is urgent, she will hold the caller on the wire until the call is traced and referred to a physician and to the police. A counselor in the district from which the call comes is notified; he completes the emergency counseling on the telephone, suggests possible courses of action, and perhaps arranges later personal consultations or refers the person to the proper agency in Chicago. In emergencies, doctors or ambulances are called. The announcement of the service and the number LOngbeach 1-9595 were publicized in the local newspapers, resulting in as many as 200 calls a day for a while.

Dr. Kenneth Hildebrand, minister of the Central Church of Chicago,[10] indicates that he is one of a number of clergymen who have committed themselves to receiving telephone calls from would-be suicides. Such a person may call a publicized number and be referred to one of the team or may call his church office number, DEarborn 2-4840, direct. A clinical psychologist is available at all times, and two psychiatrists and a mental health counselor are available occasionally. The counseling is pastoral in

[9] Personal communication, magazine articles, 1960.

[10] Ibid.

nature and entirely outpatient. Counseling sessions are continued as long as the help is needed. Once the contact is terminated, no effort is made to follow up each case.

An organization which calls itself FRIENDS, was begun in December, 1959, in Dade County, Florida.[11] The telephone number is FRanklin 4-3637, which spells out the word FRIENDS on the telephone dial. Its president is Frank Wutz, its corresponding secretary is Mrs. Elizabeth Binai, and one of its charter members is Tom Lownes who, as a reporter for a local newspaper, became interested in the problem of suicide for Dade County and was instrumental in founding the organization. A 24-hour answering service is maintained, and the caller is immediately telephoned back by a FRIENDS member to whom the call has been referred. The goal is to get the right professional help for the caller—medical, legal, psychiatric, employment, welfare, marital, religious, etc., as needed. Person to person meetings, return calls, all depend on the situation and mutual agreement between the caller and the FRIENDS member. No fees are charged. All materials, facilities, and services are volunteered. The agency operates on an extremely small budget, less than $200 per year, and no money, food or clothing are distributed. Members of FRIENDS are of both sexes, all religions, and all occupations, with ages varying from the middle twenties to the sixties. For each call handled by a FRIENDS member, a card with pertinent details is mailed to a psychiatrist, Dr. Harvey Resnik of Jackson Memorial Hospital, Miami, Florida, who serves as professional advisor and evaluator for the group. While results are to be evaluated in a systematic way, the group feels encouraged by the fact that a 24 per cent decline in suicide rate has been noted in Dade County for the 10 months the agency has been operating, and that 1960 marks the first time in eight years that the rate has failed to increase there.

SUMMARY

What general conclusions can be made from the varied information cited above? One general impression is that these suicide prevention agencies serve extremely useful, indeed vital, functions and that they hold promise of providing at least partial answers to questions about self-destruction, concerning which adequate documentation is at present lacking. One hopes that suicide prevention centers will be established in many more communities throughout the world and that support will be found for these programs.

[11] Personal communication, 1960.

PART II

The Psychotherapeutic Response to the Cry for Help

II

Introduction and Case History of Mr. A. S.

NORMAN L. FARBEROW

Suicide in its many manifestations is a problem of major importance for all therapists. The suicidal crisis, when it occurs, presents crucial moments not only to the patient but to the therapist as well, arousing as it does for the latter all the critical decisions of management, so vitally important in these instances because the balance often lies between life and death. In the light of this, it is surprising to survey the literature on suicide. Most of the writing has been anecdotal, statistical, sociological, ecological, philosophical, moral, etc. Clinical accounts have touched only infrequently on either the theoretical aspects of the problem or the techniques per se used in handling the suicidal crisis. Perusal of these accounts seems to suggest, however, that there are different basic theoretical approaches to the phenomenon of suicide and that, inevitably, these different approaches yield varying techniques in the treatment of the phenomenon. In Part II some of these different approaches are explored.

The reader will find in this part some of the more common theoretical points of view on suicide. These chapters were written by persons who either had published on the subject or had displayed special interest in suicide and who were asked by us to write on the theory of suicide and its various clinical manifestations from the point of view of the school of thought in psychiatry and/or psychology with which they were associated. No claim is made that the schools of thought represented constitute a complete listing, nor should any implication be drawn as to value of any one theory from the omissions and inclusions of theories or from the order of presentation. Presence or absence of particular theoretical points of view was dictated in some cases by some rather prosaic and practical factors, such as availability of a representative.

It was hoped that differences and similarities among the several theoretical points of view would become apparent from this procedure. The reader will, of course, want to read the chapters and to note such theoretical similarities and differences for himself. It was deemed desirable, in addition, to make such differences and similarities more explicit by asking each expert to review a case (the same case) of a person who had attempted suicide and to indicate how he would interpret this case history in light of his theoretical orientation. In addition, the contributors were asked to indicate the treatment plans, including the possible techniques that might occur to them, etc., for this particular patient.

The very selection of a case history posed some problems. It became immediately apparent that the type of data to be included in the case history was important and that the way in which these data were presented was crucial. The most desirable ideal case would be one in which all the facts were known so they might be interpreted and discussed as desired by each expert. But the variety and number of facts needed could only be gained through many long hours of therapy interviews, yielding not only cross-sectional information of relationships in many present spheres, but also genetic longitudinal information on the developmental aspects of attitudes, character, etc. But such data must be obtained by an interviewer, who would in turn have to gather such data within the framework of his own theoretical biases. This meant that legitimate questions could be raised concerning the relevancy of such data for therapists of other theoretical orientations. Even so, it was felt desirable to obtain data that were dynamically oriented and of such a nature that they could yield to theorists information which would be much more than a bare recounting of facts and figures in a chronological review. Accordingly, the case history chosen was the result of a series of diagnostic interviews by a psychiatrist with background and training in dynamic psychiatry.[1] In editing the case for distribution to the contributors, we tried to retain the facts (however biased) and to delete statements that were obvious interpretations or assumptions. We believe that it may be impossible to present a completely objective (i.e., no point of view) case history, but we have tried to come within a practical distance of this goal. This particular case was chosen not only because the patient was deemed cooperative, amenable, and communicative but also because there was an opportunity to obtain additional and supplemental data from interviews with his parents. What follows is the case history of A. S.,[2] a twenty-three-

[1] Grateful appreciation is expressed to Dr. Norman Tabachnick, psychiatrist, who obtained the anamnestic interview data from A. S.

[2] Anonymity has been preserved with changes of names, places, and other vital data.

year-old, white, male, single, college student, who had attempted suicide by ingesting about seventy-five barbiturate capsules, and who had been brought unconscious, after having been discovered in his hotel room, to the emergency ward of a large general medical hospital.

CASE HISTORY: MR. A. S.

Age, 23; sex, male; race, white; religion, Methodist; marital status, single; occupational status, college student.

General Situation at the Time Patient Was First Seen

The patient was first interviewed by the psychiatrist in a two-bed emergency ward of a large general medical hospital, after he had been there for approximately a week. The other patient in the room was comatose. There were five interviews with the patient and one interview with the patient's mother. The patient had been in a deep coma for about a week after ingesting about seventy-five barbiturate capsules. He had been in critical condition when admitted and had required a tracheotomy and forced respiration. During the first two or three days of the interviews there were some slight signs of organic brain illness, such as inability to concentrate and some impairment of memory, but these seemed gradually to improve as time went on.

Appearance

The description of his appearance may be somewhat affected by his severe state of physical illness. However, he was a slight, blond, boyish-looking person, already partially bald. During the entire week of the interviewing he appeared passive and eager to please. At times he was apparently in severe pain, but it was difficult for him to request an interruption in the interview. He seemed to emphasize the passive role to a greater degree than the illness would account for. He usually preferred to lie down, thus dramatizing his helplessness.

Circumstances Surrounding the Suicidal Attempt

When the patient was asked why he had tried to kill himself, he said, "Well, it all goes back to before I went into the Army. I had a girl friend then, Mary [who was of South American–Spanish descent]—she was a wonderful girl." He repeated this several times. "I loved her, and she loved me. She was intelligent and gracious, and I really wanted to marry her. But my folks were against this and I couldn't understand it. It was the first time that they had ever crossed me. They seemed so cold to her, both my mother and dad. I remember we wanted to get married, and mother started talking about black babies, and she said it just wouldn't be good for me. Then they accused her of being pregnant, and she really wasn't, and I remember it hurt her; it hurt her a lot. And I didn't know what to do. I couldn't go against my parents, and I couldn't understand why they were so mean. Dad would not give me the car when I wanted to take Mary out and Mary would call up. I could hear my mother answering her on the phone and she was cold and angry to her. Then I left for the Army, and after a while I wasn't feeling so bad about it. It wasn't that I forgot Mary, but it didn't bother me as much; I found another girl, and I thought that I was even in love with her. Then I came back home; Mary would call me, and my parents had the same attitude toward her, and and it brought back the whole thing that had happened two years before, and I started to feel bad again. I didn't want to stay at home and I wanted to go back to college to study sociology; but even after I got to school, I still kept thinking about my parents and then I decided I would sever relations with my family and get started on my own, but I had to get away for a while, and I remember I decided it all one afternoon. I just would have to get away, so I called a travel agent and he arranged a trip to South America for me. I thought maybe I could forget down there, so I went to South America, but I couldn't get interested in anything. I couldn't do the things that the tourists were supposed to do, and after about a week I felt it was time for me to leave, and I decided that I would come to Los Angeles and see what it was like and that maybe eventually I would be able to go to school. I had heard that there were very good schools around here. So I went to a cheap hotel and paid my weekly rent. I would look in the papers and try to get a job, but it would seem as if I just couldn't get started. I would look at them but wouldn't do any more. Then I would go to a movie and come back, and all the time my mood was getting worse, and I still had the feeling that I wanted to sever relations with my family. I had to have something bigger than myself, a feeling of understanding from home. Before I left school, I had been getting nervous and the doctor had given me some sleeping pills, and then in the couple of days before I tried to commit suicide, I went to several other doctors and got more sleeping pills. I wasn't sure at the time that I was going to commit suicide, but I did have the idea. The day that it happened I went to a movie and then came back, and I only had a quarter left and I was hungry, so I got a malted milk and had it, and that probably saved my life. Then I came up to my room, put all my stuff away, took a shower, and took the pills and lay down—and then I don't remember anything else until I started waking up at the hospital."

Chronological History

The patient was born in Kansas, the younger of two children. He has a sister who is married and who is three years older than he is. "As far as I know my mother's pregnancy and delivery of me were normal, but mother used to tell us that she couldn't have any more children afterward. There was nothing unusual that I can remember about my infancy."

The patient was asked to tell something about his parents and any other persons with whom he had much contact. "My mother is a very hard-working woman who likes to take on responsibility. She likes to excel. She likes to be the leader in clubs and be the chairman of organizations. She feels flattered when she is elected for something like this. She likes to do things alone, though, even though she might be in a group of people. She is a very intelligent woman and very hard-working, and she never gives up at anything. She liked to do most of the work around the house, and I guess both of us were somewhat pampered because of this attitude of hers. I think my sister turned out lazy because mother would never let anyone else do anything. I know I resented this at times." At this point the patient became somewhat tearful and said, "I feel all confused. Mother spent as much time with us as any other mother did—" and then was silent.

Then the patient was asked to speak about his father. "Dad was never extremely successful at anything he did, and I used to feel bad about this. He had to give up the dairy farm because he couldn't make a financial success of it. He is the kind of person who had many friends and did a lot of different things. Once he worked on an evening job, and I remember we used to go with him. Sometimes we would fall asleep, and then we would come back home and milk the cows. Finally, when the farm failed, he had to sell it, and then he worked in a general store. That hurt me a lot because my friends always had fathers who were important and were doing important things, but dad didn't stay at that job too long. At first we lived in a small house, and after a while we were able to move to a bigger one. My father did odd jobs. In the last four years he got into politics and finally got to be a foreman in the city maintenance department, but you know, even that ended up rotten. There was a scandal, and his boss had to resign, and my father lost his job. Mother used to work, and it was really because of her energy that I guess we were able to do as well as we did. Mother got sick in 1947. She had a bad liver attack and almost died. That was terrible.

"Mother was so intelligent. In a way, though, I think that mother enjoyed dad's illnesses because she liked the opportunity to work and to show that she was very competent. She is a self-denying woman and makes everyone that is around feel inferior. My dad is thankful toward her for the help that she has been to the family, but also quite resentful. He says sometimes that she has supported the family, but he likes to avoid crowds and go to clubs because she always predominates. He is not a good family man. What he likes to do is to take a car (he always likes to have a new car) and wash it, but he is not interested in working around the house; my mother has to pull him into it and tell him what to do, and he expects her to do this. I guess that I am closer to my mother. I used to take my problems to her from time to time, but not too much."

Ann, who is the sister, is 26 years old. "We were never too close. We were different personalities. We often had fights, but they weren't too serious. I would say that it was a normal relationship. She was talented in music, and she still plays well. She was interested in music. She joined the band, and she could sing, and she was very interested in church. I played the violin, but I wasn't very good. I was never active in church, but I did play trombone in the band. As far as I know, there was no favorite between us for either of our parents. Ann is still interested in the church. She is sort of a tense girl. She is divorced from her husband now. I don't know why, but she is very emotional and she was like this as a kid. I have never showed a lot of my emotions. I would feel things, but I would hide them. Sometimes we would visit relatives, but otherwise we didn't go out much and spent most of our time playing with each other."

The earliest memories patient said that he had dated to about the age of 9 or 10 years, and this is what he remembered: "This was about the time we moved into town. I remember that I fought with a neighbor kid all the time. I don't know why it was, but I was always fighting. I just had to. We would be friends in between. It seemed that I used to love to fight. I was small and would lose most of the time, but anyway I would keep on doing it. I would feel very bad when I lost. My mother would tell me that I shouldn't fight. My father sometimes also would, and I would feel uncomfortable about this; I would wonder why they wouldn't stick up for me rather than just tell me not to fight. When I was a kid, I didn't mind that I was so small. Even in high school it seemed that I didn't mind. I would play football some, and I used to tell myself that it didn't matter that I was small, but later it seems that I didn't care very much about it. At college I started to feel bad about being small. Once I even bought some elevator shoes. It seems like I didn't feel physically equal to the fellows. In regard to girls it didn't seem to matter so much, but I thought that even there I might have been liked a little better if I were taller."

When asked if he had any memories from before the age of 9 or 10, he said: "Well, I remember playing with neighbor children in the hayloft. I remember something else wonderful; we took a long trip to get a bicycle and we came back late at night, but my dad set it up for me even though it was late, and I remember we were riding it with him helping me." This seemed to be a pleasant memory, and patient was asked further about it. He said: "I don't remember it as being happy or unhappy. I remember going to school, that I would have to get up real early in the morning and get out of the cold bed. Then I would run downstairs to get dressed in front of the warm stove, but in general it seemed that everything went well at that time and everything seemed to be happy then. We finally had to sell. Dad was ill and we didn't have enough money, and we had to move into town, and then it seems I was jealous of the other kids and would fight with them all the time. At the time that we moved I knew that things weren't going well. Dad got a job in a general store. I can remember vividly I was taking violin lessons and I was playing the violin one day, and I started to cry because I wanted to go to a movie. Dad gave me the money, but then I came back because I guess I felt bad at the way I had gotten the money.

"My mother was actually my teacher during the time that we lived on the farm. My aunt was the teacher at our school. I remember, we would fix our lunches in the morning and go off to school in the car. My aunt treated all the kids the same and didn't favor us, but I used to think I was something special because my aunt was the school teacher. I used to play with the neighbors and with my sister, but when we came to the city, everything was different. I used to fight all the time, and I remember once the teacher spanked someone who had beat me up. I don't know how I felt about it. I remember feeling bad because I lost the fight; apparently some of the other kids had told the teacher, and she had come out and brought us both in and then she spanked the other boy. I don't think the other kids liked that. I didn't have too good luck in school in the city schools. My marks dropped down and they weren't so good, and in the sixth grade I almost flunked. My mother looked at my report card that day when I came home and started to cry, and dad scolded me. Things would upset her very easily, but she never would punish us. She would tell us it would worry her if we did something bad. I can't remember too well about my dad's way of handling things. When dad scolded us, I didn't resent it because mother never scolded us. I remember desperately trying to be popular. I would try to be nice and charming and everything, but it seemed as if the others didn't like me, and then I would fight with them. I graduated from grammar school at 14. Things still seemed to be the same, but after a while in high school I got a lot closer to some of the kids, but I still had a feeling that I wasn't in the real top echelon and I was trying to get in. I would want to be the leader, but I never was. After a while in high school I finally got around to accepting that I just wasn't one of the select group. I felt a little better then, and my marks went up. I didn't like to go to Sunday school, but mother told us we would have to. The reason I didn't like it was that there was a teacher there who really didn't care about teaching and didn't know how to be a good teacher. Mother was always trying to build me up and brag about me to everyone, and whenever anyone would come over she would tell them how wonderful I was."

Medical History

Patient had the usual childhood diseases. Patient had a tonsillectomy at the age of 11, and he can remember other persons were very good to him. They brought him good things to eat and malted milk. When he had whooping cough at the age of 12, he can remember choking in the living room and trying to call for someone, but he couldn't and it was a very panicky situation. Patient recalled his service experience and, particularly, his superior, who always seemed to be making fun of the patient. Finally the patient developed severe diarrhea, which was caused by nerves. "This man was everything I hated. He was tall, domineering, didn't know what he was doing, but acted as if he knew everything. He always tried to humiliate me, and I couldn't disagree with him. I couldn't stick up for myself; he would always win." Patient had minor surgery in 1950, that was not complicated. He remembers that, when he was a child, he used to have ingrown toenails, and he used to have operations on them that were painful and kept him laid up.

Sexual History

Then the patient was asked to tell something about his sexual development. He said that in high school he used to try to date the very popular girls. "They turned me down and I wouldn't ask others, so I didn't go out very often. I never went steady with any one girl in high school. There was this one particular girl who was, I think, the most popular one in school, and I kept asking her for dates all the time, but she never gave me a tumble. Then I would pretend that I didn't like to have a date with her, but that really wasn't true. Later on in my junior and senior years, I would ask other girls out and was more successful, but I never felt that I was really enjoying myself with them, that I would rather have had the other girl."

The patient said that there was never any discussion of sex by his parents in any regard, and until he had his affair with Mary in college he had never had intercourse. He guessed that he must have learned about it from the other boys, but he didn't really remember. He denied any memories of early masturbation or sexual experiences, except for this: when he was young, about 8 or 9 years old, he was going to meet a girl, who was 12 years old, in the bushes with the idea of having some sexual play, but then he had to pay a visit to his grandparents; he remembered having to call her up and call off the date, and she got really angry and said, well, they would never do it again then. In regard to masturbation he can only remember masturbating since he was in college. He remembered one time having an erection at about the age of 5 or 6; the foreskin seemed to be stuck, he couldn't get it back over the glans, and he had to call his mother to undo his foreskin. He said that he felt he really didn't need to masturbate when he was in high school, that he only seemed to awaken sexually when he was in his last years of high school and in college. In college he started masturbating and had some wet dreams and felt guilty about it.

In college he met Mary. He had known her for a long time. Mary was a South American–Spanish girl who had been adopted by one of the respected members of the community. It was in the summer between high school and college. He was going on a special date, and he asked one girl who couldn't make it; she suggested Mary, and he just tried to make sure that it would be a nice girl and a good-looking one. "And we hit it off real well, and we started going steady. When I went to college I had to take out other girls since I was in a fraternity and I was expected to, but I would always think of Mary; she was my girl. The other girl I had always tried to get in high school didn't seem to mean as much to me after Mary came. We got along very well except for my folks, who were quite resentful toward her. My dad wouldn't give me the car. Mary was the first girl I had intercourse with, and I enjoyed it very much. Then the last year before I left for the service I started college." At first he enjoyed himself. During the preceding year or so he had started feeling not so small, and he continued on this spurt of activity; then after a while it seemed as though he didn't care for school any more. He lost interest in the school work and started fighting with his dad about Mary. "I didn't actually fight. I would talk with my mother, but I wouldn't talk with my dad. Mother told me that I was wasting my time with Mary, and I decided I wanted to get away. I didn't know at that time if I blamed my parents or not, but I began to feel that I was going down again, and even though I told my friends the reason I joined the Army was to get it out of the way and to make myself eligible for the GI Bill of Rights, the real reason was to get away from the terrible problem."

Service History

"There was quite an argument at home at that time. My mother never wanted me to join the Army, but I had to join to find what I was looking for. I was sent out west. I was very lonely; Mary would write me every day, and I would wait for her letters and pounce on the mailman. I finished basic training and came home, and I remember the day that I came home I wrote to my parents that when they came to the station they should bring Mary with them, but when I arrived, they hadn't brought her. I was disappointed and resentful. Mary and I had a wonderful time. We went out every night.

"Then my next tour of duty was up north, and after I had been there a couple of weeks I decided that I wanted to get married right away. My folks said that I shouldn't get married then, that I should wait for two years, and that if I still felt like it then I could marry. They caused a lot of trouble. They went down to where Mary worked and accused her of being pregnant, and then my parents lied to me. They told me that Mary's mother was against her getting married. But I had a letter from her mother saying that she thought it was a good idea. I felt terrible about that. It was the only time it had ever happened.

"When I finished up north, I was sent east and I got a short leave to spend at home. I saw Mary again and we talked about eloping, about going to New York, but it seemed like we didn't have the nerve; then I remember one day it seemed there was just a doomed feeling about the whole situation and we knew that things would never work out. When I left her that day, I cried. The next morning, even though I had a day or two more, I packed and took off for my new station, and for a while I didn't write my parents. Then one day while I was in New York I called the hospital where I had learned my mother's sister was ill and found out that she had died, and then suddenly I felt different about things and I called my mother and told her that I would be back home and I wanted to write to her again. Then I wrote Mary and told her that we would have to break it off, and I asked her to send me my fraternity pin, but she never sent it back; I still knew that there was a tie, and when I thought of how we broke up I was resentful.

"I liked the service very much and did extremely well in it, even though I griped a lot. I became a specialist and advanced to the position of sergeant. I had people working for me. Things were going swell. All during this time I was tempted to tell my folks good-by, but I never did. I did administrative work in the service, and I was very happy except for times when I would have moods. Then my father wrote me a letter that he was buying a new car, and I asked him if I could buy his old car and he said I could; so one weekend I went down and got the car and came back to camp. Then I could drive around a lot; during the summer I went to the beaches, and I met a girl from a city near the camp. We became very close. Her family was wonderful to me and we became quite fond of each other, but in the beginning I told her that it was just in fun, that I didn't feel that I wanted to get serious. I felt myself falling in love with her, and it was very hard for me to tell her that it was love, but as time went on I knew that that was so."

Postservice History

"When I got out of the service, neither of us could accept the fact that we wouldn't see each other again. I hated to go home. I was tempted to stay with her, and her family would have loved to have me. So I decided that I would go back to school, but I didn't want to spend any time at home, so I made arrangements for a preenrollment at school; I was just at home a few days. I decided then to change to sociology. For the first couple of weeks I was happy in school, but then the same situation between Mary, myself, and my folks preyed on my mind, and I didn't feel so close to Mary; she had changed a lot. She was not considerate any more; she would say things and wouldn't care what people thought. She would hurt their feelings, and I remember feeling that this was all my folks' fault, and I blamed myself, too. I wasn't enjoying school, but my marks were up; I started feeling socially inferior again, and I couldn't study. It got so it was a real effort to study, and I hated it. I was at my nerves' end. I went to the doctor for a nerve tonic, and he gave me some sleeping pills and it didn't help; but I really don't know what was causing all the trouble at that time; that's when I decided to leave school and go to South America."

Interview with Patient's Mother

This interview was conducted with Mrs. S. at the general hospital. Her age is estimated to be in the fifties. She is of medium height, slight in build, with an air of tightness and control about her. She holds her lips quite tightly, and it seems to require positive effort for her to open them and let something out. Mrs. S. is quite neat and takes her time before answering most questions, as if to plan her answer. Mrs. S. spoke almost not at all spontaneously, but questions were asked and made very pointed in order to get specific information from her. Otherwise, her tendency was to say that everything was normal, or all right, or just as you would expect. It may be noted here that, when the parents heard of their son's critical condition, they immediately flew to Los Angeles; for the first week or so of his stay in the hospital, they were at his side night and day. This continued, although with some decrease, even after the son was pronounced out of critical condition by the hospital physicians.

"We were always very good to A., let him do whatever he wanted to, and never tried to influence him in any way. We were very pleased with him because he always was very obedient and did whatever we thought was right even though we had to exert almost no pressure on him to do so." Mrs. S. stated that, before she was married, a doctor told her that she would never be able to have children because of an obstructed tube. However, she had this adjusted, and she seemed to take some pleasure in pointing out that, even though the doctor had said she would never be pregnant, she was able to conceive. She remembered that A. seemed to be a very active child while she was carrying him. Mrs. S. stated that she and her husband had decided that they wanted children and that they were not disappointed that they did not have more children; however, they did not use birth control, and "if more had come they would have been welcome. A. was a normal child in every way. He was a very active infant and into everything." Mrs. S. said that she and her husband always treated the children equally, and that there was never an issue as to which sex would be preferable to either parent. She emphasized that both children were wanted. "When A. was a child he lived on the farm with us and was very active. He played with everything and was alert in every way. Our children were very much admired; other children would get into trouble, but A. was obedient. There were never any quarrels or arguments about what his rights were. The father and son were like two peas in a pod; they often talked together and shared interests. A. was very close to his sister. He liked to play with toys and animals on the farm and would sometimes help with the work. Finally we had to sell the farm because of my husband's health. We moved into town and rented a home, and my husband worked. A. was a very active boy; all the children liked him. He took his share of responsibility and enjoyed doing it. He was very active in sports, but unfortunately he had poor eyes; for this reason he had to leave the baseball team, even though he was a good player. He was very musical, which we enjoyed. He plays the violin and the trombone, and he enjoys this. He didn't work during the school year, but he would work summers on the farm and would save his money. He has always paid for much of his upkeep, and we have never had to ask him to do this. He wouldn't like to accept money and would rather work. We weren't too strict with the children, except for certain things, like regulating the amount of shows they went to, according to the kind of show that would come in. For example, if there was a horror movie or something like that, we would request that they did not go and they would comply. If there was a party that they were going to, they would have to be back at certain times. We didn't let them stay out until all hours. We never punished them. If occasionally they would step out of line, we would talk to them about what we wanted done. Our kids never said no when we asked them. I don't know if it was respect or what. I thought A. and his dad had always been close, but I think he is closer to me. I never knew of any problems with A. other than the usual ones. We always talked it over very completely.

"He was the kind of boy who always liked to stick up for the underdog. I remember one time a teacher flunked a student, and the girl wanted to ask the teacher what the reason for the failure had been, but she was afraid to ask; A. was quite angry at this teacher because of his unkind attitude. He wanted to strike back at the teacher, even though he felt it might mean his own expulsion from school. From a very early age he has been interested in the problems of the world; he always comes in and turns on the news and is very concerned about the terrible things that are happening. There was only one time we stepped on A. He was in the service. He had a South American girl friend. He was on furlough and started seeing this girl and decided that he wanted to get married. I said no because I felt that he was too young and there was a difference in the pattern of living. I am worried that that might be at the root of the trouble. I don't know; since A. has been home from the service, he might have been having an affair with this girl.

"A. was very nervous when he came out of the service. He had a mean officer with whom there was much difficulty, and I think that might be the reason why. He was only in school for five weeks after he got out of the service, when he suddenly decided to leave school. I remember one evening before he started school we were talking about the West Coast and his going there, but it came as a complete surprise when he did leave school. He just called me up one evening and told me that he had quit and that he felt he wanted to get away for awhile. He couldn't even take time to come home. He hadn't been doing poorly at school. I know because we went down there to bring his clothes back, and, of course, I tried to find out everything that I could about his leaving. His friends all told me that they thought he was happy and he was doing well in his studies. Nobody knew why he left."

When the interviewer first came on the ward to evaluate the situation and begin interviewing A., his parents were at his bedside. The interviewer explained to them who he was and what his function in the hospital was. Mrs. S. became quite suspicious of him and asked the chaplain who was with them if he knew the interviewer. She asked for his credentials and asked who had requested his appearance and, in general, was most reluctant about him interviewing her son. Mr. S. for the most part stayed in the background. He is a man of about 55 or 60, who is somewhat heavy and, in general, seems to be a passive person who at times steps out from behind his wife's skirts to assume some of the gruff exterior that he feels is demanded of a man; for the most part he is overshadowed by her and stays in the background. During several brief conversations with the interviewer, he tried to emphasize certain manly aspects of his own personality and he also adopted the position that A. had always been a happy and successful person.

12

Suicide: Psychoanalytic Point of View

SAMUEL FUTTERMAN

Doctor Futterman was born in 1909, and received a B.S. degree from the College of the City of New York in 1930 and an M.D. degree from the University of Geneva, Switzerland, in 1935. He had his psychoanalytic training at the New York Psychoanalytic Institute. A Diplomate of the American Board of Neurology and Psychiatry, he is also a member of the American Psychoanalytic Association and the American Psychiatric Association, and an instructor at the Los Angeles Psychoanalytic Institute. He taught in the Graduate School of Social Work at both the University of Washington and the University of Southern California. He was chief psychiatrist at the Veterans Administration Mental Hygiene Clinic, Los Angeles, from 1945 to 1952, and is now consultant to the clinic. He is vice president of the Los Angeles Psychoanalytic Society, president of the Southern California Psychiatric Society, and he is a contributor to various journals in psychiatry, psychology, and social work.

An approach to the problem of suicide, examined from the psychoanalytic point of view as developed from Freud's original theories, must start with his formulations about instinct theory. This presentation, in outlining some aspects of Freudian instinct theory, particularly the death instinct, and in summarizing some of the available psychoanalytic literature on this topic, makes no claim to be comprehensive. Further, it makes no attempt at originality; the hope is rather that a more complete understanding of the death instinct theory may help us both in our methodology and in providing a background of theory for the postulation of concepts around suicide.[1]

A glance at Freud's conception of drives will help in understanding his theoretical formulations, first proposed [6] in 1920, in which he outlined the whole problem of instinctual forces that he believed energized the mind and impelled it to activity. The less familiar word drive seems preferable to the more common term *instinct* because the aspect of human functioning it is intended to describe is distinctly different from the aspect of lower

[1] For background, history, and development of the death instinct theory by Freud, the reader is referred to E. Jones [9], pp. 266–280.

animal functioning attributed to instinct. However, the words are often interchanged, and even in this chapter it is occasionally easier and smoother to bow to custom and to talk about the death instinct as well as about aggressive drives.

Freud, in considering drives as they appeared in man, did not include the motor response (which is included in lower animals) but only the state of central excitation in response to stimulation. A drive is a genetically determined psychic constituent that, when operative, produces a state of psychic excitation or tension. This impels the individual to activity or behavior, which, in a general way, is also genetically determined but which can be considerably altered by individual experience. The attribute that drives possess of impelling the individual to activity struck Freud as analogous to the concept of physical energy. He consequently assumed the presence of a psychic energy as a part of the drives or somehow derived from them. Thus, drive and its energy are considered as purely intrapsychic phenomena and are concepts that Freud felt were needed to explain some of the observed facts of psychic functioning. The term *cathexis* was introduced as an indication of the amount of psychic energy directed toward or attached to the mental representative of a person or thing. The greater the cathexis, the more important the object is, psychologically speaking.

Stimuli, both external and internal, may arouse drives that impel the individual to activity. This activity seeks as its aim something that will result either in cessation of excitation or tension or in gratification. The motor activity that occurs as a result of the state of excitation is mediated in man by a highly differentiated part of the mind, known in psychoanalytic terminology as the *ego*. We will delay our discussion of the role of the ego in psychic functioning and state here only that the ego modifies the instinctual drives by experience and reflection, a process that differentiates man from the lower animals, where the drives are predetermined so far as motor activity is concerned. Therefore, in man, individual experience serves to modify the drives.

Freud reached the important conclusion that there were two kinds of drives, assumptions which not all psychoanalysts accept in the form in which he originally presented them [6]. Freud proposed to account for the instinctual aspects of our mental lives by assuming the existence of two drives: one was called the life instinct, or Eros, or the sexual drive; the other was called the death instinct, or Thanatos, or the aggressive and destructive drive. The former drive describes the erotic component of mental activities, and the latter gives rise to aggressive, destructive components. It is important to know that Freud emphasized that neither drive could really function independently of the other but that they are fused in variable amounts. In other words, there is no act of love that does not have integrated with it an unconscious amount of aggressive drive; the most callous act of intentional cruelty, which seems on the surface to be pure aggression, has within it some degree of unconscious erotic gratification. It should be understood that the aggressive drive is not only shown in behavior that we ordinarily think of as aggression and that the aggressive drive is no more synonymous with what we ordinarily speak of as aggression than is the sexual drive with the desire for sexual intercourse [2]. Rather, we see the derivatives in the generalization and proliferation of these drives.

Theorists have found it easier to describe the vicissitudes and genetic development of the sexual drive than those of the aggressive drive. We know, however, that the components of the aggressive drive show the same capacity for fixation and regression as have been described for the sexual drive. Thus, aggressive impulses in the very young infant may be discharged by oral activity such as biting, or in the older child, sometimes in fantasy only, by use of his penis as a weapon and means of destruction. It becomes apparent that both sexual and aggressive drives are manifested during the developmental period by fixations to oral, anal, and phallic zones and that the fusion of these drives appear in the resolution of the oedipus complex and in the formation of the superego. Ideally, fusion of the erotic impulses with the aggressive impulses relieves them of their destructive quality, permitting sublimation of these latter impulses so the individual will be able to make a positive productive contribution to his life processes. Menninger [11], whose theories of the death instinct and its relationship to suicide are well known, felt that the wish-to-die element in suicide was much more hypothetical in contrast with the clinically demonstrated existence of the other two elements, that is, the wish to kill and the wish to be killed. The condition of a fusion of the destructive and sexual drive was central to his theories, with self-destructive activity emerging when there was incomplete or inefficient functioning of the neutralizing device of love. "In a person who commits suicide, it (the self-destructive drive) suddenly bursts its bounds, springs into power, and puts an immediate end to the existence of the individual."

Some psychoanalytic authors feel that the aggressive drives can be explained without assuming the existence of a death drive. The reason is that aggression can be regarded as activity through which the organism must go in freeing itself from frustrating tensions and in surmounting the obstacles between it and the attainment of the goals of the sexual or life instincts. Or, as Bowlby has postulated [1], aggressive activity is reaction to trauma, thus representing love and hate as the relationship between a loving ego and a traumatic world. This is another way of saying that hostile impulses arise when the organism is frustrated in satisfying its other needs. It is also unquestionably true that aggression appears as a manifestation of pregenital and genital sexuality [2]. Young children, in pursuit of their pregenital sexual aims, display a great lack of consideration for the feelings of others, hostility toward the environment, sadism, aggression, and destructiveness. Although aggression, as a result of frustration of sexual impulses, has been attributed particularly to the anal phase, it becomes apparent that it is actually part and parcel of all zones, oral and phallic as well, and, in addition, that it also appears in the manifestations of the oedipus complex.

However, such clinical evidence seems much more clearly understood and accountable if viewed as manifestations of the components of both sexual and destructive urges. In the development of the child in mastering his oedipal strivings, the aggressiveness becomes incompatible with other needs and the superego appears to mediate the conflicting tendencies. The superego thus provides for the individual a higher agency of the mind, which protects him from the open expression of his own aggression. At some moment in the development of the child he experiences the ideas, fantasies, and wishes of the aggressive drive as dangerous and/or incompatible with other strivings. Anxiety appears, and guilt feelings are produced to help dispel the intolerable wishes from consciousness. In this way the mechanisms of defense are developed and used by the individual both to fend off and to transform what the ego has learned to recognize as dangerous instinctive strivings.

There is no reason why the same repression that occurs for sexual urges should not also occur for aggressive urges, with the development of similar mechanisms of defense, such as reaction formation, projection, and sublimation. Projective displacement of aggression may be responsible for much of the strain, suspiciousness, and intolerance found between individuals and nations. Aggression may also be turned inward, a process that might be seen in the bodily sphere in the development of somatic complaints or in the mental sphere as a lack of self-possession, excessive severity of the superego, depressive states, and self-destructive or suicidal tendencies.

The significance of the above for the consideration of suicidal behavior is seen clinically in the attack against the self by the melancholic, a condition that represents a real aggressive explosion directed toward the self [12]. In melancholia the reality of the object world has diminished because of the regression that has taken place. Freud has described the process in melancholia as one in which the identification of the ego with an incorporated love object takes place (as in the situation of the feeding infant) and this object becomes lost, either in reality or in fantasy [7]. Whereas, in the normal person, after a period of mourning, cathexis to other objects occurs and identification processes continue, in the melancholic situation the process becomes a regressively incorporative one with aggression appearing as a means of possession-destruction. Perhaps for this reason, the melancholic expresses very little aggression outside himself and has little relationship with the outside world. However, aggression during the height of the attack can occasionally spread to those around, enveloping them in his frenzy of ruin and massacre. Even then, the situation is usually experienced by the melancholic as a subjective occurrence. He may even think of destroying others, but the basis for this lies in the misunderstanding and confusion that, for the melancholic, now reigns between subject and object.

Other psychoanalysts have theorized that it is with the formation of object relationships that frustrations, disappointments, dissatisfactions, etc., appear as aggressive and destructive behavior. However, theorists from this monistic school (Eros only) meet with difficulty in accounting for the energy sources, resources, and distributions in conflict behavior, since a single source of energy must activate opposing activity. The dualistic school (Eros and Thanatos) overcomes such difficulties in the postulation that the death or aggressive instinct makes available a potential reservoir of energy, which, with the development of object relationships, allows aggression to go through its many vicissitudes in the form of superego formations, identifications, etc.

Object relationships assume, however, the presence of a functioning ego. Anna Freud [4] wrote (pp. 147–149):

> In clinical observation, neither sex nor aggression can be studied in pure form.... This essentially biological theory contains far-reaching social implications.... The infant develops hostile as well as loving feelings toward the mother over and above the hostility which is aroused whenever the mother frustrates the child's wishes.... The mental representatives of the two organic forces remain unrelated to each other as long as no central point of awareness is established in the personality. It is only the growth of this focal point, the ego, which results in the gradual integration of all instinctive striving and during this process may lead to clashes and realization of the incompatibility between them. According to these

views therefore the presence of mental conflicts and of the guilt feelings consequent of them presupposes that a specific and comparatively advanced stage of ego development is reached.

In the Melanie Klein school this ego development is attributed to a much earlier age, allowing the conflict to appear between these two opposing instincts earlier than Anna Freud has theorized.

In detailing the character of the death instinct, Freud reasoned from his assumption that organic matter had grown out of inorganic matter and that inanimate matter had been infused with life under some unknown cosmic influence. The tendency is for animate matter to return to inanimate matter, a retrogressive process that he felt was similar to the process of dying and the ultimate state of death. Freud stated that the death instinct similarly is essentially conservative and does not seek new experiences but rather strives for a state of complete rest. This is in contrast to the life instinct, which disturbs this rest and constantly strives for new experiences [13]. This principle was developed to accord with Freud's conception of the homeostatic principle of the ego. This principle stated, in effect, that, when excessive stimuli invade the organism, the ego reacts with an effort to reduce these stimuli to a constant level. This effort continues as long as the imbalance remains. The reactions to a disturbance of rest may be violent, as seen in the infant who will cry, scream, and kick when his rest has been interrupted. A schizophrenic in a catatonic stupor frequently reacts to the outside world with outbursts of rage and fury, which may lead to the destruction of everything within reach. Thus there are conditions in which every external stimulus is painful and is warded off by destruction. This tendency of the ego to ward off stimuli persists throughout life, diminishing in the early years but increasing again in the later, declining years of life, as exemplified in the conservative, rejecting attitude of older persons toward new impressions and experiences. The death instinct thus seeks the past, is averse to new experiences, is essentially conservative, and is under the domination of the repetition compulsion. As such it tends toward eternal rest, a tendency that may find its expression in suicide. It is the apogee, the culminating expression, of the suicide's attempt to maintain the status quo. There is a certain similarity between the repetition compulsion used in describing psychological conditions and the law of inertia, which, in describing inanimate matter under physical conditions, expresses the tendency of inorganic matter to remain in a certain stable state or to return to this state. Freud analogized that, once a behavior pattern that is suitable for the gratification of subjective needs had been found, it is repeated until it becomes automatic. It is repeated because it follows the direction of least resistance and because it requires less output of energy. It is of interest to note that this stage of Freud's theorizing had been preceded by the use of the fluid hydraulic conceptual model appropriate to the closed system theoretical thinking prevalent at that time [14]. The changeover to a more open system theoretical model did not occur until the 1920s, with the publication of *The Ego and the Id* (1923) and *Inhibitions, Symptoms and Anxiety* (1927), which resulted in the assumption by the ego of a more prominent and pervasive role in the functioning of the personality. This allowed for the concept of anxiety to emerge as a trigger or signal mechanism, of vital importance to the functioning of the ego. As already referred to above, the development of and the functioning of the ego is considered by some writers to be of vital importance in the conflict, relationship, and integration of the opposing forces of the life and death drives.

The phenomenological similarity of death to sleep or drug and intoxication states has occupied the attention of some writers. According to Lewin [10], there is some connection between ideas of sleep and ideas of death. He states that ontogenetically the wish to sleep is older than the wish to die and thus the idea of death may be a modification of the idea of sleep. There is also some connection between the artificial excitement of the drug addict, the natural excitement of manic and related states, and sleep. The drug addict's stuporous sleep represents for him the union with the breast, but this is only partly true for the manic. Suicide in both types, the drug addict and the manic, may thus represent a fusion of the ego and superego and a consequent return to the mother. In its most extreme form this would be a reproduction of the fantasy of sleep at the "good" ever-nourishing breast. Lewin develops the theme that the idea of death as a nirvana, or state of complete rest, has become related to and confused with the idea of sleep, more specifically a good sleep. The matrix of subjective experience from which the ideas that become differentiated as sleep, death, nirvana, immortality, heaven, and the oceanic feeling spring is the blank state that follows nursing and later good dreaming states. This is related to the lack of a concept of time in the unconscious, thus representing in a way the earliest days of infancy, in which there is practically no distinction of time or between annihilation and immortality. In this ecstatic sleep the immortality stems from the feeling of union with the immortal superego figure, a fusion of the ego with the superego, which repeats the original fusion with the breast. The model for immortality and happiness, union with the breast, is the "good" sleep. Certainly some forms of suicide in cases of manic depressive psychosis are influenced by this fantasy. Clinicians have noted that, in severe manic excitements, the patients hope to visit heaven or see God or the saints or have other intimations of immortality or of pleasant experiences in the other world to come. This, incidentally, is in marked contrast with the uninviting death that seems to await the pathologically depressed.

The death that comes to be feared is the "bad" sleep that is interrupted by tensions, anxieties, guilt. In the sleeper it is like the ghost who cannot rest, or like the wandering Jew who, for a sin against Christ bearing the cross, is doomed to remain alive, a curious sentence unless it is understood as analogous to a bad case of insomnia. "Good" death and "bad" death thus seem to be modeled on early subjective experiences of sleep until finally integrated into a single conception. In the final integration, the ambivalent symbolism still reveals the two ingredients; and the fact that the suicide believes in the ego's immortality represents a regression to the good sleep. Rado, in 1933 [15], also commented on drug addiction and, with the coining of the term *pharmacothymia,* remarked on how both stupor and suicide may be sequelae. He hypothesized that the patient who kills himself in pharmacothymia does so because he wishes to dispel depression forever and substitute for it an elation that could last forever. This kind of patient thus does not really kill himself but rather reaches for the immortality he feels is his through death.

Glover [8] refers to another aspect of suicidal states that seems worthy of note. Often when there is an overburdening of the psychic apparatus with instinctual energy, there occurs a building up of stasis with intolerable tension. Relief might be attempted by activity outlets such as suicide. These phenomena of bursting sensations are usually seen where the individual experiences no effective efferent discharge; this produces in him an intolerable tension with a gradually developing dread of total annihilation. It is related to early childhood fixations, usually of anal or urethral character, where the only relief seems to be one of bursting, a process that in later life might produce impulsive suicidal tendencies.

Freud [6] indicated that the organism moved with a vacillating rhythm when he referred to the instinctual drives. Later Anna Freud [4] wrote (p. 149): "In early infancy love and hate can be seen to appear in quick succession, seemingly unaffected by each other." Then Scott [16] suggested that the oscillation of the instinctual energies, in terms of one borrowing energy from the other in its expression, rather than just the succession from love to hate and vice versa was the most important concept. He felt that the damming up of sexual energy in the absence of satisfaction can lead in sequence to desire, tension, pain, and disorganization. Then (p. 237):

"... this disorganization is re-organizable but only with the energy unchanged. Consequently, when, during psychoanalysis, hate is re-organized into love, the energy of the hate will be manifested in the energy of love, and the anxiety of hate will be found equally in the anxiety of love until further analysis, further progress occurs. Similarly, with the disorganization of love, equivalent energy will appear in hate."

Scott thus seems to emphasize that the absolute quantity of energy remains unchanged despite the overt behavioral changes. This may account for much of the clinical evidence of suicidal tendencies occurring in patients where there is sudden dissolution of a love relationship and a quick oscillation to reunion with the love object after suicidal attempts. Other mechanisms also could be involved, such as the suicidal attempt as a destruction of the introjected love object, as Freud postulated in melancholia, but, in addition, the quick reparation and restoration after the attempt. Brunswick [3], in his attempt to formulate a defensive aspect of the aggressive instincts, probably had something like this in mind. Otherwise he felt that there would be an overwhelming of the organism by the aggressive instincts. He indicated that the aggressive and defensive instincts then would have both the aim of protecting the body itself and of maintaining the possibility of the satisfaction of the sexual instincts. He also indicated that defensive and aggressive drives or instincts are the most closely related physiologically, both being mediated in their emotional and functional aspects by the sympathetic division of the autonomic nervous system, in contradistinction to the libidinal instincts, which are mediated in their operation chiefly by the parasympathetic division.

Probably the most persistent unanswered question regarding suicide is the reason for the choice of this mode of expression for the resolution of the underlying conflicts. In terms of either escape or aggression, there are certainly many other resolutions within the framework of symptom, defense, character neurosis, psychosis, etc., which are all available in response to the drives and their conflicts. This has long been an unanswered problem in the consideration of psychopathology, and this chapter cannot aspire to do more than add additional questions to an already confused area. Freud addressed himself to these questions in part [5] when he attempted to clarify the primary gain accruing from a symptom, act, or illness that was used to resolve pre-existing intrapsychic conflicts and secondary gain accruing from a symptom, act, or illness after they had become well established. He distinguished between internal, intrapersonal, and external, interpersonal components in the primary gain, which combine in bringing about the symptom and the illness. Secondary gratification was then limited to those incidental and unexpected gratifications arising after the establishment of the illness or the appearance of the symptom. In the consideration of suicide as a symptom, an act, a defense, or an illness, several characteristics appear that seem to differentiate it, superficially at least, from other kinds of resolutions, despite the fact that suicide stems from the same elements of aggression in its conflict source as any other symptoms, defense, character neurosis, or psychosis. What is particular about suicide is (A) its drastic nature; the action is impressive in that it leaves such little leeway to repeat because of its effect upon the actor; (B) its gamble with success; the suicidal person deliberately risks the highest stakes he has available, his life, in a frequently casual manner; (C) its comic-tragedy aspects in failure; the action arouses many reactions, not the least of which is the sheepish, sometimes relieved, frequently hostile, and only sometimes sympathetic feelings, both in the suicidal person and in those around him; (D) its mobilization of guilt, death wishes, or fears in others; mixed in with the feelings described above are the intense reactions of those closely involved with the patient who respond to the suicidal act with feelings of guilt, fear, or with severe feelings of anger and hostility at the implied accusations communicated by the act itself; (E) its primitive character as motoric behavior; the individual, in developing from id response, first uses motor activity automatically for discharge of his tensions and gratification of his needs. With growth he learns to insert a time period between stimulus and reaction; an acquisition of certain tension tolerance is necessary to bind primitive reaction impulses. Reality judgment is necessary. For all of this a more mature, rational, less narcissistic ego is required, which is not present in the suicidal patient. The suicide fears the experience of further traumatic states.

It may be of interest to watch for these aspects of the suicidal act in the discussion of the case to follow.

THE CASE OF MR. A. S.

This case history is unfortunately lacking in necessary and important details, a situation that in part may result because the case material was obtained in a hospital setting under certain difficult situations. In the discussion of this case, therefore, an apology is offered to the reader for the fact that there may be little connecting link between the theory as discussed above and the case material.

Some of the history might be summarized as follows: The patient was described from the ages of one to five as an active, alert child, and he lived on a farm until he was about ten years of age. He was quite obedient. His aunt was the teacher in a small school, and he felt well liked up to the age of ten. Because of external conditions his family had to sell the farm and move to the city at that time. Then he began to find himself in many fights with neighbor children and had early feelings about his small size, feelings that later became quite emphasized. He had a tonsillectomy at eleven and almost failed the sixth grade when he was around twelve. At this age he also had whooping cough. Then at ages fifteen to twenty he shifted from high school to college. There were reawakened feelings about his size, and his masturbation began about this time. He seemed to have managed well in the first part of college, when there was a spurt of activity, but then he lost interest and joined the service. It was also around this time that the whole affair with Mary had started. His service record seemed to be good. Then he started back to school, felt nervous, got sleeping pills, went to South America, and within a few weeks returned to Los Angeles, where the suicidal attempt occurred.

One often raises the question in depressed and suicidal patients whether there was a loss or absence of an important figure in his childhood. In this case we have an intact family that has lived together. There is no real absent father, although we might say that the father was physically available but emotionally uninvolved. There may have been some subtle indications of intent toward suicide when he told his parents that he was going to go to the West Coast from their home in Kansas. But there was nothing subtle in his idea of going to South America after dating a South American girl for a number of years. He buys a malted milk with his last quarter before taking the pills, and malted milk also had been associated with the tonsillectomy at the age of 11. We see in all this the unconscious bid for help for his mounting tension. He tried to delay the impending explosion by trying to run or move away, but then the loss of money, added to all the dammed-up feelings produced a kind of internal catathymic crisis. He felt a kind of bursting within himself that impelled him to activity, which for him took the form of a suicidal attempt.

The oedipal nature of his relationship to Mary is seen in this case. There is a greater preoccupation with the mother than the father. Often the giving up of the mother and choosing another woman implies for the patient the risk of abandonment or death of the mother. This was seen when the death of the aunt makes him resume the union with his mother and the giving up of Mary. His irrational self wanted both parents and Mary, as when he requested that his parents bring Mary with them to the station once when he came home on a furlough. When he did attach himself to a girl in the service, it seemed this was not sufficient. He needed to attach himself to a figure that might help him break away from his mother. Mary supplied this much more than the girl to whom he was attracted in the service. For himself, the parents' attitude toward Mary was the first time that they had ever crossed him. This probably is a screen memory of many other frustrations in regard to the parents. The concept of suicide as destruction of the superego figure could be enlarged here as a punishment he was meting out to his mother for all the wrong that she had done to him.

Many points can be raised as to the motivation for treatment that would first have to be shown by this patient before a treatment program could be set up. Some may say that he does not seem to talk of any inner conflict and that projection still prevails as the dominant defense. One may also say that he showed little motivation because he did not seek advice about his problems prior to this attempt. Other questions about his motivation might indicate that his frustration tolerance was low; that he had tendencies to escape rather than to work through his problems; also that he attempted to work out his problems in a living situation and that this is what he essentially found in the situation with Mary. On the other hand, he had done fairly well in the school situation and in service, his intelligence seems adequate, and much of his need to act out in a small but serious way can be attributed to the paucity of living experiences. We also do not know what resources were available to him from the community in case he really sought help.

PSYCHOTHERAPEUTIC IMPLICATIONS

In planning any kind of psychotherapy with this patient, many factors would have to be considered. There is, for example, some question whether the psychotherapist who would continue with this patient should actually see the patient while he is still in the hospital. Careful consideration has to be applied to this question, for in a hospital setting many emergency problems come up, which the therapist should perhaps best avoid. It starts the relationship on a different level if the patient sees the therapist as making the many important decisions that must occur in a hospital setting. The changeover to an outpatient setting, whether it be clinic or office, is quite different and may prove to be distorting and confusing to the patient. This consideration may be of particular importance when the therapist has been treating the patient for some time and the occasion arises wherein the patient needs hospitalization for either a suicidal attempt or to prevent the possibility of acting out along these lines. Sometimes the patient is placed in the hospital against his wishes, though it is foreseen as a short stay. Here it would be better if a therapist who has not been treating the patient functioned as the restricting authoritative person and in this way preserved the therapeutic relationship between the original therapist and patient. This kind of planning is often overlooked but can be quite crucial.

The possibility of treating A. S. with intensive psychotherapy would have to be weighed against what is known of his ego strength, the fact that he has not had enough living experience, and the need for a more stabilized outside environment. Perhaps psychotherapy should not be interpretative but rather more supportive until the reality factors of the total situation can be worked out. Supportive therapy is not to be confused with a laissez-faire attitude, for sooner or later therapy has to be interpretative to have any kind of lasting effects. Theoretically, if the case of A. S. is a reactive depression in a neurotic person, psychoanalysis would be the treatment of choice. Even were we to think of it as a case of repetitive cycles of psychotic depressions without real hypomanic attacks, psychoanalysis might be tried, though with a great deal of caution and with the use of special techniques. Supportive therapy for the depressions has been found to be most effective at the beginning of the therapy, but later interpretations have to be tried, even during the depressive phases. As a general rule in the treatment of such cases, when the patient's unconscious tensions become more violent, it is then necessary to divert the therapy again to more superficial levels that the patient can tolerate. During the therapy we must certainly deal with the variations of all the guilt mechanisms in the patient, helping him to maintain a sense of reality for himself even in crises, in order to sustain his self-preservative defenses. In dealing with all the problems of transference with the patient, particular attention has to be directed to his fears of abandonment, to the analytic transference reactions, and to the narcissistic character of his reactions. There is a tendency to be glib in dealing with these kinds of cases along single planes, such as the concept of oral frustration. This would demand that the therapist yield to certain needs in the patient at certain times but with the realization that catering to the patient's needs does not produce a dissolution but rather a continuance of those needs. It must be stressed that, when we work with such patients, we are dealing with patients who have severe oscillations in their instinctual urges, a situation that tends to minimize when these urges are bound more to the life instincts but might quickly produce crises when they are bound to and emphasized by the death instincts.

Adjunct therapy with parents in this case or with a spouse in other cases has to be constantly thought of and regulated to the type of setting in which the therapy is conducted. Marginal interviews could be held with parents or spouse if they are sufficiently spaced so as not to produce interference in the therapy of the patient. However, if more intensive work has to be done with the parents or spouse, another therapist would be indicated.

References

1. Bowlby, J.: Aggression in relation to emotional development: Normal and pathological, paper read at meeting of the Psychiatric Section, Royal Society of Medicine, London, September, 1947.
2. Brenner, C.: *An Elemental Textbook of Psychoanalysis,* New York: Doubleday & Company, Inc., 1957.
3. Brunswick, D.: A revision of the classification of instincts, *International Journal of Psychoanalysis,* 35: 224–228, 1954.
4. Freud, A.: Notes on aggression, *Bulletin of the Menninger Clinic,* 13 (5): 143–151, 1949.
5. Freud, S.: Fragments of an analysis of a case of hysteria, in *Standard Edition,* London: Hogarth Press, Ltd., 1953, vol. 7, p. 43, footnote.
6. Freud, S.: *Beyond the Pleasure Principle,* London: Hogarth Press, Ltd., 1950.
7. Freud, S.: Mourning and melancholia, in *Standard Edition,* London: Hogarth Press, Ltd., 1955, vol. 18.
8. Glover, E.: *On the Early Development of Mind,* New York: International Universities Press, Inc., 1956.
9. Jones, E.: *The Life and Work of Sigmund Freud,* New York: Basic Books, Inc., 1957, vol. 3.
10. Lewin, B. D.: *The Psychoanalysis of Elation,* New York: W. W. Norton & Company, Inc., 1950.
11. Menninger, K. A.: *Man Against Himself,* New York: Harcourt, Brace and Company, Inc., 1938.
12. Nacht, S.: Clinical manifestations of aggression and their role in psychoanalytic treatment, *International Journal of Psychoanalysis,* 19: 201–223, 1948.
13. Nunberg, H.: *Principles of Psychoanalysis,* New York: International Universities Press, Inc., 1955.
14. Pumpian-Mindlin, E.: Propositions concerning energetic-economic aspects of libido theory, paper read at Conference on Conceptual and Methodological Problems in Psychoanalysis, New York Academy of Sciences, March, 1958.
15. Rado, S.: The psychoanalysis of pharmacothymia (drug addiction), *Psychoanalytic Quarterly,* 2: 1–23, 1933.
16. Scott, W. C. M.: Libidinal and aggressive instincts, *International Journal of Psychoanalysis,* 35: 234–238, 1954.

13

Suicide: Psychoanalytic Point of View

HERBERT HENDIN

Doctor Hendin received a B.A. from Columbia University, an M.D. from the New York University College of Medicine (1949), and a degree in psychoanalytic medicine from the Columbia University Psychoanalytic Clinic for Training and Research where he now is an instructor in psychoanalysis. As a Research Fellow in Psychiatry at Bellevue Hospital, he worked on the problem of suicide. A Diplomate of the American Psychiatric Association and the New York Society for Clinical Psychiatry, he is engaged in the private practice of psychoanalysis in New York City. He has written and published articles on the problem of suicide and is interested in the problem of homosexuality and the use of psychoanalysis as a tool for discovering the effect of changing social pressures on the individual. Currently he is participating in a research project at the Columbia University Psychoanalytic Clinic into the problem of homosexuality.

Most of any particular knowledge that I may have with regard to suicide stems from a research and therapeutic project into the problem of suicide carried on over a number of years at Bellevue Hospital. Briefly, this involved at first personally seeing and studying in detail 100 cases of attempted suicide and then seeing further cases for the purpose of checking on some of the tentative conclusions that had been formed. Finally, cases that were felt to be representative, i.e., representative of diverse clinical and motivational pictures, were selected for intensive psychotherapy for periods ranging from 1 to 3 years. The case illustrations that I will make use of, however, will also be taken from patients seen by me in private practice, since after I had been engaged in this work awhile, my colleagues referred more than the average number of suicidal patients to me. As I discovered in time, their reasons were not purely altruistic, for many of them felt that the risk involved in treating suicidal patients was a headache that they were glad to pass on.

Of the many problems and limitations inherent in this kind of project, there is one in particular that it might be well to mention. This study dealt with persons who made suicide attempts and failed, and the question may be legitimately raised as to how much these patients have in common with actual suicides. It was with this in mind that in each case the degree of suicidal intent was carefully rated.

I think that the cases that were considered as having maximum intent were as close to actual suicide as one could reasonably expect to get. For instance, there was one girl who jumped under the wheels of a subway train, had two cars pass over her, and still lived. There were two men admitted to the hospital after executing a suicide pact, in which each took 50 sodium pentobarbital tablets, 0.1 gr each. They were discovered comatose, with an accompanying suicide note, 13 hours later by a maid in their hotel. They were admitted to the hospital, where the condition of both was precarious. One died; the other lived. The one who survived was, like the girl I mentioned, included in the group with maximum intent. Furthermore, cases where the suicidal intent is not great nevertheless throw much light on the motivation in more severe cases and vice versa.

I might mention that for a long while I was troubled in this matter of suicidal intent by what word to use in order to describe suicide attempts that do not fail. Somehow using the word *successful* with regard to suicide never seemed right. George White, an editor for the Psychiatric Quarterly, solved it for me by suggesting what I think to be the most appropriate word, and that is *actual* suicide as contrasted with *attempted* suicide.

Concerning the question of intent a point has come to my attention several times only lately. Although in recent years a good deal of attention has been given to the possibility of an unconscious wish to die in persons who have fatal accidents, the exact opposite is also not uncommon, i.e., patients who wish to kill themselves and succeed in making it look like an accident. We often assume the unconscious motivation, but sometimes we are seeing a conscious motivation and the need to hide it.

However, it is mainly in treating suicidal patients that one learns something about the various motivations, conscious and unconscious, that go into suicide. They differ not only in intensity, as is suggested by variations in suicidal intent, but qualitatively in a marked way. I shall attempt to outline and illustrate some of the varying emotional motivational constellations that are seen.

Probably the most attention psychoanalytically has been paid to suicide springing out of severe depression. Freud, in observing depressed patients, called attention to the fact that depression involved rage intended for someone else that has been turned back on the patient himself. He concluded that suicide must be the ultimate form of this phenomenon and that there was no suicide without the desire to kill someone else. This conclusion was based on a study of depression in general rather than a direct study of suicide (Freud's case write-ups include reference to only one patient who made a suicidal attempt), but it has nonetheless stood up well under the test of time, although it is too often overworked and made into a cliché. In addition, Freud made his observations on depression before he had come to the conclusion that rage or aggression could be nonerotic in origin, so his paper "Mourning and Melancholia" (1917) dealing with the problem contains libidinal explanations for the retroflexed rage that are extraneous and undemonstrable. However, that should not be allowed to obscure the importance of the concept of retroflexed rage that is contained therein.

In recent years, largely through the work of Rado, we have become aware of the dependency adaptation involved in depression. The patient's rage and its retroflexion are seen to be part of a desire for, plea for, and frustration in the attempt to achieve this dependency. Rado also directed attention to the expiatory nature of the self-directed rage and its misdirected, adaptive purpose of atonement, with the hope of the patient being forgiven and reconciled with the object of his frustration. This is important to keep in mind because it correlates well with some of the motivations and fantasies of actual suicidal patients that will be discussed.

Depression has been seen by all observers in response to the loss of a loved object or a setback in life. Often, depression occurs without evident precipitating cause. In this regard, the use of the idea of the unconscious loss of the loved object to explain the latter situation seems an awkward and unnecessary construction of what we observe psychodynamically. The issue in the dreams and fantasies of such patients is the need for a particular person and the unavailability of that person, with consequent frustration, anger, retroflexion, and depression.

Depression and the dependency constellation are important because they are often seen in the forty to fifty-five age group, when actual suicide is most common. However, since so much has been written about it, what I wish to do with this group is merely to make a few points that I feel have not been sufficiently noted or stressed.

One of the factors that I have noticed more and more is the paranoid personality structure of these patients in the years prior to their depression. During the periods when these patients were not depressed or suicidal, they were invariably concerned with alleged mistreatment by others. The mistreatment was not necessarily delusionally elaborated, but the preoccupation with it was great. The patient's failures were due to mistreatment, favoritism, and corruption in varied and sundry situations. Then there would be the loss of someone or something or a setback that the patient's paranoid defenses were unable to handle, and the latent depression would make itself evident. Now the reaction became more that the patient himself is to blame, his unworthiness caused the loss, etc. The depression is seen in the context of frustrated dependency. The patient has the feeling that effort is pointless; he has never been cared for and can expect nothing. He dreams in corresponding images of frustrated dependency: food is denied him, or the supply is insufficient. There is some tendency to blame any person who is conceived of as the frustrator, but eventually this anger is retroflexed and depression is the picture. Some patients have the capacity to alternate rapidly from a depressed to a paranoid picture; with others it is more gradual.

I recently saw a patient, a man of fifty-five, who had been depressed and unable to work for several years. His story revealed the kind of paranoid trend I have indicated in the years prior to his depression, although when I first saw him only the depression was evident. In the course of therapy he became somewhat paranoid toward me, and coincidental with this his depression lifted sufficiently that he could resume work. In other words, with the therapist as whipping boy or focus for his paranoid defenses, which were in his case far preferable to his depression, he could function.

A second factor worth noting is that, when the depression is in reaction to the loss of a person, the relationship often has been a markedly dependent and symbiotic one and one in which the patient's self-esteem was contingent upon the relationship. Often there was a large element of a lifelong grandiosity in the nondepressed stage, which hid an underlying depression. This grandiosity was unable to support itself with the loss, and the depression then ensued. The loss may be of a person, money, or position. All three instances are seen. I am often asked about the suicides seen in this country in the 1930s following the stock-market collapse; of course, I cannot answer, not having seen any patients at that time. However, I can say something of several recent situations that I have seen where serious suicide attempts followed sudden financial failure. The response to the loss of money was similar to that of the loss of a person in the collapsing effect it had on the self-esteem of these patients. However, more interesting is the fact that there was often more than an analogy present in the sense that these patients felt unable to maintain relationships, very often with their wives and children, without the prestige and security they got from their money. Thus they too were reacting in a sense to the loss, or threatened or potential loss, of a human relationship.

The man who loses a large amount of money and reacts with a suicide attempt thus will often differ from the man who doesn't in that his self-esteem is more dependent on his financial position.

In addition to these points concerning some of the factors seen in depressed suicidal patients, I would like to stress the fact that the psychodynamics of depression are not sufficient to explain suicide. For one thing, a great number of suicidal patients do not show either the dynamics or the clinical features of depression. More important, many depressed patients are not suicidal. In other words, the mere fact that the problems of depression and suicide are so often seen conjointly does not justify using the dynamic formulations of depression as a blanket explanation for suicide.

The patient's attitudes and fantasies with regard to death and dying are extremely important in the motivation of suicide, whether or not depression is present. One patient made three suicide attempts, scattered over a period of some 20 to 25 years. When I saw her for the first time, following her latest suicide attempt, she was forty-seven years old. Each attempt had been more serious than the one before, and she had been extremely fortunate to survive her last one, which had been with gas. Her attempts always had some relation to an unfortunate and unsuccessful love affair. She was treated on an outpatient basis; but because of worry about the danger of suicide, we had a standing agreement, in the form of a promise to the therapist, that, were she overcome by the desire to kill herself and unable to reach the therapist, she would admit herself to the hospital. After several months of treatment, in which the same love affair that had preceded her suicide attempt was continuing unsuccessfully, the patient became acutely suicidal and did admit herself to the hospital. The night she did so she had the following dream:

"I was living in an apartment in Baltimore that I lived in 25 years ago. There were a lot of people around telling me to put on a beautiful wedding dress that was hanging on the wall, and I wouldn't put it on."

Her association was to an apartment in Baltimore where, 25 years before, her affair with a man had lasted for 2 years. Then one night he had told her he was going to marry another girl. She had decided to commit suicide and had made a suicide attempt. Everything in the dream was the same as it had been in her room at that time of the first suicide attempt. To the wedding dress in the dream she associated the fact that she always wanted one. However, the thing that impressed her most in the dream was that the wedding dress looked more like a *shroud* than like a wedding dress.

What I wish to call attention to is the fact that the patient's fantasy of a successful love relationship is included in a death fantasy, or vice versa. Her desires can only be gratified through her death. Thus death, although originally probably viewed as a punishment for something desired, has now become a necessary concomitant for the fulfillment of those desires. Interestingly enough, this patient recalled that she had had this same dream recurrently before her prior suicide attempts.

I have seen many variations of this fantasy. One woman, in contrast to the previous case, was depressed in the classical sense, i.e., lethargic, tearful, spoke little, etc. Her depression was essentially a plea for greater help from her mother. At times this plea was ingratiating, at times angry, and at times expiatory. Her depression ended with a dream in which she and her mother kissed and made up. However, two weeks later, when clinically her depression was far less evident, her suicidal trend became more apparent. She had the following dream:

"My in-laws took my wedding ring. I decided to steal it back and then commit suicide."

The patient associated to this dream the fact that her father-in-law had frequently told her that her husband did not belong to her and was on loan. She always felt that nothing had belonged to her, not even her children. She saw the woman from whom she stole the ring as her mother-in-law. However, the dream is of interest because of the light it throws on the patient's suicidal tendency; the primary factor in the dream is that she views gratification of her desires for men, in this case her husband (the oedipal implications of the dream need not be considered here), as possible only through her own death. It is this factor that I think is of cardinal significance in terms of her suicidal trend and distinguishes her depression from depression where suicide is less of a threat.

When patients have fantasies in which death is a means of gratification, suicide is a very great danger. Nor are these fantasies always unconscious. One patient was seen just after he had made a suicide attempt from which eventually he died. He said that before attempting suicide he had spent a year since his wife's death with conscious fantasies of reunion with her in death.

Expiation undoubtedly plays a role in the above fantasies, as it does in depression, mentioned earlier. Expiation is an important motivational factor in suicide whether or not a pleasurable fantasy concerning death or a depression is present. That suicide is seen as an expiatory act goes along with the interesting clinical fact that a depression often lifts after an unsuccessful suicide attempt as though some atonement had been carried out.

In going through the wards of a hospital like Bellevue and examining the youngest and often most disturbed group of suicidal patients, one can see feelings of guilt and the need for self-punishment blatantly. Their guilt preoccupations will vary from promiscuous sexual activity, incestuous fantasies, a body racked with imaginary syphilis, and misdeeds in service to, in a very deteriorated case, the feeling that he is a "bad boy." The underlying emotional theme in these patients involves their feeling worthless, no good, afraid, deserving of punishment, and filled with self-hatred for their failures, fears, and incapacities. For them suicide is a self-punishment in response to what amounts to delusions of guilt and sin. These are patients who are often apathetic rather than depressed. Their now self-directed aggression has been cut off from attempts at communication. They have given up both the idea of crying out for help and the possibility of achieving it through atonement. Their apathy doesn't lift after an unsuccessful suicide attempt, and the more the apathy, the more the therapeutic risk on an outpatient basis. This apathy has its psychodynamic equivalent in the self image that many apathetic suicidal patients have of themselves as already dead; i.e., they see themselves as dead emotionally or as walking corpses and see their suicide as giving reality to a state of affairs that already exists.

I might say, before turning to our case, a word about suicide attempts or perhaps gestures where the desire to spite or force affection from someone is the dominant motive and the degree of depression and of suicidal intent is usually minimal. These are the so-called lovers' quarrel attempts, made over incidents where the patient feels rejected. The patient says in effect: "Look what you are driving me to, you will have to treat me better." They rely on arousing guilt in what amounts to a form of emotional blackmail. They have in common with so many of the other groups the reaction to a real or threatened loss or abandonment. I should like to emphasize here that death often has the unconscious meaning of abandonment. The patient views his suicide or threat of death as a retaliatory abandonment. He says in effect: "I will abandon you as you have abandoned me," or "I will abandon you first, so if there is any abandoning to be done, I will do it." Suicide often involves some element of this, and the early life experiences of the patient in terms of abandonment and rejection are at least as important to evaluate as the way in which he learned to handle aggression.

There are surely other motivational patterns to be seen in suicide, but those described are the major ones in my experience; we can now turn to the case to be discussed.

THE CASE OF MR. A. S.

In beginning, let me state just what one can or cannot do with this kind of case history. The case is presented so as to give no bias toward any particular frame of reference. I assume this is the reason that we do not have the examining psychiatrist's diagnosis, his clinical evaluation of the patient, or statements as to the emotional contact he made with the patient or the weight he gave to the things he heard. I appreciate the danger of the bias these data might have caused, but my own opinion is that it is less of a danger than the one of excessive speculation we have to run without this information. I cannot honestly say that merely the biographical data given would have led me to say that this boy was a particular suicidal risk prior to his attempt, and I can state that this is not the case with many patients I have seen.

I might suggest in this regard that the patient or whoever brought him to the hospital should have been more thoroughly questioned so we could get an idea of his suicidal intent. His critical, comatose condition on admission is suggestive but not conclusive. How and under what circumstances he was discovered should and can usually be ascertained. What precautions did he take to prevent discovery? What strength were the barbiturate tablets he took? These are basic, elementary questions, but I am afraid they are necessary in evaluating suicidal intent and should be established with all cases of attempted suicide. Also, an attempt to evaluate the degree of depression before and after the suicidal attempt would be helpful.

What I have just said doesn't mean that I think we cannot make presumptions about this case, so long as we recognize them for that and not as definitive conclusions. I will try to suggest some of the things I think should be looked for psychodynamically, were this a case in therapy. First, we might look at what we have in this patient with regard to the dependency-rejection constellation. The boy's indecision and vacillation and inability successfully to carry through what his parents disapprove of certainly indicates a dependency problem. That it stems from his relationship with his mother is also safe to say. The tone of his remarks indicates far greater emotional preoccupation with her than with his father.

In his image of her as a person who assumes responsibility and yet does not include others, whether in organization work or at home, he indicates his feeling that in some way something was missing in their relationship together. This combination of seeing his mother as capable and yet not gratifying his needs would tend to cement him in an unhappy yet dependent position. Also, it is at this point in discussing her and indicating some hurt that he feels with regard to her that he breaks down, becomes tearful, and immediately feels the need to defend her, stating that he is sure she cared as much as most mothers. He says that in the days prior to his suicide attempt he felt the need to break with his family and yet felt strongly the need for them; here too I think he means more his mother than anyone. His need for his parents' approval conflicts with the need for the woman of his choice and results in his leaving home rather than facing the situation more directly, so he ends up with neither his mother nor Mary.

Psychodynamically, were this boy in therapy, one would be on the lookout for the kind of dreams that indicate he views choosing a woman and giving up his mother not merely as a frustration of his dependency needs for his mother but as total abandonment or death. This is further suggested in his reaction to his aunt's death, which influences him toward giving up Mary and making up with his mother. It can be assumed that it is his problems in this regard, with the loss of needed dependency, that went into his depression. If this patient demonstrates the type of fantasy I mentioned earlier, in which suicide is viewed as a means of gratification, one would look for it in this area, that is, he would see suicide as in some way fulfilling his dependency desires. It is in this connection that his remark that in the period before taking the sleeping pills he felt he wanted to have something bigger than himself, i.e., "a feeling of understanding from home," may take on importance.

Sometimes such patients are slightly paranoid and will see rejections and frustrations in everything. There is a suggestion of this in this boy's army experience, but this is insufficient to form any such conclusion. It is my impression that many patients with a history like this eventually manage the separation from their mother and form attachments to other women. However, they are the ones who are more vulnerable to suicidal reactions if they lose this woman later in life.

We also have some information with regard to his handling of aggression, although none of it is decisive. We have his continual alternation of fighting and losing and making up with a friend of his. More important, I think, there is his mother's way of handling his misbehavior by crying and feeling hurt. This is always a method of discipline that more than any other results in a turning inward or self-direction of aggression on the part of a child and concomitant guilt over it. That the patient as a child learned this at the cost of much internal conflict is indicated by the incident where he arouses his father's guilt and pity to obtain money for the movies and then feels guilty himself for so doing and returns it.

THERAPEUTIC IMPLICATIONS

In discussing the therapy of this case or of other suicidal patients, there is no intent to imply that we are dealing with something radically different from the general problems involved in psychotherapy. This is, of course, not the case; in addition, it is almost too obvious to mention that problems about suicide, as in our case, are only one aspect of the patient's total problems, and one deals with them as they emerge in therapy. However, some suicidal patients remain acutely suicidal after an attempt, and with them it is necessary to deal first and effectively with the problems related to suicide or there will be no opportunity to deal with others.

The major special concern of the therapist will be the suicidal risk, and unfamiliarity with the problem has led many psychiatrists to avoid therapy with such cases. When a patient is admitted to the hospital following an attempt, such as our patient, one is safest to start psychotherapy while the patient is in the hospital so that it becomes possible soon to see how good a therapeutic contact can be established. This is the biggest safety factor that one has, for with it plus a knowledge of the psychodynamics of suicide one can at least see when any danger is imminent.

There are several types of suicidal patients with whom this contact is particularly difficult to establish. The aggressive paranoid patients, with sudden alternations between rage and fear, particularly those who tend to act out their rage, form one such group. The apathetic patients mentioned before, in whose emotional life guilt and fear predominate and who seem cut off from any environmental communication, are another extremely difficult group to involve in treatment. These contrast sharply with the patients in whom a more truly depressive aspect is predominant, who often want help and can be rather readily involved in therapy.

With this particular case one therapeutic problem that could be reasonably predicted relates to his tendency to react to frustration by going away. For this boy, and for many persons with rejection problems, leaving or going away has an important emotional significance. He leaves home and joins the army to get away from the problem with Mary and his family. He leaves for South America, and later for Los Angeles in a similar manner, and then finally tries to leave for good. One might expect that, in the course of therapy, he would react to what he would feel were frustrations of his dependency needs on the part of the therapist with the desire to leave therapy. This is often not experienced as a desire to leave the therapist but merely as a feeling that a change in locale will solve his difficulties. If the therapist is alert to the source of this feeling, it is a problem that can usually be managed and the patient's understanding of it can serve as a helpful wedge in dealing with his dependency problems and his reaction to them.

As has been indicated, were this a case in therapy, the order in which this boy's problems were dealt with would be determined for the most part by the order in which he focused emotional attention upon them. This, in turn, would be largely determined for him by his immediate situation when he commenced therapy. Were he to have begun therapy in Los Angeles, i.e., away from his school or home, the chances are the first problems he would have had to be concerned with would revolve around working, going to school, or doing both. His difficulties with women and the problems centering around his mother, which would be more the source of his other difficulties, might well emerge only after this.

Ultimately the success of his therapy would hinge on his ability to resolve his dependency problem through understanding it, mastering it, and re-experiencing it in different terms. To some extent this might be possible in the relationship with the therapist, but finally it rests on the ability of therapy to help him establish a lasting, satisfying relationship with a woman. Sometimes these patients can form only overly dependent relationships with women, but at least they can be gotten to form them in a more satisfying and less frustrating manner than the original experience with the mother.

The criteria for his improvement would not be merely a more successful and less dependent adaptation reflected in school, work, and with a woman, but there would also have to be psychodynamic evidence of change as reflected in dreams and fantasies that reveal a less dependent and less helpless self image. Were this achieved, there would, in addition, be less preoccupation with his height on which he has focused his feelings of low masculine self-esteem.

What about the prognosis for psychotherapy with this and other suicidal patients? Naturally, since suicidal patients run the gamut of psychiatric entities, from nonspychotics to advanced schizophrenics, their prognosis is related to their underlying personality structure, although it is often possible to minimize the suicidal risk where this structure cannot be altered. Disappointments in psychoanalysis and psychotherapy in general in the first 50 years of this century have been related to our ignorance as to which cases could respond to it and as to how much improvement to expect. Perhaps in our infancy we could be forgiven our ignorance, but this will not hold true in the future. This is true in general, and it is certainly true for suicide in particular. A knowledge of the psychodynamics of suicide, of what patients can be treated with psychotherapy, and of how much improvement we can expect will improve our results. Among the suicidal patients who want help the results are encouraging.

As a closing thought, I call your attention in this regard to the fact that our hospitals could, although they do not at present, at least give priority to suicidal patients on their outpatient waiting lists for psychotherapy. Some such priority, based on urgency, seems to me to be desirable.

References

1. Freud, S.: Mourning and melancholia, in *Collected Papers,* London: Hogarth Press, Ltd., 1949, vol. 4.
2. Freud, S.: Psychogenesis of a case of homosexuality in a woman, in *Collected Papers,* London: Hogarth Press, Ltd., 1949, vol. 2.
3. Hendin, H.: Attempted suicide: A psychiatric and statistical study, *Psychiatric Quarterly,* 24: 39–46, 1950.
4. Hendin, H.: Psychodynamic motivational factors in suicide, *Psychiatric Quarterly,* 25: 672–678, 1951.
5. Hendin, H.: Suicide, *Psychiatric Quarterly,* 30: 267–282, 1956.
6. Rado, S.: Psychodynamics of depression from the etiological point of view, *Psychosomatic Medicine,* 13: 51–55, 1951.

14

Suicide: The Jungian Point of View

BRUNO KLOPFER

Doctor Klopfer received a Ph.D. in psychology from the University of Munich in 1922 and training as a Jungian analyst from Dr. Carl Jung in Zurich, Switzerland. Following ten years of teaching and research in the field of child guidance and mental hygiene in Munich, Frankfurt, and Berlin, he came to the United States in 1934. From 1934 to 1937 he was a research associate in anthropology at Columbia University; from 1937 to 1946, lecturer, supervisor of guidance, and instructor at Columbia University Teachers College; and from 1945 to 1947, an associate professor of psychology at City College of New York. Since 1946 he has been with the University of California at Los Angeles, where he has been Clinical Professor of Psychology since 1953. In addition to private practice in psychotherapy and analysis, he is a consultant in clinical psychology for the Veterans Administration, the Childrens Hospital, the Reiss-Davis Clinic in Los Angeles, and the Letterman Army General Hospital in San Francisco. He is a Diplomate of the American Board of Examiners in Professional Psychology and a Fellow of the American Psychological Association, the California State Psychological Association, and the Southern California Psychological Association, and a member of the Society of Jungian Analysts in Los Angeles. He is also a charter member and past president of the Society for Projective Techniques and since 1936 has served as editor of the *Journal of Projective Techniques.* For the past twenty years he had conducted regular summer workshops in projective techniques on both the East and West Coasts. He lectured at the C. G. Jung Institute in 1954, 1956, and 1957, and during the latter period he was also visiting professor at the University of Zurich. He is the author of *The Rorschach Technique* (New York: World Book Company, 1942; Supplement, 1946), *Developments in the Rorschach Technique* (New York: World Book Company; vol. 1, 1954, vol. 2, 1956), and has contributed in the fields of projective techniques and analytical psychology. He is presently a consulting editor for the German and Swiss *Zeitschrift für Diagnostische Psychologie,* the British *Journal of Analytical Psychology,* and the Japanese *Rorschachiana Japonica.*

Suicide inexorably involves death. Our discussion of suicide from the Jungian point of view can therefore appropriately start by quoting from Jung's essay [2] "The Soul and Death" (p. 6).

"The negation of life's fulfillment is synonymous with the refusal to accept its ending. Both mean not wanting to live; not wanting to live is identical with not wanting to die. Waxing and waning make one curve. Whenever possible, our consciousness refuses to accommodate itself to this undeniable truth."

For most of us death simply comes, but in the case of suicide we are faced with an active seeking of the termination of life. We are then faced with a most pertinent question: How can the ego, as the only center of the living organism capable of carrying the meaning of life, also become an instrument of self-destructive tendencies or acts? [1] What is noteworthy in the phrasing of this question is the "monopolistic" position thus assigned to the ego as the only carrier of the meaning of life, a theoretical position shared by most non-Jungian western personality theories, including the Freudian theory.

EGO, DEATH, AND THE MEANING OF LIFE

One of the most important contributions Freudian theory makes to modern psychology is the insight into the elaborate defensive operations of the ego against any threat to the gratification of its goals, whether such threats come from the internal world of drive impulses or from the world of external reality. We are also aware of the importance of strengthening this ego-defensive capacity and, with it, of the strength of constructive ego functioning in the general process of adjustment and maturation. But how can this same ego, reinforced by the power of life-preserving instincts, be made to face the reality of death or even be forced into the service of life-destroying impulses?

The difficulty of visualizing such a turn of events leads many psychiatrists (with or without psychoanalytic orientation) to the assumption that anybody who commits suicidal acts must automatically be insane, meaning essentially that the ego must have been at least temporarily overwhelmed by dissociative forces and, in the process, deprived of its monopolistic role. It seems to me, however, that this stretches the concept of insanity too far to apply it so automatically in all such situations.

Freud attempted to overcome this theoretical difficulty by postulating the concept of the death instinct, which vies with the life instinct in its influence on the ego. If one conceives of instincts in the naturalistic sense, in which drive impulses are derivatives of life-preserving forces, the concept of the death instinct remains rather incomprehensible, as can be seen by the fact that it has remained a highly controversial issue within all Freudian groups.

This difficult semantic situation changes fundamentally when we approach the Jungian frame of reference. Within this conceptual framework, the life-preserving forces are only a small part of the archetypal powers whose impact on our behavior and experiences we describe clinically as drive impulses of instinctual reactions. More important, the Jungian conceptualization denies the monopolistic role of the ego as the only

[1] This question is very pointedly raised and treated by Wahl [7].

center of the individual organism capable of carrying the meaning of life. The ego becomes merely the center of the *conscious* part of our personality functioning. The *self* constitutes a deeper center of the functioning of the individual human organism, maintaining the contact between the individual and the cosmos to which it belongs. From the self emanates the experience of meaningfulness.

One essential prerequisite for the conscious experience of meaningfulness is a minimal contact between the ego and the self. As long as the ego is completely engulfed in its goals of ego satisfaction or caught in a spasm of ego-defensive activity, the elation that accompanies an experience of meaningfulness of life cannot take place. Only if and when the ego can free itself from its pseudomonopolistic egocentric position and seek contact with the other center, the self, can life become meaningful. There is an increasing body of evidence, both inside and outside the Jungian way of thinking, that the more important psychological processes, especially the creative ones, demand a state of affairs that Ernst Kris [3] describes as "regression in the service of the ego"; phenomenologically, it would be more accurate to describe this same state of affairs as the abdication of the ego in the service of a more meaningful life.

One further important thought construct for the Jungian point of view in regard to suicide is the assumption that this self, which can be consciously experienced only occasionally (usually in the form of a religious experience), has both a bright and a dark side. When the dark side prevails, a situation in which death seems more desirable or less horrifying than life occurs. This state, in fact, is a necessary, although not a sufficient, prerequisite for any suicidal act.

Let us examine some of the situations in which this may occur. We are not yet talking about suicidal tendencies or acts but simply about situations in which death seems preferable to life.

1. The death of the hero or martyr is the most common and well-known of these situations, in which the life of the individual seems far less important than the preservation of the ideal.

2. Intractable pain or unbearable mental anguish make life seem so miserable that death appears largely as a liberation, regardless of what expectation a person may have regarding the hereafter.

3. Counterphobic reaction to death is closely related to the situation described above, in which the expectation of death seems so unbearable that the individual prefers an end to horror to a horror without end. Again we can refer to Wahl [7], who describes this situation very aptly.

4. Reunion with a dead loved one is sought in cases where the death of a

loved one seems to carry with it all the meaning of life. The desire to reunite with this person in death becomes so overwhelming that it does not even matter whether the individual has any concrete notion of how this reunion will take place.

5. The search for freedom, one of the most peculiar of these situations, leads to cases of completely unpredictable, almost whimsical acts of suicide, involving the desire not to be committed, not to be tied down, to life or anything it contains.

6. The search for closure, the opposite situation, is an older person's longing for death as a well-deserved closure to a rich and full life.

THE PSYCHOLOGICAL PROBLEM OF REBIRTH

In the six situations described in the preceding section, death seems to be consciously desirable or preferable, whether for rational or irrational reasons. The Jungian point of view emphasizes another aspect of death, which rarely comes to the conscious awareness of a person with suicidal tendencies: namely, the longing for a spiritual rebirth. The principle of dying and being reborn belongs to the essence of the unfolding life process. Parenthetically, we wish to emphasize that this discussion will be confined strictly within the empirical realm of psychology; there will be no attempt to transgress into the realm of metaphysics or to consider the age-old problem of life after death and reincarnation. In the present context, *rebirth* implies a spiritual rebirth experienced within the life span of the individual.

The archetypal symbol of the night journey of the hero, connected with the daily experience of the rising and setting sun, is the most general representation of this principle. Jung likes to compare the decisive phase in the analytic process of self-realization with the symbol of crucifixion. Death in this connection is clearly conceived as the death of the ego that has lost contact with the self and thus with the meaning of life. The ego has to return to the womb of the *magna mater* to reestablish this contact and to be reborn with a new meaning for life.

This process of rebirth is not without danger. The archetypal force of the *magna mater* has both life-giving and life-destroying aspects, parallel to the dark and bright side of the self. Therefore, the night journey contains always the danger of ending in destruction rather than in rebirth. If the patient is made aware of this danger and is helped to face it by the analyst, the suicidal crisis can be transformed into a profoundly healing and life-giving experience.

This explains the negative correlation between the tendency to suicide and the degree of self-realization or self-actualization reached by a person within his lifetime. The less successful a person is in being or becoming himself, the more vital energy he invests in what Jung calls the persona; the need to play a certain role, to act as one thinks other persons expect one to act. Thus, the greater will be the need for psychological rebirth when this persona-centered existence reaches the end of its usefulness. The over-investment in persona values rather than in self-realization is a corollary theoretical formulation to the I_s and I_o proposed by Shneidman and Farberow [5] in "The Logic of Suicide" and may explain the difficulty experienced by the suicidal person who leaves a suicide note in distinguishing between the self as experienced by the self (I_s) and the self as it feels itself experienced by others (I_o).

PHENOMENOLOGICAL DIMENSIONS OF SUICIDAL ACTS

In order to focus the case history under discussion and its interpretation, we must delineate the vast field of suicide phenomenologically. A brief outline of the major dimensions of suicidal attempts or actual suicides will permit us to achieve a certain topographical orientation.

Collective and Individual Suicide

The first dimension, and it will be seen that these are all dimensions dealing with polarities in which any individual case may fall somewhere between the two poles, is the polarity between *collective* and *individual* determination of suicide. We tend to think of the many cultures, societies, and religions that prohibit self-destructive acts, but there are actually a few cultures in which under certain conditions suicide is sanctioned. We need mention only the two classic examples of collectively determined suicide, the death of the hero and the death of the martyr. We all remember the *kamikaze* in World War II, the Japanese suicide pilots who deliberately crashed with their airplanes and their bombs into American ships to make sure that the bombs would reach their goal; anyone familiar with Lawrence van der Post's [6] stirring book *Bar of Shadow* will understand that this has a strong and specific affinity to certain aspects of Japanese culture. But the collective sanction of suicide is by no means limited in time and space. It is interesting to recall, as an extreme opposite example, a story about the Swiss. During the critical period of World War II, in 1940, Hitler decided to advance but could not know for sure whether it would take him 3 days, 3 weeks, or 3 months to outflank the French

Maginot Line by attacking Holland and Belgium. We know now from documentary evidence that he had an alternate plan, in case this move should fail, to march through Switzerland and attack France from the other side. The Swiss were aware of this, and hundreds of volunteers were fully prepared to destroy themselves in an attempt to blast all bridges and other forms of access into their country. It is most interesting that this was also connected with a strong religious experience. A high percentage of the Swiss population believe that what actually changed Hitler's mind and protected Switzerland from the threatened German invasion was the intervention of the only saint in their country's history, the famous Brother Klaus. There are eyewitness stories from whole battalions of Swiss militia who actually experienced the collective vision of Brother Klaus standing before them and holding the Germans off. Near the hermitage where he lived there is a monument, placed on the spot by a Swiss division, to commemorate this very experience.

Whether Brother Klaus changed Hitler's mind, or whether the success of the German march through Holland and Belgium caused him to abandon the idea of invading Switzerland, the fact remains that countless numbers of Swiss citizens would have been willing to sacrifice their lives to stop him, even temporarily. One can readily see that it makes a tremendous difference whether a suicidal act is performed under such a strong collective impulse or as an individual, personal decision, even though in each case these cultural factors will naturally play an important role. The whole sociology of suicide is one of the most fascinating areas of research.

Active and Passive Suicide

The second of these polar dimensions I wish to mention is the polarity between *active* and *passive* suicide. It may sound like a verbal contradiction to speak about passive suicide, but if one takes a simple example, namely, the tradition that the captain goes down with his ship, one has the classic design of a completely passive form of suicide (and one that is also linked closely to our first polarity). Another passive form of suicide, and one that has given rise to much literature, is the so-called accident proneness of certain persons who do not actually want to commit suicide but somehow manage to get into the path of a car that cannot be controlled. A much more recurrent and familiar form of this passive suicide is simply the tendency to let nature take its course, e.g., the will to die when faced by an incurable illness. In psychosomatic terminology, we speak of this as host compliance. In contrast, any suicide attempt or deed is without question an act *contra naturum* (against nature). This is a very important and significant distinction.

Sincere and Attention-getting Suicide Attempts

The third of these polarities is clinically the most important one, namely, *sincerity* versus the *attention-getting aspects* of the suicide attempt. Quite frequently, suicide attempts are not sincere attempts to kill oneself but simply attention-getting devices. In such cases, the act is so prepared that there is an optimal chance to be saved. For instance, there is the case of a wife who waited until she saw her husband's car drive into the garage and then quickly swallowed 17 barbiturate pills. As soon as the husband came to the door, she told him what she had done, so he could still make her stick her finger down her throat and regurgitate. As far as the meaning of suicide is concerned, it makes a world of difference whether a person plans it so there is practically no chance to be saved or there is the maximal opportunity to be saved. There are, of course, many cases where persons die entirely by accident and where persons who had no desire to be saved are saved; but the basic motivation certainly has to be considered.

Planned and Impulsive Suicide

There is a fourth polarity, a dimension that I simply call the degree of *rootedness*. How deep are the roots of any human being in life; how much is he committed to life and to relationships with others? Does he, perhaps, represent the picture that was so beautifully drawn by the French aviator, Saint-Exupéry [4], in his book *The Little Prince,* where one just takes off at will and is not really tied down by anything? Persons who have this kind of rootlessness, and some of them are brilliant and successful, have what clinically we would like to call "floating island" egos, which, under the sway of any strong current, will take off and float along with it. Such persons are capable of taking their lives purely as a whim. There seems to be no question that this kind of suicide is very different from one that is the outgrowth of deep despair. This form of suicide is often called *spontaneous* suicide. To give an inkling about its importance, I cite a recently published book, *Ausgewählte Briefe* (Selected Letters), by Gottfried Benn [1]. Benn was a German physician whom the high command of the Nazi army assigned to study cases of suicide in all three branches of the *Wehrmacht*. Benn examined between 1,000 and 1,500 cases, all with full psychiatric evaluations, and came to the conclusion, surprising both to him and to the German high command, that about 80 per cent of all these cases were spontaneous suicides, often under the influence of alcohol.

It follows from this discussion that, to understand any act of suicide or suicidal attempt, one must first determine where within these four dimensions the individual case is to be located.

THE CASE OF MR. A. S.[2]

The case of Mr. A. S. definitely belongs to the category of an active, serious suicide attempt with individual rather than collective motivation, by a person with a fairly deep-rooted ego.

For such cases, the dynamic components of the suicide pattern can be described in Jungian terms as follows:

(A) A dead-end situation prevails. Life seems to have lost its meaning; there is no way in which this could be regained except through psychological rebirth, which, in the mind of the patient, is naturally not recognized. The desire for rebirth is unconscious; only the longing for death is consciously experienced. (B) The emotional conflict largely responsible for the blocking (for the meaninglessness of life, experienced as a dead-end situation) has enveloped the ego. The ego is unable to disidentify itself from the complex that blocks further personal development. (C) The resentment about the frustrating situation is contaminated through emotional forces, which are experienced as demoniacal and thus reach murderous proportions. This is actually experienced as an uncontrollable compulsion to kill oneself. (D) This murderous disposition is combined with a corresponding loss of vitality.

In the case of A. S., there were signs of considerable vitality up to the age of twelve; after that, the vitality seems to drain out of him and returns only in feeble spurts. In persons whose vitality remains in force, usually some form of acting out, some alternative short of suicide, can be found to overcome the dead-end situation, even though it may be no more rational than the suicidal act. Where no vitality for any such active attempt to change the life situation is possible, suicide seems the only way to relieve unbearable tension.

The first striking feature in the case history is that in the short period of the interviews (five during the period of a week) the patient mentioned five times that he loved to fight and that he fought with the neighbor children all the time. Even his mother, who tried desperately to hide all negative aspects in her description of her son, mentioned that he was a very active boy, the kind of boy who always liked to stick up for the

[2] The formulations in this section are the product of the joint efforts of Dr. Marie Louise von Franz, staff member of the C. G. Jung Institute in Zurich, and the author.

underdog. This aggressive attitude suddenly disappeared approximately at the age of twelve. After that, the only clues for any assertive behavior are, first, his playing the trombone; second, his relatively successful military history; and finally, his abortive attempt to stick to his relationship with his girl friend, Mary, against his parents' opposition, an attempt that collapsed at the moment of crisis and led to his suicide attempt as suddenly as his childhood aggression disappeared.

The mother appears, both indirectly in the son's story and directly in her own interview, as an extremely domineering and castrating person, who, however, is successful in hiding these tendencies behind the mask of nonpunitive concern and martyrlike worry for her son. As one reads the entire material, one comes to feel that, even though the mother was a very modern woman and quite efficient in helping to provide for her family, in her basic emotional attitudes she comes remarkably close to the life-giving and life-taking *magna mater*. When she complains, "Because of you two I couldn't have any more children," she displays this swallowing aspect of the *magna mater*, of devouring the life she had given birth to, in a remarkable symbolic expression. Her whole attitude is such that, to put it in a rather banal way, one just could not get any fun out of life with her around.

The father completes the vicious family circle by failing repeatedly in his role as provider and by rarely speaking up for his son.

The son never realizes the true nature of his mother and therefore finds no way of expressing his mounting resentment except in ridiculously mild comments. Once during the interviews he says, "I know I resented this [the domineering role of the mother] at times"; but then he became immediately tearful and confused. He adds, "Mother spent as much time with us as any mother did" and then is silent. Even about the father he only says, "My dad is thankful toward her for any help she has given to the family, but also quite resentful." When his frustration tolerance reaches its limits for the first time, in the conflict with the parents about Mary, he runs away to the Army in order to strengthen his courage.

During his service, his mother almost forces him into taking a stand against her by using obviously foul means to separate him from his girl, Mary. First, the mother writes him that she suspects that Mary is pregnant (naturally by another man, since he was away), which was false information; then another time she writes him that Mary's parents were against the marriage, which is also a lie. He tries to free himself and plans an elopement, which produces the first crisis leading directly to his future suicide attempt. Discussing the time when he had made preparations to elope with Mary, he says, "We didn't have the nerve. Just a doomed feeling. When I left her that day, I cried." This is the most dramatic of a series of incidents that he himself describes as "going down," the symbolic expression of the desire to let himself be swallowed up by the *magna mater,* the earth mother, since he is unable to live life without her.

A relatively extraneous coincidence, the illness and death of an aunt, the mother's sister and a former teacher of his, suffices to make him break off the relationship with Mary and to come running back to mamma. After that, he does well in the service and even tries to fall in love with another girl, one more acceptable to his mother.

It is symbolically quite fitting that Mary refuses to return his fraternity pin and that he is unable to go through with marrying the other girl, even though everyone is in favor of it. He obviously is not ready to face life on his own responsibility and goes back to Mary, the only positive and warm contact in his life, in contrast with his compulsive, emotionally twisted mother.

In school, he switches to sociology, a symbolic expression of the desire to find a way to the outer collective, and even gets good grades, but finally his relationship to Mary cannot be maintained any longer. She is fed up with his dilly-dallying, and her former yielding behavior gives way to a more demanding attitude. In desperation, he runs away again, this time to South America, Mary's motherland. This symbolic escape fails completely, and he enters the last phase before his suicidal attempt. He returns to continue his studies and to look for a job, but he is "going down" for the last time. He says, "I wanted to sever relations with my family and to have something bigger than myself, a feeling of understanding from home." In convincing symbolic actions he prepares for the union with the *magna mater:* he gets a glass of malted milk, takes a shower, and then swallows the pills (around seventy-five barbiturate capsules) and lies down. The recognition that he would have to kill the mother image that holds him tied is only expressed in his feeble desire to sever relations with his family, but the only way he can accomplish this is to sever relations with his past life in his unconscious desire to be reborn.

A few words about guilt in this case might be appropriate. It can be assumed from the patient's behavior in the several interview sessions that guilt was very strongly present but unconscious. Further, in Jungian terms, the contamination of the personal shadow by the archetypal shadow, the demon, is particularly facilitated when such intense guilt feelings remain entirely unconscious. This is what seems to have occurred, as far as we can speculate, in this particular case.

PROPOSALS FOR TREATMENT PLANNING

There are some positive and active elements in the life history, some occasional flashes of ambition, and presumably a good intelligence. In the past, the positive strivings only strengthened the inversion of aggression against himself. Now they can be transformed into constructive forces, if and when he learns to free himself from the poisonous accumulated resentment against his mother and to understand the suicidal attempt as a symbolic expression of the psychological act of rebirth.

We might conclude with a few words about the general topic of countertransference or counterreactions: the feelings of the therapist for a suicidal patient or a suicidal threat. Essentially, the answer to this problem is the ability of any therapist to face up to death, either in the case of suicide or in the case of incurable disease; it depends very much on the degree to which he is able to come to a successful reconciliation with the reality of death in his own personal philosophy. The problem of the meaning of death is a crucial area in the whole discussion of suicide; this problem can be related back to the therapist and his resolutions and solutions. It seems, then, that a prerequisite for the successful treatment of suicide is to believe in something as a key to the meaning of life.

References

1. Benn, G.: *Ausgewählte Briefe* (Selected Letters), Wiesbaden: Limes Verlag, 1957.
2. Jung, C. G.: The soul and death, translated by R. P. C. Hull, in H. Feifel (Ed.), *The Meaning of Death,* New York: McGraw-Hill Book Company, Inc., Blakiston Division, 1959.
3. Kris, E.: *Psychoanalytic Explorations in Art,* New York: International Universities Press, Inc., 1952.
4. Saint-Exupéry, A. de: *The Little Prince,* New York: Harcourt, Brace and Company, Inc., 1943.
5. Shneidman, E. S., and N. L. Farberow: *Clues to Suicide,* New York: McGraw-Hill Book Company, Inc., Blakiston Division, 1957.
6. Van der Post, L.: *Bar of a Shadow,* New York: William Morrow and Company, Inc., 1956.
7. Wahl, C.: Suicide as a magical act, in E. S. Shneidman and N. L. Farberow (Eds.), *Clues to Suicide,* New York: McGraw-Hill Book Company, Inc., Blakiston Division, 1957.

15

Suicide: The Adlerian Point of View

HEINZ L. ANSBACHER [1]

Doctor Ansbacher received his Ph.D. degree in psychology from Columbia University in 1937. Subsequently, he became assistant editor of *Psychological Abstracts* and taught at Brooklyn College and Duke University. In 1946 he went to the University of Vermont, where he is now Professor of Psychology. He is a Fellow of the American Psychological Association, and a member of the American Association for the Advancement of Science and of Sigma Xi. For 1954–1955 he was awarded a Fulbright lectureship at the University of Kiel, Germany. Among his earlier interests are perception and personality and attitude research, and he has a number of publications in these areas. During the war he was with the Psychological Warfare Division, SHAEF, as a survey officer, doing attitude research with prisoners of war in England and France. Considered an authority on Adlerian psychology, he is currently president of the American Society of Adlerian Psychology and editor of the *Journal of Individual Psychology*. He wrote the article on Alfred Adler for the *Encyclopaedia Britannica,* and with his wife, Rowena R. Ansbacher, edited *The Individual Psychology of Alfred Adler* (New York: Basic Books, 1956; London: Allen and Unwin, 1958).

ADLER'S THEORY OF PERSONALITY DEVELOPMENT

A psychological theory of suicide is essentially one of its dynamics. The Adlerian theory of dynamics sees the individual as a unified and unique whole, at all times directed by one over-all striving. This striving Adler has named variously a striving from below to above, a striving from a minus situation to a plus situation, or a striving for superiority or perfection or completion. The particular name is less important than the general idea it represents: a striving for a goal of success. A second important thought here is that the concrete representation of success corresponds altogether to the subjective conception of the individual and may take on the greatest variety of forms. A third factor is that the individual is not necessarily aware of his particular goal of success and in this sense is unconscious of it. But the goal can be inferred if we study all his actions and expressions

[1] The author acknowledges his appreciation to Dr. Alexandra Adler, Mrs. Danica Deutsch, and especially Dr. Rudolf Dreikurs, all of whom read the original manuscript and the case history and made valuable comments that have been incorporated in this chapter.

together, looking for the common denominator that permits understanding them all as parts of a coherent and self-consistent picture.

All primary drives and other motives are subordinated to and in the service of this main striving. The individual cannot be considered in isolation but must be considered as part of his social context. Adler's theory is a field theory. Not only is the individual influenced by his social setting, but his actions are in turn socially effective. What occurs in one part of the field must produce effects in other parts.

Mental Disorder

The mentally healthy striving represents a contribution or an asset to the social group, whereas mental disorder is a disturbance or liability to the group. In the former, the goal of success is in accordance with common sense, makes sense to others as well as to the individual himself, and is acceptable to others. The maladjusted person, on the other hand, strives for a goal of success that represents only private intelligence, makes sense only to himself, and is thus not valid.

The striving in mental disorder has been designated by Adler as a striving on the useless side. It is useless from the point of view of society because it represents no contribution and often a liability. But it is ultimately useless also to the individual. Because he is an inextricable part of a social setting, so that almost all his partial needs, such as sex, food, security, and status, depend for their satisfaction on contributive social interaction and thus become social problems, his striving is not likely to be successful in the long run. By contrast, the striving in mental health is, on balance, essentially on the socially useful side.

Social Interest. Adler's construct in explanation of the difference between striving on the useful versus the useless side is social interest. Deficiency in social interest is the common denominator for problem children, neurotics, psychotics, alcoholics, drug addicts, prostitutes, perverts, and criminals, as well as suicides. Thus Adler established the unity of all maladjustment. Social interest is the criterion for appraising mental health.

Social interest is the capacity to understand and accept the social interrelatedness of the individual human life, to empathize with one's fellow men, and thus to be in harmony with the social world and the universe. It is not a second dynamic force, opposed to the striving for superiority, which, if a proper balance is obtained, would hold the superiority striving in check. This would be a dualistic system of dynamics, comparable to Freud's death versus life instincts. Adler's system of dynamics is monistic.

Social interest is innate in the form of a disposition, or potentiality, or aptitude, like the aptitude to read, to sing, or to swim. Like these aptitudes, it "must be trained and exercised, or its development will be stunted" [4, p. 371]. When developed, social interest, like other capacities, becomes part of the individual's goal of success. If your aptitude to ski has been developed, your striving for success will include skiing in one way or another. The capacity secondarily assumes dynamic qualities, in accordance with Allport's and Woodworth's principle of the functional autonomy of motives [3, p. 191]. Similarly, if your social interest has been developed, your goal of success will include a striving on the socially useful side.

Social interest is from the start more a cognitive than a conative factor, although it does acquire conative properties. The *apperceptive schema* of everyone is biased in accordance with his individual style of life, but the stunting of social interest makes it more narrow, incomplete, and distorted and makes the striving more self-centered. The development of social interest, on the other hand, leads to a more objectified striving, which has greater validity. In this sense Adlerian psychology is a rational psychology.

Developmental Factors. Deficiency in social interest is likely to arise in children with organ inferiorities, in those who have been hated or neglected, and in those who have been pampered. The apparent advantage of the last group turns into the opposite when the pampering situation does not prevail. The individual in all three groups is likely to see himself at a special disadvantage, not welcomed by the world or not able to obtain the special consideration that he tacitly demands. He is thus likely to develop increased inferiority feelings. Rather than learning to see himself as an equal part of a larger social setting, he is likely to see himself as a unique case in opposition to the world, considers himself living in enemy country, and develops a self-centered and heightened goal of success and a corresponding personality or style of life. Such self-centered striving for personal success is what Adler calls the *neurotic disposition.*

It must be pointed out here that environmental factors are, however, no more absolute determiners of the style of life than the biological factors. They only provide greater or lesser probabilities. The last word is spoken by the individual, who must be understood as being creative and as using in the formation of his life style the factors with which he finds himself.

The Exogenous Factor. The exogenous factor is a situation or problem that requires more social interest than the neurotically disposed person has available. His inability to meet the situation represents a threat to his self-esteem and life style, which he then moves to safeguard through symptoms.

Suicide as Symptom of Mental Disorder [2]

In view of such a general theory, the categorical differentiation between disorders is of secondary importance for Adler. The burden of diagnosis and treatment is shifted from the disease category to the individual case. Adler's psychology is very much an idiographic psychology, in which it is essential to understand how the general dynamics of mental disorder have become uniquely concretized in a given individual.

Yet there are certain similarities among cases that are to a degree characteristic for the various commonly recognized symptomatic categories. Adler's general observations regarding suicide are as follows.

Pampered Life Style. Suicidal tendencies, like depression, which is closely related, develop "in individuals whose method of living, from early childhood on, has been dependent upon the achievements and the support of others. They will always try to lean on others" [4, p. 319]. They expect and demand that others fulfill their wishes. They have a pseudoconsciousness of their value to others. They expect always favorable outcomes, are poor losers, and are unable to play the game as equal partners.

Inferiority Feelings and Self-centered Goal. "Their self-esteem from childhood on is clearly low, as can be concluded from their unceasing attempts to achieve greatest importance" [4, p. 319]. The suicidal person is ambitious and vain. The contemplation of suicide gives him the feeling of mastery over life and death. This feeling is "the supreme expression of the goal of superiority on the useless side of life" [1, p. 55]. His thinking is self-centered rather than problem- or other-centered.

Degree of Activity. Among the maladjusted the greatest amount of activity is found in criminals, where again the murderer shows more activity than the pickpocket. Among neurotics and psychotics, activity is generally low; but again differences exist within the groups. Activity is generally lowest in anxiety neurosis and schizophrenia, greater in compulsion neurosis and depression, and greatest in suicide [4, p. 165].

Veiled Aggression. "The life style of the potential suicide is characterized by the fact that he hurts others by dreaming himself into injuries, or by administering them to himself" [4, p. 324]. Occasionally suicide is combined with open aggression as in cases where it is preceded by murder. Suicide can be taken as an act of reproach or revenge. In this respect it is also similar to depression and to alcoholism and drug addiction, all of which are forms of veiled attacks on others who will have the sorrow

[2] This section is essentially based on Adler's paper on suicide [2], with other quotations interspersed as indicated.

or care. In suicide, as in depression, the life style employs complaints, mourning, and suffering to influence others by creating sympathy. Thus we also find self-accusation and begging for forgiveness, which are often included in the notes left behind.

Suicide in Mental Health

Adler recognizes that there also are persons who commit suicide who cannot be described otherwise than as well-adjusted, although such cases are conspicuously rare. "Situations in which the approximately healthy may regard suicide as the only way out are: endless suffering, inhuman cruel attacks, fear of discovery of disgraceful or criminal actions, incurable and extremely painful diseases, etc." [2, p. 49].

He further points out that suicide may appear in the form of epidemics or receive cultural sanction, as in the case of hara-kiri.

THE CASE OF MR. A. S.

If we examine the case history of Mr. A. S. in the light of the preceding theoretical considerations, we gain an understanding of how the patient arrived at an erroneous style of life and how, in view of his mistake, suicide appeared to him as a suitable means to solve a critical problem situation.

Pampered Life Style

Talking about himself and his sister, the patient says, "both of us were somewhat pampered." We learn that his mother did all the work around the house and would never ask even his sister to help with the household duties. The mother confirms in her interview, "We were always very good to A., let him do whatever he wanted to.... There was only one time we stepped on A." (when he wanted to marry Mary). Although this is not necessarily the case, a child with such a pampering mother is prone to develop a pampered style of life, as the patient indeed did.

He acquired the opinion that he could obtain everything easily with the help of others and that he could expect everything from others. Getting things from others became part of his goal of success. This is shown in a first childhood recollection, which he describes as "wonderful." "We took a long trip to get a bicycle, and we came back late at night. But my dad set it up for me, even though it was late, and I remember we were riding it with him helping me." The significance of early recollections is that they reflect the present opinions of the individual, which in this instance would be: "When things are being done for me and people help me, no matter how inconvenient it is for them, then I can go forth and things are wonderful." By contrast, when the family had moved to the city and the patient was in a school where he did not receive special consideration, his marks dropped and he almost flunked in the sixth grade. In the former school he had had his aunt for his teacher and used to think he was something special.

Wanting help from others is a recurrent theme in the case history. From a tonsillectomy at the age of eleven he remembers that other persons were very good to him. They brought him good things to eat and malted milk. From his whooping cough at the age of twelve he remembers becoming panicky when he was choking and found himself unable "to call for someone" to help him. When he wanted to take a trip, he called a travel agent "and he arranged the trip . . . for me."

Underdeveloped Social Interest

One important aspect of the pampered life style is deficient social interest. Indeed, the patient gives no evidence that he ever approached a social situation with a contributive attitude, meeting the other person on an equal level, maturely. When the family moved to the city, he was confronted with the task of establishing new social relationships. How did he go about this? "I remember desperately trying to be popular. . . . I would try to be nice and charming and everything." This sounds like condescension and hardly seems the right way. No wonder the patient did not succeed.

From the same time he remembers that the teacher once spanked another child who had beaten him and that the other children did not like this. His feeling of solidarity with the children was not great enough to regret the entire incident. All he can remember is "feeling bad because I lost the fight. . . . I was jealous of the other kids and would fight with them all the time."

The mother, according to the patient, "likes to do things alone, even though she might be in a group of people." We can understand from this that the mother was the kind of a person who is unable to teach cooperation and to develop social interest. Wanting to do everything herself, she also wanted to do everything and thus be everything for her son. The patient tells that, during the time he lived at the farm, "my aunt was the teacher at our school" but "my mother was actually my teacher."

Inferiority Feelings

Lack of social interest by itself tends to give rise to strong inferiority feelings. "Psychological tolerance depends on the strength of social ties" [4, p. 243], and their development depends on social interest. But it is equally, if not more, true that increased inferiority feelings interfere with the development of social interest. In the patient's case there were three further factors contributing to his sense of inferiority: his size, the mother's domineering nature, and the father's general weakness and lack of success.

The patient was small. The psychiatrist describes him as a somewhat slight, blond, boyish-looking person, already partially bald. Relating to the time when he was ten years old, when he fought a great deal, the patient says, "I was small and would lose most of the time." In college he started "to feel bad about being small. Once I even bought some elevator shoes. It seems like I didn't feel physically equal to the fellows." In the Army he had a superior of whom he says, "This man was everything I hated," and he begins his description of him with "He was tall. . . . He always tried to humiliate me." The patient's smallness was a thorn in his flesh.

The mother pursued for herself a goal of personal superiority rather than one of general usefulness. According to the patient, "She likes to excel. She likes to be the leader in clubs and be the chairman of organizations. She feels flattered when she is elected for something like that." Such a person, rather than making others feel as equal partners, is likely to depreciate them in innumerable subtle ways, even though overtly boosting them. To the patient she is the kind of woman who "makes everyone that is around feel inferior. . . . My dad is thankful toward her for the help that she has been to the family but also quite resentful. . . . He likes to avoid crowds and go to clubs, because she always predominates."

The father was, in the patient's eyes, ineffective, failing, and unsuccessful. The psychiatrist describes the father as staying for the most part in the background and as only occasionally stepping out from behind his wife's skirts to assume some of the gruff exterior that he feels is demanded of a man. The patient says about his father, "He is not interested in working around the house, and my mother has to pull him into it and tell him what to do, and he expects her to do this." In his relation to the outside world, "dad was never extremely successful at anything he did, and I used to feel bad about this. . . . That hurt me a lot because my friends always had fathers who were important."

And yet the patient identified with his father, in this way to some extent forming a common front against the mother, in spite of the patient's statement, "I guess that I am closer to my mother." We gather this from the good times the patient remembers having had with his father. The mother says that "father and son were like two peas in a pod, they often talked together and shared interests." When the patient said, as noted above, that his father was quite resentful toward his mother, we may well take this partially as a projection based on identification with the father.

The Goal of Personal Superiority and Masculinity

As is frequently the case in persons with increased inferiority feelings and low social interest, the patient compensated by secondary feelings of his particular value and an exaggerated goal of personal superiority.

Such a development again was fostered by the mother who, the patient says, "was always trying to build me up and brag about me to everyone, and whenever anyone would come over, she would tell them how wonderful I was." The mother told the psychiatrist, "Our children were very much admired."

Under such influence the patient developed the idea that he should be tops. He says, regarding his goals while in school, "I still had a feeling that I wasn't in the real top echelon, and I was trying to get in. I would want to be the leader, but I never was." He kept asking the most popular girl in school for dates, although she never gave him a tumble. Eventually he did go out with other girls, "but I never felt I was really enjoying myself with them, that I would rather have had the other girl."

Here we have an illustration of the "antithetical schema" of apperception [4, p. 248], the "dichotomizing judgment" [4, p. 249], or the "all or nothing" motto [4, p. 294] that Adler found typical for the neurotic individual. According to Adler [4, pp. 249–250]:

> The neurotic's striving for security, his very safeguards, can be understood when the original antithetic value-factor, namely that of insecurity, is taken into consideration at the same time. Both security and insecurity are the result of a dichotomizing judgment which has become dependent upon the fictional personality ideal and furnishes biased subjective value judgments. The feeling of security and its opposite pole, the feeling of insecurity, arranged according to the antithesis of inferiority feeling and personality ideal, are, like the latter, a fictional pair of values. They are the kind of psychological construction concerning which Vaihinger points out "that in them reality is artificially divided, that they have meaning and value only when together, but that, when taken singly, they lead through their isolation to meaninglessness, contradictions, and illusionary problems." In the analysis of psychoneuroses it often becomes apparent that these antitheses are analogous to the antithesis of man-woman taken for real. The dynamics of the neurosis can therefore be regarded, and are often so

understood by the neurotic, "as if" the patient wished to change from a woman to a man, or, in the case of a man, wanted to hide his unmanliness. These tendencies, in their varied fullness, give the picture of what I have called the masculine protest.

In the case of our patient, the antithetical schema of apperception did indeed also take the form of the masculine protest. Being small and identifying with an ineffectual father, the patient's goal of security and superiority included the idea of wanting to be a real man [4, p. 250]. He wanted to be superior as a man or, rather, what he thought a man should be.

In this light the fighting that we noted earlier, which was taken as a sign of lack of social interest, takes on additional and possibly greater significance as an expression of the patient's struggle for manliness. But he did not understand these coherences; they remained unconscious to him. This is why he could not explain why he fought so much. "I don't know why it was, but I was always fighting. I just had to. . . . It seemed that I used to love to fight." He could also not understand why his parents "wouldn't stick up for me rather than just tell me not to fight." He "would keep on doing it," although he would lose most of the time because of his small size. Here we see the small, overprotected, pampered boy who tries desperately to assert himself.

Only after he came to the end of his rope, being disliked by the other children and almost flunking in school, he began to change, trying to be popular by being nice and charming, as mentioned earlier.

In the Army, where he advanced to the position of sergeant, the patient temporarily felt successful as a man. "I liked the service very much and did extremely well in it." Yet this did not provide him with the assurance that he could later on also find his place in a masculine world, and after he was out of the Army, there was no such place with clearly defined masculine status available.

The Ruling Type

As a child the patient was very active. His early memories include milking cows, running downstairs to get out of the cold and get dressed in front of the warm stove, playing in the band, and playing football. The frequent mention of fighting with the other children completes the picture of an active boy. In his later life he copes with his important problems in the form of running away, showing activity to this extent. He leaves college twice, goes into the Army, goes on a long trip, etc. He responds to his problems with activity, although not of a constructive type. Taking his recollection as a metaphor, we can say he always tries to run away from the cold of real life to the warmth of the family stove so he can continue with the business of getting started.

In her interview with the psychiatrist, the patient's mother repeatedly confirms that the patient was very active: while she was carrying him, while he was an infant, as a young child on the farm, and later as a boy in the city.

Such relatively great activity, combined with deficiency in social interest and the expectancy that others must help him to attain the exalted position to which he feels entitled, has been described by Adler as the dynamics of what he called the ruling type [4, p. 168]:

> If confronted strongly by a situation which he feels to be in the nature of an examination, a test of his social value, a judgment upon his social usefulness, a person of this type acts in an unsocial way. The more active of this type attack others directly. . . . To this type also belong suicidals, drug addicts, and drunkards, whose [relatively] lesser degree of activity causes them to attack others indirectly. They make attacks upon themselves for the purpose of hurting others.

The description of belonging to the ruling type would seem well applicable to the patient. He characterized his satisfaction in the Army in the following words: "I had people working for me. Things were going swell." We remember he always wanted to be the leader.

His originally very high degree of activity, however, became somewhat diminished. When, still as a child, he experienced that fighting and asserting himself did not help him, partly on account of his small size, he developed, as a secondary phenomenon, the more passive attitude of pleasing others and of trying to find his place through seeking approval. At times he liked to dramatize his helplessness, as during his recovery from the suicide attempt.

The Exogenous Factor

"It all goes back to before I went into the Army. I had a girl friend then, Mary. . . . I really wanted to marry her. But my folks were against this." Mary was a South American–Spanish girl, perhaps of partly Indian or Negro descent, who had been adopted by one of the respected white members of the community. Naturally, the patient's overambitious mother would not consider such a socially "inferior" girl as being good enough for her son.

It was probably precisely this quality of social inferiority that the patient needed in a woman. Such a woman would look up to him as a man and not treat him like his mother treated his father. When persons choose partners far beneath them in social status or education, they wish, according to Adler [4, p. 437], "to establish a situation in which their partner will look up to them." Mary had indeed been very "considerate" to the patient. "Mary was the first girl I had intercourse with, and I enjoyed it very much." At that time he no longer felt so small. While he was in the Army, "Mary would write me every day, and I would wait for her letters." He had finally found the one girl who looked up to him, who treated him like somebody important and great.

Many young men are confronted with the problem of wanting to marry a girl of whom the parents disapprove and find a solution other than suicide. The patient, however, was unable to give up either his mother or Mary because he needed both women for his self-esteem.

He expressed what he considered the ideal solution when he requested that his parents bring Mary with them to the station one time when he came home on a furlough. This was a quite unrealistic and unreasonable request in view of the fact that the parents disapproved of Mary very strongly from the start. It corresponded, however, to his private logic of wanting both his parents and Mary. It was his private logic that did not permit him to "understand," as he says, why his parents were against the girl.

The inability to reconcile his parents and Mary, so he could have them both, was "the terrible problem." He tried repeatedly "to get away from the terrible problem" but did not succeed. He vacillated for two years, had a good time in the Army, and even found another girl. But the new girl, nice as she was, did not apparently give him the same support as Mary did. Thus at the end of the two years "the same situation between Mary, myself, and my folks preyed on my mind."

The Revolt of the Pampered Child

We have seen that the patient needed Mary in support of his self-esteem. But there was probably a second reason why he could not give her up, namely, the very fact that his mother was strongly opposed to Mary. If this assumption is correct, we should be able to find opposition against the mother for which clinging to the thought of Mary would give him strength.

According to Adler [4, p. 370], "For each pampered child there comes the time when even the most affectionate mother can no longer fulfill all his wishes. Then the revolt of the young despot breaks out, leading to various forms of tyranny against the weaker." Suicide in such cases is an act of aggression in the form of reproach or revenge, as stated earlier. Again according to Adler [4, p. 324], "One will seldom go wrong in determining against whom the attack is aimed when one has found who is actually affected most by it." In the present case it is undoubtedly the mother.

The wish that the mother and the father did not fulfill was to consent to Mary. "It was the first time that they had ever crossed me." This was the shock that caused the revolt to break out into the open. From then on the patient speaks repeatedly of "hating to go home" and "severing relations with the family." But being a pampered child, he did not have the courage to do so. When he expressed the generally human feeling, "I had to have something bigger than myself," he could not think of it in terms of work, study, or the love of a girl. This "something" remained for him "a feeling of understanding from home." Another time he says, "I couldn't go against my parents."

The revolt that broke out with the parents' disapproval of Mary had been smoldering for some time. There are several indications of earlier resentfulness against the mother. "I think my sister turned out lazy because mother could never let anyone else do anything. I know I resented this at times." The patient also stated that the father was quite resentful against the mother, that she made everyone around her feel inferior, and that she always predominated, as mentioned earlier. He even made the accusation that "mother enjoyed dad's illnesses, because she likes the opportunity to work and to show that she was very competent." During her visit to the hospital after her son's suicide attempt, the mother's conduct was so officious and obnoxious that she made it quite plain how she would create resentment and hostility at home as well.

But the suicide was directed also against Mary, who let him down in the end. After he got out of the service and went back to Mary, he was at first happy. But then his relationship with Mary deteriorated, and he did not feel so close to her any more. "She had changed a lot. She was not considerate any more. She would say things and wouldn't care what people thought. She would hurt their feelings, and I remember feeling that this was all my folks' fault, and I blamed myself, too." At that time he had gone back to college, and despite the fact that his marks were up, "I started feeling socially inferior again, and I couldn't study." This would seem to confirm neatly how he needed the complete support of Mary to maintain his self-esteem.

The patient then says, "I was at my nerves' end." But it was not his nerves; he was at his wits' end. The doctor to whom he went gave him sleeping pills but did not understand him, nor did the patient understand himself. In Mary he lost the only woman with whom he truly felt superior as a man, the only one who made him feel like a man. Now he felt that he had been abandoned.

The basis for his revenge feelings toward Mary is her daring to change while he was away. His subsequent decision to go to South America may be understood already as an attempt to punish her. Did he go there to find another Mary, one might ask?

Hurting Oneself to Hurt Others

Why did the patient not express his revolt and revenge through any of the other possible symptoms? Why did he resort to suicide to hurt his mother and Mary?

In answer to this question we note that the patient had for a long time incorporated into his life style the mode of operation found in potential cases of depression and suicide. Such cases typically attempt to gain their ends through appealing to the sympathy of others by playing up their own weaknesses, griefs, and sorrows. In the face of a shock experience, the less active of them may then resort to an actual depression, the more active to suicide [4, p. 168]. The patient can well be considered as belonging to the more active group, as explained earlier, who will produce the injury themselves.

The following are indications that he resorted since childhood to this mode of attack. "I was playing the violin one day and I started to cry because I wanted to go to a movie. Dad gave me the money." But he does not stop at getting his way by resorting to crying; he wants to earn further sympathy by not accepting the fruits of his victory, through showing guilt feelings. And so we learn that, after he had gone out, "I came back because I guess I felt bad at the way I had gotten the money." No wonder his mother attests, "Other children would get into trouble, but A. was obedient." Adler had explained in one of his early papers (1910) that aggression in children may manifest itself through obedience as well as defiance. "The human psyche is capable of operating in either of these directions" [4, p. 66].

A similar application of the patient's tactics is the following. "I was small and would lose most of the time when I fought with other children, but anyway I would keep on doing it. I would feel very bad when I lost." With his grief he would then go to his parents to win their support and sympathy. When neither would "stick up" for him, but simply told him not to fight, he "would feel uncomfortable."

Another example of indirect attack is almost understood by the patient himself. When he started fighting with his dad about Mary, "I didn't actually fight. I would talk with my mother, but I wouldn't talk with my dad." And further on, "I didn't know at that time if I blamed my parents or not, but I began to feel that I was going down again."

This mode of operation is, of course, the patient's own doing, but he again had the model of his mother before him. "Things would upset her very easily but she never would punish us. She would tell us it would worry her if we did something bad." When he almost flunked in school, "My mother looked at my report card that day when I came home and started to cry, and dad scolded me." To appreciate this, we must recall how much the mother was actually the dominant figure in the family. Yet at the same time, worry and crying, appeal to sympathy, was an important part of the mother's arsenal, and the patient had learned to appreciate it as a most powerful weapon. In the words of Adler [4, p. 288], "Tears and complaints—the means which I have called 'water power'—can be an extremely useful weapon for disturbing cooperation and reducing others to a condition of slavery."

Because of his self-centered, narrowly focused life style, it did not occur to the patient that he could solve "the terrible problem" by meaning something to others through looking after them. If he had loved Mary in this sense, that is, if he had really loved her, the problem would not even have arisen. Instead, he is now striking against his mother and against Mary through the puzzle of suicide but retaining the appearance of being a good boy.

The patient, being unaware of the internal coherence of his actions, is quite calm at the time of the suicide attempt, as one who does not take the responsibility for an important decision but ascribes it to others or to fate. In South America he had not been able to get interested in anything, and after a short time he went to Los Angeles, where he apparently ran out of money. "I would look in the papers and try to get a job, but it would seem as if I just couldn't get started. I would look at them, but wouldn't do any more. Then I would go to a movie and come back, and all the time my mood was getting worse, and I still had the feeling that I wanted to sever relations with my family." One day, after coming back from the movie, "I had only a quarter left, and I was hungry, so I got a malted milk." This is a replica of the malted milk he was given at the time of his tonsillectomy at the age of 11, when others were so good to him. "Then I came up to my room, put all my stuff away, took a shower, and took the pills and lay down." He was a "good and obedient" boy.

Summary

We have here a young man with a pampered life style, deficient social interest, strong inferiority feelings, and an unrealistic goal of personal superiority and masculinity. His originally great activity is tempered by a desire for approval. He reaches an impasse when his mother strongly disapproves of the girl he needs to support his self-esteem. When the girl finally lets him down, he takes revenge on both his mother and his girl by attempting suicide.

THERAPEUTIC IMPLICATIONS

All failure, according to Adler, is based on a faulty method of living, a faulty style of life. The work of the Adlerian therapist consists in bringing the bits of information about the patient, obtained from the interviews, into such a relationship that an understandable picture emerges of how this particular person dreams himself toward some form of success on the useless side of life. The therapist is usually relatively soon able to understand the patient's life style. This understanding represents the diagnosis.

Therapy consists in imparting this understanding to the patient, the assumption being that the patient will then be able to correct his mistaken life style. At the same time, the therapist must strengthen the patient's social interest and thus enable him to gain the greater independence and courage necessary for the correction of the mistake [4, p. 119].

Therapy is time consuming because the patient's schema of apperception is biased. Thus it becomes necessary to use the material from further interviews to interpret to the patient again and again how all his expressions fit his life style. "The therapist must grasp the special structure and development of that individual life with such accuracy, and express it with such lucidity, that the patient . . . recognizes his own mistake" [4, p. 335]. "Once this is accomplished, the patient will understand his specific incidents better than does the therapist" [4, p. 336]. "The cure is brought about by a correction of the faulty picture of the world and the unequivocal acceptance of a mature picture of the world" [4, p. 333]. The objective of therapy is "to enable the patient to take a better, more self-reliant attitude toward life, one which is in greater accordance with society" [2].

In the present case, one would show the patient to himself in approximately the way we have done in the preceding pages. This would have to be done gradually and tactfully, adapted to the patient's response. Treatment must be flexible. Specific measures suggested would also have to be scaled to the patient's reactions. As the patient had a "weak" father, a male therapist would probably be indicated.

The first objective would be to get the patient to see that he has been looking for protection like a child and then had sulked because he did not get enough. But he should also understand that with his old attitude he never would feel that he was getting enough and would be led to further fighting.

The next objective would be to help the patient prepare himself to stand on his own, which includes preparation for unavoidable failures and independence from the opinion of others. The therapist would encourage new efforts by the patient in the direction of self-realization by emphasizing the patient's positive qualities. He would also help the patient in formulating a vocational goal and in pursuing it. The planning should take into account that the patient is intrinsically active, that in the Army he was very happy doing administrative work, and that he always wanted to be a leader.

In this connection, and therapeutically at the same time, some kind of leadership training with role playing might be considered. There the patient would learn that being a leader does not mean "I had people working for *me*" but that instead the function of the leader is to take on responsibilities and to work *with* others, which means also to look after them.

The ultimate objective of therapy would be to change the patient's unrealistic self image into a realistic view of himself and the world. He would then be able to respect others and change his self-centeredness into other-centeredness. He would learn not to be concerned primarily with the question of "who will take care of me" but to take care of others and that this can be a pleasure. Once he has come to understand this, he will be all right.

References

1. Adler, A.: *Problems of Neurosis,* London: Routledge & Kegan Paul, Ltd., 1929.
2. Adler, A.: Suicide, *Journal of Individual Psychology,* 14: 57–61, 1958; translated from Selbstmord, *Internationale Zeitschrift für Individualpsychologie,* 15: 49–52, 1937.
3. Allport, G. W.: *Personality; A Psychological Interpretation,* New York: Henry Holt and Company, Inc., 1937.
4. Ansbacher, H. L., and Rowena R. Ansbacher (Eds.): *The Individual Psychology of Alfred Adler,* New York: Basic Books, Inc., 1956.

16

Suicide: The Sullivanian Point of View

MAURICE R. GREEN

Doctor Green was born in 1922 and received a B.S. degree in 1942, a B.M. degree in 1945, and an M.D. degree in 1946, all at Northwestern University. He was an attending psychiatrist in child psychiatry at Roosevelt Hospital from 1949 to 1957; consultant at the Institute of Jazz Studies, Inc., from 1952 to 1957; consultant at Broadwood Hall Child Care Society from 1954 to 1958; and staff psychiatrist, Low Cost Series of W. A. White Institutes from 1949 to 1958. He is a lecturer at the William Alanson White Institute of Psychology, Psychiatry, and Psychoanalysis; consultant for the Bleuler Psychotherapy Group; and staff psychiatrist, Psychiatric Clinic, Court of Special Sessions, New York. He is a Fellow of the American Psychiatric Association; a Fellow of the Academy of Psychoanalysis; a member of the American Orthopsychiatric Association; a Diplomate (in Psychiatry) of the American Board of Neurology and Psychiatry; and a member of a number of other national and state professional and scientific societies. His publications include articles on schizophrenia, psychiatric aspects of various physical diseases, and psychological disorders in blind children.

In his interpersonal theory of psychiatry, Harry Stack Sullivan attempted to organize psychoanalytic, psychobiological, and anthropological information in a description of patterns of human interaction and relatedness, as precisely as he could and in explicit detail. He saw the psychiatrist as a trained expert who participated in his patient's experience, who carefully observed this participation, and who attempted to communicate what he noticed in a way that would be helpful to the patient. In contrast with the Freudian concept, with its emphasis on generalized and predetermined biological drives, Sullivan's outlook focused on particular patterns of interaction that occur between particular persons within a particular milieu. This had nothing to do, in Sullivan's mind, with cultural versus biological factors; he simply chose to limit his field to the study of concrete experience occurring between living persons.

SULLIVAN'S THEORY OF PERSONALITY DEVELOPMENT

Sullivan was outstanding in his persistent efforts to establish his conviction that human relatedness was the very core of character and personality.

He felt that it is only in this relation between separate persons that a human being could emerge and grow. In using the term *self* to refer to selective, organizing, and defensive aspects of the function of awareness in a person's growth and development, he meant it mostly in a narrow sense. The self referred to the organized experience of reflected appraisals by the significant other persons in the course of one's life, for Sullivan used it as the ongoing self-conscious part of a person, participating and communicating at a particular time in relation with one or more other persons. In this regard, the self does not at all refer to the whole person or to the essential character or identity of a person.

A person's consciousness of himself as an entity begins very early in his life, in the beginning personifications of *infancy*. This starts with the symbolic elaboration of infantile experience of body exploration and coordination, the beginning personification of what is later called *me* and *mine*. The term *personification* refers to the symbolic elaboration of organized experience that leads to the anticipation of particular kinds of interpersonal events; so the continuity of recall with foresight is part of the structure of what is implied by "me," "mine," and "I."

This process of personification begins as far back as the recall and anticipation of sucking one's thumb and feeling the thumb being sucked, and of the movements and kinesthetic sensations of eyes, hands, mouth, feet, and so on, all of which are the beginning of a feeling of independence and autonomy. The process is associated early with the beginning personifications of "good me," "bad me," and "not me"; and these personifications, in turn, are further associated with personifications of the "good mother" and "bad mother."

The achievement of these personifications occurs during the development of language and other communicative behavior, and for Sullivan this marks the end of infancy, the beginning of *childhood*. The personified self continues to develop and grow as the personifications of "me" and "we" are augmented by an increasingly rich and more complex body of experience with the important persons in the child's life. The thrust of biological maturation, the eager play and curiosity, and the exciting responsiveness of the child to the world about him bring further and more rapid transitions in his personifications. Important additions occur early in this period simply on the basis of whether the child is a boy or a girl; and endorsement or scorn by the authority figures of the child's behavior and activities greatly affects the enduring influence on the personified self.

Other important additions occur in later childhood with the personification of playmate, in preadolescence with the personification of chum, and in adolescence with the personification of preferred sexual partners. So far as these stages have been successful, the individual's growth continues with a deepening sense of respect for himself and for others and with a wider and more expansive relatedness to his fellow men and to the world about him.

Expression in *adult life* is related to the unsolved conflicts and failures, as well as to the gratifying personifications and experience of infancy and childhood. However, Sullivan was very explicit in his concept that a man's life is never a closed system. Activities in adult life are also of great and, frequently, decisive importance; and opportunities and restrictions of the cultural milieu, as well as social conditions, play a significant role.[1]

The importance of the adult's personal relations is well recognized, especially with one's chosen mate, with one's selected friends, and with coworkers on the job. Unresolved conflicts and failures that arise out of these relationships may, in predisposed persons, precipitate mental disorder, as sometimes manifested by suicidal attempts. It is possible to define specific areas of conflict and failure in infancy and childhood, but it is more difficult to state general stages or conditions for fulfillment in adult life.

All in all, Sullivan stressed the affirmation of life as it is lived in the human world. He recognized the desirability of knowing as much as possible about the persons in one's life and of developing the capacity not only for loving but also for realizing the worth of those one loves. In contrast to this, suicide is usually a destructive activity and belongs in the category of hateful and hostile types of integration with other persons.

COMPARISON WITH OTHER PSYCHOANALYTIC THEORIES

Sullivan believed that the origins of the attitudes of patients were too complex for simple generalized formulation. Although he did formulate observable patterns of events or interaction between the patient and other persons (including the patient's introspective reports of those events), from which he derived his diagnostic syndromes, he postponed making genetic formulations, that is, formulations explaining how these predominant patterns came to assume their dominant role. He postponed doing so in order that such formulations would take a proper place in the work of a particular psychiatrist with a particular patient, without the intervention of preconceptions that might interfere with a more free and open explora-

[1] Sullivan saw the anxiety gradient as only one of several ways of learning or of organizing new experience. He mentions trial and error and eduction as well [9, p. 154].

tion. It would be useful here to examine briefly how Sullivan's thinking on this matter differed from some of the more popular psychoanalytic theories about the origins of self-destructive urges.

In 1917, Sigmund Freud wrote his classic paper "Mourning and Melancholia" [3], in which he thus described the depressive process: A person's love relationship to another is first undermined by a real injury or disappointment; as a result of this, he identifies himself with the disappointing and now abandoned loved one, so part of his own ego comes to be regarded in a way equivalent to that of the abandoned loved one. Hence, the person is angry with himself instead of being angry with the loved one, depreciates himself instead of depreciating the loved one, and injures himself in place of the loved one. The type of person who succumbs to this behavior pattern was called by Freud narcissistic—incapable of mature love and fixated at an infantile, oral level of psychosexual development. In this connection, Freud explains the tendency to suicide in terms of the turning back on the ego of the person himself of his murderous sadistic feelings toward the hurtful, abandoning loved one. Later, in 1919–1920, Freud developed his death instinct theory as a more general formulation of instinctual activity, which included suicidal behavior [2].

Karl Menninger [6], in 1938, followed Freud's sound clinical observations and similar findings of others in his description of the dynamics of suicide.

More recently, Sandor Rado [8] has critically improved Freud's theory.[2] Rado describes the depressive episode in a person's life, in an adaptational context, as a particular kind of emergency dyscontrol. He says (p. 167): "But there is one characteristic that sets aside true depression from the various forms of unrecognized atonement. This feature is the patient's non-reported fear of starvation. . . ." Rado here stresses the combination of fearful self-contempt and violent rages that overwhelm these patients, which have their source in infantile attempts to conquer the "disappointing breast" and which try to force an "ecstatically satisfying breast" to appear. From this point of view, suicide would be a miscarried attempt at destroying the disappointing (breast-mother-loved) one, in the unwitting hope of gaining intoxicating satisfaction. It is Rado's belief that the depressive episode is initiated by a real or imagined loss, which is related to earlier real injury or loss. The patient's reaction to this loss is an overwhelming one, and he is torn by coercive rage and guilty fear. The increasing guilty fear tends to split the defeated rage into a smaller part that is repressed and a larger part that becomes assimilated into the guilty fear itself. The

[2] See also the discussion of this theory by Futterman, *supra*, chap. 12.

portion of the defeated rage that is assimilated into the guilty fear is the portion that is turned against the patient himself, as Freud described it, and is expressed in remorseful bouts of self-reproach and self-contempt. This exaggerated and intense emotional disturbance incapacitates the patient and reduces him to the subjective state of a frightened and helpless young child. As a result of early infantile experiences of exaggerated fear of starvation on one hand and an orgiastic satiated engorgement on the other, the patient develops what he voices as fear of depletion or impoverishment.

The Sullivanian theory considers that a number of factors influence the drive toward suicide. Sullivan regarded the total experience of the self in its felt value as the organized aggregate of all the various developmental personifications in a person's life, both within and outside the field of conscious awareness. This aggregate is never fixed but evolves from experience and is modified more or less in the course of a person's lifetime. The conscious part of the individual's experience, to which he refers by "I," "me," and "my" in talking or thinking about himself, is very important, particularly from later childhood on, in establishing an adequate orientation to living. Though no single personification is a completely accurate description of an individual, the degree to which any personification is inadequate, false, and dissociated affects the degree to which the individual is handicapped for the process of living.

In relation to this handicap, anxiety appears, which Sullivan viewed as the main factor in personality malfunctioning. He emphasized the traumatic nature of *severe* anxiety, likening it to a blow on the head, and made it one of the central organizing principles of what could be consciously formulated by the individual. The organizing of experience directed at escaping anxiety was called by Sullivan the antianxiety system, or self system. The operations of the self system or antianxiety system were designated by Sullivan as security operations, and these, he felt, tend to interfere with growth of personality and openness to new experiences. However, in spite of this, many persons continue to develop, as explained in his statement: "If they are fortunate, their growth goes on and on; they observe, formulate, and validate more and more; and at the same time, their foresight continuously expands so that they can foresee their career line—not as it inevitably will be, but in terms of expectation and probability, with perhaps provisions for disappointment."

Sullivan felt that, in the case of the less fortunate, early experiences with others may have warped their appraisal of themselves and crippled their personality dynamisms sufficiently to lead to very serious difficulties in living, causing them to require expert professional help. There is no one-to-one correspondence between these earlier experiences and later mental disorders; in other words, Sullivan has no genetic model for a diagnostic category. Like Adolf Meyer and others, he saw the personality as being in a continuous state of development or becoming of a person and considered the entire past of his life up to the present and foreseeable future as a significant influence in this development. Thus he describes various possibilities of predisposition for mental illness.

Many other factors can contribute to anxiety and these arise from the very conditions of human existence. Some of the most commonplace precipitating factors of anxiety are the birth of children, death in the family or among close associations, new responsibilities, and actual or potential violent separation from loved ones by war, accidents, or disease. Anxiety may also arise from repeated unfortunate experiences with persons, other than the family, upon whom one is continuously dependent in some way, such as school teachers, policemen, physicians, nurses, clergymen, and others.

Sullivan considers envy as directly related to anxiety and as arising from the desire to avoid the implications of anxiety, which are worthlessness and meaninglessness. That is to say, an individual consumed with envy is a person who cannot find rest in his sense of worth, as seen in the case of A. S., and must always covet what others have, always seeking more and more. Sullivan discusses envious persons in the following terms [10, p. 130]:

> Sometimes they are people with rather small gifts but whose parents had expected them to have larger gifts, as a result of which the smallness of their gifts was brought very keenly to their attention. With other envious people, the lesson may take a different form. Instead of being taught directly by being unsatisfactory to their parents' ideals, they have been given an irrational and extravagant picture of themselves as children and as very young juveniles. Then from the beginning of the school era onward, they have constantly experienced the dissatisfaction of others with their attempt to approximate these extravagant ideals that their parents gave them. . . . As a result the envious person comes to invest with importance all sorts of things that carry prestige or approval; he needs those things, he feels, to add to what he already has to demonstrate in the world, in order to be on an even footing with others.

PATHOLOGICAL FACTORS IN INFLUENCING ATTEMPTS IN SUICIDE

Suicide may be defined as an act of more or less deliberate self-destruction. Sullivan, in line with accepted psychiatric nomenclature, regarded suicide as an unfortunate eventuality possible in a variety of clinical entities. It is the author's belief that it may also occur as mature behavior. This is exemplified by Socrates' decision to kill himself by taking the hemlock, thus carrying out the sentence of his society rather than taking advantage of the opportunity afforded him by his devoted disciples to escape into exile. However, the term *suicide* is usually not used to imply some heroic act of self-destruction, perpetrated in order to preserve certain values of a situation of greater importance to the suicidal person than the survival of his own life. The previous point is meant only to call attention to the complexity and diversity implicit in the phenomenon of the drive toward self-destruction. It is as impossible to set forth a theory of suicide as it would be to set forth a theory of murder, which in many parts of the world is not an uncommon phenomenon. Murders and suicides are committed by persons for a variety of reasons, and it would be meaningless to attempt to explain this complex diversity by a single theory. Nevertheless, certain generalizations can be made.

It is well recognized that one of the predispositions for suicide that especially concerns the psychiatrist is that caused by the *depressive syndrome,* which may manifest itself in depressive psychosis, manic depressive psychosis,[3] neurotic depressive reaction, or involutional agitated depression. When he has reached this stage, the person has come to be extremely preoccupied with self-depreciating rumination and very restricted in his thought and activity, and yet he communicates in some way his intention to destroy himself.

This syndrome must be differentiated from the less malignant neurotic conditions, which induce grown-up persons childishly and spitefully to threaten to kill themselves, as a kind of emotional blackmail, in order to avoid an unpleasant situation. Such persons can be effectively treated by firm management, as has recently been illustrated by three army psychiatrists [7]. These psychiatrists separated out a group of patients who had either threatened or actually attempted suicide, choosing those showing no evidence of depression or psychotic confusion. These patients were then told that their various demands (for transfer, light duty, discharge, hospitalization) would not be granted. Furthermore they were told that

[3] Recently, several psychiatrists who had been associated with Sullivan and Fromm-Reichmann at Chestnut Lodge described two very interesting research projects on manic depressive psychosis, one of which identified the crucial period for development of the psychosis in the process of interpersonal relationships [1]; the other described the kind of family background and early life experiences found in the manic depressive patient [5].

no one would stop them if they wanted to kill themselves, but such an act, if successful, would be punished by revoking all material benefits to their respective families and, if unsuccessful, would be punished by court martial for all of them. This was told to the patients without any hostility on the part of the psychiatrist, and none of the patients was hospitalized. In the follow-up, it was found that there was only one suicide committed among the 75 suicidal patients.

In a review of the available data on attempted and successful suicides, Dr. James M. A. Weiss [11] demonstrates the usefulness of separating attempted suicides into at least three main groups: aborted successful suicides, true suicidal attempts, and suicidal gestures. Persons in the first group seriously attempt to destroy themselves and would successfully do so if their efforts were not interrupted by a chance event, fortunate medical care, or some ignorance or ineptitude on their part. In contrast to the suicidal gesture, the aborted successful suicide is intended to accomplish the aim of the suicidal person by means of killing himself. This is usually done to hurt someone else, mate, parents, sweetheart, or some other person, as has been noted in psychoanalytic studies on the subject. At the same time, as a number of writers have pointed out, there is included in most suicidal attempts an implicit or overt cry for help, not necessarily correlated with any particular mental state or personality pattern. The suicidal act does shock and arouse the compassionate interest of those who are touched by it, whether it be friends, family, doctor, or strangers; and the foreknowledge of this compassion is an important factor in the patient's drive toward suicide. He knows that, if he lives, he will be hospitalized and some attempt will be made to help him; if he dies, those who witness the tragedy will feel sorry for him.

Persons in the second group (the true suicidal attempt) are not seriously determined to destroy themselves, but they knowingly risk the probability of destruction in a desperate gamble for some stake, hoping to win and live in spite of the danger involved. An example is the case of a woman who tried to commit suicide by turning on the gas, hoping that her husband would arrive home at his usual time. She knowingly risked the danger that he might be delayed and that she might consequently die, but she was desperate to allay his anger, which was quite justified, and to gratify her wish for dependent support.

Persons in the third group (the suicidal gesture) try to avoid any danger in making their gesture, as exemplified by one man who dramatically announced his wish to kill himself and then drank a quantity of colored water out of a bottle labeled "Iodine." This last group seems to be more or less similar to the military patients described previously, who were characterized by the attempted use of blackmail or some other way of influencing others in order to accomplish some conscious evasion or exploitation.

MANAGEMENT OF ATTEMPTED SUICIDES

The suicidal gestures of persons suffering from obsessional neurosis deserve special consideration. Obsessional neurosis, both as symptom neurosis and character neurosis, may not necessarily be part of the depressive syndrome, except that it predisposes to it. Obsessional neurosis predisposes to the depressive syndrome by reason of the illusory type of interpersonal *relation* maintained and the actual interpersonal *distance* maintained, which lead to the consequence of a considerable waste of human life. Marginal insight into this fact may precipitate the depressive syndrome in a person.

In describing his procedure for dealing with the suicidal threats that may occur during the course of psychiatric treatment of a patient with obsessional neurosis, Sullivan had the following to say [10, pp. 257–259]:

> Fear of committing suicide is sometimes one of the really impressive fears or phobias in the presenting picture of an obsessional neurotic. As soon as I have convinced myself that there is a pretty stable obsessional state *rather than an indefinite obsessional schizoid condition,* it is my practice to treat this fear very roughly—to just assume that there is practically no danger. This is partly a derivative of my feeling that to take such a thing seriously is a collaboration in the psychosis, you might say, and that it is never very profitable to give it much respect. . . .

Sullivan did not minimize the danger here but believed that with this, as with other obsessional symptoms, the therapist must be direct and forceful rather than let himself be engaged in a seesaw of obsessional maneuvering and countermaneuvering, at which the patient is more practiced and skilled. In relation to the reactive depression that occurs in a person with obsessional neurosis, Sullivan goes on to say [10, p. 269]:

> So far as suicide in such a situation is concerned, if the environment just gets up and leaves—won't have any—I assume the self-destruction is not likely to occur. Thus when I have encountered vigorous threats of suicide in retaliation for my brutality to obsessional neurotics, I have usually taken these threats as merely an invitation to real brutality. For instance, I have asked such patients to do it somewhere, if possible, where it won't put me to great awkwardness in getting somebody to remove the results.

I can illustrate this point with one of my own cases. A young doctor, found to be suffering from obsessional neurosis, came with a complaint of extreme feelings of apprehension and inadequacy in spite of his brilliant career. In the course of his treatment, he arrived at a point where his quietly grandiose assumptions of special privilege, rationalized by symptoms of fear and tension, were questioned. When he retaliated by threatening to jump out of the fourth-floor window of the office, he was told quite directly that he would get the hell beaten out of him if he made such a mess in front of the office building. This was said to him in a very angry voice, with complete conviction; and the difficult, tedious course of therapy continued without being sidetracked into a discussion about suicide.

Needless to say, diagnostic acumen is a very important factor in the treatment of these patients. Measures as just described cannot always be undertaken safely with obsessional persons who are bordering on a state of schizophrenic psychosis. Before treating them so roughly it must be known with certainty that there is not a schizophrenic element present. The risk of successful suicide in persons with beginning schizophrenia is only second to the risk in those recovering from agitated depressions. Moreover, as Clara Thompson has pointed out in a discussion of Sullivan's attitude,[4] there is often no warning at all of the suicidal drive or attempt in the course of treating patients with beginning schizophrenia.

Of course, Sullivan was not insensitive to the genuine pain, despair, and danger experienced by obsessional persons. On this point he wrote [10, p. 269]:

> When a person is attached to unreal love objects and denies the possibility of anything actually available ever equaling these objects or making up for them, I can conceive that he might feel, "What difference does it make whether I kill myself or not?" . . . but I do not think that it is usually the origin of statements about suicide made by obsessional neurotics.

In contrast with Sullivan's approach to the danger of suicide in the obsessional neurotic, his approach to this problem in the manic depressive and persons with other depressive psychoses was made very gingerly. He geared his approach to his notion of the dynamisms and appropriate therapeutic interventions for the particular states. He saw the depressive person as a very destructive force, and he wrote as follows [10, p. 297]:

> Although I have not been able to document my observations to any extent, an equally important surmise I would make is that other people must *suffer* from the depression. . . . As I have said before, very little goes on in the depressives; and

[4] Personal communication with the author.

whatever does go on is not responsive to any intelligent approach on the part of the psychiatrist to find out who is the target of his destructiveness, for all that is outside the patient's awareness. Yet all my observations indicate quite conclusively that the depressive always hits the target and usually does this, unhappily, by self-destruction . . . *that a particular person who was a destructive influence in the patient's past is the target of the patient's self-destruction. The intention is that the person shall suffer the rest of his life because the patient has destroyed himself.*

The seriously depressed patient requires hospitalization and protection from himself until he can become a viable prospect for psychotherapeutic intervention. The point at which he can be considered amenable, however, is difficult to ascertain exactly. It occurs as a working relationship is experienced with the patient, in which explanatory interpretations by the psychiatrist and responses on the part of the patient are felt meaningfully by the patient. That is to say, it occurs when greater clarity and productivity of participation in this exploratory relationship has been achieved on both sides. Improved activity and social appearance of the patient usually come about, but although these are valuable indices of progress, they are insufficient in themselves and custodial protection may continue to be necessary. The period of custodial protection can be shortened by various forms of physiological and chemical treatment, though some of these methods have serious disadvantages. It must be borne in mind, once psychotherapy *is* started, that it is very important to judge the transition point very critically, because during the early stages of recovery, as is well known, the risk of successful suicide is greatest.

Sullivan was pessimistic about the possibility of successfully initiating psychotherapy with very depressed patients, and especially with those diagnosed as manic depressive psychotics. This pessimism was based on his own personal, self-confessed difficulty in reaching the self of these patients and understanding the psychogenesis of their psychoses. On this point, he said [10, pp. 301, 303]:

> In the agitated depression I cannot get anywhere near either the self or whatever threatens the self, because of the impregnably depressive content. . . . I must simply accept the fact that the manic-depressive remains a mystery to me. . . . That does not mean I value them less as examples of human beings or as less important tributaries to the sum total of our knowledge of the governing limitations of human personality—which are insignificant compared with the magnificent possibilities of human personality. It means merely that I have discovered, from previous tests of myself as an investigative instrument, my own limitations for learning something about my fellows.

In this connection, it is interesting to note Sullivan's observations that even psychiatrists, if they are manic depressive, who may have many years of training and successfully go through a prolonged course of psychoanalysis, will still commit suicide subsequently, though usually not until they have had treatment with a colleague and arranged the suicide so that that colleague will presumably suffer from the event.

Frieda Fromm-Reichmann, a colleague and close friend of Sullivan for many years, was more optimistic about reaching depressed persons. In regard to these patients, she said [4, pp. 198 ff.]:

> These hostile impulses are frequently within the patient's awareness, as in the case of the depressed patient who said to his psychiatrist that he would have liked to kill himself if only he could have been sure that it would matter to the doctor.

Fromm-Reichmann stresses the importance of inquiring into the unhappiness, despair, and hopelessness of these patients, along with the attempt to bring into their awareness the destructive tendencies they harbored against others. She warns the psychiatrist here to pay close attention to his own attitudes and to the stake of prestige in the patient's survival and urges him to remind the patient that no other person, not even the psychiatrist, can carry the total burden of responsibility for the self-induced death of a patient. She also advises the psychiatrist to point out, early in the course of treatment, the wasteful futility of beginning any psychiatric therapy with the reservation of an escape into suicide. Naturally, she cautions, the psychiatrist should *not* share with his patients the conventional prejudice that merely thinking of suicide, or contemplating the act, is a shameful, reprehensible thing in itself.

THE CASE OF MR. A. S.

This brings us to a consideration of the patient under discussion. A. S. is a dutiful mama's boy, disappointed with himself and his father and trying hard to live up to his mother's ambitions and exaggerated expectations. Having become infantilized by this possessive controlling woman, he tried to be important through his identification with her and her ideal. He was raised by her under such powerful controls that she never even needed to threaten physical punishment in order to maintain discipline.

Whatever of the boy's self-esteem survived the subtle strangulation by his mother seemed to have found some expression in fist fights with his peers and in some rather warm, though not highly esteemed, shared experiences with his father. During his adolescence, he continually tried to achieve self-esteem by going out only with the most popular girls and refusing to be interested in any others, by jealously craving what others had, and by thinking of himself as belonging only in the top echelon of his classes at school.

A. S. was fortunate in meeting a girl of ambiguous social position, who was probably much more appreciative of his attentions than some of the other girls he might have dated. In this relationship, he was possibly as close as he ever came to really being capable of loving anyone. He was able to have successful sexual intercourse with this girl and even to plan on marriage. However, he must have known all the time that his mother would fight this, which, of course, she did.

Following this episode, the long-postponed struggle for independence and affirmation against his mother began, but he was no match for it, although he tried. He quit school and joined the army, but the relation to his parents remained the same; he thought about eloping with the girl but was over-whelmed by his old infantile feelings of futility and helplessness ("a doomed feeling"). He achieved status and authority in the army but could never muster up courage to stand up to his parents. He fell in love with another girl whose family wanted to adopt him; but a few weeks after he was home for a visit, this shallow relationship was disrupted by the old struggle: blame for his parents and himself, a feeling of smallness and inferiority, and increasing anxiety.

Then A. S. tried desperately to destroy his infantile ties to his mother by running away to a foreign country, and this attempt, of course, also failed. He wanted desperately to free himself but was helpless to know what to free himself for. He craved "understanding" from home (mother), but he grew increasingly helpless, moneyless, and depressed (depletion and impoverishment).

The hostility of A. S. toward his mother is clear from his history; so are his fear and dependency. The sense of infantile hunger emergency that Rado described might be expressed in this case by the patient's wish for a malted milk, which he credited with saving his life. His was not merely a suicidal gesture: it was a serious attempt at suicide, although fortunately aborted.

The case of A. S. brings to mind a similar case, that of a Negro patient with a similar history, who did succeed in committing suicide and who was seen by the writer for a short period before the unfortunate event. This man had a long history of lonely, dutiful submission to a detached, cold, demanding mother and later to a rigid, dominating wife. The referral was made by his internist because of his overt feelings of depression and apprehension that followed a subtotal gastric resection for a severe ulcer.

In the course of treatment, the patient realized that this depressive feeling dated back to a much earlier time in his life than he had been aware. However, he also complained frequently of being constantly taken advantage of by his employers. Gradually, it became evident that the patient was overwhelmingly burdening himself with the very work he was complaining of and was practically inviting the exploitation that he was suffering. Subsequently, the patient found, to his surprise, that he could turn over much of his work to assistants, secretaries, and others, with the complete approval of his employer. He seemed to improve, but unfortunately at this stage the treatment was interrupted by illness of the psychiatrist. After the therapist's recovery, the patient did nothing to resume treatment, though he complained to his family physician about feeling dizzy and confused. He did not speak of suicide then; neither had he threatened suicide at any time during the course of his treatment. One morning he simply shot himself in the head. In reviewing the case it seemed possible that the patient's success in freeing himself from the boss's domination and exploitation might have confronted him with his own humiliating dependency cravings and destructive rage. In addition, the burden of responsibility for his isolation from his peers and his family gained during the course of treatment must have become intolerable in the face of the temporary insecurity and disappointment with his psychiatrist. The early oral cravings, similar to those described by Rado, may have played some part in bringing on the patient's ulcer. His wife later reported that the patient had been so withdrawn from her and her family for so many years and so vain and demanding that, although she was upset over the tragedy, she could not grieve for him. Instead, she felt hurt and angry (justifiably so) at this last display of the petty rage that had so frequently burdened their relationship. She added that before the suicide she had been afraid to get in touch with the psychiatrist (myself) because of her husband's severe agitation over anything that might have been construed as interference on her part with anything that he was interested in. She revealed that the patient had openly despised his own father for his weakness and dependency and said on several occasions that he would shoot himself if he ever became like his father.

The passive oral trends of both this patient and A. S. are in line with the psychodynamics described by Freud, Fenichel, Menninger, Rado, and other psychoanalysts. In my opinion, Rado's formulation, more than that of any of the others, would be more nearly compatible, although not entirely so, with what Sullivan might have formulated about A. S. However, rather than speculations about Sullivan's thinking, what follows are my own impressions of the case.

First of all, by calling A. S. *passive,* it is not meant that he was a soft, weak person, unable to do anything for himself. As a matter of fact, among other things, this boy fought other boys; he strove after the most popular and attractive girls in school; he courted a girl of his own choice more or less successfully; and he was an aggressive executive, noncommissioned officer in the army. His passivity lay in the crucial relationship with his mother, wherein he and she were so integrated that the relationship was dominated overwhelmingly by her need to be exclusively necessary to his well-being and existence, to live vicariously through him, and to maintain the integration of the mother–infant son relationship into his chronologically adult life.

This aspect of the mother's personality was manifested by her behavior on visiting A. S. in the hospital.

In using the word *oral* (with regard to the trend of this patient), no mechanisms like fixation or regression of libido were meant. This boy was able to have sexual intercourse, but he was not able to develop any sense of worth as a person in his own right. He was as dependent on others for his self-regard as a baby is for the food that is given him. This factor of utter dependency was maintained in the pathological relationship he had with his mother, and this is the problem that would have to be faced in the course of any therapeutic intervention.

THERAPEUTIC IMPLICATIONS

This patient would probably need to maintain a testing relationship with his therapist for a very long time before he would really dare to try to relish his own powers and capacities for living and loving. In the course of this development, he might repeatedly try to imitate his therapist, to imagine himself to be the person his therapist is, and to worship him; all this as a kind of substitution for developing regard for his own powers and capabilities. The effort to imitate his therapist might also be necessary as a compensation for the deficiency in his identification with his father, and hence it might have a kind of educative function in his maturation. However, even this early stage of development in the psychotherapeutic treatment may take a long time in coming to clear confrontation.

In summing up, the treatment of A. S. should be aimed at first establishing a working relationship with him; he has to recover enough from his depression to be responsive to his psychiatrist's efforts to help him collaborate in the treatment. In this collaboration, he may at first erroneously think that he is finding the "understanding," the "magical breast." However, this transference can help prepare the way for a real understanding and insight into his relationship with his parents and with other significant persons in his life.

In the collaborative participation-observation with the psychiatrist, he can mobilize his resources, which are actually more than adequate, for living a fuller life at a more mature level of interpersonal relationships. Hence, rather than despising his own "small" efforts and looking for illusory or narcissistic esteem by dependency on his mother and identification with her, with the select group, the most popular girls, and so on, he can achieve real ego strength. This strength will come from the recognition of his limitations, his dissociated infantile conflicts, and the true nature of the enduring relationships that he has participated in throughout his life. Also, in the collaboration, the psychiatrist can share in the patient's feelings of loneliness and despair without confirming his hopelessness and without colluding in his magical expectations. The prognosis, however, must remain guarded, for the danger of suicide can only be minimized by the above-stated precautions. Indeed, the prognosis with all suicidal cases must remain guarded until the crucial point is reached in which the insights gained in therapy are worked through and integrated by the patient so he can achieve fulfillment in his daily living.

References

1. Cohen, M., G. Baker, R. A. Cohen, F. Fromm-Reichmann, and E. V. Weigert: An intensive study of twelve cases of manic-depressive psychosis, *Psychiatry,* 17: 103–137, 1954.
2. Freud, S.: *Beyond the Pleasure Principle,* London: Hogarth Press, Ltd., 1950.
3. Freud, S.: Mourning and melancholia, in *Collected Papers,* London: Hogarth Press, Ltd., 1925, vol. 4.
4. Fromm-Reichmann, F.: *Principles of Intensive Psychotherapy,* Chicago: University of Chicago Press, 1950.
5. Gibson, R. W.: The family background and early life experience of the manic-depressive patient, *Psychiatry,* 21: 71–90, 1958.
6. Menninger, K. A.: *Man Against Himself,* New York: Harcourt, Brace and Company, Inc., 1938.
7. Offencrantz, W., E. Church, and R. Elliott: Psychiatric treatment of suicide problems in the military service, *American Journal of Psychiatry,* 114: 33–41, 1957.
8. Rado, S.: Hedonic control, action-self, and the depressive spell, in P. E. Hoch and J. Zubin (Eds.), *Depression,* New York: W. W. Norton & Company, Inc., 1956.
9. Sullivan, H. S.: *Interpersonal Theory of Psychiatry,* New York: W. W. Norton & Company, Inc., 1953.
10. Sullivan, H. S.: *Clinical Studies in Psychiatry,* New York: W. W. Norton & Company, Inc., 1956.
11. Weiss, J. M. A.: The gamble with death in attempted suicide, *Psychiatry,* 20: 17–25, 1957.

17

Suicide: The Horney Point of View

LOUIS E. DE ROSIS

Doctor De Rosis was born in 1917, and received his M.D. degree from the State University of New York College of Medicine (formerly the Long Island College of Medicine) in 1942. He is a Diplomate of the American Board of Psychiatry and Neurology, a charter Fellow of the Academy of Psychoanalysis, a member of the American Psychiatric Association, treasurer of the Association for the Advancement of Psychoanalysis, president of the Association of Medical Group Psychoanalysis, and a member of the editorial board of the *American Journal of Psychoanalysis*. He began his psychiatric training at Brooklyn State Hospital and attained the position of acting supervising psychiatrist. He received further training at the New York State Psychiatric Institute and the American Institute for Psychoanalysis. He lectured at the State University College of Medicine from 1947 to 1950, and was an associate in psychiatry at the Kings County Hospital and psychiatrist at the Brooklyn and Long Island College Hospital Clinics. He is presently teaching at the American Institute for Psychoanalysis. His publications include articles on group psychoanalysis and the therapeutic process.

In its most comprehensive sense, neurosis, which includes most suicides, represents a failure in social as well as in individual growth. In its most particular sense, suicide, from the Horney point of view, represents a failure of development of the self. Nowadays no one disputes the fact that "No man is an island entire unto himself." In truth, he cannot be an island because his growth requires many hands and many hearts. Human growth is the outcome of an exquisitely continuous integration of so extensive, so intricate, and so delicate an array of processes that it strikes us as marvelous and at the same time fills us with deep reassurance. It is marvelous that it has come to pass at all.

Ordinarily we take the term *suicide* to mean the total self-destruction of the individual. Statistics tabulate only obvious and violent suicides. Actually, these are quite few compared with the numbers of persons who live out their full span and never experience the growth that results from an outwardly extending inner development. These, perhaps, should also be considered suicides, though they are much more insidious forms. For example, severely psychotic persons, with the least development of self, are the nearest to being the living dead. The chronic alcoholic who dies of cirrhosis of the liver and the drug addict who dies of septicemia might be considered similarly. No one labels it suicide if an accident-prone person has died of an accident, but how much of accident-proneness actually represents an incomplete development of self growth and thus, intrinsically, a suicide?

According to Horney, man is not born with innate destructive tendencies as Freudian and other doctrines (notion of original sin) specify. This is a confusion that probably stems from the biological-physiological processes of anabolism-catabolism and the attempt to analogize on the basis of these. The validity of the analogy is yet to be conclusively demonstrated. A similar confusion has been introduced from Darwin's theory, the survival of the fittest. I believe that this notion was transplanted into the theory of social development in such a way as to rationalize and justify ruthless competitiveness and man's brutality toward man as not only desirable but essential. In other words, if man cannot succeed, then he must capitulate to others and depend on them for his survival.

To discuss suicide from the Horney point of view, one must consider the development of neurosis, for the two spring from the same sources. As a beginning, it is helpful to consider the similarities appearing between certain cultural patterns that culminate in suicide and certain neurotically held patterns that also culminate in suicide. If the self had obtained a central position within a given culture, then it would follow that such a practice as, for example, suttee would not have been permitted in India. It would also follow that the Japanese could not favor hara-kiri or espouse the *kamikaze* practice of World War II. In these societies, the self is considered to be an adjunct to, and subordinated to, the cultural standards and other deeply rooted systems of tradition. In nondemocratic cultures and nondemocratic religious sects an individual is regarded as an agent of some greater power than his own self. This dependency requires of him a constant attentiveness to the outer world, so he becomes inordinately attuned to it. This subordinated self resembles what we observe in the neurotic person who has come to experience himself merely as an instrumentality dependent on the play of outer forces for his movement and control.

In this connection it is significant to note that various religions (Catholicism, etc.) as well as other systematized orders (British government) have made it a sin or crime to commit suicide. But this is of dubious meaning when seen from the viewpoint of self-growth. In England, a citizen is the property of the state; therefore, if one destroys himself he is depriving the king. In the Catholic system, the adherent is a soldier of Christ who is forever in its service. It is therefore a disservice to God to leave it until He permits its occurrence. The notion of the self as being primarily responsible to itself and for itself has no place in any of these systems. But clearly in this sort of an organization a person who conformed would be deterred from suicide until he was "ordered" by his king or taken by his God. Since the Catholic position enjoins the penalty of excommunication for suicide, the bargain is eternal damnation for the sake of temporary relief. The suicide rate is quite low among confirmed Catholics. A desirable goal is achieved by a means that leaves much to be explored in terms of the implications for the development of the self.

According to the Horney theory, neurotic dependency has its beginnings in the infant. This form of dependency is to be clearly distinguished from the natural dependency that characterizes the optimal relationship between the mother and her child, in which the relationship produces increasing areas of mutually stimulating and satisfying contact. The differentiation of a self in the infant is an expression of this kind of a relationship between the abundant mother and the belonging child. When, however, the mother is anxiety-ridden, she becomes a power over him instead of a partner with him. Because of her own insecurities she provides him with attitudes of anxiety, patterns of contradiction, lack of interest, out-and-out neglect, and a lack of sensitivity to his own individual needs. The infant then grows up regarding himself as a combination of plaything, invalid, and a kind of stuffing box into which things are poured and to which things are done. This is a most insidious initial impairment because it is so often regarded by our culture as the thing to do. However, the variations in these unconscious attitudes are as numerous as the number of parents involved.

What Horney found was that these attitudes on the part of the parents toward the offspring sooner or later induced, in varying degrees, a process which she called *basic anxiety*. This process is the outgrowth of the child's attempt to create some consistent position for himself. In constantly attuning himself to his parents, he becomes *outer-oriented* instead of *self-oriented*. These forms of outer-orientation eventually appear as patterns of authoritarianism, self-abnegation, or resignation. The beginning of these can be seen in the phases of neurotic development to be described below.

In one of the early phases of neurotic growth, if the child is successful in overcoming his feelings of anxiety, he begins to feel superior. He usually is unconscious of these feelings of superiority unless the parents inadvertently ally themselves with them in such a way that the child can then dare to raise them to his awareness. This, in turn, can be even more devastating, for the child entrenches his superiority feeling by making it an overt operating procedure.

Another phase of neurotic growth occurs if contradictory demands are constantly made upon the child. These generate anxiety that the child may master by learning to juggle the demands so he can satisfy them all. If he is successful, he may develop further superior feelings. If not, he finds himself constantly with the feeling of being torn within himself. These children frequently experience nightmares. Epilepsy may intervene, and other symptoms will become manifest, depending on these conflicts.

The next phase occurs when the child organizes and embellishes his feelings of superiority with all kinds of powers. This happens largely in fantasy, though it sometimes occurs with deeds as well. This is the final phase, the formation of the *idealized self,* in which the person has formalized his concepts of himself and which he now also expects others to recognize. When he lives up to his own self picture, he feels just fine. The extreme of such a state is found in the manic psychotic.

By the time anyone comes to this stage of development he has drifted far away from the development of the self. This general separatedness, this disparity between the development of the idealized self and the now more or less undeveloped real self, Horney called the *alienation of the self.* This alienation is extremely important in connection with suicide. In graphic terms it is like a no man's land where events can happen in isolation that can determine the course of the entire struggle. A sudden impulse of self-hatred in a framework of severe alienation can contribute markedly to the outcome of suicide. It is as if the self-protecting patrols are too scattered in the field to prevent a small but intense spark of self-hatred from igniting the whole ammunition supply, which then destroys everything. What we are conveying here is the shift in the balance of power in what Horney calls "the cruel and murderous battle."

The question may arise: Why do feelings of self-hatred appear in a person who is living on the basis of idealized, self-glorifying operations? The answer is that self-hatred is developed as a strategem on the part of the idealized self in order to effect its own ends in as immediate and direct a way as possible. "When trying to account for its (hatred) depth, we must realize the rage of the proud self (idealized self) for feeling humiliated and held down at every step by the (actual) self" [1]. Horney emphasized the fact that, in the end, the idealized or glorified self is still dependent on the self for its maintenance and support. She quotes one of her patients as saying, "The only difficulty I have is reality." The patient who said this came close to partial self-destruction when she had a sudden impulse to gouge out her eyes. The woman had made a premature connection with the fact that what she was doing was not only doomed to failure but absolutely ludicrous as well. Her hatred of herself was intense. Convinced that what she could not see could not hurt her, she directed her assault upon her eyes.

Many phobias may be understood as a flaring up of self-hatred, which then serves various functions. It was noted previously that self-hatred is a strategem as well as a means of punishment. The idealized self uses it as a strategem both to intimidate the self into carrying out its ends at almost any cost and to keep itself from being subjected to renewed evidences of its inadequacy. This it does by threatening the self with hate and with destruction. A patient who worked in a brewery had to quit his job because of intense fears. Actually, he had suffered a severe dressing down, which he had no way of avenging. The phobia then provided him with a way of getting out of the job and, incidentally, of staying alive.

Sometimes, however, if the intensity (and vindictiveness) of the self-hatred is great and the possibility of its discharge nonexistent, and if the person has an extensive alienation from his self, suicide can ensue, sometimes by design, sometimes by accident. One patient in a fit of panic drove his fist through a pane of glass and severed his radial artery, so he almost bled to death. Another patient kicked at his reflection in a mirror and knocked the whole thing on his head, causing himself severe cuts and contusions. Another drove his car into a tree, too late to stop it when some awareness of his actions came into being. In the phobias the self saves itself by avoiding those areas where the idealized self might be reminded of its defects.

A word might be said in connection with vindictiveness. Here Horney's theory illustrates another phase of neurotic development, which is in a certain sense the counterpart of the glorified or idealized self. This is called the *despised* or *hated self*. In its purest form, it is met with in psychotic patients such as the patient who burned his arm in hot water because this was the hand with which he had sullied the idealized self by masturbating. In other ways, the hated self is important in certain phases of suicide, in that the hatred is not limited to a single part but is extended to the whole physical self, so total destruction is the outcome. In the novel by Oscar Wilde, *The Picture of Dorian Gray,* the author describes what is actually the battle between the glorified and the despised selves. The hero stabs at the portrait, as if wanting to destroy his connection with mortality (his humanness) as well as with his despised self. Similarly, certain patients complain of being eternally bored. But if one looks underneath, one finds in them a seething cauldron of hate, hate at the world for not recognizing them as well as hate at the self for not getting them this recognition. In therapy, this may appear in the form of hate for the doctor for not giving them fast and painless answers for their "problems." Such problems may range from getting them a husband with certain qualifications to guaranteeing them that they will never experience feelings of unreality or of anxiety again. What the patient is really demanding is that the doctor relieve the prized idealized self of any indignities or evidences of inadequacies. Thus, the female patient will deplore not being married by the time she is thirty, and the male patient will bewail his lack of achievement. Homosexual patients fear losing their partners. It is a fairly common occurrence in our culture for the remaining partner in such a relationship to follow suit in the event of the other's death. The suicide is caused by the resurgence of deep feelings of self-hatred, which could be kept in check only as long as the other partner was available to fill the gaps within his own being. The person in question could know himself only as the agent of an outer relatedness with his partner; all else had no meaning for him.

Horney would also classify many feats of daring and heroism under the heading of unconscious self-destructive moves. In these cases it is as if the idealized self, unbelieving of its mortality, toys with the self, disporting as one would with an object. The idealized self enjoys the spectacle of suspense and danger that the poor self goes through as it tries to respond to inordinate demands. These patients feel that unless the self and others are exposed to daredevil escapades and thrills, life is meaningless. An engineer patient with numerous phobias, who had mentioned suicide often, extolled the courage of the man who had killed himself while playing Russian roulette. His feeling was that, if he could be as brave as this man, he would no longer have to be an analytic patient. This kind of development occurs in those persons whose lives have become increasingly boring and empty.

In her penetrating article, "A Psychoanalytic Understanding of Suicide," Elizabeth Kilpatrick [4] postulates that there are three main underlying factors that prompt the suicidal act. These are hopelessness, alienation, and suffering. I agree that all these factors do operate in all suicides, and I add one or more additional factors to be considered. One is the concept Horney postulated, the *search for glory,* a concept I believe to be one of the most important of the factors described by Dr. Kilpatrick. The search for glory is diametrically opposed to the development of the self. The emphasis in our culture of "what's in it for me" usually means "what is in this or that which can further my cause toward glory?" Its relationship to previously discussed material is seen in the fact that boredom is quickly experienced by such persons when nothing is happening to gratify this search for glory, and thrill seeking may be resorted to in order to obtain a feeling of high excitement and feed the glory-seeking self. It might be speculated that much of the abracadabra of certain religious and political organizations owe their appeal to this same search for glory, in which their activity is made to pass for reality. Intriguing as these notions might be, they are beyond the scope of this presentation, except to suggest my feeling that this search for glory probably lies at the basis of many of the social ills that beset man today.

Another factor that makes the search for glory pertinent in the consideration of suicide is that suicide often results when the individual sets out on this search alone and ends up foiled and frustrated. One is impressed by the solitary quality of persons who have committed suicide. It seems significant that persons who band together to make the achievement of glory a common goal are less likely to commit suicide when the project fails. And suicide is seldom heard of among persons who have attached their dream of glory to a larger one, such as a supernatural one. There is fresh strength to be found from the fact of persons being together, even though the new strength is marshalled for a renewed effort toward the glorious but false heights.

Another form of suicide occurs in which, as the idealized self drifts more and more away from reality and the self and experiences in ever-increasing amounts its frustration and hate, it comes to invest the self with ugliness and slothfulness. It is a form of slow suicide in which the self is subjected to all the indignities imaginable in a slow, grinding, and implacable manner. Some of these people are found in the Bowery, or anywhere bums are located. They let themselves become literally lousy and usually are soaked in alcohol. The alcohol also has a narcotizing effect, but the narcotization is made necessary by the inner self-destruction, which would otherwise find no mitigation.

Sometimes we find a curious contradiction in these persons. They show a mixture of what is obvious deterioration and self-neglect, and at the same time they appear, at least on the surface, quite cheerful. What we might be witnessing here is a dual development. The idealized self is dragging down the self and deriving some vindictive pleasure from the process at the same time. An example comes to mind of one such patient who was very obese. He would eat everything in sight, partly because it allayed his yawning feelings of emptiness; but largely he would eat like the court buffoon who was required to eat by the king even though he were to become nauseated. He dared not regurgitate, for it would bring on even more painful feelings of self-hate. As his analysis got under way, he left his homosexual partner with whom he had conducted a relationship in which some kind of self-preservation had been possible. He moved down to the Bowery and lived in isolation in a flop house. He gradually became more and more inaccessible in the sessions. Shortly, I was told that the patient was at the hospital, having attempted suicide by cutting his wrists. Subsequent follow-through revealed that the patient had had a flash of awareness just prior to the suicidal act in which he had seen himself undergoing what he himself had labeled a cynical deterioration. Unfortunately, this awareness was a premature one. These are some of the dangers to be guarded against in analyzing a patient. The patient had used this piece of awareness against his self rather than in behalf of it. He had heaped new insult upon himself. The suicidal act was the outcome of a sudden flash of rage against himself. In fact, as soon as he had done it, the patient, on seeing, as he said, "the flowing of the redness," was recalled to his senses and at once took the necessary steps to stop the bleeding and took himself to the hospital for treatment. This event marked a turning point in his growth, for the "flowing of the redness" symbol of living never left him again.

The patient in this case, A. S., draws our attention to another form of self-destruction that merits mention. It is important because it is both unobtrusive and widespread. Horney found that a person can "silently but actively collaborate toward his own moral deterioration." It stems partly out of the general widening of the rift between the idealized self and the self (alienation), but it is also coupled with an active interest within that person that is set against integrity. Integrity comes to be looked upon as an expression of weakness, a stupid self-presentation that lays one open to attack and ridicule. Cynicism is a quality to be cultivated. Some patients, if they could put their feelings into print, would, indeed, make Machiavelli appear a rank amateur. The chief difficulty arises because the object of their cynicism is not the outer world but their own selves. It is bad enough if the self is made to suffer incidentally to all the neurotic processes described, but it is far more crippling if the self becomes the target for the output of cynical distortion and devaluation.

To this point we have described two of the main forms of relatedness of this outer orientation to life, i.e., the despotic or authoritarian, which includes aggressiveness, and the self-abnegating. Horney also described a third mode of relating, which she called the *resigned orientation.* These persons deny the self, and the very process becomes a way of living with which these persons present themselves to the outer world. These persons cannot endure expressions of any feelings, for this gives the lie to the pervasive muting of their being. They have no goal except to shrink the self with increasing effectiveness until it is snuffed out of existence altogether. These extreme forms of resignation occur in the schizophrenic who sinks himself into catatonia.

It is understandable that of the three chief orientations to life that replace selfness, that is, the aggressive, the self-abnegating, and the resigned, it is predominantly the first, the aggressive, that takes the active step toward self-destruction. When the self-abnegator dies, it is because he neglects himself in his need to inflate others, through which he expects to survive and even to glory; the resigned person, as in the case of the catatonic and in the case of various psychosomatic syndromes, dies because of inaction, by default as it were, rather than by action.

Parenthetically, it can be shown that in history, active suicide has been significant in those cultures where importance was placed on the pursuit of power over others, possessiveness, or prestige. The neurotic development has a field day when there is sanction, perhaps even by law, of any of these drives. Mass suicides have occurred since time immemorial in both Western and Eastern cultures under the sanction of culture and law, and legalized homicides found in certain Western cultures today are, I believe, the outcome of similar drives rationalized in the dress of certain philosophies—philosophies that are now given precedence over life itself.

The question may be posed whether suicide is ever justified. A well-developing self seldom, if ever, has recourse to suicide as a solution for its continuity. However, it has been argued that under certain conditions of extreme privation and suffering, when the outcome is hopeless, a person may choose the solution for himself as the final act of his own choice. I feel that, in the same way a person takes many kinds of steps to protect his self, a hopelessly suffering person may take such a step as suicide as a final act of self-defense. It is well known how unmitigated suffering can disintegrate the self, and it is the preservation of the self that is the aim of the person who elects suicide at these times. But here again, many important questions are introduced that are not within the scope of this paper to discuss.

In her previously quoted paper, Dr. Kilpatrick also writes concerning security versus pseudosecurity. She contrasts (p. 14): ". . . the individual who is able to accept the exigencies of life with those of the individual who feels overwhelmed by unsurmountable difficulties. The former has a strong incentive for living and for creative growth. . . . Life is full of possibilities to the end." On the other hand, ". . . the neurotic person feels that this is a hostile world. . . . Such an individual, permanently anxious, tense and beaten, and to whom every new situation is a threat, will easily relinquish his hold on life." The suicide of the person whose hold on life is very tenuous is to be sharply distinguished from the rare suicide of the person who elects to terminate his own being. In the latter instance, the person who elects this course of action does so out of a full sense of responsibility and not out of a yawning feeling of endless angry futility. The "incentive for living and creative growth" is a characteristic that we believe to be the sole and exclusive attribute of a well-developing self. Dr. Kilpatrick alludes to such qualities as wholeheartedness and, by implication, to "openness." All these define the firm, well-rooted development of the self from infancy to senescence.

We have outlined briefly some of the major neurotic factors that Horney found related to the problem of suicide, those leading directly to the act as well as those less noticeable and perhaps even more important.

THE CASE OF MR. A. S.

A. S.'s self-growth was severely crippled under the influence of his particular parents. Of course, this influence, in and of itself, does not account for the path his over-all development has taken. Attempts are often made to account for the entire span of a person's life by explaining his present dilemmas with references either to genetic theory, to instinct theory, or to a theory in which the determining parent-child relationship is felt to continue the same throughout life. These theories, however, omit the new self that is constantly growing, acting and reacting in its own behalf, no matter how outwardly imperceptible this process may be. We feel that no amount of understanding, let alone treatment of a patient, could have meaning or feasibility without attention to the constantly emerging self.

The mother of A. S. was especially important in his life. The beginnings of the development of A. S.'s self were strongly affected by this mother, who was herself driven by diverse and opposed needs. She viewed herself as suffering, patient, community-minded, and self-sacrificing. She had suffered at the hands of a husband who had not produced so she had had to take on his share of the burden. It is a fair surmise that she unconsciously sought and married such an ineffective man. As a result, she developed inner conflicts with deep feelings of frustration and resentment. Her thwarted ambitiousness found some outlet through her children, a characteristic of many parents who live vicariously through their children. She needed to mold A. S. into a pattern that would be sure to succeed so he could acquit himself better than she had. "My mother looked at my report card that day when I came home and she started to *cry*. Things would upset her very easily but she never would punish us. She would tell us it would *worry* her if we did something bad." This sounds innocuous enough. Is it not natural for a parent to be worried if her children do poorly at school? But this "worrying" will have a different meaning for a child who can only interpret it as another shortcoming in the eyes of his parent.

A. S.'s mother makes the relationship even more difficult by not using punishment, so she leaves him with no way of getting relief from his feelings of guilt and no way of redeeming himself in the eyes of his mother. Let it be clearly understood, punishment is not being advocated; but structure and discipline for the *child's* sake are important conditions in a child's growth.

A.S.'s self was so unformed, "almost no pressure" was required before he would surrender his own remaining wishes. "We were very pleased with him because he was very obedient and did whatever we thought was right, even though we had to exert almost no pressure on him to do so." Show us a child who is always obedient, and we will see a child who has traveled a long way from his center, from selfhood. Of course, disobedience per se is not evidence of self-development. However, disobedience can be a sign of resistance offered by a remaining core of self to the irrational, unfeeling, ego-centered demands of a parent. In due time, the mother had the pleasure of seeing in her son the outcome of her unconscious moldings, though she would insist he is the product of his own self-creation. An example of the mother's unwitting crushing of A. S.'s self occurs in connection with his affair with the South American girl, Mary. "I said no because I felt that he was too young and there was a difference in the pattern of living." This "difference" in the "pattern of living" is all she needed to feel justified in abrogating whatever vestige of "rights" A. S. might still have reserved for himself. However, she blithely overlooks this by her feeling ". . . that that affair might be at the root of the trouble," thereby disavowing any responsibility for her son's suicidal attempt. If A. S. had been able to develop enough self-assertiveness, he probably would not have had to resort to suicide in order to resolve his dilemma. When a patient is in a position to exact demands, he will not, in all likelihood, attempt suicide. If someone does succeed in crushing this outlet for feelings of self-denigration, then the chances of suicidal outcome are greatly increased.

Fortunately, A. S.'s spirit was not wholly crushed in childhood. If it had been, he could not, paradoxically enough, have developed to the extent that makes suicide possible. Evidence for A. S.'s spirit can be seen in his need constantly to fight. "I don't know why it was, but I was always fighting. *I just had to.*" At the age of nine years, he was still fighting to maintain some ownership of inner feelings of self. What he sought was self-affirmation, but, unfortunately, all he could receive from his parents was whatever was in keeping with their notion as to what a proper boy *should* be like. Additional evidence that A. S. was still out for self-growth (however distorted it was becoming) can be seen in his interest in "the underdog." A. S. was actually trying to acquire additional strength by belonging to a minority, feeling that he would be able to fight for them and therefore for himself. This gave him some outlet for his self-assertiveness by keeping it within the framework of the right and good.

There is a pathetic allusion to his inner feelings of smallness when he says, "When I was a kid, I didn't mind that I was so small." Of course, A. S. could not know that his smallness, while it may have been a physical fact of his existence, had also become a catchall for his *feelings* of smallness. Actually, he was *feeling the paucity of inner growth.* The only time we have some evidence of a remotely pertinent interest in his personal being on the part of his mother occurs when she remarks, "I don't know if it was respect or *what*" (that prompted her children to obedience). But it is a passing doubt, for she could not take an interest in her son's self when she lacked the same interest for her self.

The father seems the least important figure in the family constellation. The patient presents him as a person who just loved to wash a new car and who constantly "went along" with the mother. He seems to be a simple person, given to little involvement with others, which apparently included his own family. However, if there are any vestiges of some warm feelings within the family, they came from him. These were in evidence with the purchase of the bicycle, which he allowed A. S. to ride even though the hour was late. Beyond this, the father seems to have exerted little influence in the development of A. S., other than perhaps by default.

It will be recalled how A. S. felt after he had received movie money from his father. He was unable to make use of it because he had gotten the money by crying. Such a maneuver seemed like a failure to his idealized self because it made him feel dishonest, and his guilt feelings were the result of his going back on his picture of himself as honest. He then punishes himself by depriving himself of the movie. In this way he restores himself in his father's eyes, but, more importantly, he effects an inner restoration. It will be recalled how much A. S. regarded himself as a fighter. It is contemptible if a fighter cries. What is more important to us is that the crying might well have been an expression of spontaneity of feeling. However, linked as it was with feelings of contempt, this spontaneity within his self is discredited. Without spontaneity of expression, the self is deprived of one of its most important avenues of growth. By self-denial, he is able to come to terms with his idealized self but only at the cost of impoverishing himself. Thus, the way toward suicide is already being developed, for suicide is the final act of self-denial.

When A. S. was asked for the reasons for the suicide attempt, he could not give a direct answer. Instead, he talked about his love affair with Mary. A. S. was not at all aware of the extent to which this alliance would affront his parents. "I couldn't understand this [disagreement]." There are certain questions that occur at this point. Was A. S. really so dependent on his parents for approval of his interest in Mary as would appear at first sight? Is this dependence to be viewed as a direct dependence on them, or is it rather indirect in the sense that it now reflects symbolically the play of inner motives now experienced by A. S.? Why did Mary come to assume the importance she did for him? Is Mary simply a person with whom A. S. wanted to form a relationship, or was she a symbolic avenue for the exercise of other drives, which heretofore had not found a sufficiently adequate symbol through which they could be expressed?

An answer to the last question may be found in the scarcity of feelings expressed by A. S. in describing his relationship with Mary. He spoke of her, for example, as being intelligent and gracious; he said that she was a "wonderful girl" and that he enjoyed sexual intercourse with her, but these seem to contain no real expression of feeling. It is strongly implied, therefore, that the extent and depth of the relatedness between him and Mary was largely determined by inner processes within A. S. with which Mary could become only superficially involved. If it had been otherwise, if he had been free to have involved himself with Mary, he would have been able to resolve his dilemma one way or the other. It is my belief that A. S. was largely involved with a symbolic representation of Mary, which had little similarity to the girl herself. This is somewhat borne out when he finds Mary to be "changed a lot." "She was not considerate any more. She would say things and wouldn't care what other people thought. She would hurt their feelings." In other words, his view of Mary precluded any capacity on her part to stand up for herself, to feel free to disregard other people if they hurt her, etc. It might be speculated that this symbolic composite of Mary was that of a patient, long-suffering, withal gracious creature who was to be wholly free of aggressive and hostile feelings. A. S.'s reaction is to leave Mary, but he quickly feels the ineffectiveness of this solution. He tries one solution after another until the conflict produces the constellation of inner drives that could be put to rest only by the suicidal act. Yet, when the patient describes the events that precede his suicidal attempt, one is not impressed by any amount of inner turmoil, except with such allusions as "My mood was getting worse." What A. S. is expressing here is the alienation he has experienced. The further a person evolves away from the center of his being or selfness, the deeper and more extensive become these feelings of alienation. A. S. had traveled far from his self, as he reports his detachment and separation. Patients will report dreams in which they are sitting at their own funerals with no feelings noted, though they can describe the casket, etc., in great detail. Others will recite how unmoved they felt at the loss of a supposedly loved one. One patient described in detail what happened to his forearm as he held it under boiling water, how the skin discolored, etc., as if he were describing how a chicken is barbecued. He had no recollection of pain. In this man, there was so deep a degree of alienation that he no longer owned even his sensory perception of himself.

Though A. S. was amply aware of his mother's need to be well regarded by the community, his being drawn to Mary was independent of his need to please his mother. It was a desire to relate himself to the underdog. However, for A. S. there existed an equally powerful, though more in the background, drive to excel and to belong to the best. His mother, with the mention of "black babies," was able to activate in him his own fear of losing caste, his own drive to excel in the community, to be well thought of, etc. This was the conflict that tripped off the chain of succeeding events, culminating in A. S.'s suicidal solution.

A. S. presents to us, in considerable depth, one particular constellation of events, the occurrence of which can lead an already weak self to take the last and final solution. It is roughly comparable to what the strongest of selves may choose when they are being subjected to hopelessly interminable suffering from which they can perceive no escape. The performance of a suicidal act in such an individual would terminate suffering that was extreme and after that person had reasonably exhausted all other avenues of solution. Clearly, such was not the case in the problem of A. S. Yet, from his point of view, this was precisely the position in which *he* found himself, so for him the solution of suicide was the only available one. The condition in A. S. leading him to the feelings of profound hopelessness arises out of the implacable operation of the irresolvable conflict we have described. To be caught in a state of hopeless entanglement engenders the most severe kind of suffering. These persons thrash about ceaselessly in their attempt to find an out, and this thrashing only serves to tighten the knot. It causes the patient to go into a slow freeze. "It would seem as if I just couldn't get started." "My mood was getting worse." Sometimes a patient's going into a depression has the effect of keeping him from the suicidal act, just as it keeps him from doing much of anything else. It explains why we must be alert when the depressed patient, especially if there is a history of suicidal attempt or even mere consideration of it, begins to bestir himself. Frequently his stirrings are the outcome of a reactivation of some aspects of the inner conflict. When the inner conflict is activated, it will be accompanied by varying degrees of anxiety that the patient will be unable to account for or to tolerate. A weak self such as A. S.'s has a very low tolerance to anxiety. It could be said that A. S. had an aversion to experiencing anxiety because it would interfere with the picture within his idealized self that stated that efficiency and calm must not be disturbed. Such persons drive themselves to quick and easy solutions to allay their anxiety, with the common result of getting themselves into more and more untenable positions.

There was also much of the "search for glory" in A. S. He was mostly alone; we have no reports of his having had any friends. His love affair with Mary heightened certain aspects of his search for glory to the extent that its failure meant suicide. In A. S.'s dreams of glory, he saw himself in the splendid role of uplifting Mary from her menial "underdog" position. It helped that Mary possessed attributes that fitted into the picture. She was gracious and intelligent, a proper person to be at his side during the struggle. When a person who is out for glory first fastens onto a person to help him, he becomes totally oblivious to any negative qualities that might also be present. A. S. was totally blind to those other qualities in Mary, which became more apparent to him later; his realization of them could only have been greeted with dismay. The self-assertiveness in Mary could have no place in a consort who was envisioned as silently and lovingly admiring him from a distance. Assertiveness brings another person too close in too many unpredictable ways that are intolerable, since they will tend to clash with the idyllic picture that the person is out to make real.

Let us recapitulate the course of A. S.'s development. He is born into a family whose members are themselves severely neurotic. His mother early burdened him with the responsibility of fulfilling her demands, demands that were imparted more by implication than by explicit statements. In addition, these demands were contradictory in character, as, for example, extolling kindness and charity and, *sotto voce,* insisting on a competitive and perhaps even ruthless excelling. The boy grows up trying to reconcile these double standards and resorts to his own special ways of reconciling them. He evolves an idealized self that substitutes for his true self, and he then embarks on a career of making it successful and meaningful. Part of this attempt concerns his reaching out for a partner in the form of a woman, Mary. He turns to her for some affirmation of his being the accomplished self (idealized self) with which he has wholly identified his being. Mary seems eminently able to provide this affirmation. A. S.'s idealized self expands under her "love." In addition, A. S. has the opportunity to expand his idealized self by helping to make Mary into a more acceptable member of the community by marrying her. There is a misadventure at this point that dooms his "progress." His mother, who is the external symbolization of another way of life, throws her weight upon an aspect of his idealized self that he had suppressed. Mary was not the proper person, she says. Princes only marry princesses. The conflict within the idealized self begins to rage, and A. S.'s self, called upon to make an impossible effort, is caught in a net of hopelessness and suffering from which he can extricate himself only by shutting off all demands on himself and by ending his servitude in eternal sleep. His form of suicide is not a violent one, such as the suicide of a deeply vindictive person might be. It is the suicidal effort of a person looking for respite and not for restitution.

THERAPEUTIC IMPLICATIONS

Essentially, the procedure in treating a suicidal patient is similar to that utilized in the conduct of any analysis. However, as was previously indicated, the suicidal patient, living on the edge of life as it were, must be given special attention until these tendencies are markedly reduced. In other words, all efforts are bent in the direction of working out and resolving the unconscious processes that bear upon this possible outcome. The hidden sources and nuances of the self-hatred, of the feelings of hopelessness, and of intolerable, albeit unvoiced, suffering must be tracked down. The analyst needs to be alert when his patient begins to come out of a depression, for, as was indicated elsewhere, this is also a time when self-hatred can be activated. The aim is not to prevent its activation but to keep it within manageable proportions, so as to make use of it in the therapeutic process.

What must be watched for are all the important idealizations that have a bearing on the generation of self-hatred. The amount of pride invested in these idealizations determines the extent to which the patient will feel a loss at their failure. And with each failure is always the attendant self-hate. Does the patient have any avenues available for ridding himself of the hostile feelings other than those directed toward his own self? Does he throw these feelings off on others or onto objects? Is the therapeutic relationship on a sufficiently well-grounded basis that the patient can safely vent his spleen on the doctor and still be able to return? A patient once came to me armed with an Army revolver, which he put equidistant between us. He was giving the two of us an even break. The therapy at that moment consisted mainly in remaining clear of any areas that he could construe as an attack upon him. He had been so accustomed to hostility from the outside that, in not receiving it, he obtained all the support he needed and his self-hatred was able in due time to subside.

In general, if the patient is a suicidal person whose orientation is on the aggressive side, we avoid the areas closest to those aspects of his idealized self that are heavily charged with neurotic expansiveness. To touch upon them would merely cause an activation of some neurotic goodness, which would then produce self-hatred or result in a reinforcement of the aggressiveness per se.

In the case of the suicidal patient who clearly hitches his wagon to the star of another and who has failed at this pursuit (the self-abnegating patient), it is essential that he find in the doctor a person with whom he can ally himself in case of need. The patient's dependence is clearly established as an aspect of the therapeutic relationship. The patient will push this to the limit of his need. The amelioration of this dependency then becomes an essential part of the therapeutic process, but in the interval we work wherever we can on more accessible aspects, such as his various prides and pseudorelations. All this lays the groundwork for the approach to the main areas of neurotic involvement.

If drugs are used, their use should be decisive. To give these persons inadequate amounts only serves to deepen and prolong rather than relieve, albeit temporarily, their truly intolerable burden. What greater terror can there be than suddenly to be confronted by the feeling of disintegration without a single clue as to identity, without a single hold on anything firm? And yet these can be the hours that may serve to create the bond between the doctor and the patient that can bear the load of the future treatment the patient and doctor will undergo. Oftentimes, when the patient is the most disturbed, he is also the most accessible. It remains for the doctor to find his way through the miasma of terror to the little remaining self and take his stand beside it. If he is able to do this, the therapeutic process will be well begun.

As in all analyses, for that matter in all social relationships, the person-to-person or doctor-to-patient relationship is probably the single most potent factor in the therapeutic process. It must convey to the patient by all means available that the doctor is on the side of the patient's self. For a long time, the patient will probably construe this to mean that the doctor is there in behalf of his idealized self because he is usually unaware of any other self. Nevertheless, sooner or later, the patient will begin to make some excursions away from this idealized self. It is at these times that the doctor's values will have their deepest meaning for the patient's recovery. Only a self that is realizing itself can relate pertinently in the development of another less matured self. The doctor-patient relationship is one where the rights of the respective individuals must be clearly specified always. The fact that the relationship of doctor and patient is based on equality depends on this process. However, it is not inconsistent with equality that the doctor assumes the larger burden at the outset of protecting the patient's fledgling self from whatever would undermine it. We also know that the patient himself is usually well equipped with his own ways of handling his difficulties, so this task is not as extensive as may appear at first. This is not so true, however, in the case of the suicidal patient. In him, the inner forces are too pointedly deployed, not by accident but by design, against the self per se.

If the analyst can exercise this feeling for equality in its most comprehensive sense, along with all his therapeutic acumen, then he will be in a position to render the suicidal patient the optimal service he requires. Of all persons, the suicidal patient has probably suffered most at the hands of a tyranny that has all but reduced him to the status of a slave, and a hated one at that. He is, therefore, the most sensitive to the inner insensitivity of the outer world that masquerades in numerous disguises but has its origin in disrespect, unconscious or otherwise. As the patient grasps the basic fact of equality of the relationship, he will be encouraged and enabled to expose his weaknesses. In the course of exposing them, he gains insight into himself; as he gains the necessary insight, he can reclaim not only his illusions, which have now far outlived their usefulness, but the right to growth of his proper self, which once more has the reins of its own development in its own hands.

References

1. Horney, Karen: *Self Analysis,* New York: W. W. Norton & Company, Inc., 1942.
2. Horney, Karen: *Our Inner Conflicts,* New York: W. W. Norton & Company, Inc. 1945.
3. Horney, Karen: *Neurosis and Human Growth,* New York: W. W. Norton & Company, Inc., 1950.
4. Kilpatrick, Elizabeth: A psychoanalytic understanding of suicide, *American Journal of Psychoanalysis,* 1: 13–23, 1948.

18

Suicide: The Personal Construct Point of View

GEORGE A. KELLY

Doctor Kelly completed his undergraduate education at Friends University and Park College and pursued graduate studies at the University of Kansas, the University of Minnesota, and the University of Edinburgh. He received his Ph.D. from the State University of Iowa in 1931. During World War 2 he was commissioned in the Navy as an aviation psychologist, and since 1946 he has been a professor of psychology at the Ohio State University. A member of the national, state, and local psychological societies, he is a former president of the American Board of Examiners in Professional Psychology, as well as of the Clinical and Consulting Divisions of the American Psychological Association, and a former chairman of the Education and Training Board of the Association. He has served as a consultant to the Navy and the National Institute of Mental Health. He is a member of the Veterans Administration Special Medical Advisory Group. In 1955 he published a two-volume work, *The Psychology of Personal Constructs* (New York: Norton, 1955).

Personal construct theory assumes that life's vicissitudes do not thrust their singular meanings upon us; rather that it is we ourselves who must contrive to make sense out of whatever happens. If there seems to be genuine singularity in life's meanings, it stems primarily from the singularity of our own thinking. The events, on their part, never cease to be open to a host of alternative constructions.

TRUTH AS A HUMAN INVENTION

From this point of view human truth is never something discovered and wrapped up to keep; it is always invented and subject to day-by-day improvement. All that is discovered is some practical consistency between one's anticipations and their apparent outcomes. It runs like this: We invent a meaning. We impose it upon some events that happen in our immediate vicinity. This is fun, and we are often content to stop at this point. But if we have a skeptical streak in us and want to test validity, as well as enjoy the ecstasies of appreciation, we use our meaning to make a flat prediction; and then we stand back to see what happens.

Testing Truth by Making Predictions

A series of successful predictions is likely to lead us to believe, though not always, that our meaning has a substance all its own. We may even forget how it was derived and claim that we ran across it one day, quite by accident, lurking amid the predicted events. Yet, as a plain matter of fact, all that we ought to say is that what happened looked enough like what we expected to happen to satisfy our sense of similarity. And, as for the degree of truth to be credited to our invention, the safest thing to say is simply "so far, so good."

The matching of predictions against outcome is the essential feature of scientific method. More specifically, the method involves the generation of hypotheses out of theory or prior observations, conceptualization or abstraction, occasional experimental manipulations (controls) in order to maximize or minimize certain variations in events, explicit predictions, observation of outcomes at as low a conceptual level as possible (objectivity), reconciliation of predictions with outcomes, revision of constructs, and continual repetition of part or all of the cycle. One way of stating it is to say that science requires the reconciliation of predictive principles, abstracted at as high a conceptual level as possible, with concrete outcomes, identified at as low a conceptual level as possible.

As we see it, science is but a special case of human enterprise, and scientific method is but a special instance of human psychological method. Personal construct theory is an effort to get at the heart of the matter by stating the general case for human psychological method. If personal construct theory succeeds, its full statement will embrace the whole range of human psychological effort, from scientific progress, on the one hand, to existentialistic anguish, on the other.

Validation

If we look at man as an inventor of truths or, perhaps better, as a construer of events, we are bound to wonder if this means that he has any obligations except to his own whims. Or do the hard facts of life occasionally intervene to bring him back to his senses? From the position of personal construct theory we would argue that the facts never intervene. Perhaps we had better say that the *events* never intervene, since we are talking about raw reality.

It is the person himself who intervenes on behalf of reality. He makes his prediction of things he expects to happen. This has to be based on relatively high levels of abstraction. When he sees what actually does happen, according to his own lights, of course, he has something at hand that he can perceive at a relatively low level of abstraction. Now he can *validate* his construction of events. If what appeared to happen seems to be inconsistent with what he expected, he usually concludes that his expectations were at fault and sets about to correct them. Thus he checks his thinking against reality. But this validation is of his own doing. Reality, itself, goes its own way, oblivious, and lets him fret as he pleases over his ability to predict it.

What Truths Did A. S. Invent?

When we undertake to base a psychological theory on this kind of logic, interesting things begin to happen. Take the biographical events in the life of A. S. Under such theorizing, these events—the actual events—suddenly loom up not as themselves forces molding the outlook of the young man but as the grounds he used for the meanings he invented and as the outcomes against which, over the years, he must so often have checked his anticipations. The recollections he reported to his interviewer, recollections that presumably paralleled certain actual occurrences, were the verbalizable explications that most readily came to mind in his effort to lend verisimilitude to what he now felt and believed.

The events he described were important not because of what they did to him but because of what he had made out of them and what he was then making out of them. Always it was he who invented the meanings, whether verbalized or unverbalized. From such personalized constructs he projected his versions of what was about to happen next. Always he altered his own course to fit, right up to the very last.

SUICIDE AS A VALIDATING ACT

It is often helpful to strip human behavior of pathological interpretations. Health and illness are exceedingly prejudicial terms, and more often than not, when we use them, we succeed only in beclouding the relevant issues. It is much more enlightening to look at any human act in terms of how and what it fits and the ends it accomplishes.

Take suicide, for example. Instead of treating it as something evil, pathological, or nonsensical, we can understand it far better if we look at the act itself and what it accomplishes from the point of view of the person who performs it.

Death as an Implicit Choice in Everyday Life

Suppose we examine suicide first in the context of a basic question about death. Let us state it this way: Under what conditions of outlook would anyone seek death rather than life? By stating our question in this manner, we shall be inquiring after a psychological principle rather than a simple situational determinant.

Certainly it is not so unusual for persons to stack their cards in favor of death. Some do it for a social cause. Some do it because it is expected of them, as in battle. Some do it for fun, as on the highway. Some do it to avoid the guilt of being a few minutes late for an appointment. Some do it in sheer exasperation. Some do it in beautiful resignation. Mothers often risk their lives to bear children, and it is not uncommon to find both parents risking their health, and lives, to support those children in competitive luxury. Indeed, if one looks around him, he can see lives being sacrificed on every hand, and for little reasons as well as for big ones.

Socrates, according to the political logic of his time, had his choice between conceding his error in order to bargain with the court in the matter of his sentence or reaffirming his convictions intact by voluntarily taking his own life. If he accepted the verdict of guilt in order to save his skin, it meant that he had been talking through his hat. He could then no longer live as if truth were his principal pursuit. If he drank the hemlock, it meant that he still was reaching into the future for truth and that others were invited to dedicate their lives to the same quest. And they did. His choice was to validate what he had taught, and thus to validate the life he had lived. Would we otherwise have had a Plato, followed by an Aristotle? Was not Socrates' suicide, in the light of these great lives that followed, an act of sublime anticipation?

Jesus, who undoubtedly was greatly influenced by Socrates' example, validated his life in much the same way. It appears that he too could have avoided what happened to him. Yet he deliberately made up his mind to accept crucifixion. To do so seemed to him altogether necessary if he was to make it perfectly clear that the way he lived was more vital than the mere fact of personal survival. Thus he, like Socrates, invited death to validate his life. He is consistently reported by his biographers to have put the general proposition this way: "For whoever wants to preserve his life will lose it, and whoever loses his life for me will preserve it. What good does it do a man to gain the whole world and lose or forfeit himself?"

Socrates and Jesus certainly are not unique in their use of death to validate the essentials of their lives. Thousands upon thousands of others, in all the succeeding centuries, have used death in the same way. They, too, have seen their concluding acts as the natural outcomes of their convictions, expressed under the circumstances in which they found themselves.

When Is It Suicide?

Probably, when it comes right down to it, we are apt to say that a person has committed a mere suicide, rather than performed a dedicated act, when it seems clear by our own lights that the problem he faced had a better solution. We think *we* would have known better. Perhaps so. Nevertheless, the fact remains that none of the alternatives that beckon so clearly in our own minds was quite so visible in his. So the suicide makes *his* choice, and not *ours*. We say it was a bad one? We are possibly right; it might have been a "bad" choice. But that does not tell us much. To understand his act we need to know what he died for. What personal constructions of life and truth, what anticipations formulated from his structured world seemed to be validated by so drastic an act.

In a broad sense, each of us gives his life for something, something noble or something ignoble, though mostly something in between. Some do it decisively in one abrupt and frightening gesture. Some do it slowly and unobtrusively, sacrificing themselves little by little. Some face death outright; others stumble in its general direction. To seek to die well is an object of the full life, and those who fail to live well never succeed in finding anything worth dying for. Thus life and death can be made to fit together, each as the validator of the other.

What Was There in A. S.'s Life That Was Worth Dying For?

Shall we not look at A. S.'s suicidal attempt in these validational terms? What was it his effort appeared to validate? There is no indication that he was ever asked this question in any of its forms. Apparently the event was interpreted clinically from the outset as an incident in some way characteristic or inevitable in his style of life.

But if we are to employ the style-of-life paradigm, where do we look for the style?; in the bare record of events?; in deviations from the way we ourselves would have dealt with such events if we had been in A. S.'s shoes?; or do we look for deviations from the way we think "normal" persons would have handled such events? Perhaps, in place of style, we would prefer to look for some alien psychopathology or disease process that invaded this young man's psyche. Since personal construct theory leads us to deal with A. S.'s problems in terms quite different from any of these, and thus to ponder over questions never put to him, we shall have to be content only to speculate about what it was his act sought to validate or at most to make precarious inferences from the slimmest of available evidence.

TWO LIMITING CONDITIONS: REALISM AND INDETERMINACY

We have seen how a suicidal attempt can be regarded as an act designed to validate one's life. As such, it is a bid to extend life rather than actually terminate it; to extend its essential meaning, that is. But there are two conditions of personal construction under which the actual abandonment of one's life seems like the sensible thing to do. The first is when the course of events seems so obvious that there is no point in waiting around for the outcome. The score has become so lopsided there is no reason to stay through to the end of the game. The other is when everything seems so utterly unpredictable that the only definite thing one can do is abandon the scene altogether. It has ceased to be a game with perceptible rules.

The former condition is one where realism has been carried to its ultimate conclusion: fatalism. Suicidal attempts under this condition are often successful. The latter is the condition of total anxiety, and the suicidal attempt, not so often successful in this instance, is a desperate bid for some kind, any kind, of certainty. It is indeed striking that these should be the two limiting conditions for the sustenance of life; on the one hand, the sense of knowing everything worth knowing and, on the other, knowing nothing worth knowing. Yet, since the very essence of life is the use of the present to bridge the past with the future, any construction that makes such an undertaking futile serves psychologically to destroy life. Once this destruction has already taken place, the question of whether the person keeps on breathing or not becomes a side issue. Psychologically he is already dead.

To be sure, there are other considerations that contribute to the psychological understanding of suicide, hostility, impulsivity, guilt, etc., but these we can treat as secondary matters. Before we take up some of these other theoretical constructs, let us speculate on how the two limiting conditions of realism and indeterminacy might have affected A. S.

What Did A. S.'s Personal Construct System Lead Him to Expect?

In any effort to understand a suicidal attempt we look first to see what we can learn about the personal construct system of the person involved. Did A. S. see himself in the clutches of fate, or was he so hopelessly uncertain about what was to become of him that any kind of certainty seemed better than utter chaos? If his attempt was an effort to abandon his life, rather than validate something in it, which of the two life-destroying constructions did he employ?

We have said that A. S.'s personal constructs served to project his day-to-day anticipations. That is the basic assumption of personal construct theory. Pursuant upon these anticipations there were undoubtedly some rude discoveries—a whole succession of them. But did they confirm his worst expectations and thus lead him to realistic despair? Or did they continually confound him and thus leave him overwhelmed with uncertainty?

In either case he might have been challenged by the outcomes to devise new meanings and so to come to grips with life. But in this he seems to have failed, although there is some possibility that he tried to find new meanings in his study of sociology during the few weeks between leaving the Army and making his trip to South America. In any event, he at last made his ultimate bid for certainty, whether to foil his fate or to forge it with his own hand. But, as chance would have it, even this dismal prediction was to fail to materialize. Or did it? The reported interviews give no clear clue as to what he really expected to happen.

So let us say that it was not the events of his life that led A. S. to the crossroads. He arrived there as the result of a series of perceived relationships; relationships between what he was able to construe and predict, on the one hand, and what he discovered was happening, on the other. It was the result of how little he was able to reconstrue after the outcomes of all his earlier expectations became apparent.

Whether life, up to this point, had treated A. S. well or not is quite beside the point. Even the question of reinforcements in his series of learning trials is not an issue. Indeed, such a line of reasoning would probably lead us to the logical conclusion that he could not possibly have done what he did. What is important is his personal construction of the world about him and the fact that the sequence of events appeared either to invest that construction with inexorable validity or to threaten its utter collapse. There could even have been some of both features.

For him the decision to commit suicide was, at that moment in the cheap hotel room, the most obvious thing to do. Of course, he may have thought otherwise later. What matters here, as in all psychological problems, is that one's personal constructions at the time of decision seem so completely dictated by the obvious that there are no practical alternatives left to explore.

WELL-KNOWN WORDS THAT VANISH

Learning and Reinforcement

Perhaps it would be helpful to mention some of the conventional psychological notions that one soon abandons along the way when one sets out to pursue the implications of personal construct theory. It is already clear that *biographical events* are not seen as having any meaning, except as meaning is imposed upon them, as in the case of A. S.'s biography and the personal meanings he must have imposed. So *reinforcement,* as a construct, must be abandoned also. In some respects *validation* in personal construct theory takes the place of *reinforcement,* although it is a construct of quite a different order. *Validation* is the relationship one senses between anticipation and realization, whereas in conventional theory *reinforcement* is a value property attributed to an event. Even *learning* as a construct gets sloughed off, partly because it has become so badly cluttered with ambiguous meanings and partly because there seems to be no segment of the life process that one can properly isolate from the rest and designate specifically as *learning.*

Motivation

Personal construct theory has a peculiar relationship to the so-called dynamic theories in psychology. Because it starts with the assumption that man's being is measured in the dimension of time rather than in the dimension of space only, any special set of terms formulated to rationalize the fact that one is alive is simply redundant. Constructs of *motivations, drives, forces, needs,* and even *stimuli,* together with the whole class of *psychodynamics,* drop out of the system of discourse. This makes personal construct theory, in one sense, an all-out dynamic system. Movement is built into its underlying assumptions about the essential nature of man. But for those to whom a dynamic theory can be identified only by a liberal sprinkling of terms implying forces operating upon the person, either from within him or from without, personal construct theory will seem as nondynamic as Kraepelin, or even more so.

Feeling and Emotion

The constructs of *feeling* and *emotion,* for more than two thousand years so deeply entrenched in all our European systems of discourse, also drop out when we apply the assumptions of personal construct theory rigorously. Furthermore, the semantic division we customarily make between *affect* and *intellect* is no longer required, a feature of the theory that greatly disturbs some psychologists, possibly because it threatens to put them into the uncomfortable position of having nothing left to talk about or because they interpret this development as signifying a return to pre-Freudian ways of describing human behavior.

A Cognitive Theory?

Yet personal construct theory sustains no necessity for distinguishing sharply between those psychological processes that appear to follow classic formulas of reasonableness and those that do not, nor between those that are signalized by words and those that can only be portrayed by enactment, nor even between those that appear to be soundly organized and those that appear to be disorganized. It assumes that the only logic we have available to us is that which is devised by human minds; thus what is logical is an extension of what is psychological. It would therefore disclaim being either a *cognitive* theory or a *noncognitive* theory. It would be as much misunderstood if it were classed as *behavioristic* as it would be if it were classed as *rationalistic*. In brief, the point of departure in personal construct theory is at such a philosophical level that none of the usual pigeon holes for the quick and easy filing of all new psychological theories as fast as they appear will serve as a neat container for it.

NEW TERMS OF REFERENCE FOR UNDERSTANDING SUICIDE

Having abandoned so many of the terms customarily employed in talking about suicidal behavior (*feelings, emotions, needs, psychodynamics, motivation, learning, reinforcement, stimulus, cognition, irrationality, disorganization*) we seem to have little left from conventional psychology to draw verbal pictures with. Before we can come up with anything very illuminating about A. S., we shall have to replenish our vocabulary. To a considerable extent we shall depend upon refurbished terms, old words with revised meanings. But some words will have to be new, at least new in the context of precise psychological discourse. Fortunately we can limit ourselves here to those terms that need to be applied to the case at hand and leave the rest of the lexicon of personal construct theory to our more persistent readers.

Let me say a word in general about the kind of dimension used by personal construct theory. The emphasis is placed on the use of axes of reference that are abstract, i.e., mathematical in the broad sense, rather than concrete. The theoretical task is to place the problems of psychology within the framework of meaningful dimensions rather than into nosological back wards. Only thus can one properly envision directions of change and movement.

So our terms, although they inevitably categorize our ways of looking at a patient, do not presume to categorize the patient himself, nor do they even pre-empt his behaviors. For example, if we construe him in reference to *hostility*, it is the construct of *hostility* that is impounded, and not the patient or his acts. Certainly we do not say that the patient is to be stuffed alive into the *hostility* bin. Nor do we say that he has come down with an attack of *hostility*. *Hostility* is our own axis of reference, like length or height, along which a measurement can be taken in order to get a clearer idea of the proportions of human behavior.

Dilation versus Constriction

Since we have already defined *validation* in connection with our rejection of the constructs of reinforcement and learning, let us turn next to another systematic construct that is important in the understanding of suicide: *dilation* versus *constriction*. In his search for personal constructs upon which to base his anticipations, a person sometimes broadens his area of concern, hoping that by grasping at more and more things he can come across something that will help him make better sense out of the onrush of events. Often his outreaching is indiscriminate. Whether it is or not, we still describe it as *dilation*.

When he moves in the opposite direction, we call it *constriction*. A person *constricts* when he attempts to shrink his world to manageable size, as when he pulls the bedcovers over his head or attempts to stop the clock by committing suicide. It is not uncommon to find a person exhibiting violent movement along this axis. Often such movement is taken to indicate the so-called manic depressive psychosis by those who think behavior is a disease.

Anxiety

Anxiety, from the standpoint of personal construct theory, is the sense of chaos. More specifically, it is the sweeping awareness of events for which it seems one has no adequate constructs. Lacking constructs for anticipating them, one seems helplessly caught up in events, with no idea of what posture to assume while waiting for them or what to do after they arrive. Clinically, anxiety has long been described as having a free-floating quality, not ever being clearly identified with one object or one set of objects.

Threat

Threat, the subjective experience, is distinguished from *anxiety*. A person is *threatened* when he finds himself on the brink of a deeply significant change in himself. Often the impending state of affairs is all too plausible, as in the case of the reformed alcoholic who knows too well what will happen to him if he takes the first drink. Often the sense of threat is identified with what appears likely to be the precipitating cause of the metamorphosis, but the threat experience itself has to do with what seems about to happen in the region of one's core construct system. Quite often, for example, a patient is deeply threatened by a realization of what is likely to occur to him as a result of therapy. The therapist finds this hard to understand. Even the realization that the change will be for the better and result in his being happier does not necessarily make it less threatening to the patient.

Basic Postulate and Choice Corollary

Personal construct theory does not use the notion of motivation. Because man is conceived from the outset as inhabiting the dimension of time, that is to say, conceived as alive and in motion, one does not need to conjure up motivating forces to push him around. We are then left with the task of explaining only the directions his motion will take.

But this also falls into place neatly enough, once we have ventured the initial leap to a *basic postulate.* That postulate is that a person's processes are psychologically channeled by the ways in which he anticipates events. We can elaborate this statement by a series of ensuing corollaries.

The channels for anticipating events are called *constructs.* They are guides to the future, and anybody who wants to face up to life had better have an ample stock of them on hand at all levels of consciousness. When it comes down to making everyday choices, it seems obvious that a person will choose those alternatives that promise to provide either of two things: greater extension of his construct system or better definition of it. This is what we call the *choice corollary,* and it takes care of what is left over after the *basic postulate* drops the bottom out from under motivation.

This is not to say that a person will behave according to classical laws of logic. Far from it. We can be sure that neither Aristotle nor Thomas Aquinas behaved that way in their private lives. Rather, he behaves according to his own system, and that is something that has to be understood in psychological, not logical, terms. Nor does it add anything to say that he behaves in response to pleasure and pain, unless one wants to define pleasure tautologically as what we seek and pain as what we try to avoid. Moreover, constructs are not necessarily put into words, either symbolically or explicatively. Indeed, one is always impressed with how extensively persons anticipate the future in terms for which they have no speech.

Hostility

Now we can talk about *hostility.* Sometimes matters come to such a pass that one finds himself on the brink of an overdue and far-reaching revision of his construct system. His predictions have gone awry. Evidence against the validity of his constructs mounts in overwhelming proportions. In desperation he may have tried dilation to see if, in a broader context, he could grasp the elusive veridity in his way of construing the world. He may have tried constriction to see if he could find localized confirmation of his outlook. A. S. appears to have tried both. But if neither of these nor any of the other exploratory methods works, he may be confronted with a difficult choice: either to revise the very foundations of his construct system or somehow to force events to prove him right. When, on the one hand, his deeply shaken constructions have to do with his understanding of other persons and, on the other, he chooses to extort confirming evidence from them, we call it *hostility.*

This, of course, is a strikingly unusual definition of *hostility.* But *hostility,* as any psychological term, ought to help us understand the predicament in which a person has found himself and not be used merely to label a person as dangerous. The construct's referent, from this point of view, is not the desire to injure someone; the injury is incidental; it is rather an extortioner's trick designed to preserve the psychological status quo and to relieve him of the responsibility of revising his outlook. *Hostility* may, of course, be directed against a threatening object, threatening because it appears on the verge of precipitating a deep-seated change in oneself. Certainly it is often found in the reactionary person who must shore up a crumbling system of values. But it may be found as well in the radical reformer who demands that the world at large furnish him with what he thinks his home in particular did not.

Guilt

There is one term yet to go: *guilt.* The definition is a little more complex. To get at it we first have to understand *role* from the standpoint of the psychology of personal constructs. Let us suppose that one person attempts to understand another, not merely as a behaving object or merely in terms of stimulus input and response output, but as another person who himself has an outlook tingeing all his perceptions of the world about him. If, seeing the other person in this manner, a person goes on to regulate his own behavior in reference to such a subsuming construction, then he is enacting a social *role.*

In the course of his life a civilized man is likely to base a considerable proportion of his behavior on such an interpretation of those with whom he lives. It becomes a key to his expectations for himself. His own life makes sense in terms of such *role* constructs. It loses sense when they are invalidated. If the turn of events seems to leave him high and dry with no true *role* left to him, he suffers in a peculiar way. We call that experience *guilt*.

A. S.'S PERSONAL CONSTRUCT SYSTEM

Two recurrent themes stand out from the details reported in the protocol provided in the case of A. S.: his inability to understand why it was his parents crossed him for the first time when he tried to establish a close relationship with Mary, and his frequent recall of fighting during childhood. In elaborating the first of these he says, "It was the first time that they had ever crossed me. . . . And I didn't know what to do. I couldn't go against my parents, and I couldn't see why they were so mean." This theme is repeated in later sections of the protocol.

Anxiety in the System

The extent of his perplexity (the full range of events involved) is not elaborated in the protocol, but we may reasonably infer that he was pinpointing an illustrative instance in a construction that ranged much further than the particular events he emphasized. In personal construct theory a widespread sense of such confusion is called anxiety. Certainly it becomes clear as one reads the protocol that there must have been many areas in which he felt the undercurrent of confusion: in school, in looking for something to do in South America, and during his halfhearted search for employment in Los Angeles. They were all caught up in the same chaos. Let us, therefore, not be too hasty in saying that the particular domestic events in which this confusion seems focused were the material causes of his anxiety. As we have already said, personal construct theory does not deal with events of this order as if they were psychological causes.

Invalidation Deep in the System

The likeliest interpretation of the anxiety is that his anticipations were invalidated on a large scale, so large, in fact, that the truth of some very basic constructs had to be called into question. Since such basic constructs are often not couched in words, he was probably confronted with a revision of outlook for which he had inadequate verbal tools.

But how did the invalidation happen on so vast a scale? For one thing, it seems, as he reported it, that he had long looked to his mother as a principal source of validation. Validation seems to have been a function she was ready and eager to serve, both in her family and in her community. She enjoyed responsibility. This service as a personal validator for his ventures seems to be what they both meant when they agreed that he seemed "closest" to her.

A. S. puts his finger on this matter when he says, "I think my sister turned out lazy because mother would never let anyone else do anything. I know I resented this at times." At this point the interviewer reports that he became somewhat tearful and said, "I feel all confused. Mother spent as much time with us as any other mother did—" and then was silent.

In this passage A. S. seems to be about to come to grips with the fact that somehow his mother had become the custodian of all his validational evidence, thus shutting off any venture designed to check reality elsewhere. This, of course, was precisely what led up to the sense of confusion. He says he was "confused" in just so many words. Yet he cannot quite put the blame on her for he vaguely senses that it was not what she did that produced the turn of events. What he does not quite understand is how it was that his own use of his mother as a validator made him so vulnerable to the collapse of all that he had built on the evidence she supplied.

To be sure, he had long tried to validate his anticipations elsewhere: the frequent fights are evidence enough of that; but the outcomes generally seem to have run against his expectations. Only in interaction with his mother did his constructions seem to lead to consistent outcomes. And the only adventures of which she seemed to disapprove, prior to Mary, were the fights. By the time he became an adult these simple aggressive attempts had been quite thoroughly invalidated, both because he lost the fights and because his parents failed to take his side in them.

A. S. did not give up. To say that would be to fall back on traditional motivational doctrine, which, from the standpoint of personal construct theory, is obsolete. He was alive and hence active. If his aggression appeared to fail him, it was because the alternatives he construed for himself turned it off into ineffectual channels.

By the end of high school he says he was "desperately trying to be popular." Even though his mother was "always trying to build me up and brag about me," he was still looking elsewhere for validity. At last he seems to have made intimate contact with the outside world when he met Mary. Now he had a project of his own that he was successfully testing out on its independent merits. Moreover, Mary's own aggressiveness (". . . when I wanted to take Mary out and Mary would call up") provided him with validation firm enough to test his weight on. So he inched his way out on new ground.

It was at this point that he was overwhelmed with invalidational evidence from home. It was not merely that his parents disapproved; what was vastly more threatening than that was their apparent metamorphosis. They also became unpredictable. Everything he thought he knew about them and his relationship to them fell apart. They not only withheld the keys to the car; they took away his keys to the truth. He could no longer understand them. Indeed, how could he now understand anything? The fact that they invalidated his understanding of them was far more devastating than their mere disapproval.

And so it always is. To face disapproval, punishment, pain, or a dismal succession of unrewarding outcomes is one thing. These are matters man can partly understand and hence often bears without complaint. But to face chaos is another thing. Even the bravest shudder on the brink of utter emptiness. What worse chaos can one face than sudden chaos where always before there has been firm certainty and the loving confidence of one's home.

To dwell on A. S.'s loss of Mary would be to miss the point. The void was not the place that Mary had filled; it was the place his parents had filled. Moreover, this was no physical place that had been emptied. Even the death of both of his parents would have disturbed him less. What he had lost was something that could never be restored, even by abandoning Mary, even by receiving daily comfort from his parents, even by marrying a girl of whom they approved. He had lost a deep sense of validity for the way he had once ordered his world. This is what he seems to be saying to his interviewer.

Dimensions of Threat

Threat, the sense of imminent change in one's core construct system, often lies at the roots of disturbed behavior. Although there must have been moments when A. S. felt that there were deep changes in the immediate offing (certainly on the eve of suicide he must have felt so), there is very little in the protocol to suggest exactly what he thought was about to happen to him. The story is, instead, primarily one of chaos or anxiety with little so clearly structured as threat looming up before him.

To be sure, the frequent fights throughout childhood and early adolescence imply threat. Yet, except to say he fought when he found he was not liked, he gives us little clue as to any consistent type of taunt or hazard that occasioned the fights. Then, too, there was the superior in the Army. In this case the dimensions of threat are more clearly spelled out: "This man was everything I hated. He was tall, domineering, didn't know what he was doing, but acted as if he knew everything. He always tried to humiliate me, and I couldn't disagree with him. I couldn't stick up for myself; he would always win."

Look at the constructs used and then at the contrasts they implied. The implication was that A. S. was about to be cast in a part that was "short," "dominated," in which he might "know what he was doing but could not act that way," "humiliated," "unable to disagree," "unable to stick up for himself," and "always the loser." This passage probably describes better than any other the axes along which he felt himself always in danger of being transformed. More than that, they suggest some of the well-defined slots in which he might try to rattle back and forth himself.

Later, if he felt that he had achieved some basic changes in his way of life by leaving the orbit of his family, and if then also he saw himself about to slip back into that all too plausible orbit, he would have sensed threat and might have taken extraordinary measures to stave off the relapse. But there is no clear indication of this or, indeed, that he later saw himself on the verge of any clear shift in psychological position. Yet threat is never something to be overlooked in a case where violent action has been taken, and it certainly would be a mandatory topic of psychotherapeutic exploration in the case of A. S.

Vacillation between Dilation and Constriction

A. S.'s movements along the axis of dilation and constriction are important for his therapist to note. For the most part, the record seems to indicate that his method of dealing with perplexity was to constrict; that is to say, he tended to limit rather than to expand his world of concern. But there were marked exceptions. His shift to the study of sociology certainly suggests dilation, although the protocol does not say what had been his previous plan. Certainly his trip to South America seems not only to have been an impulsive venture with little systematic planning behind it, but also a combination of dilation and constriction; dilation because it would open up a whole world of new experiences, and constriction because it would shut him off from present matters he felt he could not handle.

The trip seems to have been his last desperate bid to deal with his problems en masse. If he could have found some semblance of structure there, as he had found the time before when he packed himself off to the Army, the effort might have succeeded. But there was no ready-made way of life waiting for him in South America; only more chaos.

All this suggests one of the problems that would continually have to be faced in therapy. As long as his dependence on his therapist was safe and his world of important realities constricted to the therapy room, matters might be expected to go along smoothly. When the time came to venture out of doors there would be the danger of impulsive movements along the old dilation-constriction axis. Such movements would confront both himself and his therapist with unanticipated developments and catch both of them unaware.

On the face of it, suicide is always a constrictive gesture. What needs to be kept in mind is that constriction is movement toward one end of an axis, the other end of which denotes dilation. To be free to move in one direction along this axis implies freedom also to move readily in the opposite direction. Together these poles define an avenue of movement, sometimes almost the only avenue of movement clearly open to a disturbed person.

INTERLOCKING RELATIONS BETWEEN GUILT AND HOSTILITY

Not all psychological systems employ the constructs of guilt and hostility. Among those that do, an interlocking relationship is usually assumed to exist between them. Hostility is often seen as a way of alleviating one's feelings of guilt; guilt, in turn, commonly follows the realization that one has acted in a hostile fashion.

Personal construct theory, as we have seen, conceptualizes these two types of experience in its own particular way; a way consistent with the assumptions and structure of its systematic position. For one thing, hostility and aggression are kept clearly distinct from each other. Clinical descriptions, therefore, come out in a somewhat different form.

Distinguishing between Hostility and Aggression

Aggression, in personal construct theory, is more nearly synonymous with adventuresomeness, especially adventuresomeness involving high stakes and persistent action along a single chosen line. Hostility, as we have already said, is a last-resort effort to achieve validation in one's interpersonal realm by means of extortion, by a misleading manipulation of the data rather than by revision of the constructs that have proven themselves faulty.

Both A. S. and his father appear to have been threatened by A. S.'s mother. A. S. speaks of their "resenting" her efficiency. Better stated, they were threatened by the form her aggression took. For father as well as for son, she served as a constant reminder of their precarious hold upon life's initiative and the ever-present possibility of finding themselves to be confirmed incompetents. Undoubtedly they were threats to each other too, for each could see in the other an image of himself that was much too plausible for comfort.

In the presence of this sense of threat they could have been anxious, aggressive, or hostile; perhaps a little of each. With A. S. it seems to have been mostly anxiety, the feeling of chaos. But to the extent that he expressed his experience as resentment and took active measures to cope with the threat, he was aggressive. And not to be overlooked are the evidences of sporadic aggressiveness that appear all through the biographical record. The indications of hostility are less clear, but then hostility is usually hard to detect from bare protocol.

The Interviewer's Impression of Passivity

The interviewer was impressed with A. S.'s emphasis of the "passive role." He also notes that it was difficult for A. S. to request an interrruption in the interview, even though he was apparently in severe pain at times. But how shall we interpret these two observations? Was he simply assuming the position that doctors expect of patients in hospitals? Was it a gesture of helplessness or of aggressive eagerness to get a job done by being a doctor's patient if necessary? The clinical evidence on this point would come more from the way he led out in steering the course of the interviews than from the posture he assumed or his failure to complain. He seems to have complained ("griped") enough in the service. Besides, there are cultural differences here that often mislead a clinician.

Another matter must also be taken into account. A clinician's theoretical orientation affects the way he sees things. Since personal construct theory makes a clean distinction between hostility and aggression, A. S.'s failure to show obvious hostility in the clinical situation would not weigh against the perception of aggressive tendencies or of impulsive vacillation along this axis. But still A. S.'s range of positions with reference to the axis of aggression remains undetermined. It is left for the psychotherapeutic series to clarify this critical point.

We must not neglect still another consideration. The protocol reports "some slight signs of organic brain illness, such as inability to concentrate and some impairment of memory, but these seemed gradually to improve as time went on." From what we know generally about organic brain involvements of this type, we are led to expect associated changes with respect to aggression, changes more marked than those taking place with respect to hostility, which is an additional reason for keeping the two constructs separate in our thinking. We have to remind ourselves that

A. S. may behave more aggressively as he recovers. If so, some of the conspicuously missing evidences of hostility may come to light also.

Signs of Hostility

Whenever a clinician deals with a suicidal attempt, he most certainly has to be alert to the hostile strivings that may be expressed in the act. Too often the suicidal person uses both his verbal warning and his actual suicidal attempt to extort validating evidence from those upon whom he has come to depend for the confirmation of his social outlook. One can never be quite sure about this until one has examined closely the case at hand.

Of course, the conclusion is quite simple, if one always assumes that hostility is the tendency to hurt or destroy something. In that case we say that the suicide was obviously a matter of hostility turned inward. Usually we go further and say that it turned inward because it could not successfully turn itself outward. This is perfectly painless logic; any clinician can follow it.

But personal construct theory does not lead one to reason this way. The definition of hostility is different; furthermore, it is not envisioned as a directive force but rather as a reference axis in terms of which behavior can be judged. When we look at A. S.'s act in this manner, we seek to discover what he was trying to achieve. What did he expect would happen? If he thought his act would force his parents to concede to his position, there would be evidence of hostility. If, in some remote way, the act was perceived as producing a kind of artificial validity for his construction of life, that also would be evidence of hostility. Perhaps he was trying to prove his mother a murderer. But we have no such evidence at hand. There is not even a report of a suicidal warning being expressed by A. S. Besides, as we said before, hostility is a matter that is hard to elaborate adequately during the early stages of clinical contact.

Control by Guilt

To feel that one has ordered one's life by understanding the outlooks of others—that is awareness of role. To sense that one's role has been lost—that is guilt. This is not to say that a person feels guilty when he fails to conform to the expectations of others; it is rather when he fails to conform to those expections of himself that he has based on his perception of what others believe and understand.

Guilt resembles anxiety, although personal construct theory makes a qualitative distinction between them. The loss of social role, the role one has defined for oneself in the light of genuine social perceptions, is what lies at the core of guilt. A person does not face conceptual chaos, as in anxiety, but social excommunication in his own realm of values. Thus, in guilt, he senses himself being cut off from the means of interpersonal confirmation and hence from his contact with social reality.

Perhaps the clearest instance of guilt in A. S.'s anamnesis is the experience of finding that his mother's sister had died in the New York hospital before he had got around to calling on her. We have to infer this experience, of course, but his quick ensuing shift of attitude and his immediate effort to adapt to his mother's wishes regarding Mary strongly suggests that he suffered sharp pangs of guilt on this occasion.

Here, too, we see the classic relation between guilt and hostility. In response to the guilt feelings he had written Mary to "break it off," and he had asked for his ring to be returned. When it became apparent that there was still a tie between himself and Mary, he says he was resentful. Guilt had tricked him. How could he handle his mother so he would not be tricked again? Thus he felt guilty because he had aggressively deserted his mother at a time when her sister was dying, and he felt hostile because the guilt feeling had brought him back into tow.

There is no evidence in the protocol to indicate how he felt about the effect of his suicidal attempt on his role. He had tried to kill his mother's son; did he feel guilty about that? Or did it seem as if he could thus restore a childhood role, exemplified, perhaps, by the nourishment of his mother's attention or even by the two malted milks that seem to play such a symbolic part of his portrayal of deeper cravings.

We must keep in mind also that he had begun to structure his role in terms of other figures. Mary and the girl with whom he felt himself in love during the last year of service were doubtlessly involved. So was his sister, presumably. Even his sister's divorce could have been involved in some way. Certainly his failure to marry either Mary or the other girl must have given him some sense of having fallen below the standards he had recently erected for himself founded on his feelings for them.

One sentence in this part of the protocol seems worth exploring much further. In speaking of the second girl he is quoted as saying, "I felt myself falling in love with her and it was very hard for me to tell her that it was love, but as time went on I knew that that was so." Had he reached a point where the sense of being in love was threatening, or could he not speak of such feelings without experiencing guilt? Later, in Los Angeles, was this remembered inability to admit a loving relationship between himself and another person a contributor to his loss of role, his sense of guilt? Perhaps he could not tell her that he loved her because to do so would be to conform to his parents' outlook toward Mary, and the substitute mate would always be a living reminder of his failure to confirm his own way of life.

QUESTIONS

Was He Trying to Terminate His Life or Validate It?

We return to the fundamental issues posed earlier. Is there anything that would lead us to believe that A. S. had dedicated his life to some purpose that would have to be abandoned if he remained alive? Certainly we have little to go on, but if there was such a purpose, it might have been to establish his independence as a person. He was broke; he had just spent his last quarter. He could have asked for help, but that seems to be the thing that he was determined not to do. To go without food would have brought persons clattering to his relief, and he probably was already acutely aware of doctor bills. If, indeed, there was a firm line that he was continuing to follow, it seems that it must have been the line of independence. Whatever we infer from the protocol at hand, however, the matter is one that only the subsequent psychotherapeutic series could clarify.

Consider the two limiting conditions for terminating one's own life: complete realism or complete chaos. Of the two, the latter seems to be much the more likely condition in A. S.'s case. He must have felt himself confronted with inexorable reality at the moment he bought his last malted milk, but the picture as a whole is one of chaotic outlook, or anxiety, as it would be called in terms of personal construct theory. It seems likely that he was trying to terminate his life more than to validate it.

Interestingly enough, two of his last acts, the purchase of the malted milk and the bath, seem to be directed by deep-seated constructions. The constructs involved were probably preverbal; that is to say, they were not of an order that could easily be labeled or even easily talked about. He remembers the malted milk as one of the good things he was brought to eat after his tonsillectomy at age eleven. There is also a passage in the protocol that seems to express preverbal constructs: the one that tells of getting up early in the morning and running downstairs to get dressed in front of a warm stove. Somewhere among these elements the clinician might expect to find vaguely formulated constructions that would help him to reconstruct A. S.'s state of mind just before swallowing the barbiturate capsules. Such a reconstruction might throw light on A. S.'s basic structure and hence upon his basic resources.

"Something Bigger than Myself"

The expression "needing something bigger than oneself" is an over worked cliché in inspirational discourse, but A. S. gives it a personal meaning by following it with the appositional phrase "a feeling of understanding from home." He had come to depend upon this feeling of understanding as his evidence in hand for most of his construction of life and particularly for his construction of role relations. To say that one feels the need for something bigger than oneself is to say what is probably true of all of us. What is bigger than self is the whole world of reality and the sense of being validly in touch with it. To be out of touch with it is to be out of touch with the future and to realize that life's bridging of past and future has failed to cross the chasm. In the broadest possible sense, A. S. was saying that he needed the restoration of the only sure contact he had ever felt with the world of reality.

But Why Didn't He Get a Job?

If A. S. had been able to establish for himself the single purpose of becoming independent, matters might not have turned out as they did. Such a purpose wavers badly when one's whole system of truths appears to have lost its validity. He says, "I would look in the papers and try to get a job, but it would seem as if I just couldn't get started. I would look at them, but wouldn't do any more. . . . And all the time my mood was getting worse, and I still had the feeling that I wanted to sever relations with my family." Under these conditions his efforts were much too much taken up with the internal struggle to allow him to shine his shoes and put up a proper front to an employment interviewer. The task that confronted him could not be reduced to the dimension of job hunting.

Why Did He Go to South America?

The one role relationship outside his family that seems to have taken any kind of root at all was with the girl of South American extraction. Moreover, his parents' objection to her was on stereotyped grounds; they made it plain that their way of life could not be reconciled with her presumed way of life. If he was to abandon his old stakes altogether, what more likely place was there to go than the one identified with the antithetical way of life.

To be sure, it was an ill-considered venture. He admits himself that he decided upon it all one afternoon. Besides, one must remember that by this time Mary had become inconsiderate and that he felt this was his folks' fault. Perhaps in South America there was more of the kind of person Mary once was.

PSYCHOTHERAPEUTIC PLANS

Psychotherapeutic plans always have to take into account the personal constructs of the therapist as well as of the client. Perhaps it is even more important to take the therapist into account, because clients cannot always be depended upon to keep their therapists in line. This is by way of saying that, if A. S.'s therapist is a psychoanalyst, it would be best to lay out the therapeutic plans in analytic terms rather than to risk the confusion of trying to follow personal construct plans seen through psychoanalytic spectacles.

From the standpoint of the psychology of personal constructs the task of psychotherapy is to restore and accentuate those universal psychological processes that characteristically make life an ongoing proposition. The client needs enough structure to lay his wagers, channel his aggressive efforts, and accept his losses. He needs to experiment with some idea of what is at stake. He needs access to various forms of reality to be used as validational evidence. He needs to have a methodology for dealing with his world piecemeal instead of in catastrophic terms. He needs role relationships so he can sift out social outcomes and maintain himself as a distinct individual, related to but distinguishable from other persons. He needs basic structure that will not be too much shaken by life's daily vicissitudes. Finally, he needs to look upon the objective of his therapy not as a terminal state of well-being but as a course of action to be embarked upon and continuously replotted throughout his life.

Immediate Therapeutic Issues to Be Faced

In this case there is the matter of medical rehabilitation. The schedule for whatever structural repair is required following the tracheotomy will have to be fitted into the psychotherapeutic plans. Presumably there will also be physical medicine treatment required. Assuming all treatment will soon move from an intramural to an extramural basis, there will be the matter of living arrangements and employment to be considered. There will also be immediate adjustment problems to be faced: the way he will account for himself to employment interviewers and to new acquaintances; how he will make use of recreational and educational resources; how he will manage his psychotherapeutic interview appointments.

If he is to be treated in a Veterans Administration mental hygiene clinic he must be labeled a service-connected disability case. Whether or not his military service was in any way involved, the very notion of service-connected disability is prejudicial to psychotherapy, especially in a case of this sort and especially as psychotherapy is understood from the position of personal construct psychology. It suggests, most unfortunately, that his psychological difficulties were caused by external events rather than by the way he had dealt with those events.

If all these practical assumptions are correct, we think of A. S.'s psychotherapeutic program being set up on an outpatient basis. Ideally the program should be initiated immediately and the long-range plans laid out as definitely as possible, while A. S.'s recent experience is still fresh in his mind and before the beginning of another type of adjustment takes shape. Certainly the relationship to his therapist, so important in this particular case, needs to be established immediately, and it should be clear to him that it will be maintained even after he is shifted to an outpatient basis. In some ways the experience he has had serves the function of shock treatment, and, as with shock treatment, the sooner the psychotherapeutic relationship is established the better. Too often there is a tendency to wait until the patient is in contact. But this is a mistake; one should start before the patient has come back into full contact with the everyday world.

Elaboration of the Construct System

At the present stage we know too little about A. S.'s personal construct system to be able to anticipate accurately what reformulations will be needed and how he will come to make them. Personal construct psychology leads us to try to work out these matters on the client's own terms rather than in terms of dogmatized versions of reality or psychodynamics. This makes the task less technical and more one of creative conceptualization. Client and therapist work as a construing team rather than having the therapist wait patiently for the client to come around to his way of thinking.

A. S. seems to be articulate enough to be able to express large portions of his outlook in words. In addition, he seems willing to venture into areas of confusion where words fail him but in which he can at least express himself by gesture and tears. With this combination of useful skills, so valuable in any client undergoing therapy, it should not be too difficult to get some of the preverbal constructs expressed at a precise enough level to be examined and tested.

This is only our surmise. If he begins to deal with matters in sweeping terms of unworthiness and generalized hostility, the therapist will be in for a long, long series. If it appears that there is danger of this happening, it will be important to keep the elaboration of the construct system well compartmentalized and approach any kind of sweeping insight with caution. Especially must one keep in mind the two slots already mentioned in which he might impulsively vacillate: dilation-constriction and aggression. Until the nature of these two construct dimensions is more fully known, the therapist will have to be doubly alert.

Establishment of Working Relations with Parents

One difficult issue will have to be settled by the therapist early in the game. Will he and the client try to establish a working role relationship with the parents, or will they keep the field constricted to minimize interaction with the parents? This decision can be postponed for a time, until there is a further exploration of the client's social resources, but not for long.

The chances are that therapy cannot reach down to a stable construct foundation unless the former course is taken. There is so much construing at the level of nourishment and primitive guilt that it is hard to imagine a simple substitution of an adult world of role relationships. Even if the therapist undertakes to accept a heavily dependent transference role, the parents, both mother and father, are still much too clearly part of A. S.'s world to be ignored.

A. S. will not like this, I suspect. He will object, especially when he begins to feel that he has got a fresh grip on life. Every time the relations with the parents are explored he will perceive the old threats standing there before him: the mother keeping tight possession of the keys to reality and truth and the hapless father with whom he must identify in spite of himself. It will not be a comfortable picture, and he will probably become quite annoyed with his therapist for holding it up in front of him.

But the picture is one he painted; it is not a photograph of his family; and this he must come to understand. It can be painted in other ways that are no less accurate and far more revealing. Furthermore, the new picture can be validated by aggressive exploration of the two parental personalities. It will take skill on the part of both members of the psychotherapeutic team, but it will be the way to make sense out of the new outlook and it will provide deep roots for the new personality structure.

It is customary for therapists to take a dim view of parents, especially of mothers. Because mothers play an important part in the personality development of clients, it is easy for therapists to imagine themselves in competition with them. Clients often anchor their inadequate construction in their mothers, and thus it seems to client and therapist both that those constructions were foisted upon this poor mortal by a designing witch.

Personal construct theory by its basic position permits us to see through this subject-predicate error. Let us hope the theory can be used to avoid the error in the case of A. S. as he is helped to reconstrue his mother. Besides, it is quite likely that the person who has suffered most in this case is not A. S. but his mother. She has both guilt and anxiety to cope with. As she is an aggressive person, she may try to handle her situation by aggressive hostility and thus cut herself off from sympathy and support. But that will not mean she is to be abandoned by a wise therapist or by a perceptive son. So it is with the father too. What more did he need to confirm the picture of his own inadequacy?

This is not the place to elaborate on the techniques that are derived from personal construct theory. Certainly, each therapist will use the theory to invent techniques that would not occur to others. Under a personal construct regimen clients often devise their own techniques. This is as it should be; for what good is therapy if it turns out clients who are mentally aseptic and unable to conceptualize for themselves any new ways of coping with life, either good or bad? What good would it do A. S. to be extricated from his present confusion if he were to be left high and dry without the ingenuity to invent his way out of the next mess he gets into? Let us hope that psychotherapy will land him on his feet and arunning—forward, that is.

References

1. Kelly, G. A.: *The Psychology of Personal Constructs,* New York: W. W. Norton & Company, Inc., 1955.

19

The Nondirective Handling of Suicidal Behavior [1]

SOLOMON DIAMOND

Doctor Diamond was born in New York City in 1906, and received a B.S. degree from New York University in 1927, and M.A. and Ph.D. degrees from Columbia University. He served as psychologist in the Vocational Advisory Service, New York City, and as counselor in several veterans guidance centers. A Diplomate in Counseling Psychology of the American Board of Examiners in Professional Psychology, he is now Professor of Psychology at Los Angeles State College where, at the time his contribution was written, he was also an active member of the college counseling staff. He is the author of *Personality and Temperament* (New York: Harper, 1957) and *Information and Error* (New York: Basic Books, 1959).

I do not approach the problem of suicide as one who has thought intensively about it, still less as one who has done research in this area. I come to it as a college counselor, who from time to time faces the problem directly in the form of a student client who confides his suicidal impulses or intentions. This very morning, a student whom I have seen half a dozen times stood with his hand on the doorknob, as he was about to leave my office, and "remembered" that one of the things he had meant to tell me about, which had been slipping his mind week after week, was that some time ago he had given serious thought to the question of suicide. Next week, this will be a topic of our discussion.

I have a week to prepare. Shall I speculate further on the dynamics of his problem? It is not trivial, and it is not implausible that it should lead to a genuine suicidal act. Nevertheless, I cannot imagine how my better understanding of it will help me to deal with this new facet of his behavior. Shall I give him reassurance, telling him that many quite normal persons toy with the idea of suicide or even experience suicidal obsessions without being in danger of actual suicide? Shall I admonish him, pointing out the

[1] Dr. Carl E. Rogers has been kind enough to read the original draft of this chapter, and I have taken advantage of his insightful criticism to correct certain defects. Of course, this does not imply that he is in agreement with all of its present content.

serious consequences to members of his family? Shall I reason with him about the futility of such a desperate last measure, which cuts off the possibility of attaining any of the satisfactions that life still holds? Shall I distract him, leading our discussion into other areas, hoping to arouse positive motivations? Shall I stall matters while I arrange to have him take a battery of projective tests in order to appraise the seriousness of the situation? Shall I ask him for further details and for his associations with the thought of death, hoping that I shall be able to give him insight into the fact that it is not really death he seeks in suicide but some symbolic satisfaction? Shall I plan to make a few suggestive allusions of my own that may serve as subtle reminders that suicide, like many other melodramatic acts, turns out to be less romantic in the execution than in the plan?

Of course, I shall do none of these things. I shall remind him at the start of the hour that he had mentioned thinking about suicide, in order to dispel any notion he may have that I am reluctant to talk about this subject. From then on, I shall pursue the problem as far as he permits me, keeping all my responses as far as possible in the pattern described as *reflection of feeling.* I shall do this not because I have an abhorrence to every other possible procedure but because in my experience this method has been effective. If I follow any of the other procedures mentioned in the preceding paragraph, I shall only be playing a role that parents and teachers and well-meaning friends have played before me, in the discussion of other schemes, if not of this one. He may seem to accede to my wisdom, but I know that meanwhile a defensive wall will be hardening around the deeper motives to this act. I know that I shall be forcing him deeper into the loneliness that is part of those motives and which others have not been able to dispel. Instead of this, my plan must be to let him see that, by exposing this added aspect of his self, he has enabled me to understand him more fully than before and thus to appreciate him more genuinely than I could have done without knowing this. I shall count on the motivating force of his need to be understood.

I am one of those counselors who is described as *nondirective* by his colleagues, his clients, and his students but whose actual allegiance to the methods of client-centered therapy is less than absolute. Not only do I permit myself an occasional question, but I am not always successful in suppressing the insight that reaches me before the client, and I am aware that my reflections characteristically include more guesswork than a good Rogerian would condone. Above all, I do not qualify as nondirective in the sense of being content that each client shall dispose of his own life as he sees fit. When I meet the possibility of suicide, I find myself wishing to prevent it. In this instance, as in many others, my reliance on the reflection of feelings is opportunistic rather than principled. It is possible, therefore, that I have not the right to present the case for the use of the client-centered approach in the psychotherapeutic treatment of suicidal behavior.

For Rogers, there is an essential connection between the permissive, democratic, client-centered philosophy that has respect for the client's objectives as its cardinal principle and the techniques that he recommends. He writes [1, p. 421]: "Client-centered counseling, if it is to be effective, cannot be a trick or a tool. It is not a subtle way of guiding the client while pretending to let him guide himself. To be effective, it must be genuine."

It is, in fact, not difficult to recognize the essential historical connection between the philosophy and the method. One must concede that its strategy, the constant focus on the client's feelings and personal meanings with avoidance of reassurance and other subtle forms of directiveness as well as of outright urging and suggestion, grew out of this respect for the client as a self-directing person. It does not follow that its tactics will be ineffective in the hands of a therapist who does not fully espouse the nondirective philosophy and the theories of personality that have grown up around it. Why may they not serve the skillful psychotherapist, even when he is directively minded? This question has considerable import for counseling generally, but it is especially relevant to any discussion of the handling of suicidal persons. Each of us recognizes that there is some point at which he ceases to feel free to permit the client to decide his own actions. For some, this point is reached as soon as we have decided that the client is immature. For others, it is not approached until the client plans seriously to perform violence upon another person. For most of us, it is reached when he plans violence upon himself. At this point, facing a matter of life and death, we feel that we must do something, whereas being nondirective seems to imply doing nothing. Emotionally, we are stirred to adopt some more directive procedure.

Rogers has left no doubt about the fact that, for him, the declaration of suicidal intent is no adequate provocation to a change of method. On this point, I shall quote him at length [2, p. 46 ff.]:

> Where life, quite literally, is at stake, what is the best hypothesis upon which to act? Shall the [therapist's] hypothesis still remain a deep respect for the capacity of the person? Or shall he change his hypothesis? If so, what are the alternatives? One would be the hypothesis that "I can be successfully responsible for the life of another." Still another is the hypothesis, "I can be temporarily

responsible for the life of another without changing the capacity for self-determination." Still another is: "The individual cannot be responsible for himself, nor can I be responsible for him, but it is possible to find someone who can be responsible for him." ... Does the counselor have the right, professionally or morally, to permit a client seriously to consider psychosis or suicide as the way out, without making a positive effort to prevent those choices? ... To me it appears that only as the therapist is completely willing that any outcome, any direction, may be chosen—only then does he realize the vital strength of the capacity and potentiality of the individual for constructive action. It is as he is willing for death to be the choice, that life is chosen.

Nevertheless, one may wonder if the last words quoted do not imply that even Rogers feels a *more complete* willingness that life shall be the choice. When I cling to the reflection of feelings in such a situation rather more rigorously than I ordinarily do, it is because of my conviction that the choice for life will be facilitated.

Next week, when the student whom I saw this morning will tell me about his thoughts on life and death, it will not be difficult to share in a measure and to reflect with sincerity the particular shadings of guilt, pessimism, despondency, self-derogation, desperation, and the like that have been associated with his suicidal thoughts. In my responses, I shall strive to fulfill one of the six conditions that Rogers [3] has recently defined as necessary and sufficient for therapeutic personality change: namely, that "the therapist experiences an empathic understanding of the client's internal frame of reference and endeavors to communicate this experience to the client." Surely, it would be futile to attempt to communicate any other set of ideas or feelings in the hope that the client may find these attractive and thus be persuaded to a change of conduct: In forming my responses, I shall follow these rules: (A) always reflect the worst and (B) express empathy and not a spectator's appraisal. I should like to expand on these rules, because I believe that the literature of client-centered counseling has not given sufficient attention to such problems of technique. Perhaps one must approach the problem of technique somewhat as a trickster in order to formulate it in these specific terms.

That one must always reflect the worst is a general rule that takes a lot of the guesswork out of counseling. The non-nondirectivists have always delighted in pointing out that even the technique of reflection has its directive aspect, because the therapist must decide what part of the client's communication shall be reflected. In fact, however, to reflect anything but the worst, whatever is most pessimistic, most foreboding, most self-condemnatory in the client's utterance, whatever is most unacceptable by the standards of his own self-concept, is to be guilty of a form of reassurance, on the one hand, because exclusion seems to imply that this is a relatively unimportant element in the communication, and of exhibiting a reluctance to talk of unpleasant subjects, on the other. The bright cheery remark and the casual event, and even the sincere expression of hopeful optimism, can always be ignored safely. But anything that hints of fear or trouble must be reflected at its first mention without minimizing intent. It is this sort of utterance that costs the client most effort, and therefore it would be as gauche to ignore it as to praise the store cake and fail to taste the dainties our hostess has made with her own hands.

That reflections must express empathy, and not appear to be the comments of a spectator, is also clear. Here, the tone of voice and the nuances of posture are quite important, but there is a matter of language that deserves some attention. The reflection of a statement of suicidal intent should never take such a form as "you want to do away with yourself" or "you can't see anything in life worth living for." The second person pronoun should enter very rarely into the counselor's vocabulary. One must be ready to share the feeling, whereas such statements disown it. Therefore one says, without equivocation, "it would be good to be through with living" or "there's nothing worth living for." One says it as if he has been convinced by the client's fate and as if ready to include this dismal outlook upon life as a part of one's own philosophy. Less than this would not be adequate acceptance. In short, one does not describe the client's point of view as it looks from a leather-covered armchair, but one enters into his world.

I do not feel myself dishonest if all the while I hold the inward hope that this person, whose worth I value and whom I truly respect as a person, will experience a change of heart or an influx of new courage. Occasionally, I have felt a strong temptation to notify some person—a parent, or a landlady, or a husband—that this unhappy patient should be watched. The belief that this decision is one for the person alone to make is one that I cannot hold with conviction; but I can pretend to myself that I believe it in order to refrain from taking what would be, I am sure, a foolish step and one that would only precipitate further difficulties.

THE CASE OF MR. A. S.

Up to this point, we have discussed only the handling of expressed suicidal intent on the part of clients being seen in therapy. However, the greater danger of suicide lies most certainly with those deeply troubled students who do not come to the counselor's office. Such a case was A. S., who when he found that "it was a real effort to study . . . went to the doctor for a nerve tonic." He received some sleeping pills, which didn't help, and then he went off on his disappointing South American junket.

If at this time A. S. had been successfully referred to the counseling office, the story he had to tell would have been very much like one that I find in my records. This student (let us call him B. T.) came for counseling, as many others do, because he had been having trouble concentrating on his studies. In the words of A. S., he did not know "what was causing all the trouble at that time," and he expected no more than a few suggestions that would help him to keep his mind from wandering—a sort of psychological nerve tonic. He was twenty-two, perhaps the very age at which A. S. dropped out of college. He too was quite youthful in appearance, for he spoke of his frequent annoyance when others mistook him for nineteen. He had the same sort of efficient and domineering mother and the same sort of passive father, whom he described as "just there," a sort of fixture in the home. He had the same history of feelings of inadequacy, which in this case were based in part on a disabling illness in childhood. There was the same feeling that his parents did not trust his abilities, which was expressed in uncertainty whether they really wanted him to continue in school. There was the same immediate conflict: the pledge of marriage to a lower-class sweetheart and reluctance to oppose his mother, who looked upon her as unsuitable. Give or take a few nonessential facts, the history of A. S. up to the time when he quit college might have been the disguised history of B. T. There was no mention of suicidal impulses (which apparently would not have figured in A. S.'s story at the same juncture), but B. T. did state that his father had attempted suicide at least twice and had been ineffectual in this as in everything else. There could be no doubt that he feared he had inherited much of his father's instability.

I saw B. T. only three times. However, he came to see his relations to both his girl friend and his mother with a new objectivity, and he reported at the last of these sessions that he was burning the midnight oil successfully. It is not unlikely that a similar outcome would have resulted if A. S. had gone to the counseling office with his study problem instead of taking sleeping pills from the doctor. The therapy was a warm interest, with a complete absence of guidance or advice. He decided to move into an apartment with a friend, away from home, but this rather standard bit of environmental therapy was his own idea, not even hinted at by me. The technique was almost solely reflection, but, as I confessed earlier, it was a brand of reflection that includes a bit of guesswork now and then; that is, I color my own responses with feeling tones or elements of general experience that seem close to expression in the client's thinking, and this pushes him into exploration of his feelings somewhat faster than he might otherwise progress. I do not believe that this violates Rogers' necessary and sufficient conditions, already cited above, that "the therapist experiences an empathic understanding of the client's internal frame of reference and endeavors to communicate this experience to the client."

To illustrate, I shall give a typical series of counselor responses that might occur in the first interview with such a student. To his statement that he "can't concentrate," I am likely to answer, "When you try to study, other thoughts keep coming into your mind." When he has incorporated this much into his account of his difficulties, the reflection advances to the form, "all kinds of worries keep popping into your head." This sometimes leads to a denial, which I accept. "The things that bother you while you are reading are not really worries, just anything at all." But, of course, the mention of worry is just as effective, shall we say in the unconscious or as a determinant of associations, in the negative as in the positive form. Soon there is an admission of something that does resemble a worry. This permits me to say, "This thing that is bothering you keeps pushing into your mind when you are trying to study." Before long, the process of studying slips into the background, the client is talking about less academic matters, and I can limit myself to the accurate reflection of his feelings. This is, I must confess, a rather directed procedure, but it is one I would not know how to manage without the help of Rogers. Without the technique of reflection, I would be reduced to asking questions, and every question would set up a block to free expression.

However, A. S. did not get to see a counselor. He received some pills, then dropped out of college in midsemester, and went off to South America. Returning, he went to Los Angeles, vaguely intending to enter one of the colleges there. But he did nothing about this and spent his days aimlessly thinking about finding a job, while his money dwindled away. With a little more strength or a little more money, he might have gone a step further with his plan, and the college counselor might still have had his chance. Later, A. S. described the therapy he needed at this time. He wanted "a feeling of understanding from home." This simple phrase is reminiscent of a series of childhood and adolescent rebuffs. We remember how as a little boy he kept getting into fights, even though he usually lost and hated to lose, and he could never understand why his parents did not take his side. Later, he did not understand why they did not rejoice in his success at gaining a sweetheart. Because he needed their approving understanding so much, he kept creating opportunities for it to take place, even though it never did. Surely, if the counselor had been fortunate enough to get his chance at this point, his most necessary function would be to fulfill that need as far as it lay in his power to do so. That is, he would have had to follow the rules laid down by Rogers, regarding the essentials of therapy. At this time, it is probable that there would have been confessions of suicidal intent. They would be met by reflections, phrased and spoken in a manner that would diminish none of their serious import. This would be no matter of 3 hours' counseling. But if the old, old hunger for a "feeling of understanding" were satisfied, even though not from home, the strength of the compulsion to create opportunities for it would be reduced. In this minimal sense, at least, it would be reasonable to expect a therapeutic change of personality.

The reader will have been disappointed if he expected to find a general theory of suicide as a part of the justification for the use of the client-centered method in dealing with suicidal behavior. On this point, too, we may listen to Rogers directly. After listing the essentials of any kind of psychotherapy, he specifically excludes certain factors as nonessential. Among these [3, p. 100 ff.]:

> It is *not* stated that these conditions apply to one type of client, and that other conditions are necessary to bring about psychotherapeutic change with other types of client.... It is *not* stated that special intellectual professional knowledge ... is required of the therapist.... It is *not* stated that it is necessary for psychotherapy that the therapist have an accurate psychological diagnosis of the client.

I do not fully agree with all the *not* statements just quoted, but this is not the place to discuss them. Like most psychologists, I would like to believe that my special professional knowledge has some utility in the counseling situation, but perhaps Rogers is correct in supposing that this is more a wish than a fact. However, it is undoubtedly true that any psychologist who turns to the client-centered method in dealing with such a critical problem as suicide does so because he is in agreement with Rogers' basic premise that what are most important are the dynamics of growth and cure and that these are basically the same with all our clients.

In final summary: whatever the sources of the difficulties that led A. S. to his suicide attempt, a counselor operating within the general framework of client-centered therapy could have met the situation adequately, and with a minimum of risk, if this young man had come for help. In such a case as this, the most pressing social problem is not to improve our therapeutic skills but to arrange the opportunity for using them.

References

1. Rogers, Carl R.: Significant aspects of client-centered therapy, *American Psychologist,* 1: 415–422, 1946.
2. Rogers, Carl R.: *Client-centered Therapy,* Boston: Houghton Mifflin Company, 1951.
3. Rogers, Carl R.: The necessary and sufficient conditions of therapeutic personality change, *Journal of Consulting Psychology,* 21: 95–103, 1957.

20

Summary

NORMAN L. FARBEROW

The purpose of this chapter is to review and summarize the materials presented in Part II. It is apparent that in perusing these chapters the reader will have been able to observe a number of skilled artisans at work on the same subject, providing him with the opportunity of peering over their shoulders as each worked at his task. It might be likened to the opportunity of having a group of artists, each representative of a different school of painting, explain the mode and manner that are the basis for the constructions of his school, then describe how this would apply to painting a particular subject, and then actually paint a picture of that subject for us. More than that, in this instance each artist has used the same model for his painting. What emerges is always more or less recognizable as the original object, but the painting as a whole is slightly different for each artist. The purpose of this chapter may now be sharpened: it is not to enunciate a *new* theory of suicide or even a synthesis of pre-existing theories but rather to present here in one chapter résumés of the eight points of view presented in Part II of this volume and to note their similarities and differences in theoretical focus and practical (psychotherapeutic) application.[1]

Each reader will have reflected on some of the similarities and differences that appeared between the various viewpoints and the resulting pictures and will have noted the way particular facets have been emphasized,

[1] Critical evaluation of each theory is not attempted in this chapter. For comprehensive summaries, discussions, critiques, and integrations of the theoretical formulations, the reader is referred to Hall and Lindzey [1], who discuss all the theories except Kelly's, and Munroe [4], who discusses the psychoanalytic theories. The complete presentation of Kelly's personal construct system may be found in his two volumes published in 1955 [2].

other patterns have been outlined, and still others have been ignored. But it is difficult to hold these contrasts and similarities in mind unless they are selected and outlined, as this chapter hopes to do for the reader.

The presentation below follows this outline:

I. Theoretical approaches to suicide
  A. Theoretical bases of suicide
  B. Significant suicidal dynamics
II. Analyses of the case of Mr. A. S.
  A. Qualitative descriptions
  B. Quantitative descriptions
III. Therapeutic implications
IV. Epilogue

THEORETICAL APPROACHES TO SUICIDE

Although each contributor represents a different theoretical point of view, it is obvious that the presentations must reflect the individual theorist as well. In other words, it is impossible to separate the general theories from the specific theorists presenting them. It is inevitable that each theorist will integrate, modify, and select from the theory with which he is identified elements compatible for him and tend either to eliminate or disregard what he cannot use. This, of course, does not apply to Dr. Kelly's chapter, where he is the originator of the specific theoretical approach discussed. Thus, any theory presented by an adherent becomes a general presentation of its concepts and formulations colored and tinged with the personal perceptions and reflections of that proponent.

Theoretical Bases of Suicide

Psychoanalytic (Futterman)

Theoretical background. The aggressive, destructive drive, or the death instinct (Thanatos), is postulated as another source of energy along with the sexual drive, or the life instinct (Eros), and is subject to the same kinds of vicissitudes. A key concept is that neither drive operates independently of the other, but they are fused in variable amounts, the fusion relieving the aggressive impulses of their destructive quality and permitting sublimation. The death instinct is characterized as essentially conservative, avoiding new experiences, and striving for a state of complete rest; it seeks the past and is under the domination of the repetition compulsion.

Theoretical bases of suicide. Fundamentally, the basis for suicide lies in the mere fact of a death instinct, which in its constant seeking of eternal rest may find expression in suicide. Futterman refers to some of the formulations by psychoanalytic theorists of the ways in which the drive seeks and finds expression; e.g., Menninger has distinguished three elements as essential in all suicidal behavior: the wish to kill, the wish to be killed, and the wish to die. Suicidal behavior emerges when a diffusion of the aggressive drive from the sexual drive occurs so destructive behavior can emerge. The process in the melancholic, where there is a real aggressive explosion directed toward the self, is described as a regressively incorporative one, with aggression appearing as a means of possession-destruction. Self-destruction occurs because of the confusion between subject and object. Lewin's ideas about sleep, the fantasy of sleep at the "good" ever-nourishing breast, as a model of immortality, happiness, etc., are related to cases of suicide in manic depressive psychosis and the drug addict. Rado's concept of pharmacothymia and its relation to suicide is described in terms of efforts by the person to dispel depression forever and to substitute for it an elation that could last forever. Glover's discussion of bursting sensations that may result in suicide because of overburdening of the psychic apparatus with instinctual energy is related to the internal catathymic crisis. The attempts to relieve such sensations may appear as impulsive suicidal tendencies. A state that may help the occurrence of suicidal behavior is one in which there is a rapid oscillation of feelings leading to disorganization in the personality. Love and hate may appear in rapid succession (in Scott's formulations) so each borrows energy from the other in its expression. This helps us to clarify the appearance of suicidal tendencies in patients where there is a sudden dissolution of a love relationship and a quick oscillation to reunion with the love object after the suicidal attempt.

Suggested classifications. Describing the nature of the phenomenon of suicide, its characteristics seem to be the following: (A) it is drastic; (B) it gambles with success; (C) it has comic-tragedy aspects in failure; (D) it mobilizes guilt, death wishes, etc., in others; and (E) as motor behavior, it is primitive in character.

Psychoanalytic (Hendin)

Theoretical background. Hendin's psychoanalytic view falls within the framework of Freudian psychodynamics, but it specifically excludes the postulation of a destructive drive as a separate motivating force. His focus is in keeping with modifications of earlier Freudian instinct psychology toward an ego or adaptational psychology.

Theoretical bases of suicide. Freud's basic contribution toward suicide and depression was the concept of retroflexed rage. However, we have learned much since. Depression itself we now see as a dependency adaptation with the self-directed rage viewed as a reaction to frustrated dependency. Expiation is now considered an important aspect of the psychology of depression (Rado), as is the pre-paranoid personality structure of many depressed patients. Depression, however, is not the *sine qua non* of suicide, and the psychodynamics of depression are not simply equivalent to the psychodynamics of suicide.

The whole dependency constellation, whether depression is present or not, and attitude toward rejection and abandonment are as important as the ways in which aggression is handled in understanding suicide. Equally significant and most neglected psychodynamically are the patients' attitudes and fantasies toward death and dying. Great suicidal danger exists when the patient, consciously, in dreams, or in fantasies, views death as a source of gratification. The danger is also great when the patient is apathetic and views himself as already dead. In addition, death may also be viewed as a punishment and suicide as an atonement. Abandonment and death may be equated and the suicide may signify a retaliatory abandonment.

Jung (Klopfer)

Theoretical background. The monopolistic role of the ego is denied, and the self is described as the deeper center that maintains the contact between the individual and the world. There must be minimal contact between ego and self in order for life to be meaningful. Danger occurs, however, because the self has both a bright and a dark side; the latter, when it prevails, may make death seem more desirable than life.

Theoretical bases of suicide. The person with suicidal tendencies has longings, rarely conscious, for a spiritual rebirth. In suicide, death is seen as the death of the ego, which has lost contact with the self and must return to the womb of the *magna mater* to reestablish contact and to be reborn. The danger is that the archetypal force of the *magna mater,* which has both life-giving and life-destroying aspects, may result in self-destruction rather than rebirth. The suicidal act occurs when (A) a dead-end situation prevails, with the feeling that life has no meaning and that meaning can be regained only through psychological rebirth; (B) the ego is enveloped by the conflict; (C) the resentment may reach murderous proportions with rage directed against the person "responsible," in which case suicide may then be an attempt to prevent such murderous acts; and (D) a lack of vitality makes it impossible to find some acting-out substitute to release the tension.

Suggested classifications. Some sample situations when death (not necessarily by suicide) may seem more desirable than life are (A) the possibility of a hero's or martyr's death; (B) intractable pain or unbearable mental anguish; (C) counterphobic reaction to death, when death seems so horrible that a person prefers an end to horror to a horror without end; (D) reunion with a dead loved one; (E) the search for freedom, where the desire is not to be tied down to life or anything it contains; and (F) the search for closure, where an older person may long for death as a well-deserved closure to a rich and full life.

Some of the phenomenological dimensions of the suicidal act are (A) collective versus individual suicide, where the culture sanctions suicide so it may even be performed under a strong collective impulse rather than under individual personal decisions; (B) active versus passive suicide, where, as an example of the latter, the captain may choose to go down with his ship; (C) sincere versus attention-getting suicidal behavior, where the motivation and the intent become important in understanding the act; and (D) planned versus impulsive suicide, where the degree of rootedness is important and where suicide may occur on the basis of a whim.

Adler (Ansbacher)

Theoretical background. The individual must be seen as part of his social context and as a unique, unified whole, striving for a success that he defines in his own subjective terms, all of which he may not be aware of. As some of the characteristics of adjustment, such factors as mental disorder striving, mental health striving, and adequacy of social interest, which is the capacity to understand and to accept the social interrelatedness of the individual human life, must be evaluated. Social interest is seen as innate in the form of dispositions or attitudes that, when developed, becomes part of the individual's goal of success. Exogenous factors in situations may require more social interest than the neurotically disposed person has available, resulting in threat to self-esteem and the formation of protective symptoms.

Theoretical bases of suicide. The following characteristics occur in suicide, although they may also appear in many other symptomatic disorders in varying patterns: (A) pampered life style, in which suicidal tendencies develop in persons whose method of living has always been dependent on the achievements and the support of others; (B) inferiority feelings and self-centered goals, where self-esteem is low and suicide may offer the feeling of mastery over life and death; (C) degree of activity, which is high among suicides; and (D) veiled aggression, in which the suicide hopes to hurt others by hurting himself and maneuvers to influence others by creating sympathy. Although rare, there are cases of suicide among well-adjusted persons, as in situations where there is endless suffering, inhuman cruel attacks, or incurable and extremely painful disease. Epidemics of suicides may occur, in which cultural attitudes toward suicide are important.

Sullivan (Green)

Theoretical background. By focusing on patterns of interaction that occur between particular persons within a particular milieu, human relatedness emerges as the core of character and personality. The self grows out of the organized experience of reflected appraisals by the significant others in a person's life, with personifications as the symbolic elaboration of organized experience which lead to the anticipations of particular kinds of interpersonal events. Personifications occur throughout life, so unresolved conflicts occurring at different times may, in predisposed persons, precipitate mental disorder, sometimes manifested by suicidal attempts. Genetic formulations of personality are not attempted because these would interfere in the interaction between patient and therapist.

Theoretical bases of suicide. Suicide, as a destructive activity, belongs in the category of hateful and hostile types of integrations with other persons. Freud's (early, 1918), Menninger's, and Rado's formulations on suicide are considered as sound. Additional factors important in suicide are anxiety, which is a result of inadequate personifications and which may produce antianxiety systems that may actually interfere with growth; and envy, which occurs when the person cannot feel a sense of his own worth. The various depressive syndromes, such as depressive reaction or involutional agitated depression, indicate extreme preoccupation with self-depreciating thoughts and are of especial concern. Special treatment must be considered for those who threaten suicide as a kind of emotional blackmail in order to avoid an unpleasant situation. Also, there are situations in which suicide could be called mature behavior. It is apparent that no single theory can account for all suicides.

Suggested classifications. Green finds most useful the classification suggested by Weiss, which divided attempted suicides into three groups: aborted successful suicide, true suicidal attempts, and suicidal gestures.

Horney (De Rosis)

Theoretical background. Neurosis is seen as a failure in social as well as individual growth, with suicide as one type of failure of the development of the self. Man is not born with innate, destructive tendencies. Basically, if the infant is given an anxiety-free abundant environment, there will be spontaneous development and growth. However, culture, religion, political, and similar forces may cooperate with parents or parental figures to produce distorted forms of self-development. The process of neurotic development involves the arousal of basic anxiety, a condition in which the child, as he attempts to create some consistency for himself in his world, learns to orient himself outwardly, a state of outer-centeredness. As the child maneuvers to overcome this basic anxiety, he succeeds on certain levels and may develop feelings of superiority, but new sources of anxiety appear in the contradictory demands made upon him. An idealized self develops, encompassing self-expectations and appraisals of expectations of others. Alienation of the self occurs with the disparity between the development of the idealized self and the development of the self. There are three main forms of outer orientation to life: (A) despotic and authoritarian, (B) self-abnegating, and (C) resigned.

Theoretical bases of suicide. Four main factors underlie suicide: (A) hopelessness, (B) suffering, (C) alienation, and (D) search for glory. A sudden impulse of self-hatred in a framework of severe alienation may initiate suicidal behavior. Feats of daring and heroism, which may occur as part of the search for glory, may be unconscious self-destructive moves in that they reflect the inability of the idealized self to accept its immortality. A slow form of suicide occurs when the idealized self invests the self with ugliness and slothfulness, degrading the self, as occurs with bums and alcoholics. Another form of self-destruction occurs when the person "silently but actively collaborates toward his own moral deterioration." This also is based on alienation, with the person cynically opposed to integrity, which he considers a form of weakness. Other factors important in suicide are cultural mores, values of life, and concepts of life and death. A hopelessly suffering person may take steps toward suicide, in which case it becomes a means of preserving the self, which may be disintegrating from the uninterrupted suffering.

Suggested classifications. Suicide occurs in different ways depending on the form of outer orientation: (A) despotic and authoritarian persons take the active step toward suicide; (B) self-abnegators die through neglect of the self in the search for others to fill self-esteem; (C) resigned persons die by inaction or by default. Active suicide is apparent in cultures where pursuit of power is important.

Personal Construct (Kelly)

Theoretical background. The personal construct theory assumes that we impose the singularity of our own thinking on life's events and that these events actually can be construed in many different ways. Each person validates his reality in terms of his own personal constructs. The theory discards well-known words such as learning, motivation, feeling, emotion, needs, and stimuli and redefines others.

Theoretical bases of suicide. For each suicide the question has to be asked: What was the person trying to validate by his action? The choice of death by a particular person as a solution to his problems must be seen from *his* constructions. Two conditions under which suicide seems sensible are realism, where the course of events seems so obvious there is no point in waiting for the outcome, and indeterminacy, where everything seems so unpredictable that one might as well abandon the scene. Terms important in the understanding of suicide are (A) the basic postulate and choice corollary, or the psychological channeling of a person's processes by the ways in which he anticipates events, with the tendency to choose alternatives that seem to provide more validity to his construct system; (B) dilation versus constriction, as when a person grasps at more and more things or restricts himself to fewer and fewer things in the hope of making better sense out of events; (C) anxiety, the sense of chaos with feelings of helplessness; (D) threat, the result of finding oneself on the brink of a deeply significant change in the self; (E) hostility, or the extortion of confirming evidence for the validation of the individual's personal constructions to preserve the status quo; and (F) guilt, or the feeling the person is left with when his perceptions of demands upon him from others are invalidated and he feels he has no role left and that he is thus cut off from the means of interpersonal confirmation.

Nondirective (Diamond)

Consistent with the nondirective approach, Diamond offers no theoretical framework for viewing suicide but concentrates instead almost entirely on the therapeutic process and the philosophy with which nondirective counseling functions. This philosophy is based upon the fundamental tenet of respect for the client as a self-directing person and a conviction in the dynamics of growth and cure within each individual. This is effected by avoiding all forms of directiveness and by focusing on the client's feelings and personal meanings.

Significant Suicidal Dynamics

Some dynamics and their relation specifically to suicide seem to appear both frequently and consistently in the discussions by the contributors. In order to see the relative significance and specific roles attributed to each dynamic, each contributor's comments about it have been summarized and grouped with the comments by the others about that same dynamic, allowing ready comparison for differences and similarities.

Dependency

Dependency is noted frequently as an important factor in the constellation of motives important for suicide or as significant in the general make-up of the personality in which suicide can appear. *Futterman* does not elaborate specifically on dependency, but his references to Rado's and Lewin's formulations about the fantasy of sleep at the "good," ever-nourishing breast, and the frustrations from inability to achieve this state, seem to be directly related to dependency behavior. *Hendin* stresses the nature of the dependency adaptation in depression, particularly that the rage and depression seen in severely depressed patients is part of the drive for dependency that has been frustrated. A paranoid personality structure in the person facilitates the frustration of the dependency. Loss of a symbiotic relationship in which the person has been very dependent on another for self-esteem contributes to suicidal impulses. *Klopfer* indirectly implies the dependency element when he says that the suicidal act can be seen as a symbolic process of rebirth, reestablishing the early pattern of an acceptable dependent relationship from which he can once again develop. *Ansbacher* refers to the pampered life style, in which suicidal tendencies develop in persons whose method of living from early childhood has been dependent upon the achievements and the support of others. They expect and demand that others will fulfill their wishes. *Green* refers to persons whose early experiences with others may have sufficiently warped their development that predispositions for illness may occur. Anxiety, which is for Green one of the important factors in suicide, arises from repeated unfortunate experiences with persons upon whom one is continuously dependent in some way. *De Rosis* describes the neurotic dependency fostered in the child that results in an outer-centeredness, or a relationship to life in which the person is overly dependent on persons and objects outside of himself. In suicidal behavior, a form of outer-orientation that he calls self-abnegation results in death that comes about because the person neglects himself in pursuit of the esteem of others. Cultural influences enter in that some religions, governments, and other systematized orders have idealized self-abnegation. Suicides then may be either many or few, depending on the way the authorities have formalized it. Although for *Kelly* dependency is a term that would probably drop out of his system as a motivational referrent no longer necessary, it still might be implied in his use of the concept of validation, in which a person may have learned to base much of his behavior on his interpretations of what is expected of him from a particular person. Without this validation, chaos and confusion appear. Kelly points out how A. S.'s mother was the principal validator of his constructions, so without her he could not make sense of his life.

Aggression and Hostility

Because the terms *aggression* and *hostility* are so frequently used interchangeably, both are grouped together as a general concept in examining the roles they play in the presentations of our contributors. *Futterman's* presentation of Freudian theory on suicide, of course, based as it is on the postulation of a separate aggressive, destructive drive, makes the role of aggression and hostility central for the consideration of suicide. It is in terms of the tracing of the vicissitudes of the aggressive drive and its varying relationships with the sexual drive that many Freudian theorists now concern themselves. Menninger, in particular, elaborates the role of the aggressive drive in suicidal behavior, feeling that within it can be seen at least three elements: the wish to kill, the wish to be killed, and the wish to die. Self-destructive activity emerges when there is incomplete or inefficient functioning of the neutralizing device of love. The earlier (1918) Freudian formulation of hatred expressed toward a rejecting or abandoning (lost) introjected love object falls in this category. In melancholia, aggressive explosions may occur as a result of the identification of the ego with an incorporated love object that has become lost either in reality or fantasy. For *Hendin* aggression is usually seen in reaction to frustrated dependency and its self direction may serve coercive, retaliatory and expiatory motives. *Klopfer* refers specifically to the building up in the person of resentment from the frustrating situation until, with the addition of other emotional forces, the resentment reaches a demoniacal level with murderous proportions, and uncontrollable impulses to kill oneself are experienced. *Ansbacher* refers to the veiled aggression of the suicidal person and his desire to hurt others by injuring himself. Suicide is an act of reproach or of revenge in that it takes the forms of veiled attacks on others who will be most affected by it. *Green* includes among the neurotic conditions those in which persons childishly and spitefully threaten or attempt to kill themselves as a kind of emotional blackmail in order to avoid an unpleasant situation. Green also describes Rado's formulation of the depressive episode as one in which there is a real or imagined loss related to earlier real injury or loss. The reaction is coercive rage and guilty fear, with the increasing fear splitting the defeated rage into a smaller part that is repressed and a larger part that becomes assimilated into the guilty fear itself. The portion that is assimilated into the guilty fear is the portion that is turned against the individual himself. This latter hypothesis is, of course, similar to the earlier theory of Freud, in which the now hated, introjected love object is the aim of the suicidal activity. Green adds to this that in depressives the particular person who was a destructive influence in the patient's past is the target of the present self-destruction. *De Rosis* describes the condition of alienation in which there is a disparity of development of the idealized self with respect to the relatively undeveloped self. A sudden impulse of self-hatred may cause the person to act against himself. This occurs because the idealized self seeks to effect its own ends as directly as possible and uses the self-hatred to intimidate the self into carrying out its needs. Vindictiveness in a person will occur from his demands that his prized idealized self be spared from indignities. *Kelly* redefines the term hostility to fit within his theoretical system, but it seems to include the elements of aggression and hostility as they are generally conceptualized. For him it is not a directive force but rather one axis in the general construct system of the individual along which his behavior can be judged. It is the extortion of confirming evidence for the validation of the individual's personal constructions. In this way the individual arranges his world so he can continue as he has, preserving the status quo and relieving him of the responsibility of revising his outlook.

Guilt

Guilt is mentioned frequently in the literature as a feeling that is of significance in the understanding of suicidal activity. Some of our contributors assign it an important role; others mention it barely or not at all. *Futterman* refers briefly to guilt in the description of the development of the superego. The child, in mastering his oedipal strivings, finds the aggressiveness derived from his destructive drive incompatible with other needs, and the superego is formed to mediate the conflicts. Guilt feelings (and anxiety) are produced to help dispel intolerable wishes from consciousness. They are used to fend off and transform what the ego has learned to recognize as dangerous (destructive) instinctual strivings. *Hendin* stresses the factor of expiation as a motivational force, a kind of self-punishment for the anger felt toward a disappointing object. By punishing himself the person hopes to be forgiven and reinstated. In the sicker patients the guilt of sin takes a delusional form and the self punishment appears as almost an end in itself without any hope of being forgiven or reinstated. *Klopfer,* in discussing the case of A. S., notes how intense, unconscious guilt feelings may facilitate the contamination of the personal shadow by the archetypal shadow. *Green* implies guilt feelings when he describes the depressive syndrome, which is so important in suicide and in which the individual has come to be extremely preoccupied with self-depreciating rumination. Although *Kelly* uses the term guilt, it is also redefined within the framework of his theory and refers to the feelings a person has when he feels no true role has been left for him. This occurs when he fails to conform to those expectations of himself that he has based on his perception of what others believe and understand and results in his feeling cut off from the means of interpersonal confirmation. Life makes sense in terms of various role constructs; when these have been invalidated, life no longer makes sense and the person suffers from guilt.

Anxiety

Although anxiety is a broad and general term, several of the contributors make explicit mention and place particular emphasis on this element in suicidal behavior. *Futterman* talks about the building of tension within the patient to the point where an internal catathymic crisis may take place; he relates it to Glover's postulations of bursting sensations that may result from an overburdening of the psychic apparatus with instinctual energy. He also refers to the anxiety of the child as, in his development, he experiences the ideas, fantasies, and wishes of the aggressive drive. The anxiety (and guilt feelings) that results helps in the development of defenses for handling such impulses. *Klopfer* refers to the ego being enveloped by conflict and being unable to disidentify itself from it when the emotional conflict that is largely responsible for the blocking makes the person feel that life is a meaningless, dead-end situation. *Green* states that, among the factors influencing the drive toward suicide, Sullivan specifically pointed to severe anxiety as an extremely important element in personality malfunctioning that may lead to suicidal behavior. *De Rosis* underlines the concept of anxiety as a basic one in terms of neurotic growth. Anxiety is extremely important in the development of the idealized self, which can be disparate from the true self, so alienation appears a very dangerous state in relation to the possibility of suicide. *Kelly* calls anxiety the sense of chaos; a state of total anxiety occurs when the person feels that everything in life is indeterminate. One has no personal constructs available for events, so one is at the mercy of the events. The suicidal attempt is often a desperate bid for some kind of structure or certainty.

Suicide and "Adjustment"

Whether or not suicide can occur in relatively mentally healthy persons has long been a bone of contention. There are some who have argued that the mere fact of suicidal behavior is evidence in itself of psychosis, irrationality, mental illness, etc. If suicidal behavior per se is made equivalent to insanity, then such a conclusion must (tautologically) follow. However, if it is accepted that some emotional disturbance can occur in well-adjusted persons or that culture, religion, ethics, etc., can be powerful factors in determining the behavior, then the concept of healthy suicide [2] becomes possible. *Ansbacher* states there are cases of suicide in which the person could be considered well-adjusted, although such instances are rare. He sees these kinds of suicides occurring in such situations as endless suffering, inhuman cruel attacks, and incurable and extremely painful diseases. Suicides may also appear in the form of epidemics or receive cultural sanction, as in the case of hara-kiri. *Klopfer* lists situations where death seems desirable, such as intractable pain in which life can seem so miserable that death appears as a liberation, and the search for closure, in which an older person longs for death as a well-deserved closure for a rich, full life. He points, too, to cultural influences that may sanction the act, where suicide is an accepted form of behavior and not an indication of emotional ill health. He refers specifically to the hero's or martyr's death and to the traditional, passive kind of suicide, such as the captain going down with his ship. *Green* states his belief that suicide may occur as mature behavior and cites the example of Socrates' taking hemlock. *De Rosis* makes the point that a person may choose to kill himself under certain conditions of extreme privation and suffering when the outcome is hopeless. This is felt to be a form of self-protection undertaken by the hopelessly suffering person. Unmitigated suffering can disintegrate the self, and suicide is elected as a way to preserve the self. He states that "it would appear to be well within the province of the self to take its own life as

[2] The concept of logical suicides is elaborated in "The Logic of Suicide" [5].

the final act of self-responsibility." *Kelly* describes how suicide may be a validating act and how some persons for different reasons stack the cards in the way they live in favor of death, such as guilt, exasperation, and serene resignation. For him, too, Socrates validated his life by choosing the hemlock, and Jesus validated his life by choosing crucifixion. In these cases, suicide becomes a natural outcome of convictions.

ANALYSES OF THE CASE OF MR. A. S.

Another method of examining the various approaches to suicide was effected by presenting each contributor a copy of the same anamnesis of a person who had attempted suicide, Mr. A. S., a twenty-three-year-old Caucasian. The reader has already seen from the presentations in the preceding chapters how each writer described what he thought occurred in A. S. within the framework of his theory. We may summarize the descriptions of A. S. in at least two ways. The first method, which might be called qualitative, groups the comments about A. S. made by each contributor in terms of the elements previously mentioned as significant in suicidal behavior. The second method, more or less quantitative in nature, presents the results of ratings or sortings of items about A. S. by most of the contributors. This was done by use of the Q-sort, a procedure that asks (and limits) each judge to describe the patient by means of the same set of descriptive statements.

Qualitative Descriptions

In examining the case of A. S. from the viewpoint of each contributor, only a few of the many areas referred to can possibly be discussed. To some extent these are the dynamic areas of significance in suicide outlined in the previous section. The following section notes how each contributor sees these dynamics functioning in A. S.

Dependency

All contributors see A. S. as a dependent person and that it was his mother on whom he was most dependent and who was the most important person in his family. *Futterman* mentions that A. S. cannot run the risk of abandonment or the possibility of death of the mother and that his irrational self wanted both parents and Mary, his girl friend. *Hendin* remarks that, for A. S., giving up the mother may have amounted to abandonment or death. The dependency-rejection constellation was very clear, with the inability to carry out successfully what his parents disapproved of further indicating the intensity of the dependency. *Klopfer* states that A. S.

could not face life on his own responsibility and made only abortive attempts to declare his independence. His desire in the suicidal attempt was to let himself be swallowed up by the *magna mater* because he felt he could not live his life without her. *Ansbacher* points to how much A. S.'s mother spoiled him, resulting in the pampered life style, in which he felt he could obtain everything easily with the help of others. The main conflict was seen as one in which A. S. was trying to hold on to (and remain dependent on) both his parents and his girl friend. *Green* calls A. S. a dutiful mama's boy and feels that he was infantilized by the mother. The struggle is likened to the infantile hunger emergency described by Rado. A. S. was utterly dependent on others for his self-regard. Green indicates, however, that, although one might call A. S. passive, it did not mean that he was a soft, weak person, unable to do anything for himself. *De Rosis* outlines the entire course of outer-centeredness that characterized the development of A. S., with the mother again specified as the principal agent who never let the patient be anything other than dependent on her. *Kelly* indicates that the mother was the principal validator for the patient's construct system and that, although he tried to validate his anticipations elsewhere, it was only with his mother that his constructions would lead to consistent outcomes. *Diamond* refers to the fact that A. S. seemed constantly to need his parent's approval and understanding.

Hostility and Aggression

Futterman sees A. S.'s suicidal act as, in part, an attempt to destroy the superego figure (his mother) for all the wrong that he felt she had done him. *Hendin* refers to the retroflexion of aggression that has occurred. *Klopfer* feels that some of the patient's behavior is an attempt to kill the mother image that is holding A. S. tight. He describes also the aggressiveness that the patient showed until he was twelve years old. *Ansbacher* sees in A. S. the revolt of the pampered child and strong indications of a smoldering resentment against the mother. With such persons a time is always reached when even the most affectionate and giving of mothers can no longer supply all the aggressive demands of the child. A. S. is the ruling type, but his activities are mostly of the nonconstructive variety. A. S. uses aggression against himself, hurting himself in order to hurt others, a mode of offense he learned from his mother. *Green* indicates how A. S. continually tried to fight his mother and could not, and he stressed the continuing hostility toward the mother that the patient felt. *De Rosis* mentions the early fighting as indicative of a small amount of self-development but sees A. S. mainly as a person who never could be self-assertive. However, the suicide attempt itself is seen as a search for respite rather than restitution, with no basis in what he calls vindictiveness. *Kelly* refers to the sporadic aggressiveness on the part of A. S. in reaction to the feelings of threat he experienced in relation to his mother. However, Kelly, like De Rosis, sees no substantial evidence of hostility, within his use of the term, specifically as A. S.'s efforts to extort validating evidence from the world for his constructs. Kelly sees the suicide attempt as an effort to terminate life rather than trying to validate it.

Relationship with His Girl Friend

The girl friend, Mary, was seen as serving different purposes and filling different needs. *Futterman* stresses the oedipal nature of the relationship with Mary and how A. S. was attempting to attach himself to a figure that might help him in freeing himself from his mother. *Klopfer* feels he gained strength from Mary for his opposition toward his mother and that he sought in Mary the positive, warm mother he desired. *Ansbacher* feels that the relationship with Mary gave him the strength to attempt to revolt. *Green* says A. S. was fortunate in meeting Mary, who appreciated him, and that she was important in allowing him the opportunity to try to love someone else. *De Rosis* and *Kelly* feel differently from the others; Mary was, in their opinions, relatively unimportant. De Rosis saw the alliance with Mary as superficial, for he feels that A. S. couldn't really involve himself with anybody and was using her within his needs to rescue the underdog; Kelly saw A. S. as using Mary merely as a filler for the void that his parents had left.

Other Significant Factors in Mr. A. S.'s Suicide Attempt

A number of other factors were noted by the different contributors as more or less significant in the case of A. S. *Futterman* feels that in A. S. there was a continuous building of tension that resulted in an internal catathymic explosion, which then required some activity on his part, in this case, a suicide attempt. *Klopfer* stresses the unconscious desire to be reborn and mentions that in the change of A. S.'s studies to sociology may be seen the symbolic expression of the desire to find a way to the outer collective. *Ansbacher* describes the underdeveloped social interest, the inferiority feeling, and the goal of personal superiority of A. S. He also singles out the exogenous factor present, specifically running out of money. *Green* stresses the envious craving in A. S. of what others had. *De Rosis* sees the patient as without hope, alienated, and suffering and as involved in the search for glory for some means to aggrandize his feelings of self.

Kelly sees much anxiety and chaotic confusion in A. S.'s system as a result of his parents' actions in invalidating his constructions. As a result he felt guilty (loss of role constructs), and he was left with the task of finding new meanings for his life.

Quantitative Descriptions

The Q-sort procedure was selected as a way of quantitatively presenting the similarities and differences in viewing A. S. that occurred among the contributors. This is a technique, devised by Stephenson [6], that requires each rater to sort the same items, previously selected as relevant and descriptive for the task at hand, into categories ranging from *most* characteristic to *least* characteristic for a specific patient. In general, the main purpose of employing the Q-sort is to enable persons of different points of view to indicate their judgments of the same person in terms of the *same* traits or items. The number of items to be placed in each step is predetermined so fewest items are in the extremes and most of the items are in the middle steps. In our procedure, nine steps and 76 items were used.[3] The items used are reproduced in Table 20-1. The following distribution of items in each of the nine steps was required: 3, 5, 10, 12, 16, 12, 10, 5, and 3, where the first step was *most* characteristic of A. S. and the last step was *least* characteristic of him. One advantage of the Q-sort is that it forces all raters to have identical means (average) and standard deviations (dispersion), thus permitting rapid intercorrelations without the complexities involved with varying distributions. Six of the contributors to Part II completed Q-sorts for A. S.

Table 20-1 lists each Q-sort item and indicates the rating (from 1 to 9) given to each item by each sorter.

By viewing in Table 20-1 the items placed in the extreme steps, 1 and 2 and 8 and 9 (which indicates which items were considered very characteristic and which not at all characteristic), it is possible to see how each rater described A. S. Each rater had to place three items in each of steps 1 and 9 and five items in each of steps 3 and 8. Table 20-1 also indicates that 13 of the 76 items were rated in either step 1 or 2 by at least two of the raters. Assuming that this indicates some measure of agreement in describing A. S., we can see (from items 1, 6, 17, 20, 27, 34, 48, 60, 63, 70, 71, 75, 76) that the patient is seen most characteristically as one who likes interaction from others and seeks companionship but cannot respond effectively, so his relationships are superficial and his interactions are slight. He behaves passively even when affection is shown to him, he

[3] Items were obtained from previous study by Little and Shneidman [3].

Table 20-1

Items and Their Rank as Q-sorted for Mr. A. S. by Contributors

Item	Rank						
	Futterman	*Klopfer*	*Ansbacher*	*Green*	*Kelly*	*Diamond*	*Average*
1. He likes and seeks the companionship of others	4	2	3	3	2	3	3
2. He usually withdraws in social situations	2	6	5	4	6	4	5
3. He is obviously uncomfortable in his contacts with authority	4	3	6	5	5	1	4
4. He gives in immediately when attacked	6	4	5	4	6	7	5
5. He seems to adapt to his environment quite well	6	5	6	5	7	8	6
6. Nearly all his interpersonal relationships are superficial	2	7	4	3	1	4	4
7. He meets aggression from others with counteraggression	9	5	5	8	3	5	6
8. He has very few friends	4	4	2	3	3	3	3
9. He blames himself when criticized	1	3	4	3	5	5	4
10. He has difficulty in relating to people	4	5	5	4	3	1	4
11. His contacts with authority are marked by strife	4	5	5	8	7	4	6
12. He draws into himself in interpersonal situations	5	4	6	2	5	3	4
13. He has quite a few relatively warm interpersonal relationships	4	4	7	7	9	6	6
14. He does not invest affect in his interpersonal relationships	3	8	5	5	5	5	5
15. He is constantly fighting his environment	4	7	7	7	6	6	6
16. He is rather cold and impersonal in his interactions with women	5	8	7	5	5	2	5
17. He goes out of his way to please people	6	1	6	2	5	3	4
18. He accepts rather passively any impositions made upon him	2	3	5	5	4	6	5
19. His social adjustment seems satisfactory	7	5	6	5	8	8	7

TABLE 20-1

ITEMS AND THEIR RANK AS Q-SORTED FOR MR. A. S. BY CONTRIBUTORS (*Continued*)

Item	*Rank*						
	Futterman	*Klopfer*	*Ansbacher*	*Green*	*Kelly*	*Diamond*	*Average*
20. He tends to retreat from the stress and strain of everyday living	7	5	1	3	1	3	3
21. He meets the demands of his environment in a rather reasonable fashion	6	5	6	5	7	8	6
22. He escapes in fantasy when threatened	3	4	3	1	5	4	3
23. He tries to manipulate those around him to serve his own ends	4	7	2	3	3	6	4
24. He is uneasy and uncomfortable around other men	5	5	4	2	3	3	4
25. He becomes quite aggressive in most social situations	6	6	7	8	5	5	6
26. He generally feels accepted by others	6	6	6	9	9	7	7
27. He behaves rather passively in most situations	3	2	1	3	4	5	3
28. He responds well to most of his environmental demands	6	3	6	6	5	8	6
29. He reacts in a hostile and aggressive fashion in his interpersonal contacts	6	7	7	8	4	6	6
30. He is unable to recognize affection when it is offered to him	3	8	7	4	5	4	5
31. He retreats when people become aggressive toward him	3	4	3	4	6	5	4
32. He competes very strongly with father figures	6	5	7	6	6	5	6
33. He gets along quite well with his superiors	6	3	5	3	5	9	5
34. He withdraws immediately at the slightest hint of rejection	5	3	5	1	7	2	4
35. He becomes actively hostile when he is criticized	9	6	5	6	4	4	6
36. He is only mildly responsive to friendly approaches from others	3	7	4	3	3	2	4
37. He is generally composed and at ease with authority figures	6	5	5	5	6	9	6

Item	Rank						
	Futterman	Klopfer	Ansbacher	Green	Kelly	Diamond	Average
38. He is quite responsive when people show an interest in his welfare	7	3	2	4	4	3	4
39. He faces unpleasant situations in a direct manner	5	7	9	7	9	7	7
40. His immediate response when threatened is to fight back	8	6	6	9	3	5	6
41. He gets along well with most people	7	6	6	5	7	6	6
42. He responds gratefully to positive gestures from others	5	2	3	5	4	3	4
43. He is quite passive in most of his interpersonal contacts	7	4	2	3	4	3	4
44. He adapts easily to social situations	5	5	6	5	7	8	6
45. His friendships seem rather stable and have relatively few conflicts	6	6	7	7	8	7	7
46. His relations with mother figures are fairly happy	9	4	3	7	2	5	5
47. He yields meekly to the demands of others	2	4	4	4	6	6	4
48. He responds immediately to any show of tenderness or affection	2	1	5	6	4	4	4
49. Rejection from others only makes him more aggressive	8	6	6	7	3	5	6
50. He is tactful and considerate with other people	4	3	4	6	5	5	5
51. He runs away from hostility in others	4	2	3	4	3	5	4
52. He seems to handle criticism quite well	5	5	5	9	8	7	7
53. Friendly gestures from others arouse his suspicion and hostility	5	7	7	7	7	5	6
54. He is quite responsive to social stimuli	8	4	4	5	6	4	5
55. He rarely responds to positive gestures from others	5	7	8	6	7	7	7
56. He runs away from any show of tenderness or affection	7	9	7	5	5	7	7
57. When others show an interest in him, he immediately becomes aggressive and demanding	8	8	5	7	4	5	6

TABLE 20-1

ITEMS AND THEIR RANK AS Q-SORTED FOR MR. A. S. BY CONTRIBUTORS (*Continued*)

Item	*Rank*						
	Futterman	*Klopfer*	*Ansbacher*	*Green*	*Kelly*	*Diamond*	*Average*
58. He has little difficulty in dealing with other people	4	6	3	6	8	6	6
59. He is responsive to the needs and wishes of others	5	3	5	6	7	4	5
60. He likes to have people show an interest in him	3	2	3	1	2	1	2
61. He avoids any display of friendliness on the part of others	5	9	8	6	6	6	7
62. He responds in a realistic fashion to hostility from others	7	6	9	7	8	7	7
63. He responds passively to any positive gestures made toward him	3	6	4	5	2	2	4
64. He actively seeks social contacts	7	4	5	4	3	6	5
65. Even the mere presence of other people produces immediate withdrawal in him	5	7	8	7	6	5	6
66. He tries to dominate other people	8	9	4	4	4	3	5
67. He gets along quite well with other men	5	4	3	6	7	7	5
68. He actively rejects affection from others	5	8	9	6	6	7	7
69. Almost any social situation arouses aggressive behavior on his part	7	5	8	8	5	4	6
70. He seems quite meek in most of his interactions with others	1	1	3	4	4	4	3
71. He shows decreasing involvement in social contacts	3	5	1	2	1	6	3
72. He adapts fairly easily to authority demands	7	3	2	4	4	9	5
73. He becomes negativistic when people show a friendly interest in him	5	7	8	6	6	5	6
74. He is rather neutral toward others	4	6	4	5	5	6	5
75. He is rather reserved in most situations	1	5	4	2	5	4	4
76. He accepts affection passively	3	5	4	5	2	2	4

withdraws readily, he is very sensitive both to rejection and to show of affection, and he tries to please others in his relationships with them. If the average of the ratings for each item is obtained, eight items with a rating of 1 to 3 are found. Six of these duplicate the items obtained by the other method as most characteristic, and the other two items (8 and 22) add that A. S. felt he had few friends and tended to escape into fantasy when threatened.

Looking at the items considered to be least characteristic of the patient, 12 items were consistently placed in the last two steps (8 and 9) by two or more of the raters. These items (7, 19, 26, 39, 40, 52, 57, 61, 62, 66, 68, 69) describe A. S. as one who could not handle criticism or be realistic about hostility directed toward him and who could not dominate others, face unpleasant situations directly, or fight back and be counteraggressive under threat. He was not a person who felt either accepted or socially adjusted. Also, when items with *average* ranks (also shown in Table 20-1) of 7, 8, or 9 are examined, 10 items are obtained with 7 of these duplicates of those found previously. The three new items (45, 55, 56) add that A. S. was unstable in his friendships and had many conflicts but did respond to positive gestures and to show of affection from others.

It is of interest to note that only three items evoked real disagreement among the raters as evidenced by the fact that the same item was ranked in both the first two and the last two steps by two of the raters. These items (16, 46, 72) indicated marked differences of opinion as to whether the patient's relationships with mother figures were happy, whether he was impersonal with women, and whether he adapted easily to authority demands.

Some items describing A. S. were very consistently rated by the contributors; that is, they were either placed in the same scale step by four or more of the raters or the range in rating each item was no more than two. For example, two items were given the same rank by four of the six raters (53, 14), and eight other items were relatively consistently rated (8, 60, 32, 41, 45, 53, 60, 8). The contents of these items, however, do not change the description of the patient already obtained.

The question of how the contributors agreed among themselves may be seen from Table 20-2, which presents the intercorrelations among the six raters who did the Q-sorts for A. S. The reader will note at least two important facts about the figures presented in this table. The first is that there are no negative correlations; that is, in no case did any one expert rate an overwhelming number of items in more or less direct opposition to the way any other expert rated them. Another way of saying this is that

TABLE 20-2
INTERCORRELATIONS BETWEEN CONTRIBUTORS ON Q-SORTS FOR MR. A. S.

Contributors	*Futterman*	*Klopfer*	*Ansbacher*	*Green*	*Kelly*	*Diamond*
Futterman		.21	.21	.38	.06	.23
Klopfer			.48	.33	.16	.13
Ansbacher				.53	.56	.28
Green					.38	.33
Kelly						.50
Diamond						

all the experts tended to rate the same items on the characteristic side and the same items on the noncharacteristic side, though they may not have placed them in exactly the same steps.

On the other hand, the intercorrelations are all relatively low, ranging from .06 to .56, with a median correlation of .33. This seems to indicate that none of the experts tended to agree consistently with any of the others in the way in which he described A. S. using these particular personality items, even though the tendency was consistent, as mentioned above, to place the items on the same side of the scale.

It is possible to state, very roughly, that certain raters were more or less like other particular raters in their ratings by arbitrarily defining those correlations of .48 and above as *more* alike and those correlations of .21 and below as *less* alike (the upper and lower quarters of the distribution) and those correlations in between as intermediate. Table 20-3 shows this

TABLE 20-3
INTERCORRELATIONS BETWEEN CONTRIBUTORS ON Q-SORTS FOR MR. A. S.

Contributors	*Futterman*	*Klopfer*	*Ansbacher*	*Green*	*Kelly*	*Diamond*
Futterman		—	—	0	—	0
Klopfer			+	0	—	—
Ansbacher				+	+	0
Green					0	0
Kelly						+
Diamond						

with + indicating those more alike, — indicating those less alike, and 0 indicating those intermediate.

It may be unnecessary to remind the reader that the statistical findings indicated above refer to the individual raters and do not necessarily accrue to the schools they represent.

THERAPEUTIC IMPLICATIONS

This section summarizes the therapeutic implications for the treatment of A. S.'s suicide attempt and of suicidal behavior in general, as presented by the several contributors. In presenting their suggestions most of the contributors offered both specific suggestions for the treatment of A. S. and practical and theoretical suggestions that are generally useful in the therapeutic management of self-destructive behavior.

Futterman

Futterman stresses the need to examine the important question of motivation for treatment of A. S. as one would for any patient. Although A. S. gives some negative indications of motivation for therapy in his lack of inner-directed concern, continued use of projection, low frustration tolerance, and ready tendencies to escape rather than working through, there are some positive signs in terms of good intelligence, good school record, and adequate service record. The kind of psychotherapy decided on is important, and for A. S. supportive rather than intensive psychotherapy is suggested because it has been found to be most effective for depressions at the beginning of therapy. It may include or lead to interpretations, but the therapist must be ready to postpone these if the patient's tension rises too high. He must be prepared for severe oscillations in instinctual urges, with the possibility of sudden severe crises occurring without warning. In neurotics with reactive depressions psychoanalysis may be the treatment of choice, with the therapist being ready to work with guilt feelings, problems of transference, and feelings of abandonment. Depressed patients make considerable demands to which the therapist may yield at times, but he should be aware that this does not dissolve the needs but rather helps to continue them. The important question of whether the therapist who would treat the patient in therapy should also see him in the hospital is also raised. Futterman feels (in contrast to Hendin and Kelly) that there are too many disadvantages to such a procedure, such as distorting and confusing the relationship for the patient and involving the therapist in the authoritative emergency situations that arise in the hospital. If the patient has been in treatment and then is hospitalized, it is even more important for the therapist to avoid the restricting authoritative role and to preserve, as much as possible, the original therapeutic relationship. Adjunct therapy with the patient's relatives always presents a problem, but occasional interviews with parents or spouse could be held if they are spaced so as not to interfere in the therapy of the patient. If the relatives need therapy, they should be sent to another therapist.

Hendin

Dealing with suicidal patients does not imply a radically different approach from general problems encountered in psychotherapy. Suicide is but one aspect of the patient's total problems. It must be dealt with first and effectively, however, or there may be no opportunity to deal with the others. The two biggest safety factors are to start therapy while the patient is in the hospital after an attempt (to see how soon a good therapeutic contact can be established) and to know the psychodynamics of suicide. For all cases of attempted suicide, it is extremely important to evaluate the suicidal intent. This can be done with more thorough questioning of the patient regarding the method, motivation, and the nature of the suicidal action. The suicidal patients with whom contact is most difficult to establish are the apathetic patients and the very aggressive paranoid patients. The degree of depression before and after the suicidal attempt should be evaluated along with the nature of the dependency-rejection constellation. The patient's attitudes toward death and dying and his fantasies in this regard must be watched. Dreams in which death is seen as a source of gratification are particularly important.

Because A. S. has shown the pattern in the past of running away in reaction to his frustrations, one might expect that in the course of therapy he would react to what he would feel as frustrations of his dependency needs on the part of the therapist with the desire to leave therapy. The correct handling of this tendency might well serve as a wedge in dealing with his dependency problems and his reaction to them. The order in which the problems come up within A. S.'s therapy would depend on the immediate situation when he began therapy, but ultimately therapy must revolve around his difficulties with women and his problems with his mother. Success of the therapy will depend on his resolving his dependency problem and in the establishment of a lasting, satisfying relationship with a woman. Success in therapy would be indicated not only by changes in behavior at school, work, and with a woman but psychodynamically in dreams and fantasies indicating a less dependent, less helpless self image. Were this achieved there would, in addition, be less preoccupation with his height on which he has focused his feelings of low masculine self-esteem.

Klopfer

The general goal of any therapy is to free the ego of its pseudomonopolistic, egocentric position and allow it to seek contact with the self. Suicidal patients must be taught to understand the suicidal attempt as a symbolic expression of the psychological act of rebirth and have to be informed about the danger that the night journey may end in destruction rather than in rebirth. A. S. must be taught to free himself of the anger against his mother so he can understand the above and can reach the point where he can use some of his positive elements more constructively, e.g., ambition and good intelligence. An important aspect for any therapist to consider in working with a suicidal patient is his own (the therapist's) ability to face up to death, for the counterreactions (or countertransference) of the therapist toward the suicidal patient may interfere in the treatment. The therapist must be able to come to a successful reconciliation with the reality of death in his own personal philosophy.

Ansbacher

The objective of therapy is to enable the patient to take a better, more self-reliant attitude toward life. Cure is effected by correcting the faulty picture of the world the patient has, allowing him to accept a mature picture of the world, and strengthening his social interest. The task of the therapist is to understand the patient's style of life and to impart this understanding to the patient. For A. S., one would show him to himself, getting him to see that he has been constantly seeking protection and resenting it when he did not get enough, although he could probably never be satisfied anyhow. Also, the patient might be helped toward some constructive activity by emphasizing his positive qualities, including pursuit of a vocational goal. Training for leadership by role playing might be considered. Through learning to view himself more realistically, he might learn to respect others and to wish to take care of them instead of demanding that they take care of him.

Green

In general, the therapist should treat suicidal fears and threats in obsessional neurosis very roughly, directly, and forcefully, first making certain there is no indefinite obsessional schizoid condition. To take such threats seriously in the former condition is to collaborate with the neurosis. In contrast, the therapist should be very cautious in his approach to depressive psychoses and manic depressions, feeling free to use hospitalization, if necessary, to protect the patient. Sharp diagnostic skill is needed in both instances to know when therapy can reach the patient and when collaborative participation can occur. Sullivan remained pessimistic about therapy with manic depressive psychotics, feeling he could not reach them, but Fromm-Reichmann felt that one could try to help them become aware of the destructive tendencies they felt toward others and to inquire into their depressive feelings. The therapist must not feel that suicide is shameful and reprehensible. He must be aware of his own needs to cure the patient and be able to tell the patient that no other person can be totally responsible for the suicide of someone else. The patient should be made to realize that therapy would be wasteful if he is beginning therapy with the reservation of an escape into suicide.

In the treatment of A. S., the first goal is establishing a working relationship so he can respond to and collaborate with the therapist. He has to learn to understand his relationships with his parents and with others, to give up his dependency on his mother, and to recognize his own limitations and infantile conflicts. The therapist collaborates by sharing the patient's feelings of loneliness and despair without agreeing to the hopeless feelings and colluding with the magical expectations. During the patient's maturation in therapy, one might expect the patient to test the therapist and to imitate him. The latter might serve a positive, educative function. Prognosis for A. S., as with all suicidal patients, would be guarded until the crucial point is reached at which the insights gained in therapy are worked through and integrated by the patient.

De Rosis

As in all therapy, the therapist-patient relationship is the most important single factor. The therapist must convince the patient he is on the side of the patient's self and not that of his idealized self. The therapist must accept the fact of equality of selves, even though he has assumed the burden and the responsibility of helping another person. The therapist must be constantly on the alert for feelings of self-hatred, hopelessness, and intolerable suffering. To do this he must watch for the kind of idealizations that, unattained, produce self-hatred. He has to evaluate the possibilities for discharge of these feelings by the patient, not only in the general environment, but also on the therapist. In the aggressive person, the therapist must approach carefully those areas the patient might have idealized, because frustration in these will produce self-hatred. For the self-abnegator, he should allow the patient to ally himself and to depend, using these devices to work through his problems. The therapist has to estimate and evaluate the amount of self present, and if it is felt to be insufficient, supportive rather than interpretive therapy is called for at first. If the patient seems able to express and to exact demands, the danger of suicide is less. Particular care must be paid in depressions when the person seems to be emerging from the depressed state. If drugs are used by the therapist, he should use adequate amounts, for inadequate dosages for persons filled with the sense of incipient disintegration will deepen and prolong their feelings of anxiety rather than relieve them.

Kelly

Generally speaking, the task of psychotherapy is to help the patient approach the various forms of reality to be used for validating his system, providing him with both a methodology for handling his world and with role relationships that will help him distinguish his own individuality. He must learn that the goal of therapy is not a final state of well-being but a continuing course of action constantly to be changed as needed. Personal construct theory tries to help patients devise their own techniques so they can handle future problems. The personal constructs of the therapist are extremely important and must be taken into account in considering the therapeutic plans.

For A. S., medical rehabilitation, not only for his immediate suicidal attempt but also for whatever other physical conditions may be present, will be important. Living arrangements, employment, recreational and educational resources, and management of his interviews for psychotherapy must all be considered and discussed. It is important that therapy should start immediately with long-range plans made as definite as possible, thus firmly establishing the relationship to his therapist. It would be a mistake to wait too long to start therapy. A. S.'s personal construct system needs to be reformulated in his own words, a task at which both patient and therapist should work together. A. S. seems to be verbal enough to be able to conceptualize himself in this way. If A. S. continues to employ terms of unworthiness and hostility, elaboration of the construct system must be kept well compartmentalized and the therapist must be on the lookout for impulsive vacillation along dilation-constriction and aggression dimensions. As long as A. S. feels dependent and safe with his therapist in the therapy room, matters may be smooth but venturing outside to other situations may cause such impulsive vacillations. It seems probable that the parents will have to be included in the therapy plans, for they are still too important in A. S.'s world to be ignored. A. S. may object to this but can be brought to see the usefulness and the necessity.

Diamond

Discussing suicidal behavior as it occurs clinically, Diamond concentrates on the process within the therapy. He feels the therapist must have an empathic understanding of the client's internal frame of reference and must try to communicate this to the patient. Reflection of feeling is seen as the most useful technique, permitting the therapist to avoid the roles that parents, teachers, and well-meaning friends have played before. The motivating force in the therapy will be the patient's need to be understood. Although Carl Rogers feels that a therapist must be completely willing that a client may choose any outcome or direction and that a patient's statement of suicidal intent is no adequate provocation for a change of method, Diamond states that he does not feel content that each client can dispose of his own life as he sees fit; Diamond finds himself wishing to prevent it. Reflection of feelings is used as a technique with the conviction that the choice on the part of the patient for life will be facilitated. In giving responses, these two rules are to be followed: (A) Always reflect the worst; not to do so is either to reassure (by implication it is unimportant) or to indicate reluctance to talk of unpleasant subjects; (B) Express empathy and not a spectator's appraisal; share the feeling through the tone of voice and the nuances of posture and language. The above would serve for the patient with expressed suicidal intent, but actually the greater danger lies with those disturbed persons who do not get to the counselor's office, as with A. S. In such cases as these, the most pressing problem is to arrange the opportunity for employing therapeutic skills. If the therapist adopts the client-centered method for dealing with critical problems such as suicide, it is because he must agree with Rogers that the dynamics of growth and cure, which are basically the same with all persons, are the most effective in treating such problems.

Summary

Summarizing the therapeutic implications briefly, the recommendations and cautions raised by the contributors for special consideration deal with such aspects as the need to evaluate carefully the suicidal intent (Hendin) and the degree and intensity of the patient's depression (Futterman, Hendin, Green) and to note carefully the nature of the dependency-rejection constellation (Hendin). Suicidal behavior in obsessive schizoid patients, depressive psychotics, manic depressives (Green, Futterman), aggressive paranoid patients, and anxious persons with apathy and guilt (Hendin, Kelly) is especially significant. In the course of the treatment, the therapist must watch carefully the period when the patient seems to be emerging from the depression (De Rosis) and be alert for sudden alternations in feelings of fear, rage, and love (Futterman, Hendin, Kelly) and especially sensitive in anticipating and handling the patient's demands and testing of him in the relationship established (Futterman, Hendin, Green, De Rosis, Kelly). He should be alert for tendencies of the patient to demand of himself as well, producing feelings of worthlessness and self-hatred (De Rosis) and note carefully the kind of dreams reported by the patient, particularly when the dream implies that death will be a source of gratification (Hendin). Special importance is attributed by the therapist to knowing what his own feelings are toward death and suicide (Klopfer, Green, De Rosis, Kelly, Diamond). If the patient is depressed, supportive rather than interpretive therapy might be considered (Futterman, De Rosis), although if there is no evidence of psychotic tendencies, the suicidal threats and fears may be treated rather roughly (Green). The patient may be taught the symbolic meanings of his action, apprised of the real danger of dying from his act (Klopfer, Green), and encouraged to take more self-reliant attitudes toward life (Ansbacher). The patient has a faulty picture of the world, and he should be helped to see it differently (Ansbacher, Kelly). Therapy of the patient may be helped by seeing the relatives (Futterman, Kelly), but no attempt should be made by the patient's therapist to treat them (Futterman). There is a difference of opinion about treating the suicidal patient in the hospital, with the feeling that to do so would interfere with the therapeutic relationship to be established (Futterman) contrasted with the recommendation that to delay starting therapy is undesirable and that the time in the hospital should be used to evaluate the patient's motivation for therapy (Hendin, Kelly). The therapist should deal actively and directly with the patient's practical problems of work, school, etc. (Hendin, Ansbacher, Kelly). Some of the techniques suggested include psychoanalysis for neurotics (Futterman), physiological and chemical treatment (Green, De Rosis) (with the caution that, if drugs are used, they should be used in adequate amounts) (De Rosis), role playing (Ansbacher), and reflection of feeling (Diamond).

In general, it becomes apparent that, although there is no one kind of treatment that could be selected and singled out as appropriate for all suicides, there is considerable agreement as to the general lines along which therapy would proceed. The treatment will vary depending upon the kind of patient, the nature of the suicidal attempt, and the theoretical framework within which the therapist operates. This diversity, however, should not be misinterpreted; rather the findings imply that a therapist who manifests sensitivity, warmth, interest, concern, and consistency, within his own theoretical framework, may be of inestimable value to the suicidally troubled patient.

EPILOGUE

Before concluding this chapter, it would be of interest to tell what had happened to A. S., a question that undoubtedly has occurred to many readers. The unfortunate fact is that his fate is unknown to us. A. S. was discharged from the hospital three days after the interviews were concluded and, despite strong and urgent recommendations both to him and to his parents to seek further help or to continue his contact with the interviewer, was not heard from again. Further attempts to trace him to a local address were unsuccessful, and he and his parents simply seemed to have disappeared from Los Angeles. The likelihood is that they have returned to their small midwestern town; at any rate, letters sent to them there have been unanswered. At least he has not appeared on the suicide lists of the Los Angeles County Coroner to date.

Although it is regrettable that follow-up information is not available, it does serve to point up a serious problem in the current modes of treatment for persons who attempt suicide. This lack of follow-up is typical of the hundreds of cases that appear in a large metropolitan hospital over a single year. In Los Angeles, the county hospital treated over 500 cases of attempted suicide in 1957, and the city emergency hospitals treated over 1,500 such cases. As in most similar large county and emergency hospitals, the usual treatment is primarily medical and emergency in nature (gastric lavage, suturing of cuts and wounds, or removing of bullets), after which the patient is discharged immediately, most often back to the environment that fostered the very constellation of factors precipitating the suicidal attempt. Unless he has gone, on admission, to the psychiatric ward, if one exists in the hospital, there is most often complete absence of psychiatric contact and little appreciation of the emotional state of the suicidal person's special problems. If anything, he is often the recipient of overt hostility and rejection by many of the hospital personnel. This may be because an attempt at self-destruction often touches on repressed sources of guilt and anger in the persons around him who become involved. In hospitals, the feelings are frequently "why work so hard to save a person who has just tried to put himself out of reach of help" or "this person is so ineffectual he couldn't even do an adequate job of killing himself."

A. S. would have had no psychiatric contact while in the hospital, had he not just happened to be there at the time when our psychiatric team, collecting data for our continuing study of suicide, was there. It may be noted here that, with the aid of a U.S. Public Health Service project grant, we have established a suicide prevention service (see Chapter 2) designed to meet the needs of patients admitted to a hospital in an emotional suicidal state by, after comprehensive interviews and examination, referring them to appropriate therapeutic resources within the community in response to their clearly implied cry for help.

References

1. Hall, C. S., and G. Lindzey: *Theories of Personality,* New York: John Wiley & Sons, Inc., 1957.
2. Kelly, G. A.: *The Psychology of Personal Constructs,* New York: W. W. Norton & Company, Inc., 1955.
3. Little, K. B., and E. S. Shneidman: Congruencies among anamnestic and psychological test data, *Psychological Monographs,* 73: 1–42, 1959.
4. Munroe, Ruth L.: *Schools of Psychoanalytic Thought,* New York: The Dryden Press, Inc., 1955.
5. Shneidman, E. S., and N. L. Farberow: *Clues to Suicide,* New York: McGraw-Hill Book Company, Inc., 1957.
6. Stephenson, W.: *The Study of Behavior: Q-Technique and Its Methodology,* Chicago: University of Chicago Press, 1953.

PART III

Bibliography

Bibliography on Suicide, 1897-1957

Compiled by
NORMAN L. FARBEROW AND EDWIN S. SHNEIDMAN [1]
with the assistance of
EUGENE A. BOUVIER

This bibiography contains the references for publications on suicide which have appeared during the period from 1897 through 1957. The year 1897 was chosen as a starting point because it was the year in which Durkheim's great work, *Le Suicide,* was first published. As a work of great importance in the application of scientific procedures, it marked a turning point in the kinds of published material on suicide which had preceded it. The bibliography concludes with the year 1957 because, at the time the list was being prepared, this was the latest year for which one could reasonably be certain that practically all of the published titles had been listed.[2]

This bibliography contains references both in foreign languages and in English from the period 1927 on. For the most part, the references from 1897 through 1927 are in English only. This is because a comprehensive bibliography by Rost (see Psychological-General section) listing about 3,750 items, appeared in 1927, and it was felt that it was unnecessary to duplicate the foreign language items listed in Rost. The English language references are listed, however, in order to present them all in one place, and because the Rost book, now out of print and in very few libraries, is difficult to obtain. However, it is available in the Library of Congress, and

[1] Acknowledgment and sincere appreciation is expressed to Mr. Eugene A. Bouvier, M.A., who, in his capacity as bibliographer, devoted considerable attention and care to the thousand-and-one details in his efforts to obtain reasonably accurate listings.

[2] It is anticipated that, as the opportunity presents itself, supplementary lists will be published, bringing the bibliography up to date.

the reader is referred to it for articles in English which appeared before 1897 and for articles in foreign languages which appeared prior to 1927. The references are presented in the format of American Psychological Association Publication Manual, which follows the procedure of listing in order: name(s) of author(s), title, and reference source. If the source is a book, the place, publisher, and the year are shown. If the reference is a journal, the year, volume number, and the inclusive pages are shown.

Some attempt has been made to group the references. The headings have purposely been made large and comprehensive, so that only four categories are employed. Inasmuch as the judgment as to which category was to receive which article often had to be made on the basis of the interpretation of the title or as an inference from the reference source, it is possible that some of the articles have been placed in an incorrect category. In addition, many articles contained material which would have allowed them to be classified in more than one category, so that the decision as to which one they most readily belonged sometimes became quite arbitrary. The reader is therefore urged, in his use of the bibliography, to check all the sections for the particular reference he is seeking, rather than assume it is missing because it does not appear in the section first checked.[3]

The Psychological-General classification contains items which are primarily psychological, psychiatric, psychoanalytic, psychodynamic, diagnostic, prognostic, etc. In addition, references which were more or less general in scope were included in this category.

The Sociological category contains references which are generally sociological, anthropological, and economic in approach. Publications which are primarily statistical, tabular, and normative for different groups classified in different ways, such as nationality, race, religion, occupation, etc., are found in this category.

The Medical-Legal category contains references which are primarily medical, legal, or both, in content. Publications concerned with general medical problems in suicide, forensic medicine, statutory aspects and implications of suicide, differential diagnoses between suicide and other modes of death, and relationships with financial and/or insurance proceedings are found in this category.[4]

[3] The editors would be both grateful and appreciative were any reader to send to them any references which have been inadvertently omitted.

[4] References describing organic and physiological aspects of diagnosis and treatment of suicidal wounds, many of them short medical descriptions of single interesting and unusual cases, have not been included because of space limitations. They may be obtained from the editors upon request.

The Philosophical-Religious classification includes items which are concerned with the philosophical, ethical, religious, moral, and general historical considerations in suicide.

Some general impressions gained while compiling the bibliography are as follows:

1. Medical and surgical procedures in the handling and treatment of suicidal cases continue to receive a major share of the space devoted to suicide, particularly in foreign medical journals.

2. Researches into the etiology of suicide continue. Attempts have been made to approach the phenomena of suicide from different viewpoints, such as communication theory, information theory, ego adaptational theory, etc. All these represent continued attempts to discover meaningful and significant factors for earlier recognition and treatment.

3. Sociological investigations continue to examine in detail the occurrence of suicide in various geographic locations and among specific groups, with more and more attention directed toward the group of attempted suicides.

4. Publications focusing on practical clinical procedures in therapeutic care, management, and treatment of suicidal persons both in outpatient and inpatient settings continue to appear.

5. The possibility of identification of suicidal persons by means of psychological tests has been relatively unexplored, possibly because of the very ambiguous results obtained so far.

6. There is a growing sophistication in the continuing search for better and alternative definitions and taxonomies of suicide in terms of more meaningful concepts and rubrics.

7. There seems to be a growing awareness of the significance and importance of the general practitioner in the early detection of suicidal patients, inasmuch as it is he who most often comes into initial contact with them. This important conclusion has emerged from researches studying the presuicidal activity of the suicidal patient.

8. There is a pressing need, as pointed out by a number of investigators, for education of the lay public and also of professional personnel concerning the many aspects of suicide.

PSYCHOLOGICAL—GENERAL

A family of suicides. Med. Rec., N.Y., 1901, 60, 660–661.

A modern Dido. Med. News, N.Y., 1904, 85, 176.

Abraham, K. Notes on the Psycho-analytic Investigation and Treatment of Manic-Depressive Insanity and Allied Conditions. (Selected papers on psycho-analysis.) London: Hogarth, 1927.

Achille-Delmas, F. Psychologie pathologique du suicide. (The pathological psychology of suicide.) Paris: Alcan, 1933.

Adler, A., et al. Über den Selbstmord Inbesondere den Schüler-Selbstmord. (Suicide, especially among students.) Diskussion des Wiener Psychoanalytischen Vereins, Wiesbaden: J. F. Bergmann, 1910.

Adler, A. Selbstmord. (Suicide.) Int. Z. Indiv.-Psychol., 1937, 15, 49–52.

Aisenscitat. J. Le cause del suicidio. (The causes of suicide.) Morgagni, 1931, 13, 608–617.

Alexander, F. The need for punishment and the death instinct. Int. J. Psychoanal., 1929, 10, 256–269.

Alexander, L. The commitment and suicide of King Ludwig II of Bavaria. Amer. J. Psychiat., 1954, 111, 100–107.

Allison, W. L. The relation of suicide to insanity. Texas St. J. Med., 1907/08, 3, 308.

Alvárez Villamil, V. El suicidio infantil. Sus causas. Su patogenia. Sus remedios y su clasificación como hecho moral. (Infantile suicide; its causes, pathogenesis; prevention and classification as moral action.) Pediat. esp., 1929, 18, 8–13.

Anchersen, Maria. (Amnesia and progressive dementia following attempted suicide by hanging.) Ugeskr. Læg., 1915, 77, 683–700.

Anderson, C. Aspects of pathological grief and mourning. Int. J. Psychoanal., 1949, 30, 48–55.

Anderson, W. Suicide; its causes and prevention. Pacif. med. J., 1908, 51, 539–551.

Annecchino, F. P. (Suicidal psychosis in children and adolescents.) Rif. med., 1926, 42, 614–615.

Arieff, A. J., McCulloch, R., and Rotman, D. B. Unsuccessful suicidal attempts. Dis. nerv. Syst., 1948, 9, 174–179.

Arnoštka, R. (Suicidal obsession.) Čas. Lék. čes., 1922, 61, 780–783.

Attempted suicide. Lancet, 1952, 1, 1059–1060.

Auden, G. A. Unusual form of suicide. J. Ment. Sci., 1927, 73, 428–430.

Audiffrent, G. Du suicide. (Theory of suicide.) Arch. Anthrop. crim., 1902, 17, 389–402.

Baader, I. Bedeutsame psychische und soziale Ursachen des Selbstmordes bei Kindern und Jugendlichen. (Significant psychic and social causes of suicide in children and adolescents.) Mschr. Kinderheilk., 1955, 103, 55–56.

Bachrach, A. J. Some factors in the prediction of suicide. Neuropsychiatry, 1951/52, 1(4), 21–27.

Bafico, J. B. Del suicidio. (Suicide.) Sem. méd., B. Aires, 1934, 2, 159–168; Día méd., 1946, 18, 866–873.

Bakwin, H. Suicide in children and adolescents. J. Pediat., 1957, 50, 749–769.

Ballard, J. W. Suicide. Delaware St. med. J., 1938, 10, 74–77.

Ballasteros, A. Suicides in adolescence. Proc. 4th int. Cong. ment. Hlth, 1951, 281–289.

Bandel, R. Selbstmord und Alkoholismus. (Suicide and alcoholism.) Münch. med. Wschr., 1928, 75, 1465–1466.

Banen, D. M. Suicide by psychotics. J. nerv. ment. Dis., 1954, 120, 349–357.

Barbé, A. (Suicide and homicide obsession impulse.) Encéphale, 1921, 16, 304.

Barker, L. F. Alleged attempt at suicide by a woman of seventy-one who stated that she had grown desperate regarding her economic situation; discussion of the mental state. Int. Clin., 1930, 3, 64–67.

Barrancos, A. De una rara impulsión suicida. (Consideraciones sobre el suicidio en los alienados.) (An unusual suicidal impulse. [Comments on suicide in the insane.]) Rev. Criminol., B. Aires, 1928, 15, 682–692. A propósito de una rara impulsión suicida. Consideraciones sobre el suicidio en los alienados. (Unusual impulsion to suicide. Comments on suicide among the insane.) Act. prim. Conf. lat.-amer. Neurol., 1929, 2, 103–112.

Batchelor, I. R. C. Alcoholism and attempted suicide. J. ment. Sci. 1954, 100, 451–461. Psychopathic states and attempted suicide. Brit. med. J., 1954, 1, 1342–1347. Repeated suicidal attempts. Brit. J. med. Psychol., 1954, 27, 158–163. Attempted suicide. (One of: Emergencies in general practice.) Brit. med. J., 1955, 1, 595–597. Suicide. Med. ill., 1955, 9, 436–438. Management and prognosis of suicidal attempts in old age. Geriatrics, 1955, 10, 291–293.

Batchelor, I. R. C., and Napier, Margaret B. Attempted suicide in old age. Brit. med. J., 1953, 2, 1186–1190. Broken homes and attempted suicide. Brit. J. Delinq., 1953/54, 4, 99–108. The sequelae and short-term prognosis of attempted suicide. The results of a one-year followup of 200 cases. J. Neurol. Psychiat., 1954, 17, 261–266.

Beardsley, G. L. The fad of self-murder. Med. Pr., 1904, 20, 385–392.

Bell, C. R., Bond, H., et al. Suicide: social, forensic, and psychological aspects. Milit. Surg., 1932, 71, 399–403.

Bender, Lauretta. Children preoccupied with suicide. *In* Lauretta Bender, Aggression, hostility, and anxiety in children. Springfield, Ill.: Charles C Thomas, 1953, 66–90.

Bender, Lauretta, and Schilder, P. Suicidal preoccupations and attempts in children. Amer. J. Orthopsychiat., 1937, 7, 225–234.

Ben El Mouffok Abderrahman. Le suicide non pathologique. (The non-pathological suicide.) Paris: Rodstein, 1933.

Benham, H. A. Some remarks on suicides in public asylums. J. ment. Sci., 1903, 49, 447–453.

Bennett, A. E. Prevention of suicide. Calif. Med., 1954, 81, 396–401. The physician's responsibility in the prevention of suicide. Dis. nerv. Syst., 1954, 15, 207–210. Methods for prevention of suicide. Mod. Med., Minneap., 1955, 23 (4), 140, 142.

Bercio. Ein Fall eigenartiger geistiger Veranlagung einer Selbstmord-Kandidatin. (A case of singular intellectual talents of a female suicide-candidate.) Arch. Krim-Anthrop., 1905, 18, 348–350.

Berdiaev, N. A. Le suicide. (Suicide.) (Trans. Elizabeth Bellenson.) Le Cep, 1954.

Bergler, E. Problems of suicide. Psychiat. Quart. Suppl., 1946, 20, 261–275.

Berk, N. A personality study of suicidal schizophrenics. Unpublished doctoral dissertation, New York Univ., 1949.

Bermann, G. Der Selbstmord als Rache. (Suicide as revenge.) Mschr. Psychiat. Neurol., 1930, 77, 297–309; Sem. méd., B. Aires, 1931, 38, 899–907.

Bernfeld, S. Selbstmord. (Suicide.) Z. psychoan. Pädag., 1929, 3, 355–363.

Bien, E. Vorgeschichte eines Selbstmordes. (Previous history of a suicide.) Psychoanal. Praxis, 1932, 2, 137–142.

Birnbaum, M. Der Selbstmord. (Suicide.) Gesund. Wort u. Bild, 1905, 2, 318–326.

Birstein, J. Zur Frage des Selbstmordes. (On the question of suicide.) Zbl. Psychoan., 1912/13, 3, 593–595. W. M. Garschin's Traum; eine neuropsychologische Studie zur Frage des Selbstmordes. (W. M. Garschin's dream; a neuropsychological study of the question of suicide.) Zbl. Psychoan., 1913/14, 4, 432–442.

Bischler, W. Selbstmord und Opfertod. (Suicide and sacrificial death.) Imago, Lpz., 1936, 22, 177–195.

Bishop, F. B. Neurasthenia and suicide. Nat. med. Rev., Wash., 1898/99, 8, 437–440.

Blumer, S. Selbstmord und Witterung. (Suicide and weather.) Gesundh. u. Wohlf., 1945, 25, 89–111.

Boisen, A. T. Personality changes and upheavals arising out of the sense of personal failure. Amer. J. Psychiat., 1925/26, 5, 531–551.

Bosch, R., Jr. Profilaxis del suicidio. (Prophylaxis of suicide.) Sem. méd., B. Aires, 1920, 27, 431–433. El suicidio patologico. (Pathologic suicide.) Sem. méd., B. Aires, 1920, 27, 405–414.

Boulin, R., Guéniot, M., and Lapresle, C. Le suicide chez les diabétiques. (Suicide in diabetics.) Hyg. ment., 1956, 45, 233–240.

Boye, B. (Frequency of neuroses and number of attempted suicides cared for at Sabbatsberg Hospital during the years 1926 to 1933.) Nord. med. Tidskr., 1935, 9, 252–257.

Brandejs, M. Zvláštni případ sebevraždy. (Peculiar case of suicide.) Čas. Lék. čes., 1898, 37, 552.

Brandstätter, J., and Kisser, F. Ein Beitrag zur Frage des Selbstmordes. (Contribution to the theory of suicide.) Dtsch. Z. ges. gerichtl. Med., 1924, 4, 237–247.

Brantmay, H. Recueil de faits; tentative de suicide d'une fillette de 9 ans. (Recollection of fact; suicide attempt of a 9-year-old girl.) Z. Kinderpsychiat., 1944, 11, 81–82.

Bremer, F. W. Zur Vererbung der Selbstmordneigung. (Hereditary transmission of suicidal tendency.) Arch. Psychiat. Nervenkr., 1925, 73, 168–185.

Brend, W. A. The mental condition preceding suicide. Practitioner, 1919, 103, 401–411.

Brie. Zur Kenntnis der Psychosen nach Strangulationsversuch. (Toward recognition of psychoses following a strangulation attempt.) Ärztl. SachverstZtg., 1904, 10, 449–456.

Brill, A. A. The concept of psychic suicide. Int. J. Psychoanal., 1939, 20, 246–251.

Broida, D. C. An investigation of certain psychodiagnostic indications of suicidal tendencies and depression in mental hospital patients. Psychiat. Quart., 1954, 28, 453–464.

Bromberg, W., and Schilder, P. The attitude of psychoneurotics toward death. Psychoanal. Rev., 1936, 23, 1-25.

Brun, R. Über Freuds Hypothese vom Todestrieb; eine kritische Untersuchung. (Freud's hypothesis concerning the death instinct; a critical study.) Psyche, Stuttgart, 1953, 7, 81–111.

Buckle, D. Attempted suicide. Med. J. Aust., 1942, 1, 154–155.

Bunzel, Bessie. Suicide. Encycl. soc. Sci., 1934, 14, 455–459.

Buschan. Zur Selbstmordfrage. (On the suicide question.) Arch. KrimAnthrop., 1903, 13, 233.

Caba, P. Teoría del suicidio. (Theory of suicide.) Rev. Psicol. Pedag. apl., Valencia, 1953, 4, 75–102.

Cahen, Eleanor R. A transitory psychotic episode in a man following the accidental death of his wife. Case Rep. clin. Psychol., 1951, 2, 42–50.

Caldas, M. Examen médico-psicológico de los predispuestos al suicidio. (Medico-psychologic examination of patients inclined to suicide.) Act. prim. Conf. lat.-amer. Neurol., 1929, 2, 35–61.

Carelli, A. Di alconi pseudo-suicidi. (Pseudosuicides.) Policlinico, 1919, 26, 559–562.

Carmichael, B. Death wish in daily life. Psychoanal. Rev., 1943, 30, 59–66.

Carp, E. A. D. E. (Protective measures against suicide.) Ned. Tijdschr. Geneesk., 1941, 52–56.

Carr, J. L. Suicide. Int. Rec. Med., 1957, 170, 613–620.

Carrette, P. Sensibilité physique et anxiété au cours des tentatives de suicide. (Physical feeling and anxiety during attempted suicide.) Ann. méd.-psychol., 1941, 99(2), 64–69.

Carstairs, G. M. Attitudes to death and suicide in an Indian cultural setting. Int. J. soc. Psychiat., 1955, 1(3), 33–41.

Cashman, W. M. Suicide due to promotion depression; a case report. Nav. med. Bull., Wash., 1943, 41, 1412.

Catalán, E. Suicidio por obsesión en un psicasténico. (Suicide from obsession in a psychasthenic.) Rev. Criminol., B. Aires, 1926, 13, 291–295.

Catalano-Nobili, C., and Cerquetelli, G. Il suicidio. Studio statistico e psicopathologico. (Suicide. A statistical and psychopathological study.) Rass. neuropsich., 1949, 3–68.

Cavalca, G. G. Il suicidio nella pubertà. (Suicide in puberty.) Riv. sper. Freniat., 1957, 81, 712–761.

Centenarians and suicide. Boston med. surg. J., 1912, 167, 142.

Chadwick, Mary. Notes upon the fear of death. Int. J. Psychoanal., 1929, 10, 321–334. Über Selbstmordphantasien. (Suicidal phantasies.) Z. psychoan. Pädag., 1929, 3, 409–422.

Chatterji (Chatterjee), N. N. Ideas of suicide in schizophrenia. Samīkṣā, 1951, 5, 121–127.

Chavigny, M. Deux cas de suicide accidentel (les anomalies du sens génital). (Two cases of accidental suicide [anomalies of the genital sense].) Ann. méd.-psychol., 1931, 89, 79–81.

Chmela, Z., and Kohout, L. Zvláštni případy sebevražd. (Unusual cases of suicide.) Čas. Lék. čes., 1951, 90, 1471–1473.

Choroshko. (See Khoroshko.)

Clark, L. P. A study of the unconscious motivations in suicides. N. Y. med. J., 1922, 116, 254–263.

Claude, H. and Masquin, P. Tenatives amnésiques de suicide au cours d'états obsessionels. (Amnesic suicide attempts during obsessional states.) Ann. méd.-psychol., 1932(1), 424–428.

Clausager-Madsen, M. (Nosocomial suicides in Danish psychiatric hospitals during years 1932–1941.) Nord. Med., 1943, 17, 8–11.

Cleaver, J. H. Prevention of suicide. Med. Her., St Joseph, 1930, 49, 47; 95.

Cleckley, H. Semantic dementia and semi-suicide. Psychiat. Quart., 1942, 16, 521–529. Suicide rarely carried out. *In* H. Cleckley, The mask of sanity. St. Louis: Mosby, 1950.

Clemmesen, C. Nosocomiale Selbstmorde an den Irrenanstalten Dänemarks 1922–1931. (Nosocomial suicides in the institutions for the mentally diseased in Denmark, 1922–1931.) Acta psychiat., Kbh., 1933, 8, 509–512.

Cleveland, S. E. Three cases of self-castration. J. nerv. ment. Dis., 1956, 123, 386–391.

Collective suicide. Brit. med. J., 1898, 2, 1181.

Colom, G. A., and Levine, M. H. Self-inflicted pre-frontal lobotomy; report of a case. J. nerv. ment. Dis., 1951, 113, 430–436.

Comyn, G. Suicide. Aust. med. Gaz., 1899, 18, 496–499.

Courbon, P. Pseudo-suicide par dépit. (Suicide for spite.) Ann. méd.-psychol., 1931, 89, 32–36. Psychophysiologie du suicide. Le suicide non pathologique. (Psychophysiology of suicide. Non-pathological suicide.) Ann. méd.-psychol., 1934, 92(2), 384–397.

Courbon, P., and Fail. Le suicide par logique démentielle et les autres aspèces de suicides des aliénés. (Suicide by demented logic and other kinds of suicide among the insane.) Bull. Soc. clin. Méd. ment., 1927, 15, 99–101.

Courbon, P., and Rousset, S. Impulsions au suicide chez un vieillard épileptique. (Impulsions to suicide in an old epileptic patient.) Ann. méd.-psychol., 1936, 94(1), 766–770.

Courchet, J. L. Le suicide: essai d'étude psychanalytique. (Suicide: attempt at a psychoanalytic study.) Évolut. psychiat., 1955, No. 3, 467–482.

Crasilneck, H. B. An analysis of differences between suicidal and pseudo-suicidal patients through the use of projective techniques. Unpublished doctoral dissertation, Univ. of Houston, 1954.

Crichton-Miller, H. The psychology of suicide. Brit. med. J., 1931, 2, 239–241.

Cunha Lopes. (Aiding subjects with suicidal tendencies.) Arq. Serv. nac. Doenç. ment., Rio de J., 1941 (n. v.).

Curtin, R. G. A study of the influence of climate upon suicide. Trans. Amer. climat. (clin.) Ass., 1909, 25, 141–155; Med. Her., New Albany, 1910, 28, 193–198.

DaCosta Doria, J. R. Suicidos que chamam mais a attennção em consequencia dos neios empregados. (Suicides of interest because of unusual means used.) Brasil-med., 1939, 53, 1017–1019.

Dahle, M. (Unusual suicide attempt.) Med. Rev., Bergen, 1938, 55, 128–132.

Dahlberg, G. Suicide, alcohol, and war. Acta genet., 1948/49, 1, 191–198.

Dahlgren, K. G. On suicide and attempted suicide. Lund, Sweden: Lindstedts, 1945.

Dalma, J. El suicidio como fenómeno de contagio mentale. (Suicide as a phenomenon of mental contagion.) An. Med. púb., 1952, 4, 355–377.

Damaye, H. Idée de suicide latente ou spontanée chez un confuse. (Latent or spontaneous ideas of suicide in a confused person.) Rev. Psychiat., Paris, 1907, 11, 245–248. Note sur un cas de suicide. (Note on a case of suicide.) Rev. Psychiat., Paris, 1904, 9, 330–333.

Davidson, G. M. The problem of suicide. Med. Rec., N.Y., 1934, 139, 24–28. The mental state at the time of suicide. Psychiat. Quart. Suppl., 1941, 15, 41–50.

Da Villa, F. Osservazioni su 40 casi di suicidio. (Observations on 40 cases of suicide.) Igiene ment., 1926, 6, 4–18.

Davis, J. L. Suicide, with some illustrative cases. J. Amer. med. Ass., 1904, 43, 121–123.

Davis, N. S. What is the cause of increased number of suicides, homicides and murders? Quart. J. Inebr., 1903, 25, 65–67.

Deb., A. K. Suicide and homicide in relation to sexual difficulties. Indian med. Rec., 1946, 66, 134–135.

De Bie, J. De zelfmoord. Voordracht gehouden te Antwerpen. (A suicide lecture given in Antwerp.) Mechelen: P. Rychman, 1909.

De Boer, W. Neuere Arbeiten über Psychologie und Psychopathologie des Selbstmordes und der Selbstbeschädigungen. (Recent work on the psychology and psychopathology of suicide and automutilation.) Fortschr. Neurol. Psychiat. Grenzg., 1949, 17, 483–502.

De Fleury, M. La conception moderne du suicide. (Modern conception of suicide.) Bull. Acad. Méd., 1924, 92, 1160–1174. L'angoisse et l'appel de la mort. (The anguish and appeal of death.) Rev. sci., 1924, 62, 673–677.

Delay, J., Deniker, P., and Barande, R. La réaction de suicide chez les épileptiques. Correlations avec la "dangerosité" des sujets. (Suicidal reaction in epileptics. Correlations with the "dangerousness" of the patients.) Ann. Méd. lég., 1957, 37, 150–155. Le suicide des épileptiques. (Suicide of epileptics.) Encépahle, 1957, 46, 401–436.

Del Greco, F. Sulla mentalità dei suicidi (saggio). (The mentality of suicides. [Essay.]) Manicomio, 1916, 31, 1–16.

Delmas, A. Psychopathologie du suicide. (The psychopathology of suicide.) Médecine, 1931, 12, 154, 157–158.

Demay, G., and Sizaret, A. Tentatives répétées de suicide, séquelles d' alcoolisme subaigu (impulsions post-oniriques). (Repeated attempts at suicide following subacute alcoholism [post-confusion impulsions].) Ann. méd.-psychol., 1930, 88, 67–70.

de Oliveira, X. De la profilaxis del suicidio. (The prevention of suicide.) Arch. Brasileiros, 1927.

de Pietra Santa. Suicide et folie suicide. (Suicide and insane suicide.) J. Hyg., Paris, 1897, 22, 229–233.

De Rosa, D., and Corsino, G. A proposito di un raro impulso suicida. (On the motive of an unusual suicidal impulse.) Note Psichiat., Pesaro, 1950, 76, 241–250.

Desbordes, J., and Laurent, J. Suicide chez un persécuté halluciné. (Suicide in a sufferer from persecutory hallucinations.) Ann. Méd. lég., 1942, 22, 213–215.

Deshaies, G. Psychologie du suicide. (Psychology of suicide.) Paris: Presses Universitaires de France, 1947. Des causes et conséquences du suicide. (The causes and consequences of suicide.) Ann. méd.-psychol., 1949, 107(1), 259–270. Les doctrines du suicide. (Theories of suicide.) Évolut. psychiat., 1952, 1, 41–54.

Despert, J. Louise. Suicide and depression in children. Nerv. Child, 1952, 9, 378–389.

Deutsch, E. Über Kinderselbstmorde. (Child suicide.) Arch. Kinderheilk., 1903/04, 38, 37–56.

Devereux, G. Primitive psychiatry; funeral suicide and the Mohave social structure. Bull. Hist. Med., 1942, 11, 522–542.

Devine, H. Some observations on a case with impulsive obsessions of suicide and automutilation. Arch. Neurol. Psychiat., Lond., 1909, 4, 300–310.

Dexter, E. G. Suicide and the weather. Pop. Sci. Mon., 1900/01, 58, 604–615.

d'Heucqueville, G. Etiologie et prophylaxie du suicide. (Etiology and prevention of suicide.) Bull. méd., Paris, 1931, 45, 551–553. Comment prevenir un suicide. (How to prevent a suicide.) Pr. méd., 1932, 40, 307–308.

Dieudonne. Schülerselbstmorde. (Student suicides.) Med. Welt, 1929, 3, 1210–1213.

Dillon, F. A practical note on suicide. Brit. med. J., 1934, 2, 1098–1100.

Dogliani, P. La psicologia del suicidio negli alcoolisti. (Psychological aspects of suicide of alcoholics.) Nevrasse, 1955, 5, 409–430.

Donalies, G. Zur Frage der Selbstmordprophylaxe durch Unterricht. (Suicide prevention by teaching.) Gesundh. u. Wohlf., 1951, 31, 515–528.

D'Ormea, A., and Campioni, V. Doppio suicidio convertitosi in omicidio e mancato suicidio (psiconevrosi da trauma cranico di guerra). Studio pertico. (Double suicide changed into homicide and failed suicide [psychoneurosis from head wound in war]. Expert study.) Rass. Studi psychiat., 1921, 10, 260–288.

Dreikurs, R. Zur Frage der Selbstmordprophylaxe. (The question of suicide prevention.) Z. Psychiat., 1930, 93, 98–114.

Drewry, P. H., Jr. Some aspects of suicide. Virginia med. Mon., 1942, 69, 252–256.

Dubitscher, F. Der Suicid—Unter besonderer Berücksichitigung versorgungsärztlicher

Gesichtspunkte. (Suicide—with special consideration for the point of view of the asylum physician.) Stuttgart: Thieme, 1957.

Dublineau, J. Suicide et folie. (Suicide and insanity.) Proph. ment., 1929, 6, 42–49.

Ducosté. De l'épilepsie consciente et mnésique et en particulier d'un de ses équivalents psychiques: le suicide impulsif conscient. (Conscious and mnesic epilepsy and in particular its psychic equivalents: conscious impulsive suicide.) Thèse, Bordeaux, 1898/99.

Dunton, W. R. Suicides and suicidal attempts among mental cases. Maryland psychiat. Quart., 1913/14, 3, 23–31.

Dupouy, R., and Richard, H. Une tentative étrange de suicide. Considérations sur le suicide "favorise." (A strange attempt at suicide. Considerations on "favored" suicide.) Ann. méd.-psychol., 1932, 90(2), 173–178.

East, G. R. A case of melancholia with attempted suicide. Brit. med. J., 1911, 1, 870.

Eckstein, E. Der Selbstmord in Heilanstalten. (Suicide in sanataria.) Z. Balneol., 1913–14, 6, 283–290.

Ehinger, M. Histoire d'une tentative de suicide. (History of a suicide attempt.) Rev. méd. Suisse Rom., 1938, 58, 547–548.

Eidelman, J. R. Prevention of suicide. J. Mo. med. Ass., 1951, 48, 441–446.

Eissler, K. R. The psychiatrist and the dying patient. New York: International Universities Press, 1955.

Elfeld, P. F. Abnormal reactions resulting in suicide. Delaware St. med. J., 1934, 6, 96–100.

Eliasberg, W. Über ätiologisch ungeklarte, zum Selbstmord führende Depressionen von characteristischem Verlauf. (Etiologically obscure depressions of characteristic course, leading to suicide.) Ärztl. SachverstZtg., 1931, 37, 193–198.

Ellenberger, H. Der Selbstmord im Lichte der Enthno-psychiatrie. (Suicide in the light of ethno-psychiatry.) Mschr. Psychiat. Neurol., 1953, 125, 347–361. Psychologische Beziehungen zwischen Verbrecher und Opfer. (Psychological relationships between criminal and victim.) Z. Psychother. med. Psychol., 1954, 4, 261–280.

Elsässer, G. Zur Frage des "Familien und Selbstmordes." (The problem of family murder and suicide.) Allg. Z. Psychiat., 1939, 110, 207–219.

Epstein, J. Über die Bedeutung der Wiederholungsphasen principiell gleicher unlustbetonter Prozesse als Suicidmotiven. (Concerning the significance of repetition phases of processes, fundamentally of equally unpleasant feeling tone, as suicide motives.) Psychol. u. Med., 1930, 4, 200–203.

Estapé, J. M., and Delgado Correa, B. Herencia neuro-psicopática suicida, intoxicatión arsenical y polineuritis en una niña de 13 años. (Neuropsychopathic hereditary tendency to suicide, arsenic poisoning and resulting polyneuritis in a girl of 13.) Arch. Pediat. Urug., 1932, 3, 270–272.

Ettlinger, Ruth W., and Flordh, P. Attempted suicide: experience of five hundred cases at a general hospital. (Trans. S. H. Vernon.) Acta psychiat., Kbh., 1955. Suppl. 103.

Eulenburg, A. Kinder-und Jugendselbstmorde. (Sammlung Zwangloser Abhandlungen aus dem Gebiete der Nerven-und Geisteskrankheiten, 1913/14. Bd. 10, Heft 6.) (Child and adolescent suicide. [Collection of unsolicited papers from the department of nervous and mental diseases.]) Halle: Marnold, 1914. Das sexuelle Motiv bei den Schülerselbstmorden. (The sexual motive in student suicides.) Z. Sexualwiss., Bonn, 1916/17, 3, 473–483.

Euzière, Vidal, J., and Mas, P. Troubles délirants chez un saturnin. (Delirious confusion in a somnambulist.) Arch. Soc. Sci. méd. biol. Montpellier, 1934, 15, 577–581.

Evans, J. T. Case report of an amateur artist. J. nerv. ment. Dis., 1955, 121, 480–485.

Evershed, R. Insomnia and suicide. Lancet, 1914, 2, 1494.

Evrard, A. Een geval van zelfmoord a deux. (Case of double suicide.) Belg. Tijdschr. Geneesk., 1954, 10, 1186–1189.

Fabretti, C. Il suicidio di una vacca. (The suicide of a cow.) G. Soc. vet. ital., 1897, 46, 407–411.

Fairbank, R. E. Suicide. J. Amer. med. Ass., 1932, 98, 1711–1714.

Farberow, N. L. Personality patterns of suicidal mental hospital patients. Genet. Psychol. Monogr., 1950, 42, 3–79.

Farberow, N. L., and Shneidman, E. S. Attempted, threatened, and completed suicide. J. abnorm. soc. Psychol., 1955, 50, 230.

Farnsworth, H. R., and Ferguson, L. W. The growth of a suicidal tendency as indicated by score changes in Bernreuter's Personality Inventory. Sociometry, 1938, 1, 339–341.

Farrar, C. B. Suicide. Edgewood med. Monogr., 1950, 1, 25–36; J. clin. exp. Psychopathol., 1951, 12, 79–88.

Federn, P. Selbstmordprophylaxe in der Analyse. (Suicide prophylaxis in analysis.) Z. psychoan. Pädag., 1929, 3, 379–389. Die Diskussion über "Selbstmord," inbesondere "Schüler-Selbstmord" im Wiener Psychoanalytischem Verein im Jahre 1918. (The discussion on "suicide," in particular "suicide of school-children" in the Vienna Psychoanalytic Group in 1918.) Z. psychoan. Pädag., 1929, 3, 333–344.

Fels, J. Siebenhundertundzwanzig Selbstmorde und Selbstmordversuche, Zusammengestellt aus der Lemberger freiwillingen Rettungsgesellschaft. (Seven hundred and twenty suicides and suicide attempts collected by the Lemberg volunteer lifesaving society.) Dtsch. klin.-therap. Wschr., 1906, 3, 805, 833, 863.

Fernandez, Savio H. Motivos del suicidio. (Motives of suicide.) Policía secr. nacl., Habana, 1942/43, 11, 228.

Ferraz, A. J. Estudos neuro-psychiatricos. (Neuro-psychiatric studies.) S. Paulo: Impressora Ltda., n.d. [1940?]

Ferrer, C. O., and Cabas, M. A. Consideraciones sobre el suicido y sur tentativas en los alienados internades. (Suicide and suicidal attempts in insane patients.) Bol. Asilo Alien. Oliva, 1934, 22, 175–193.

Ferrio, C. Un caso presumibilmente storico di suicidio por acrofobia. (A presumably historical case of suicide from acrophobia.) Note Psichiat., Pesaro, 1929, 17, 481–494.

Feudell, P. Epikrise zu 700 Selbstmordversuchen. (Epicrisis of 700 suicidal attempts.) Psychiat. Neurol. med. Psychol., 1952, 4, 147–152.

Finn, M. E. Study in suicidal attempts. J. nerv. ment. Dis., 1955, 121, 172–176.

Fisch, M. The suicidal gesture: A study of 114 military patients hospitalized because of abortive suicide attempts. Amer. J. Psychiat., 1954, 111, 33–36.

Fish, N. Case history of a near suicide. J. Maine med. Ass., 1953, 44, 72–73.

Fisher, J. T. Suicide. Calif. St. J. Med., 1923, 21, 126–127.

Fisher, S. The value of the Rorschach for detecting suicidal trends. J. proj. Tech., 1951, 15, 250–254.

Fisher, S., and Hinds, Edith. The organization of hostility controls in various personality structures. Genet. Psychol. Monogr., 1951, 44, 3–68.

Flanagan, N. B., and Sullivan, D. J. Recognition of potential suicide. Sth. Med. Surg., 1942, 104, 66.

Fleck, U. Über Selbstmorde und Selbstmordversuche bei Postencephalitikern mit Bemerkungen über die Persönlichkeitsänderung der erwachsenen parkinsonistischen Postencephalitikern. (On suicides and suicidal attempts in postencephalitics, with some considerations concerning the change of personality in adult parkinsonian postencephalitics.) Arch. Psychiat. Nervenkr., 1933, 99, 233–300.

Flournoy, H. Une curieuse tentative de suicide avec emmurement volontaire. (A curious attempted suicide by voluntary immurement.) Schweiz, Arch. Neurol. Psychiat., 1946, 56, 221–232.

Fomaca, G. Il suicidio negli isterici. (Suicide in hysterics.) Riv. sper. Freniat., 1910, 36, 1–35.

Fornasari di Verce. Suicidi e fallimenti. (Suicides and bankruptcy.) Arch. Psychiat., 1897, 18, 616–618.

Forster, E. Wann muss der praktische Arzt Suizidneigung vermuten und wie verhält er sich dann. (When the physician must suspect suicidal intent and how he prevents it.) Münch. med. Wschr., 1933, 80, 766–769.

Fortanier, A. H., and Speyer, N. ("Balance" suicide; auto-observation written after taking poison by a person committing suicide.) Ned. Tijdschr. Geneesk., 1935, 79, 2639–2640.

Frank, L. M., and Hurley, T. J. Evaluation of the suicidal risk. Conn. St. med. J., 1955, 19, 305–308.

Frankl, V. Selbstmordprophylaxe und Jugendberatung. (Prevention of suicide and youth counseling.) Münch. Med. Nschr., 1929, 76, 1675–1676.

Fribourg-Blanc, A., and Scouras. La réaction suicide chez les débiles et les déséquilibrés dans l'armée. (The suicide reaction among the feeble and unbalanced in the army.) Ann. Méd. lég., 1931, 11, 662–665.

Friedjung, J. K. Zur Frage des Kinderselbstmordes. (The problem of child suicides.) Z. Kinderforsch., 1930, 36, 502–519. Das Kind als Selbstmörder. (Suicides of children.) Bereitschaft, 1930, 10, 83–85.

Friedlander, K. On the "longing to die." Int. J. Psychoanal., 1940, 21, 416–426.

Friedmann, P. Sur le suicide. (On suicide.) Rev. franç. Psychanal., 1935, 8, 106–148.

Füllkrug, G. Die Flucht vom Leben. (The flight from life.) Berlin-Dahlem: Wichern-Verlag, 1928.

Furbush, E. M. Mental disease, suicides and homicides. Ment. Hyg., Concord, 1917, 1, 406.

Garma, A. Psychologie des Selbstmordes. (Psychology of suicide.) Imago, Lpz., 1937, 23, 63–95; Rev. Psiquiat. Crim., B. Aires, 1940, 5, 279–296. Sadismo y masoquismo en la conducta. (Sadism and masochism in human conduct.) Buenos Aires: Asociación Psiconalitica, 1943. (Trans. S. B. Kutash) J. clin. Psychopath., 1944/45, 6, (I) 1–36, (II) 355–390, (III) 493–508; 1945/46, 7, (IV) 43–64.

Garnet, R. W., Jr. The threat of suicide. Virginia med. Mon., 1953, 80, 455–458.

Garnier, P., and Colilan, P. Séméiologie et traitement des idées de suicide. (Symptomatology and treatment of suicidal ideas.) Gaz. Hôp., 1900, 73, 1287–1290.

Garrard, R. L. Self-mutilation. Edgewood med. Monogr., 1950, 1, 92–101.

Gauger, K. Zu den Begriffen Tiefenpsychologie und Psychotherapie; dargestellt an einem Suicidversuch. (Concepts of depth psychology and psychotherapy as represented in a case of attempted suicide.) Med. Klinik, 1953, 48, 100–102.

Geisler, Erika. Selbstmord und Todessehnsucht im Kindesalter. (Suicide and death-longing in childhood.) Psychiat. Neurol. med. Psychol., Leipzig, 1953, 5, 210–216.

Gerstner, H. Enkele opmerkingen over het handschrift van Zelfmoordenaars. (Further observations on the handwriting of suicides.) Tijdsch. wetenschap. Graphol., 1931, 3, No. 4.

Ghysbrecht, P. F. Le suicide du poète Heinrich von Kleist; essai d'analyse. (The suicide of the poet Heinrich von Kleist; tentative analysis.) Ann. Méd. lég., 1953, 33, 283–293; Fol. psychiat. neerl., 1954, 57, 182–194. Betrachtungen über den Doppelselbstmord. (Remarks on double suicide.) Psychol. Beit., 1957, 3, 94–107.

Giani, P. Del suicidio. (Suicide.) Note Psichiat., Pesaro, 1926, 14, 337–368.

Giannelli, V. Sui tentativi di suicidio nei dementi. (On suicide attempts among the insane.) Rass. Studi psichiat., 1931, 20, 257–279.

Gille, M. Les suicides bizarres. (Bizarre suicides.) Rev. prat. Biol., 1925, 18, 233–239.

Gilli, R. Forme infrequenti di suicidio; il doppio suicidio per amore. (Rare form of suicide; double suicide for love.) Arch. Antrop. crim., 1946, 66, 11–34.

Givens, A. J. The evolution of the suicide. Hahnemann. Mon., Phila., 1912, 47, 890–899.

Glover, E. Notes on the psychopathology of suicide. Int. J. Psychoanal., 1922, 3, 507–508. Some observations on suicidal mechanisms. Psychoanal. Rev., 1928, 15, 89–90. On the early development of the mind. New York: International Universities Press, 1956.

Godding, W. W. Suicide. Nat. med. Rev., Wash., 1898/99, 8, 192–196; Trans. med. Soc. D.C., 1899, 3, 74–78.

Godin, A. Suicide ou sacrifice? Recherches sur le désengagement en psychologie normale et criminale. (Suicide or sacrifice? Investigation on disengagement in normal and criminal psychology.) Psyché, Paris, 1948, 3, 1048–1063.

Gohrbandt, E. Über den Freitod. (On voluntary death.) Arch. klin. Chir., 1957, 287, 349–351.

Gold, L. B. Suicide of a psychotic patient in therapy. Unpublished manuscript, Brentwood Med. Library, VA Center, Los Angeles, Calif., 1957.

González Mas, R. Suicidio; introduction a la psicología del desaliento. (Suicide; introduction to the psychology of discouragement.) Med. y Cirug. Guerra, 1956, 18, 337–343.

Gordon, R. G. Certain personality problems in relation to mental illness with special reference to suicide and homicide. Brit. J. med. Psychol., 1929, 9, 60–66.

Gorriti, F. Caracteres del suicidio psicopático. (Characteristics of psychopathic suicide.) Sem. méd., 1937, 2, 158–160.

Gosselin, J. Y., and Gervais, M. Suicide et aliénation mentale. (Suicide and mental derangement.) Laval Méd., 1956, 21, 784–792.

Gould, G. M. The mysteries and sources of suicide. Biogr. Clinics, Phila., 1907, 5, 183–229. A strange and illogical case of suicide. Med. Stand., 1907, 30, 594; Biogr. Clinics, Phila., 1910, 6, 201–206.

Grasso-Biondi, I. Del suicidio-infortunio. (The suicide mishap.) Riv. Infort., 1948, 35, 446–458.

Graute, P. Alkoholismus und Selbstmord. (Alcoholism and suicide.) Allg. Z. Psychiat., 1939, 111, 47–62.

Greenbank, R. K. Communication of suicidal thoughts. Canad. psychiat. Ass. J., 1957,

2, 150–153. Unexplained mental phenomena regarding suicide. J. nerv. ment. Dis., 1957, 125, 131–132.

Griffith, F. Thoughts on suicide. Alien. & Neurol., 1909, 30, 253–261.

Gruhle, H. W. Selbstmord. (Suicide.) Leipzig: Theime, 1940.

Gutheil, E. A. Dream and suicide. Amer. J. Psychother., 1948, 2, 283–294.

Guttmann, E. Suicidal head injuries. J. ment. Sci., 1943, 89, 85–91.

Habermann, P. Über einen Selbstmordversuch eines elfjahrigen Knaben. (Suicide attempt of an eleven year old boy.) Arch. Kinderheilk., 1950, 139, 130–133.

Hachlaender, F. Ärtze und Lehrer über Schülerselbstmorde. (Physicians and teachers on juvenile suicide.) Z. psychoan. Pädag., 1927, 1, 188–191.

Haggard, H. R. The anti-suicide bureau. *In* H. R. Haggard, Regeneration; being an account of the Salvation Army in Great Britain. London: Longmans, Green, 1910, pp. 151–164.

Halbwachs, M. Le suicide et les maladies mentales. (Suicide and mental disease.) Rev. philos., 1929, 108, 321–360.

Hall, G. S. Thanatophobia and immortality. Amer. J. Psychol., 1915, 26, 550–613.

Hall, J. K. Human behavior. The call to the boatman. Sth. Med. Surg., 1947, 109, 371–372.

Hanford, J. H. Suicide in the plays of Shakespeare. Modern Language Ass. of Amer., 1912, 27, (n.s. 20), 380–397.

Harbin, R. M. Suicide. Med. Rec., N.Y., 1906, 70, 462.

Hardy, H. N. Suicide of a young married woman. Med. Pr., 1912, 93, 589.

Harris, R. L., Buven, A. E., and Irwin, I. Ceramics as occupational therapy for patients with suicidal tendencies. Occup. Ther. Rehab., 1949, 28, 231–244.

Hartelius, H. Suicidförsök ur psykiatrisk synpunkt. (Suicide attempts from psychiatric point of view.) Nord. Med., 1955, 53, 226–233. Suicide in Sweden 1925–1950: A statistical analysis and psychodynamic interpretation. (Trans. Erica Odelberg.) Acta psychiat., Kbh., 1957, 32, 151–181.

Hayakawa, S. I. Suicide as a communicative act. Etc. Rev. gen. Semant., 1957, 15, 46–51.

Hayashi, S. (Opinion on three cases of suicide or death from other cause.) Kyo-rin-no Shiori, 1901, 13, 338–344.

Heimerzheim, W. Über den Selbstmordversuch bei nichtpsychotischen Persönlichkeiten. (Suicide in non-psychotic personalities.) Düsseldorf: Nolte, 1933.

Henderson, D. K. The social and individual prophylaxis of suicide. Int. Congr. ment. Hyg., 1937, 2, (2), 85–104. Suicide. Edinb. med. J., 1938, 45, 245–263.

Hendin, H. Attempted suicide; a psychiatric and statistical study. Psychiat. Quart., 1950, 24, 39–46. Psychodynamic motivational factors in suicide. Psychiat. Quart., 1951, 25, 672–678. Suicide. Psychiat. Quart., 1956, 30, 267–282. What the pastor ought to know about suicide. Pastoral Psychol., 1953, 4, 41–45.

Hendrick, I. Suicide as wish-fulfillment. Psychiat. Quart., 1940, 14, 30–42.

Hertz, Marguerite R. Suicidal configurations in Rorschach records. Rorschach Res. Exch., 1948, 12, 1–56. Further study of "suicidal" configurations in Rorschach records. Rorschach Res. Exch., 1949, 13, 44–73.

Hill, G. A. Suicide and insanity. Proc. Amer. med.-psychol. Ass., 1904, 274–283.

Hill, G. H. Observations concerning suicide. Trans. Iowa med. Soc., 1898, 16, 271–276.

Hiltner, S. Suicidal reflections. Pastoral psychol., 1953, 4, 33–40.

Hintermann, R. Ursachen des Selbstmordes bei Jugendlichen. (Causes of suicide of adolescents.) Thesis, Zürich, 1953.

Hirschfeldt, M. Analyse der in den Jahren 1919 bis 1929 in Allgemeinen Krankenhaus St. Georg, Hamburg, zur Aufnahme gelangten Selbstmordfälle. (Analysis of admissions diagnoses of successful suicide cases in St. Georg General Hospital, Hamburg, in the years 1919 to 1929.) Psychiat.-neurol. Wschr., 1932, 34, 229–235.

Hoffman, F. L. Suicide. Ref. Handb. med. Sci., N.Y. 1917, 8, 13–18.

Hoffman, J. The care and management of the suicidal patient. Bull. U. S. Army med. Dep., 1948, 8, 888–891; Surg. Circ. med. Sec. Far East Command, 1943, 3, 6–9.

Holzberg, J. D., Cahen, Eleanor R., and Wilk, E. K. Suicide: A psychological study of self-destruction. J. proj. Tech., 1951, 15, 339–354.

Homburger, M. Der Einfluss der Schundliteratur auf jugendliche Verbrecher und Selbstmörder. (The influence of trashy literature on juvenile criminals and suicides.) Mschr. KrimPsychol., 1909, 6, 145–164.

Hösli-Widmer, Luise. Beitrag zur Frage des Doppelselbstmordes. (Contribution to the question of double suicide.) Inaug. Diss., Zürich: Leeman, 1950.

Hove, H. Reddede selvmordspatienters skaebne; an efterundersogelse af 500 patienter. (Fates of intercepted suicides; follow-up of 500 cases.) Ugeskr. Læg., 1953, 115, 645–646.

Hoven, H. À propos de quelques cas de suicide. (Some cases of suicide.) Acta neurol. belg., 1948, 47, 253–258; Scalpel, Brux., 1948, 101, 429.

Howard, M. Q. Recognition and treatment of suicidal tendencies. Trans. Amer. ther. Soc., 1934, 34, 64–70.

Hoxie, G. H. My suicides. Med. Times, N.Y., 1944, 72, 282–283.

Hughes, C. H. Suicide. Trans. med. Ass. Mo. 1896–97; 1898, 537–545; Alien. & Neurol., 1897, 18, 502–509. The neurotic salvage of suicide. A sequel to "Suicide" in October (1897) number. Alien. & Neurol., 1898, 19, 104–115. Suicide pacts. Alien. & Neurol., 1907, 28, 423. Suicide by crucifixion. Alien. & Neurol., 1910, 461–462.

Hurwics, E. Ursachen und Wege zur Bekämpfung des Selbstmordes ganzer Familien. (Motives and methods of suicide of entire families.) Neue Generation, 1916, 12, 362–368. Der Liebes-Doppelselbstmord. (Double love suicide.) Neue Generation, 1917, 13, 264–268.

Hussa, R. Selbstmord nach Mord. (Suicide following murder.) Psychiat.-neur. Wschr., 1930, 32, 243–249.

Ichok, G. Il suicidio. (Suicide.) Biol. med., Milano, 1935, 11, 269–293.

Imberciadori, E., and Manganaro, D. Su di un caso di impulso coatto al suicidio; studio clinico. (A case of obsessive impulsion for suicide; clinical study.) Rass. Studi psichiat., 1954, 43, 550–554. Del suicidio; rassegna sintetico-critica. (Suicide; critical review.) Riv. Pat. nerv. Ment., 1955, 76, 65–180.

Ireland, W. W. On the causes of the increase of suicide. J. ment. Sci., 1899, 45, 451–466.

Israel, L. Les malades dangereux pour eux-mêmes. (Patients dangerous to themselves.) Strasbourg-méd., 1956, 7, 841–845.

Israel, L., and Cahn, R. Un suicide d'adolescent. (Suicide of an adolescent.) Cah. Psychiat., 1957, No. 12, 84–95.

Israeli, N. Outlook of a depressed patient, interested in planned gambling, before and after his attempt at suicide. Amer. J. Orthopsychiat., 1935, 5, 57–63.

Jackson, D. D. Suicide. Sci. Amer., 1954, 191(5), 88–96.

Jamieson, G. R. Suicide and mental disease: A clinical analysis of one hundred cases. Arch. Neurol. Psychiat., Chicago, 1936, 36, 1–12.

Jamieson, G. R., and Wall, J. H. Some psychiatric aspects of suicide. Psychiat. Quart., 1933, 7, 211–299.

Jankau, V. Selbstmord nach Unfall. Beitrag zu der Lehre von den postkommotionellen Zustandbildern. (Suicide following accident; contribution to the study of post-concussion states.) Z. ges. Neurol. Psychiat., 1930, 130, 148–159.

Jantz, H. Schizophrenie und Selbstmord. (Schizophrenia and suicide.) Nervenarzt, 1951, 22, 126–133.

Jensen, V. W. Evaluating the suicide impulse in the university setting. Jl-Lancet, 1955, 75, 441–444.

Jenter, Marie T. Der Schusselbstmord der Frau. (Shooting suicide of women.) Inaug. Diss., Zürich. Doetinchem: Misset, (1948?).

Joël, E. Über Selbstbetäubung und Selbtvernichtung. (Addiction and self-destruction.) Dtsch. med. Wschr., 1926, 52, 1082–1084.

Johnsen, G., and Vogt, E. Selvmordforsøk med gift; 306 tilfelle hos 278 pasienter. (Suicide by poison; 306 cases in 278 patients.) Nord. Med., 1950, 43, 1013–1017.

Jones, E. Das Problem des "Gemeinsamen Sterbens," namentlich mit Bezug auf den Selbstmord Heinrich von Kleist's. (The problem of "dying together," especially with reference to the suicide of Heinrich von Kleist.) Zbl. Psychoan., 1910/11, 1, 563–567. On "dying together," and an unusual case of "dying together." *In* Jones, E., Essays in applied psychoanalysis. London: Hogarth, 1951, pp. 4–15, 16–21.

Jones, R. Two cases of abdominal surgery in the insane from attempted suicide. J. ment. Sci., 1903, 49, 299–303.

Jourdan, E. Hysterie et suicide. (Hysteria and suicide.) Rev. Hypnot., Paris, 1908/09, 23, 144–150.

Julier. Zweifelhafte Selbstmorde. (Doubtful suicide.) Arch. Kriminol., 1929, 84, 114–117.

Kahn, M. H. Autobiography of a suicide patient. Med. Rev. of Rev., N.Y., 1931, 37, 665–667.

Kalischer, H. Leben und Selbstmord eines Zwangdiebes. Ein psychoanalytischer Beitrag zum Problem "Verbrechen und Strafe." (Life and suicide of a kleptomaniac. A psychoanalytic contribution to the problem "crime and punishment.") Z. psychoan. Pädag., 1929, 3, 363–379.

Kallman, F. J. Zur Häufigkeit und psychopathologischen Motivierung des Selbstmordes bei Zwillingen und alleinigen Kindern. (Frequency and psychopathological motivation of suicide in twins and only children.) Mschr. Psychiat. Neurol., 1949, 117, 280–288.

Kallman, F. J., and Anastasio, Mary M. Twin studies on the psychopathology of suicide. J. Hered., 1946, 37, 171–180; J. nerv. ment. Dis., 1947, 105, 40–55.

Kallman, F. J., De Porte, J., De Porte, Elizabeth, and Feingold, Lissy. Suicide in twins and only children. Amer. J. hum. Genet., 1949, 1, 113–126.

Kellner. Beziehungen zwischen kindlichen und jugendlichen Selbstmord und geistigen Anomalien. (Relations between child and juvenile suicide and mental anomalies.) Z. Behandl. Schwachsinn., 1919, 39, 135–142.

Khoroshko, V. K. Samoūbiystvo dīeteĭ. S predisloviyem G. I. Rossolimo. (Suicide of children. With preface by Rossolimo.) Moskva, 1909.

Kielberg, S. (Some attempts at suicide in children and young people.) Bibl. Læg., 1937, 129, 137, 177.

Kilpatrick, Elizabeth. A psychoanalytic understanding of suicide. Amer. J. Psychoanal., 1948, 8, 13–23.

Kiørboe, E. Suicide and attempted suicide among old people. J. Geront., 1951, 6, 233–236.

Kircheisen, F. M. Selbstmörder Napoleon? (Napoleon suicidal?) Münch. med. Wschr., 1933, 80, 503–504.

Kleinschmidt, H. J. The death of Elpenor; on a distinct type of self-destructive reaction in a rejected youth. J. Hillside Hosp., 1956, 5, 320–327.

Kline, C. L. Suicide; implications for the general medical man. Wis. med. J., 1950, 49, 1111–1113.

Knigge, F. Aberglaube und Verbrechen. (Superstition and crime.) Z. ges. Neurol. Psychiat., 1939, 166, 271–286.

Kohlmann, T., and Stepan, H. Zum Problem des Aufdeckens von Selbstmordtendenzen in Projektionstests (Rorschach-und Szondi-Versuch). (The problem of detection of suicidal tendencies through projective techniques [Rorschach and Szondi tests].) Wien. Z. Nervenh., 1955, 12, 54–78.

Kohout, J. (Two strange cases of suicide.) Čas. Lék. čes., 1931, 70, 20–27.

Koupernik, C. Trois adolescents et la mort. (Three adolescents and death.) Concours méd., 1957, 79, 2567–2572.

Kovalev, A. I. (A case of amnesic symptoms after attempted suicide.) Zh. nevropat., 1929, 22, 213–222.

Kratter, J. Zur Psychologie und Psychopathologie des Selbstmordes. (The psychology and psychopathology of suicide.) Arch. Psychiat. Nervenkr., 1918, 59, 484–492.

Krenberger, S. Selbstmorde und Entweichungen von Kindern und Jugendlichen. (Suicide and running away of children and adolescents.) Eos, Wien, 1928, 20, 122.

Kruger, Alice K. Direct and substitutive modes of tension-reduction in terms of developmental level. An experimental analysis by means of the Rorschach test. Unpublished doctoral dissertation, Clark University, 1954.

Kühne, D. Zur Rache als Selbstmordmotiv. (On revenge as a suicide motive.) Globus, 1898, 74, 166.

Kupper, W. H. A study of suicidal soldiers in the European Theatre after V-E day. J. nerv. ment. Dis., 1947, 105, 299–303.

Kürbitz, W. Alkohol und Selbstmord; nebst einigen Bemerkungen über die Zurechnungsfähigkeit der Trinker. (Alcohol and suicide; in addition a few notes concerning the responsibility of drinkers.) Allg. Z. Psychiat., 1907, 64, 579–611.

Ladame, P. L. Selbstmord und Huntington'sche Chorea. (Suicide and Huntington's Chorea.) Neurol. Zbl., 1911, 30, 217.—Abstract.

Lafora, G. R. (Suicide in dementia praecox.) Siglo méd., 1917, 64, 686.

Laignel-Lavastine, Bouvet, M., and Follin. Amélioration de l'état mental, à la suite d'une tentative de suicide par pendaison. (Improvement in mental condition following attempted suicide by hanging.) Bull. Mém. Soc. méd. Hôp. Paris, 1940, 56, 512–515.

Laignel-Lavastine, d'Heucqueville, G., and Gautier, M. Tentative de suicide par la hache, d'un alcoolique, au début d'une paralysie générale. (Attempted suicide by hatchet, of an alcoholic, at the outset of a general paralysis.) Ann. méd.-psychol., 1934, 92 (1), 741–742.

Laignel-Lavastine, d'Heucqueville, G., and Sambron, J. J. Tentatives de suicide répétées chez un instable déprimé sans travail (présentation du malade). (Repeated attempted suicide of an unstable, depressed unemployed person [presentation of the illness].) Ann. méd.-psychol., 1936, 94, (1), 218–222.

La Moal, P. Suicide; chantage au suicide chez l'enfant et l'adolescent. (Suicide, threat of suicide in child and adolescent.) Thèse, Paris, 1944. L'enfant excité et deprimé. (The excited and depressed child.) Paris: Pr. universitaires, 1953.

Lasch, R. Rache als Selbstmordmotiv. (Revenge as a suicide motive.) Globus, 1898, 74, 37–39.

Laughlin, H. P. Depression: some dynamic and clinical features of depressive character defenses, psychoneurotic depression, and suicide. Med. Ann. D.C., 1953, 22, 653–671, 696. Suicide; impulse and remorse. Quart. Rev. Psychiat., 1953, 8, 19–26.

Laupts. Une enquête sur le suicide; un genre de suicide; le suicide sans motifs (melancholié intermittente bénigne). (An inquiry into suicide; one kind of suicide; suicide without motive [benign intermittent melancholia].) Ann. méd.-psychol., 1897, 5, 38–49.

Laurès, G. Syndrome confusionnel consécutif à une tentative de suicide par submersion. (Confusional syndrome following an attempted suicide by drowning.) Clinique, Paris, 1911, 6, 517.

Lawson, D. E. Why man commits suicide. Hygeia, Chicago, 1940, 18, 296–299.

Lebensohn, Z. M. Self-inflicted bullet wound of frontal lobes in a depression with recovery. Amer. J. Psychiat., 1941, 98, 56–62.

Legrün, A. Die Handschrift jugendlicher Selbstmörder. (The handwriting of young suicides.) Schrift u. Schreiben, 1930, 2, 70–73.

Leibbrand, W. Der Selbstmord der Charlotte Stieglitz. (Suicide of Charlotte Stieglitz.) Dtsch. med. Wschr., 1934, 60, 1929–1931. Warum starb Ferdinand Raimund? Zu seinem hundertjährigen Todestag am 6. September 1936. (Why did Ferdinand Raimund commit suicide? On the hundredth anniversary of his death, September 6, 1936.) Psychiat.-neurol. Wschr., 1936, 38, 650–652.

Letourneau, C. U. Precautions and responsibilities in handling patient suicides. Hospitals, 1953, 27 (Jan.), 80, 82, 84, 86, 88.

Leuthold, H. Eine Schülerin denkt an Selbstmord. (A schoolgirl thinks about suicide.) Z. psychoan. Pädag., 1929, 3, 436–438.

Levi Bianchini, M. Il suicidio e l'omicidio degli alienati internati negli ospedali psichiatrici. (Suicide and homicide among insane interned in a psychiatric hospital.) Arch. gen. Neurol. Psichiat., 1933, 14, 205–278.

Levinson, B. A. Some thoughts on suicide. W. Lond. med. J., 1931, 36, 226–230.

Levy, S., and Southcombe, R. H. Suicide in a state hospital for the mentally ill. J. nerv. ment. Dis., 1953, 117, 504–514.

Lévy-Valensi, J. Note sur le suicide du duc de Bourbon (1830). Étude de psychopathologie historique. (Note on the suicide of the Duke of Bourbon [1830]. Psychopathological historical study.) Bull. Soc. franç., Hist. Med., 1927, 21, 195–200. Suicide et homicide pathologiques. (Pathological suicide and homicide.) Progr. méd., Paris, 1928, 43, 1389–1394.

Lewis, A. Social aspects of psychiatry. Part I. Edinb. med. J., 1951, 58, 214–230; Part II, 231–247.

Lewis, N. D. C. Studies on suicide. I. Preliminary survey of some significant aspects of suicide. Psychoanal. Rev., 1933, 20, 241–273. Studies on suicide. II. Some comments on the biological aspects of suicide. Psychoanal. Rev., 1934, 21, 146–153.

Lewis, O. F. Would-be suicides. Charities, 1907, 18, 80–82.

Liebermann, L. P. Three cases of attempted suicide in children. Brit. J. med. Psychol., 1953, 26, 110–114.

Lind, W. A. T. Suicide. Med. J. Aust., 1927, 1, 679–681.

Lindemann, E., and Greer, Ina M. A study of grief: emotional responses to suicide. Pastoral Psychol., 1953, 4, 9–13.

Lindemann, E., Vaughan, W. T., and McGinnis, Manon. Preventive intervention in a four-year-old child whose father committed suicide. *In* G. Caplan (Ed.), Emotional problems of early childhood. New York: Basic Books, 1955, pp. 5–30.

Lindhardt, M. Selvmordshyppigheden i Danmark. (Suicide frequency in Denmark.) Ugeskr. Læg., 1949, 111, 342–345.

Lindner, R. M. The content of the Rorschach protocol. *In* L. E. Abt and L. Bellak (Eds.), Projective Psychology. New York: Knopf, 1950. Pp. 75–90.

Lindsay, D. S. Suicidal risks in hospital and community. Canad. Hosp., 1955, 32, 55.

Lipschutz, L. S. Some administrative aspects of suicide in mental hospital. Amer. J. Psychiat., 1942, 99, 181–187.

Lipton, M. A. The recognition and management of psychiatric emergencies. Med. Clin. N. Amer., 1954, Jan., 143–166.

Lochte, T. Selbstmord durch Erhängen. Ausführliche Niederschrift des geplanten Selbstmordes vor der Ausführung. (Suicide by hanging. Detailed notes of a planned suicide, previous to the completion.) Dtsch. Z. ges. gerichtl. Med., 1922, 730–732.

Loewe, E. L. Suicid. (Suicide.) Med. Welt, 1928, 2, 164.

Loewenberg, R. D. Suicide. J. clin. Med., 1937, 2, No. 4. Suicide in twins. J. nerv. ment. Dis., 1941, 93, 182–184.

London, L. S. Psychogenesis of a schizoid manic. J. clin. Psychopath., 1949, 10, 27–49.

Lopes Junior, E. Suicidio e higiene mental. (Suicide and mental hygiene.) Arq. policia civ. S. Paulo, 1944, 8, 351–355.

Lorand, A. S. Der Selbstmord von Miss X. (The suicide of Miss X.) Z. psychoan. Pädag., 1929, 3, 430–436.

Loux, N. L. Some clinical aspects of suicide. R. I. med. J., 1953, 36, 248–250; 252 passim.

Lowrey, L. G. An analysis of suicidal attempts. J. nerv. ment. Dis., 1920, 52, 475–481.

MacErlean, D. A. Some aspects of suicide. Irish J. med. Sci., 1934, 241–254.

MacKeith, S. A., and Parfitt, D. N. Suicide after treatment as voluntary patients. Brit. med. J., 1938, 2, 451.

Mahrer, Myriam. Quando noi morti ci destiamo. Contributo alla fisico-psicologia del suicidio. (When we die and live again. A contribution to the physio-psychology of suicide.) Arch. Antrop. crim., 1930, 50, 161–196.

Manganaro, D. Un caso di suicidio familiare. (A case of familial suicide.) Riv. Pat. nerv. ment., 1957, 78, 1078–1081.

Mangili, C. In tema di suicidio "combinato." (On the theme of "combined" suicide.) Arch. Antrop. crim., 1934, 54, 562–570.

Mann, A. M., and Wittkower, E. D. A case of depression with attempted suicide treated at a general hospital. Canad. med. Ass. J., 1953, 68, 381–383.

Mapes, C. C. Notes on suicide. Detroit: Warren, 1897; Med. Age, 1897, 15, 555–560.

Marc. Réflexions sur le suicide. (Reflections on suicide.) Bull. Soc. méd. St Luc, 1934, 40, 85–95.

Martínez Gómez, S. Concomitancias en un conato de suicidio. (Concomitant factors in a case of attempted suicide.) Galicia clin., 1950, 22, 663–669.

Maschka. Beitrag zur Enquête über den Selbstmord. (Contributions to the inquiry on suicide.) Z. crimAnthrop., 1897, 1, 511–519.

Mason, P. Suicide in adolescents. Psychoanal. Rev., 1954, 41, 48–54.

Masserman, J. H. A note on the dynamics of suicide. Dis. nerv. Syst., 1947, 8, 324–325. Emotional reactions to death and suicide. Amer. Practit. 1954, 5, 41–46.

Massignan, I., and Zamparo, D. Rivelazione di tendenze suicide; studio Rorschach. (Revelation of suicidal tendencies; Rorschach study.) Rass. Neuropsichiat., 1953, 7, 333–338.

Mattioli-Foggia, C., and Pollini, L. G. Sulle psicosi dei naufraghi e sui mancati suicidi per impiccamento. (On the psychoses of shipwrecked persons, and on fruitless attempts at suicide by hanging.) Note Psichiat., Pesaro, 1948, 74, 65–70.

May, G. Selbstmord und Selbstmordversuch bei Kindern und Jugenlichen. (Suicide and attempted suicide by children and juveniles.) Diss., Basel, 1935.

Meerloo, A. M. (Attitude of physician towards patients with suicidal tendency.) Ned. Tijdschr. Geneesk., 1933, 77, 31–37. Über die Beurteilung der Selbstmordneigung. (On the judging of the tendency toward suicide.) Z. ges. Neurol. Psychiat., 1933, 144, 222–244.

Meng, H. Gespräche mit einer Mutter über Selbstmord. (Talks with a mother about suicide.) Z. psychoan. Pädag., 1929, 3, 344–355.

Menninger, K. A. Suicides. J. Kans. med. Soc., 1928, 28, 6–10. Psychoanalytic aspects of suicide. Arch. Neurol. Psychiat., Chicago, 1931, 25, 1369–1372. Psychoanalytic aspects of suicide. Int. J .Psychoanal., 1933, 14, 376–390. Some clinical examples of indirect suicide. Sth. med. J., 1935, 28, 356–360. Purposive accidents as an expression of self-destructive tendencies. Int. J. Psychoanal., 1936, 17, 6–16. Organic suicide. Bull. Menninger Clin., 1937, 1, 192–198. I. Psychological aspects of the organism under stress. II. Regulatory devices of the ego under major stress. J. Amer. Psychoanal. Ass., 1954, 2, 280–310.

Menninger-Lerchenthal, E. Das europäische Selbstmordproblem; eine zeitgemässe Betrachtung. (The European suicide problem; a timely consideration.) Wien: Deuticke, 1947. Selbstmordproblem und Psychohygiene. (Mental hygiene and the problem of suicide.) Wien. Beitr. Hyg., 1955, 4, 203–226.

Metelmann, K. Die monatlichen Selbstmord-Sterbeziffern unter den Gesichtpunken der Jaenschchen Typologie. (The number of monthly suicides from the points of view of Jaensch's typology.) Z. angew. Psychol., 1934, 47, 376–386.

Meyer, E. Zur Verhütung des Selbstmordes, insebesondere der Jugendlichen. (Prevention of suicides especially among juveniles.) Münch. med. Wschr., 1929, 76, 1459–1460.

Michl, W. Selbstmordversuche eines Kleinkindes. (Suicide attempts by a small child.) Zbl. Psychother., 1941, 13, 58–60.

Mignardot, J., Ramée, F., and Aubry, P. Impulsions au suicide répétées, conscientes et mnésiques, chez un grand épileptique. (Repeated impulsions to suicide, conscious and mnesic, of a grand mal epileptic.) Ann. méd.-psychol., 1936, 94(2), 44–54.

Mills, C. A. Suicides and homicides in their relation to weather changes. Amer. J. Psychiat., 1934, 91, 669–677.

Milner, M. A suicidal symptom in a child of three. Int. J. Psychoanal., 1944, 25, 53–61.

Miner, J. R. Suicide and its relation to climatic and other factors. Amer. J. Hyg., 1922, Monogr. Ser., No. 2, 1–140.

Minogue, S. J. Symptoms preceding suicide. Med. J. Aust. 1936, 2, 598–600. Attempted suicide. Med. J. Aust., 1942, 1, 209–210.

Minovici, M. Cas de folie communiquée. Suicide collectif par l'oxyde de carbone (10 personnes appartenant à la même famille.) (Case of communicated insanity [collective suicide by carbon monoxide by a family of 10 persons].) Ann. Méd. lég., 1929, 9, 459–476.

Moll, A. E. Suicide; psychopathology. Canad. med. Ass. J., 1956, 74, 104–112.

Moloney, J. C. The biospheric aspects of Japanese death by suicide. Samīkṣā, 1949, 3, 104–124.

Moore, M. Alcoholism and attempted suicide; a report of 143 cases. New Eng. J. Med., 1939, 221, 691–693.

Morgenthaler, W., and Steinberg, Marianne. Letzte Aufzeichnungen von Selbstmördern. (Last writings of suicides.) Schweiz. Z. Psychol. Beih., 1945, No. 1.

Moss, L. M. Prognosis of the suicidal patient. Arch. Neurol. Psychiat., Chicago, 1955, 74, 336–337.

Moss, L. M., and Hamilton, D. M. The psychotherapy of the suicidal patient. Amer. J. Psychiat., 1956, 112, 814–820.

Mudge, G. P. Inheritance of suicidal mania; the families of A. and B.; pedigree Chart I. Mendel J., 1909, 1, 11–19.

Mühl, Anita M. America's greatest suicide problem. A study of over 500 cases in San Diego. Psychoanal. Rev., 1927, 14, 317–325.

Müller-Küppers, M., and Schilf, E. Beiträge zur Kinderpsychologie, III. Selbstmord bei Kindern. (Contribution to child psychiatry, III. Suicide of children.) Psychiat. Neurol, med. Psychol., Lpz., 1955, 7, 42–45.

Mumortseff, A. N. (Contemporary pessimism and suicide.) Sovrem. Psikhiat., 1914, 8, 861–881.

Murray, C. D. A recent case of "dying together." Psychoanal. Rev., 1931, 18, 63–68. Suicide in a fit of temporary insanity. J. R. Army med. Cps., 1909, 13, 437.

Nacht, S. Instinct de mort ou instinct de vie? (Death or life instinct?) Rev. franç. Psychanal., 1956, 20, 405–416.

Näcke, P. Merkwürdige Selbstmordarten. (Remarkable kinds of suicide.) Arch. Krim-Anthrop., 1904, 16, 338. Selbstmord bei Tieren. (Suicide in animals.) Arch KrimAnthrop., 1904/05, 18, 91–93. Aberglauben als Grund von Selbstmord. (Superstitution as the basis for suicide.) Arch. KrimAnthrop., 1911, 42, 170.

Nakamura, R. Suizide und Psychopathie. (Suicide and psychopathy.) Psychiat. et Neurol. japon., 1940, 44, 33–34.—Abstract.

Nelken, J. (Nervous and psychic disturbances due to gunshot wounds of head in attempted suicide.) Lek. wojsk. (J. Polish Army med. Cps), 1931, 17, 3–24. (Nervous and psychic disturbances due to gunshot wounds of head in attempted suicide.) Roczn. Psychjat. (Psychiat. Annu., Warsaw), 1932, 135–172.

Nencini, R., Reda, G. C., Schiavi, F., and Alliani, E. Symposium di psycologia clinica;

il P. F. test di Rosenzweig in trenta tentativi di suicidio. (Clinical psychology symposium; Rosenzweig's P-F test in thirty suicide attempts.) Arch. Psicol. Neur. Psich., 1953, 14, 289–306.

Nikolski, D. P. (Suicides among students.) Prakt. Vrach, 1915, 14, 308, 320, 345, 382.

Oates, W. E. The funeral of a suicide. Pastoral Psychol., 1953, 4, 14–17.

Obersteg, J. I., and Marzetta, B. Zur Frage Selbstmord und Witterung. (The question of suicide and weather.) Dtsch. Z. ges. gerichtl. Med., 1957, 46, 18–26.

Obici, G. Un caso di doppia suicida. (Case of double suicide.) G. Psichiat. manic., 1903, 31, 1–12.

Obiglio, J. R. La huelga del hambre. (The hunger strike.) Rev. Asoc. méd. argent., 1932, 46, 587–596.

O'Connor, W. A. Some notes on suicide. Brit. J. med. Psychol., 1947/48, 21, 222–228.

Offenkrantz, W., Church, E., and Elliott, R. Psychiatric management of suicide problems in military service. Amer. J. Psychiat., 1957, 114, 33–41.

O'Hara, W. E. A case of suicide. Lancet, 1904, 2, 1178.

Oliven, J. F. The suicidal risk: Its diagnosis and evaluation. New England J. Med., 1951, 245, 488–494. Suicide prevention as a public health problem. Amer. J. publ. Hlth, 1954, 44, 1419–1425; Amer. Practit., 1955, 6, 229.

O'Neal, Patricia, Robins, E., and Schmidt, E. H. A psychiatric study of attempted suicide in persons over sixty years of age. Arch. Neurol. Psychiat., Chicago, 1956, 75, 275–284.

Oppler, W. Die Zunahme der Suizidversuche und ihre Gründe. (The increase in attempted suicide and its basis.) Arch. Psychiat. Nervenkr., 1927, 82, 95–109.

Oulès, J., and Soubrier, R. Mélancolie conjugale. (Conjugal melancholy.) Ann. méd.-psychol., 1954, 112(2), 778–780.

Pacheco, J. N. J. Suicide; its causes and prevention. Indian med. Gaz., 1936, 71, 720–723.

Palmer, D. M. Factors in suicidal attempts, a review of 25 consecutive cases. J. nerv. ment. Dis., 1941, 93, 421–442.

Palmieri, C. B. Tentato omicidio ed effettuato suicidio in un paralitico progressive malarizzato. (Attempted homicide and completed suicide by a paretic under malarial therapy.) Note Psichiat., Pesaro, 1940, 69, 163–172.

Parnell, R. W., and Skottowe, I. Toward preventing suicide. Lancet, 1957, 272, 206-208.

Peculiar methods of suicide. Lancet, 1901, 2, 921.

Peller, S. Über die weibliche Selbstmordhandlung. (Suicidal behavior in women.) Arch. Frauenk. KonstitForsch., 1932, 18, 59–67. Menarche, Menstruation und Selbstmordhandlung. (Menarche, menustruation and suicidal behavior.) Wien. med. Wschr., 1935, 85, 175–179, 205–207.

Peller-Roubiczek, L. E. Zur Kenntnis der Selbstmordhandlung; psychologische Deutung statistischer Daten. (On the understanding of suicidal behavior; psychological significance of statistical data.) Imago, Lpz., 1936, 22, 81–90.

Perezalonso, G. El suicidio. (Suicide.) Nicaragua: Léon, 1947.

Perl, K. Die psychiatrische Bedeutung der Selbsttötung in Westfalen im Vergleich mit andern deutschen Gauen. (The psychiatric significance of suicide in Westphalia in comparison with other German districts.) Arch. Psychiat. Nervenkr., 1939, 110, 253–290.

Pessin, J. Self-destructive tendencies in adolescence: report of a case. Bull. Menninger Clin., 1941, 5, 13–19.

Petrus, J., and Balaban, A. B. Special psychiatric problems of the paraplegic; report of a case of attempted suicide by a paraplegic. Amer. J. Psychiat., 1953, 109, 693–695.

Phelps, E. B. Neurotic books and newspapers as factors in the mortality of suicide and crime. Bull. Amer. Acad. Med., 1911, 12, 264–306.

Pilcz, A. Zum Lehre vom Selbstmord. (Theory of suicide.) Jb. Psychiat. Neurol., 1905, 26, 294–310.

Pilgrim, C. W. Insanity and suicide. Amer. J. Insan., 1906–07, 63, 349–360.

Piotrowski, Z. A Rorschach Compendium. Utica: State Hospital Press, 1950.

Pipal, K. Zwei unterbliebene Selbstmordversuche. (Two unrepeated suicide attempts.) Z. psychoan. Pädag., 1929, 3, 438–442.

Placzek, S. Die Selbstmörderpsyche. (The psyche of suicides.) Z. Psychother. med. Psychol., 1915/16, 6, 299–310.

Plügge, H. Über suizidale Kranke. (Suicidal patients.) Psyche, Heidel., 1951, 5, 433–450.

Podolsky, E. The paranoid murderer. Samīkṣā, 1956, 10, 65–69.

Pollack, B. A study of the problem of suicide. Psychiat. Quart., 1938, 12, 306–330.

Popoff, N. M. (School suicides.) Vrach. Gas., 1912, 19, 1413–1415.

The potential suicide. Lancet, 1951, 2, 1026–1027.

Powers, D. Suicide threats and attempts in the young; psychological management. Amer. Practit., 1956, 7, 1140–1143.

Pozner, H. Suicidal incidents in military personnel. Brit. J. med. Psychol., 1953, 26, 93–109.

Pratt, Carolyn. A validation study of intropunitive and extrapunitive signs on the Rorschach Test, based upon records given by suicidal and homicidal subjects. Unpublished doctoral dissertation, Purdue Univ., 1951.

Pressler, [C]. Le suicide chez les enfants. (Suicide among children.) Thèse Méd., Strasbourg, 1928/29; Strasbourg-méd., 1929, 89, 477, 511.

The prevention of suicide. Brit. med. J., 1918, 1, 514.

Proal, L. Le crime et le suicide passionels. (Crime and suicide of passion.) Paris: Alcan, 1900. L'éducation et le suicide des enfants. (Education and suicide of children.) Paris: Alcan, 1907.

Prudhomme, C. The problem of suicide in the American negro. Psychoanal. Rev., 1938, 25, 187–204; 372–391. Epilepsy and suicide. J. nerv. ment. Dis., 1941, 94, 722–731.

Puusepp, L. Selbstmord bei Schülern. (Student suicide.) Dorpat: J. Mällo, 1926.

Quaet-Faslem. Grenzfälle und Selbstmordgefahr. (Borderline cases and suicide risk.) Psychiat.-neurol. Wschr., 1924/25, 26, 177–179.

Quintard, E. Hermann de Vienne, chirurgien du roi René d'Anjou. (Hermann de Vienne, surgeon of the King René of Anjou.) Arch méd. Angers, 1903, 7, 451–458.

Rabin, A. I. Homicide and attempted suicide: a Rorschach study. Amer. J. Orthopsychiat., 1946, 16, 516–524.

Raines, G. N., and Thompson, S. V. Suicide. Some basic considerations. Dig. Neurol. Psychiat., 1950, 18, 97–107.

Raphael, T., Power, Sadye H., and Berridge, W. L. The question of suicide as a problem in college mental hygiene. Amer. J. Orthopsychiat., 1937, 7, 1–14.

Ratsimamanga. Contribution à l'étude psychopathologique du mobile du suicide dans la paralysie générale. (A contribution to the psychopathological study of the impulse towards suicide in general paralysis.) Thèse Méd., Montpellier, 1928/29.

Rau, H. Der Selbstmord. (Suicide.) Neue Heilk., 1902, 14, 105.

Raub, E. S. Psychological studies over a three year period before and after leukotomy of a homicidal and suicidal schizophrenic. Case Rep. clin. Psychol., 1951, 2, 39–49.

Raven, Alice. Murder and suicide as marks of an abnormal mind. Sociol. Rev., 1929, 21, 315–333.

Read, C. S. The problem of suicide. Brit. med. J., 1936, 1, 631–634.

Redlich, E., and Lazar, E. Über kindliche Selbstmörder. (Child suicides.) Berlin: Springer, 1914.

Rehfeldt. Über den Selbstmord. (Suicide.) Med. Welt, 1929, 3, 1205–1209.

Reichard, Suzanne, and Tillman, C. Murder and suicide as defenses against schizophrenic psychosis. J. clin. Psychopath., 1950, 11, 149–163.

Reitler, R. Eine infantile Sexualtheorie und ihre Beziehung zur Selbstmordsymbolik. (Theory of infantile sexuality in relation to symbolic suicide.) Zbl. Psychoan., 1911/12, 2, 114–121.

Reitman, F. On the predictability of suicide. J. ment. Sci., 1942, 88, 580–582.

Ribeiro, R. Colocaçao familiar inadequada. Tentativa de suicídio de menor. (Inadequate familial situation. Attempted suicide by a minor.) Neurobiologia, 1944, 7, 68–77.

Ricci, G. C. Modalità di tentativo di suicidio rivelatrici di una demenza paralytica. (Method of attempted suicide revealing dementia paralytica.) Riv. Pat. nerv. ment., 1957, 78, 1176–1178.

Rico, E. Psicología de dos suicidios. (The psychology of two suicides.) An. neuropsiquiat. Bogotá, 1943, 1, 227–234.

Riese, W. Über den Tod Heinrichs von Kleist. Eine Untersuchung auf Grund der Briefe und des Aktenmaterials zugleich ein Beitrag zur Psychopathologie des Doppelselbstmordes. (Death of Heinrich von Kleist. Investigation based on letters and documents; contribution to psychopathology of double suicide.) Allg. Z. Psychiat., 1932, 96, 270–312.

Rieti, H. Sobre la patogenia del suicidio. (Pathogenesis of suicide.) Rev. Criminol., B. Aires, 1925, 12, 32–39.

Riggs, C. E. Two borderline cases; with subsequent sudden development of intense suicidal propensity. Proc. Amer. med.-psychol. Ass., 1901, 262–267.

Ring, A. H. Factors in suicide. Bost. med. surg. J., 1921, 185, 650–656.

Ringel, E. Praktische Selbstmordprophylaxe. (Practical suicide prevention.) Wien. Arch. Psychol. Psychiat. Neurol., 1951, 1, 149–161. Ein Beitrag zur Frage der vererbten Selbstmordneigung. (Hereditary tendency to suicide.) Wien. Z. Nervenheilk., 1952, 5, 26–40. Der Selbstmord, Abschluss einer krankhaften psychischen Entwicklung; eine Untersuchung an 745 geretteten Selbstmördern. (Suicide, conclusion of a diseased psychic development; a research on 745 rescued suicides.) Wien: Maudrich, 1953.

Ringel, E., and Rotter, H. Zum Problem des Selbstmordversuches im Rausch. (The problem of attempted suicide in alcoholic intoxication.) Wien. Z. Nervenheilk., 1957, 13, 406–416.

Ringel, E., Spiel, W., and Stepan, M. Zur Selbstmordtendenz bei Kindern. (Suicidal tendencies of children.) Wien. Z. Nervenheiik., 1952, 5, 344–354. Untersuchungen über kindliche Selbstmordversuche. (An investigation of suicide attempts of children.) Prax. Kinderpsychol. Kinderpsychiat., 1955, 4, 161–168.

Rizzo, E. M. Un caso di tentato suicidio; narcoanalisi, Rorschach, TAT, daseinanalyse. (A case of attempted suicide; narcoanalysis, Rorschach test, TAT, and existential analysis.) Rass. Studi psichiat., 1954, 43, 685–717. Il tentativo di suicidio degli schizofrenici nella prospettiva fenomenologica esistenziale. (Attempts at suicide considered in the light of existential phenomenology.) Riv. Pat. nerv. ment., 1957, 78, 105–120.

Roalfe, W. R. The psychology of suicide. J. abnorm. soc. Psychol., 1928/29, 23, 59–67.

Robins, E., Schmidt, E. H., and O'Neal, Patricia. Some interrelations of social factors and clinical diagnosis in attempted suicide: A study of 109 patients. Amer. J. Psychiat., 1957, 114, 221–231.

Robinson, H. M. The case of suicide. N. Amer. Rev., 1932, 234, 303–308.

Rodiet, A. Ceux qui veulent se tuer. (Those who want to kill themselves.) Progr. méd., Paris, 1932, 2021–2025.

Rodríguez, F. Influencia del alcoholismo sobre el suicidio en Buenos Aires. (Influence of alcoholism on suicide in Buenos Aires.) Arch. Psiquiat. Crim., B. Aires, 1905, 4, 531–547.

Roe, Janet. (Pseud.) I was born at 18 in America. Psychiat. Quart. Suppl., 1947, 21, 94–107.

Roger, H., and Boudouresques, J. Troubles psychiques et intoxication par le thallium. (Mental disturbances and thallium poisoning.) Ann. méd.-psychol., 1949, 107(1), 287–289.

Rogers, A. W. A discussion of the suicide problem. Wis. med. J., 1909/10, 8, 186–187.

Rolle, G. La genesi del suicidio. (Genesis of suicide.) Osped. maggiore, 1928, 16, 315–323.

Rondepierre, J., Letailleur, M., and Leulier. Un cas de pseudo-suicide épileptique. (Case of pseudo-suicide of an epileptic.) Ann. méd.-psychol., 1944, 102(2), 305–307.

Rosen, A. Detection of suicidal patients: An example of some limitations in the prediction of infrequent events. J. consult. Psychol., 1954, 18, 397–403.

Rosen, A., Hales, W. M., and Simon, W. Classification of "suicidal" patients. J. consult. Psychol., 1954, 18, 359–362.

Rosen, H. Regression hypnotherapeutically induced as an emergency measure in a suicidally depressed patient. J. clin. exp. Hypnosis, 1955, 3, 58–70.

Rosenberg, L. J., and Aronstam, N. E. A contribution to the study of suicide. Med. Age, 1902, 20, 5–8.

Rosenblum, M. P., and Silverman, J. J. Self-induced mediastinal emphysema in a psychotic. An attempt to commit suicide by means of the Valsalva experiment. J. nerv. ment. Dis., 1947, 105, 414–419.

Rosenzweig, S. Unconscious self-defense in an uxoricide. J. crim. law Criminol. Police Sci., 1956, 46, 791–795.

Rossi, A. E. Los suicidios de niños y la profilaxia mental. (Suicides of children and mental hygiene.) Rev. argent. Neurol., 1927, 1, 350–353.

Rost, H. Bibliographie des Selbstmords, mit textlichen Einführungen zu jedem Kapitel. (Bibliography of suicide, with textual introductions to each chapter.) Augsburg: Haas and Grabherr, 1927.

Rowland, G. An unusual method of suicide. J. ment. Sci., 1909, 55, 324.

Sacchini, G. Il "suicidio" nei soldati ricoverati nell 'ospedale militare psichiatrico di Mombello. (Suicide by recovered soldiers at the military psychiatric hospital of Mombello.) Arch. Antrop. crim., 1918/19, 39, 27–63.

Sacerdote, A. Il suicidio dei ragazzi in Italia. (Suicides of young boys in Italy.) Arch. Antrop. crim., 1913, 34, 166.

Sadger, J. Ein Beitrag zum Problem des Selbstmords. (Contribution to the problem of suicide.) Z. psychoanal. Pädag., 1929, 3, 422–426. Zur Frage des gemeinsamen

Sterbens. (Doppelselbstmord.) (The question of common death [double suicide].) Allg. ärztl. Z. Psychother. 1929, 2, 65–72.

Sakheim, G. A. Suicidal responses on the Rorschach test: A validation study. Protocols of suicidal mental hospital patients compared with those of non-suicidal patients. J. nerv. ment. Dis., 1922, 55, 105–111.

Salinger, F., and Jacobsohn, H. Psychische Störung nach Strangulations-versuch. (Psychic disturbances following strangulation attempt.) Z. ges. Neurol. Psychiat., 1927, 110, 372–382.

Salmon, T. W. A psychiatric study of suicide. Arch. Neurol. Psychiat., 1921, 7, 389–395; J. nerv. ment. Dis., 1922, 55, 105–111.

Sanhueza, F. Suicidio en los niños. (Suicide in children.) Arch. Hosp. Niños Rob. d. Rio, 1949, 17, 166–173; Pediat. Amér., 1951, 9, 414–421.

Sastre Lafarga, G. Estudio psicopatológico del suicidio. (Psychopathologic study of suicide.) Med. clín., 1947, 9, 223–229; Acta méd. hisp., 1948, 6, 244–226.

Savage, G. H. On the relationship between suicide and insanity and the after-effects of an attack of mental disorder. Med. Mag., Lond., 1905, 14, 731–747; 1906, 15, 13, 76.

Saving the potential suicide. Lancet, 1957, 272, 203.

Schachter, M. Étude d'une obsession d'infanticide et de suicide chez une jeune femme de 27 ans. (Infanticidal obsession and suicide of a young 27-year-old woman.) Arch. int. Neurol., 1949, 68, 21–26. Suicide, tentatives de suicide et personnalités des suicidés; notes critiques et contributions clinicopsychologiques. (Suicide, suicide attempts, and personalities of suicides; critical notes and clinicopsychologic study.) Strasbourg-méd., 1947, 107, 333–339. Neurosis suicida agresiva y eczema pruriginoso crónico; contribución a la dermatología psicosomática. (Aggressive suicidal neurosis and chronic pruritic eczema; contribution to psychosomatic dermatology.) Actas luso-esp. Neurol., 1954, 13, 98–105. Évolution et transformation utilitaire, d'une névrose dépressive et suicidaire. (Evolution and utilitarian transformation of a depressive and suicidal neurosis.) Acta psychother. psychosom. orthopaedag., 1955, 3, 277–283. Conduites ou névroses suicidaires, et test de Rorschach. (Behavior in suicidal neuroses and the Rorschach Test.) Encéphale, 1957, 46, 146–165.

Schachter, M., and Cotte, S. Tentatives, chantages et vélleités de suicide chez lez jeunes. (Attempts, simulations, and obsessions of suicide in the young.) Criança portug., 1951, 10, 171–195.

Schackwitz, A. Selbstmordursachen. (Causes of suicide.) Dtsch. Z. ges. gerichtl. Med., 1927, 10, 312–321.

Schaefer, H. [Schäfer]. Der Fall Brunke. (The Brunke case.) Psychiat.-neurol. Wschr., 1906/07, 8, 37, 216.

Schaeffer, H. Suicide et chantage au suicide chez l'enfant et l'adolescent. (Suicide and threat of suicide in child and adolescent.) Pr. méd., 1945, 53, 90.

Scheele, H. Über psychopathieähnliche Zustände und Selbstmordneigung bei der Huntingtonschen Krankheit. (Possible psychopathic states and the tendency toward suicide in Huntington's disease.) Z. ges. Neurol. Psychiat., 1931, 137, 621–628.

Schenk, J. G. Personality traits of twenty women committed to a state hospital following suicidal attempts. Smith. Coll. Stud. soc. Work, 1940, 11, 176–177. Abstract.

Schermers, D. Zelfmoord bij kinderen en jeugdige personen. (Suicide of children and juvenile persons.) Med. Weekbl., 1913/14, 20, 505–507.

Schilder, P. Psychotherapy. New York: Norton, 1951.

Schletter, E. Zur Psychologie des Selbstmordes. (On the psychology of suicide.) Int. Z.

Indiv.-Psychol., 1929, 7, 7–14. A contribution to the psychology of suicide. Indiv. Psychol. Bull., 1946, 5, 119–124.

Schmideberg, Melitta. A note on suicide. Int. J. Psychoanal., 1936, 17, 1–5; Psychoanal. Rev., 1948, 35, 181–182.

Schmidt, E. H., O'Neal, Patricia, and Robins, E. Evaluation of suicide attempts as guide to therapy. Clinical and follow-up study of 109 patients. Amer. Practit., 1954, 5, 803–805. J. Amer. med. Ass., 1954, 155, 549–557.

Schmidt, F. Suizide und Suizidversuche im Verlaufe von Psychosen. (Suicides and attempted suicides in the course of psychoses.) Bonn: Trapp, 1932.

Schmidt, G. Erfahrungen an 700 Selbstmordversuchen. (Investigation of 700 suicide attempts.) Nervenarzt, 1938, 11, 353–358. Selbstmordversuche Jugendlicher. (Suicide attempts among adolescents.) Allg. Z. Psychiat., 1939, 112, 32–43.

Schneider, E. Die Todes- und Selbstmordphantasien Tom Savyers. (The death and suicide phantasies of Tom Sawyer.) Z. psychoan. Pädag., 1929, 3, 389–400.

Schneider, K. Selbstmordversuche. (Suicide attempts.) Dtsch. med. Wschr., 1933, 59, 1389–1391. Selbstmord und Dienstbeschädigung; Schizophrenie und Dienstbeschädigung; drei Gutachten. (Suicide and schizophrenia as service-connected disabilities in veterans; opinions in three cases.) Nervenarzt, 1950, 21, 480–483.

Schneider, P. B. Quelques aspects de la tentative de suicide. (Various aspects of attempted suicide.) Gaz. méd. port., 1950, 3, 839–854. Recherches catamnestiques sur la tentative de suicide. (Catamnestic studies of attempted suicide.) Bull. schweiz. Akad. med. Wiss., 1954, 10, 143–155. La tentative de suicide; étude statistique, clinique, psychologique et catamnestique; avec une analyse statistique de Ch. Blanc. (The suicide attempt; statistical, clinical, psychological and catamnestic study; with a statistical analysis by Ch. Blanc.) Paris, Neuchâtel: Delachaux and Niestlé, 1954.

Schultz, J. H. Zur Psychologie des Selbstmordes; Selbstvernichtung als Kampf gegen körperliches Leiden. (On the psychology of suicide; self-destruction as an attack on bodily suffering.) Nervenarzt, 1952, 23, 67–68.

Schuschny, H. (Suicides among students.) Orv. Hétil., 1912, 56, 1067–1069.

Schütz, R. Ein Beitrag zum Problem des Selbstmordes mit besonderer Rüchsicht auf Schleiermacher. (Contribution to the problem of suicide with special regard to Schleiermacher.) Z. ReligPsychol., 1911, 5, 24–34.

Seegen, M. Schülerselbstmorde. (Student suicides.) Int. Z. Indiv.-Psychol., 1933, 11, 152–153.

Selbstmord einer zehnjährigen Mutter. (Suicide of a ten-year-old mother.) Neue Generation, 1928, 24, 32.

Selbstmorde. Vjber. wiss.-human. Kom., 1911/12, 3, 77, 194, 317–320.

Sell, W. Mitteilung Zweier durch die näheren Tatumstände bemerkenswerter Fälle von Selbsterhängen. (Report of two cases of self-handing in remarkable circumstances.) München, 1931.

Serin, Suzanne. Les suicides d' enfants. (Suicide among children.) Hyg. ment., 1927, 22, 33–37. Causas, tratamiento y profilaxia de las ideas de suicidio. (Causes, treatment, and prevention of ideas of suicide.) Arch. Med. Cirug., 1928, 29, 386.

Shankel, L. W., and Carr, A. C. Transvestism and hanging episodes in a male adolescent. Psychiat. Quart., 1956, 30, 478–493.

Shapiro, L. B. Suicide: psychology and familial tendency; report of a family of suicides with history and discussion. J. nerv. ment. Dis., 1935, 81, 547–553.

Shields, E. A. Depression, then suicide. Amer. J. Nurs., 1946, 46, 677–679.

Shimshony, Z. Chronischer Alkoholismus und Selbstmord. (Chronic alcoholism and suicide.) Diss., Bern, 1940. Chronischer Alkoholismus und Selbstmord; ein Beitrag zu Bandels Theorie über den Einfluss des Alkoholismus auf die Selbstmordsterblichkeit. (Chronic alcoholism and suicide; a contribution to Bandel's theory on the influence of alcoholism on the suicide mortality.) Schweiz. med. Wschr., 1941, 71, 1429–1433.

Shneidman, E. S., and Farberow, N. L. Clues to suicide. Publ. Hlth. Rep., Wash., 1956, 71, 109–114. Some comparisons between genuine and simulated suicide notes in terms of Mowrer's concepts of discomfort and relief. J. gen. Psychol., 1957, 56, 251–256.

Shneidman, E. S., and Farberow, N. L. (Eds.) Clues to suicide. New York: McGraw-Hill, 1957.

Sichel, M. Der Selbstmord im Felde. (Suicide in the field.) Z. ges. Neurol. Psychiat., 1919, 49, 385–392.

Siebert, H. Betrachtungen über den Selbstmord. (Reflections on suicide.) Mschr. Psychiat. Neurol., 1918, 43, 296–315.

Siegal, L. J., and Friedman, J. H. The threat of suicide. Dis. nerv. Syst., 1955, 16, 37–46.

Siewers, A. B., and Davidoff, E. Attempted suicide: a survey of 150 patients admitted to two general hospitals. J. nerv. ment. Dis., 1942, 95, 427–441. Attempted suicide: a comparative study of psychopathic and general hospital patients. Psychiat. Quart., 1943, 17, 520–534.

Sifneos, P. E., Gore, C., and Sifneos, A. C. A preliminary psychiatric study of attempted suicide as seen in a general hospital. Amer. J. Psychiat., 1956, 112, 883–888.

Sigwart, W. Selbstmordversuch während der Geburt. (Suicide attempt during birth.) Arch. Psychiat. Nervenkr., 1906, 42, 249–256.

Simon. Epilepsie, délire alcoolique, mélancolie, tentative de suicide et paralysie générale chez le fils d'une mère alcoolisée, d'un père suicidé, lui-même étant syphilitique et alcoolique. (Suicide attempt and general paralysis of a syphilitic, alcoholic daughter of an alcoholic mother and a father who committed suicide.) Arch. Neurol., Paris, 1905, 19, 104–109.

Simon, A. Selbstmord und Dienstbeschädigung. (Suicide and service-connected injury.) Ärztl. SachverstZtg., 1926, 32, 339–344. Selbstmord und Kriegsdienst. (Suicide and military service.) Med. Klinik, 1927, 23, 841. Selbstmord und Kriegsgefangenschaft. (Suicide and military captivity.) Ärztl. SachverstZtg., 1927, 33, 60–65. Selbstmord bei einem Amputieren und die Beziehungen von Selbstmord und Sexualleben. (Suicide by an amputee and the relation of suicide and sexual life.) Ärztl. SachverstZtg., 1929, 35, 311–317. Letzte Briefe von Selbstmördern und ihre Verwertung bei der Begutachtung. (Last letters of suicides and their utilization by expert opinion.) Ärztl. SachverstZtg., 1930, 36, 69–73. Schädelverletzung, Alkoholismus und Selbstmord. (Cranial injury, alcoholism, and suicide.) Ärztl. SachverstZtg., 1930, 36, 135–140.

Simon, W. Attempted suicide among veterans. A comparative study of fifty cases. J. nerv. ment. Dis., 1950, 111, 451–468.

Simon, W., and Hales, W. M. Note on a suicide key in the Minnesota Multiphasic Personality Inventory. Amer. J. Psychiat., 1949, 106, 222–223.

Sisler, G. C. The treatment of suicidal attempts. Canad. med. Ass. J., 1956, 74, 112–115.

Smith, F. H. Suicide and sunshine. Lancet, 1908, 2, 837.

Smolaga, J. O samobójstwie w przebiegu psychozy schizofrenicźnej. (Suicide in the course of schizophrenia.) Przegl. lek., 1951, 7, 412–417.

Sobotka, J. Sebevraž dětí. (Suicide in children.) Čas. Lék. čes., 1957, 96, 102–104.

Some further remarks concerning suicide. Med. Rec., N.Y., 1901, 59, 1001–1002.

Sommer, R. Psychiatrische Untersuchung eines Falles von Mord und Selbstmord mit Studien über Familiengeschichte und Erblichkeit. (Psychiatric investigation of cases of homicide and suicide with studies of family histories and heredity.) Clin. psych. nerv. Krankh., 1906, 1, 6–25.

Sorhegui, R. La muerte temida y deseada al mismo tiempo; observación clínica. (Death feared and desired at the same time; clinical observation.) Arch. méd. Cuba, 1956, 7, 47.

Southard, S. The minister's role in attempted suicide. Pastoral Psychol., 1953, 4, 27–32.

Spann, W. Selbstmord und atmosphärische Umwelt. (Suicide and atmospheric surroundings.) Dtsch. Z. ges. gerichtl. Med., 1955, 43, 528–544.

Speijer, N. Eine Untersuchung nach den Triebgrundlagen des Selbstmordes. (An investigation of the basic motives for suicide.) Psychiat. neurol. Bl. Amst., 1937, 41, 272–294; Apeldoorn, Netherlands: Apeldoornsche Bosch, 1937.

Sperry, Bessie M., Staver, Nancy, and Mann, H. Destructive fantasies in certain learning difficulties. Amer. J. Orthopsychiat., 1952, 22, 356–365.

Spratling, W. P. A unique case of automatic or unintentional suicide in an epileptic. N. Y. med. J., 1906, 84, 16.

Staehelin, J. E. Über Selbst- und Gemeingefährlichkeit. (On danger to self and society.) Praxis, 1947, 36, 616–621.

Stearns, A. W. Suicide in Massachusetts. Ment. Hygiene, N.Y., 1921, 5, 752–777. Suicide. New Engl. J. Med., 1931, 204, 9–11. Cases of probable suicide in young persons without obvious motivation. J. Maine med. Ass., 1953, 44, 16–23. Accident or suicide? J. Maine med. Ass., 1955, 46, 313–320, 336–337 passim.

Stegman, A. Beitrag zur Lehre vom Selbstmord. (Contributions to the study of suicide.) Mschr. Psychiat. Neurol., 1907, 22, (Erg.-Heft), 109–114.

Stekel, S. A. On suicide. Amer. J. Urol., 1918, 14, 337–350.

Stengel, E. Suicide. In G. W. T. H. Fleming (Ed.) Recent progress in psychiatry, 1950, vol. 2, 691–703. Attempted suicide. Brit. med. J., 1952, 1, 1130. The social effects of attempted suicide. Canad. med. Ass. J., 1956, 74, 116–120. The risk of suicide in states of depression. Med. Pr., 1955, 234, 182–184. Enquiries into attempted suicide. Proc. roy. Soc. Med., Long., 1952, 45, 613–620. A new approach to the social psychology of suicide. Bull. Brit. Psychol. Soc., 1957, 33, 29.

Stengel, E., and Cook, Nancy G. Recent research into suicide and attempted suicide. J. forensic Med., 1954, 1, 252–259.

Sterba, Editha. Der Schülerselbstmord in André Gides Roman "Die Falschmünzer." (The schoolboy suicide in André Gide's novel "The Counterfeiters.") Z. psychoan. Pädag., 1929, 3, 400–409; Amer. Imago, 1951, 8, 307–320.

Sterba, R. Spinne, Erhängen, und Oralsadismus. (The spider, hanging, and oral sadism.) Psychoanal. Beweg., 1932, 4, 268–274.

Stevens, J. W. Suicide. J. Tenn. med. Ass., 1916, 9, 137–141.

Storch, H. D. Psychische und nevröse Störungen nach Sèlbstmordversuch durch Erhängen. (Psychic and nervous disorders after suicide attempt by hanging.) Kiel, 1909.

Strauss, E. B. Suicide. Brit. med. J., 1956, 2, 818–820.

Strauss, E. B., and Teare, R. D. Suicide. Trans. med. Soc. Lond., 1956, 72, 194–205.

Strecker, E. A. Suicide. Philad. Med., 1942/43, 38, 805

Strecker, H. P. Body-length-leg ratio in the general population and in mental hospital patients and its possible significance in suicide. J. ment. Sci., 1936, 82, 38–42.

Strömgren, E. Mental sequelae of suicidal attempts by hanging. Acta psychiat., Kbh., 1946, 21, 753–780.

A student suicide. Bost. med. Surg. J., 1927, 196, 491.

The styles in suicide and homicide. J. Amer. med. Ass., 1919, 73, 1367.

The suicidal fever. Lancet, 1902, 2, 410.

The suicidal soldier. Army med. Dep. Bull., 1945, No. 49, 2.

Suicide. Encyclopedia of Religion, and Ethics. New York: Scribner's, 1921, 21–40.

Suicide—A leading cause of death. J. Amer. med. Ass., 1952, 150, 696–697.

Suicide and attempted suicide. Brit. med. J., 1956, 2, 813–815.

Suicide and its means. J. Amer. med. Ass., 1897, 28, 130–131.

Suicide and its prevention. Med. News, N.Y., 1903, 83, 658.

Suicide and temporary insanity. Lancet, 1952, 2, 985.

Suicide collectif. Ann. méd.-psychol., 1897, 55, 331–333.

The suicide of Alfred Sellgrén. Med. Exam. Pract., 1904, 14, 76.

The suicide of a medical man following a groundless accusation. Lancet, 1910, 2, 858.

Sullivan, W. C. Alcoholism and suicidal impulses. J. ment. Sci., 1898, 44, 259–271. Cases of suicidal impulse in conditions of cerebral automatism. J. ment. Sci., 1899, 45, 338–343. Alcoholism and suicidal impulses. Quart. J. Inebr., 1900, 22, 17–29. Relation of alcoholism to suicide in England with special reference to recent statistics. J. ment. Sci., 1900, 46, 260–281. Inebriety and suicide. Brit. J. Inebr., 1903/04, 1, 25–28.

Sweringen, H. V. Suicide. Lancet-Clinic, 1899, 43, 271–273.

Tallman, F. T. The doctor's role in the preservation of mental health. J. Amer. med. Ass., 1954, 155, 827–831.

Tamburini. Obsessions sexuelles au suicide. (Sexual obsessions to suicide.) Cong. int. Neurol. Psychiat., 1897, 1, 105.

Teicher, J. D. A study in attempted suicide. J. nerv. ment. Dis., 1947, 105, 283–298.

Terman, L. M. Recent literature on juvenile suicides. J. abn. Psychol., 1914, 9, 61–66.

Tholuck, H. J. Selbstmord und Wetter. (Suicide and weather.) Beitr. gerichtl. Med., 1942, 16, 121–151.

Thorner, H. A. The mode of suicide as a manifestation of fantasy. Brit. J. med. Psychol., 1938, 17, 197–200.

Thurner, F. K. Suizid und Testzeichnung. (Suicide and drawing tests.) Z. exp. angewand. Psychol., 1956, 3, 439–457.

To be or not to be: success and failure in suicide attempts. What's New, 1957, No. 198, 5–7.

Többen, H. Über Selbstmorde Jugendlicher. (Youthful suicides.) Dtsch. Z. ges. gerichtl. Med., 1930, 14, 499–516.

Toulouse, E. Le suicide. (Suicide.) Proph. ment., 1929, 6, 91–96.

Touroff, N. B'ayot hahitabdut, mechkar psychologee, sotsiologee. (Problems of suicide, a psychological and sociological study.) Tel Aviv: D'vir, 1953.

Trakhtenberg, A. G. O samoubiystrakh sredi uchastshikhsya. (Suicide among students.) Zh. russk. Obshch. Okran. nar. Zdrav., 1909, 19, 41–53.

Tramer, M. Selbstmord im Kindesalter. Erhängungversuch eines 13 jährigen Knaben. (Suicide in childhood. An attempt at hanging by a 13-year-old boy.) Z. Kinderpsychiat., 1942, 9, 115–119; 1943, 9, 151–155. Zur Frage des Selbstmordversuches und Lebensüberdrusses im Kindesalter (Kasuistisches). (Attempted suicide and disgust with life in childhood [case studies].) Z. Kinderpsychiat., 1949, 16, 109–120.

Trillot, J., and Bernardy, J. Suicide retardé d'un meutrier; étude criminologique. (Delayed suicide of a murderer; criminological study.) Ann. Méd. lég., 1956, 36, 159–163.

Tubio Ovide, J. M. Consideraciones sobre el suicidio. (Considerations on suicide.) Arch. Med. leg., B. Aires, 1945, 15, 416–428; Rev. Asoc. méd. argent., 1945, 59, 1212–1216; Salubr. y Asist., 1945, 4, 85–97.

Ulett, G. A., Martin, D. W., and McBride, J. R. The Rorschach findings in a case of suicide. Amer. J. Orthopsychiat., 1950, 20, 817–827.

Un suicidio améno. (A droll suicide.) Minerva med., 1940, 31(2), 592.

Vaičiūnas, V. (Suicide and its causes.) Medicina, Kaunas, 1936, 17, 380–385.

Velasquez, J. O. Familiärer Selbstmord und psychopathische Vererbung. (Familial suicide and psychopathic heredity.) Rev. Criminol., B. Aires, 1935, 22, 681.

Verginella, A. Sulla rarità del suicidio negli sportivi practicanti. (On the rarity of suicide among practicing sportsmen.) Med. Sport. Educ. fis., 1954, 8, 488–492.

Verner, M. Suicidné tendencie u chorých. (Suicidal tendencies in patients.) Psychol. Časopis, 1953, 1, 279–291.

Viallon. Suicide et folie. (Suicide and insanity.) Ann. méd.-psychol., 1901, 14, 19–34, 210–224, 376–386; 1901, 15, 21–36, 219–229, 379–392; 1902, 16, 234–254, 394–403; 1903, 17, 55–73, 239–249, 394–413; 1903, 18, 28–37.

Vitanza, A., Church, E., and Offenkrantz, W. Suicide: a review of the literature, 1945–1956. Int. Rec. Med., 1957, 170, 678–683, 697–699.

Vivaldo, J. C., and Barrancos, A. Suicidio y demencia precoz. (Suicide and dementia praecox.) Rev. argent. Neurol., 1927, 1, 408–418.

Volbert, H. Selbstmord und Alkohol. (Suicide and alcohol.) Hefte z. Unfall., 1956, 52, 36–40.

von Balázs, J. Menstruation und Selbstmord. (Menstruation and suicide.) Psychiat.-neurol. Wschr., 1936, 38, 407–409.

von F–, R. Barnsjälfmord. (Suicide of children.) Hälsovännen, 1908, 23, 233–236.

von Maday, S. Zur Psychologie der Lebensmüden. (On the psychology of those wearied of life.) Int. Z. Indiv.-Psychol., 1929, 7, 88–94.

Wahl, C. W. Suicide as a magical act. Bull. Menninger Clin., 1957, 21, 91–98.

Walker, W. K. A case of matricide and attempted suicide with brief psychologic analysis. J. nerv. ment. Dis., 1908, 35, 144.

Wall, J. H. The psychiatric problem of suicide. Amer. J. Psychiat., 1944, 101, 404–406. Recognition of suicidal drives and tendencies in patients. Med. Rec. Ann., San Antonio, 1953, 47, 737.

Warburg, Bettina. Suicide, pregnancy, and rebirth. Psychoanal. Quart., 1938, 7, 490–506.

Waxberg, J. D. Study of attempted suicides in psychotic patients: a dynamic concept. Psychiat. Quart., 1956, 30, 464–470.

Weber, Hilda. Suicidal impulse and value of psychological treatment. Practitioner, 1937, 139, 168–177. Suicide and human element in therapy. Med. Pr., 1938, 196, 115–120.

Weber, L. W. Über Familienmord (erweiterten Selbstmord). (Family death (expanded suicide).) Münch. med. Wschr., 1917, 64, 55.

Weichbrodt, R. Der Selbstmord. (Suicide.) Mschr. Unfallheilk., 1933, 40, 175–181; Basel: Karger, 1937.

Weiss, J. M. A. The gamble with death in attempted suicide. Psychiatry, 1957, 20, 17–25.

Westcott, W. W. On suicide. Trans. med.-leg. Soc., Long., 1904/05, 2, 85–98.

Westra, J. J. Suicide. J. Indiana med. Ass., 1941, 34, 546–548.

Wexberg, E. Zur Psychopathologie des Selbstmordes. (On the psychopathology of suicide.) Nervenarzt, 1928, 1, 288–296.

White, Mary A., and Schreiber, Hanna. Diagnosing "suicidal risks" on the Rorschach. Psychiat. Quart. Suppl., 1952, 26, 161–189.

Whitmire, C. L. Suicidal attempts of psychotic patients. U.S. Veteran's Bur. med. Bull., 1930, 6, 309–316.

Wigton, H. A. Early recognition of suicidal tendencies. Neb. St. med. J., 1940, 25, 226–228.

Wiingaard, P. Forgiftninger og forgiftningsselvmord på en psyckiatrisk modtageafdeling. (Poisoning and suicide by poisoning in a psychiatric reception department.) Ugeskr. Læg., 1949, 111, 346–349.

Wile, I. S. Further considerations on suicide. Amer. J. Orthopsychiat., 1937, 7, 235–239.

Wilker, K. Die Selbstmorde Jugendlicher. (Juvenile suicides.) Z. Kinderforsch., 1913, 324–325.

Williams, E. Y. Some observations on the psychological aspects of suicide. J. abnorm. soc. Psychol., 1936/37, 31, 260–265.

Williams, T. A. The prevention of suicide. Amer. J. Insan., 1914/15, 71, 559–571.

Wilson, D. C. The psychopathology of suicide. Neuropsychiatry, 1951/52, 1, (4), 17–20.

Wilson, H. Suicidal compromises: psychopathy and rehabilitation. Brit. med. J., 1942, 1, 9–12.

Winfield, D. L., and Sparer, P. J. Preliminary report of the Rosenzweig P-F Study in attempted suicides. J. clin. Psychol., 1953, 9, 379–381.

Winslow, F: Suicide considered as a mental epidemic. Bull. med.-leg. Cong. 1895, N.Y., 1898, 334–351; Med.-leg. J., N.Y., 1896/97, 14, 72, 141.

Wisse, J. Selbstmord und Todesfurcht bei den Naturvölkern. (Suicide and the fear of death among primitive peoples.) Zutphen: Thieme, 1933.

Wittels, F. Heinrich von Kleist—Prussian Junker and creative genius: a study in bisexuality. Amer. Imago, 1954, 11, 1–31.

Wolf, H. Suicide notes. Amer. Mercury, 1931, 24, 264–272.

Wolfahrth, P. Der Selbstmord als psychologischer Tatbestand bei Dostejewski. (Suicide as a psychological fact in Dostoyevski's works.) Mschr. KrimPsychol., 1934, 25, 244–255.

Wood, J. M. S., and Urquhart, A. R. A family tree illustrative of insanity and suicide. J. ment. Sci., 1901, 47, 764–767.

Woolley, L. F., and Eichert, A. R. Notes on the problems of suicide and escape. Amer. J. Psychiat., 1941, 98, 110–118.

Wright, R. D. Suicide—a problem in social medicine. Neuropsychiatry, 1951/52, 1, 4, 4–16.

Yonge, C. F. Suicide; some of its causes and preventatives. Int. J. Ethics, 1905/06, 16, 179–189.

Yost, O. R. Basic facts concerning suicide. J. S. C. med. Ass., 1952, 48, 86-93.

Y. Y. Suicide. New Statesman, 1929, 32, 659–660.

Zadek, Mildred. Suicidal attempts in an obsessive-compulsive involutional male. Case Rep. clin. Psychol., 1949, 1, 35–39.

Zeckel, A. Hypnotherapy in a case of amnesia with suicide attempt. Psychiat. Quart., 1951, 25, 484–499.

Ziemke, E. Zum Tode durch Sprung ins Wasser aus grosser Höhe. (Zugleich ein Beitrag zur Psychologie des Selbstmordes). (On death through leaping into water from a great height. [Also a contribution to the psychology of suicides.]) Dtsch. Z. ges. gerichtl. Med., 1928, 12, 346–360.

Zilboorg, G. Clinical problems of suicide. Int. Z. Psychoanal., 1935, 21, 101 (summary). Differential diagnostic types of suicide. Arch. Neurol. Psychiat., Chicago, 1936, 35, 270–291. Suicide among civilized and primitive races. Amer. J. Psychiat., 1936, 92, 1347–1369. Considerations on suicide, with particular reference to that of the young. Amer. J. Orthopsychiat., 1937, 7, 15–31. The study of suicide. Med. Rec., N.Y., 1938, 147, (3) *in* Open Forum, Feb. 2; 9, 11, 13.

Zsakó, I. (Problem of suicides in various mental disorders.) Gyógyászat, 1929, 68, 763–768.

Zuboff, I. O. (Suicide.) Vrach. Gaz., 1912, 19, 1573, 1630.

SOCIOLOGICAL

Adriasola, G., Kaempffer, A. M., Leyton, A., Maria, J., and Opaso, A. Epidemiología de las muertas violentas. (Epidemiology of violent death.) Rev. chil. Hig., 1952, 14, 219–227.

Albrecht, H. Der Selbstmord in Deutschland. (Suicide in Germany.) Arch. Kriminol., 1927, 80, 242–245. Selbstmord und Wirtschaftskrise. (Suicide and economic crises.) Mschr. KrimPsychol., 1931, 22, 567–569.

Alpert, H. Suicides and homicides. Amer. Sociol. Rev., 1950, 15, 673.

Anomalies of suicide. J. Amer. med. Ass., 1913, 61, 1721–1722.

Anzures, P. An analytical study of cases of suicide. J. Phil. Is. med. Ass., 1927, 7, 235–242.

Backlin, E. (Suicides in state hospitals for the insane in Sweden during the years 1901–1933.) Hygiea, Stockh., 1937, 99, 65–100.

Bailey, W. B. Suicide in the United States 1897–1901. New Engl. Yale Rev., 1903, 12, 70–89.

Bandel, R. Der bevorzugte Rückgang, der Selbstmord-sterblichkeit während der Alkoholknappen Zeit bei der Nichtjüdischen männlichen Bevölkerung in Preussen. (Decrease in suicides among male gentiles in Prussia during times of scarcity of alcohol.) Z. Hyg. Infektkr., 1930, 111, 699–702.

Bauer, F. Unfälle und Selbstmorde durch die Eisenbahn. (Accidents and suicides on railroads.) Inaug. Diss., Zürich: Fluntern, 1951.

Bauer, H. Suicide and public health. Calif. Med., 1953, 79, 422–424.

Bayreuther, H. Über den Selbstmord in der Nachkriegzeit; ein Untersuchung von 1200 Fällen aus einer süddeutschen Grossstadt. (Post-war suicide; study of 1200 cases in a large city of South Germany.) Arch. Psychiat. Nervenkr., 1956, 195, 264–284.

Beech, M. W. H. Suicide amongst the A-Kikuyu of East Africa. Man, 1913, 13, 56.

Beeley, A. L. Juvenile suicide. Soc. Serv. Rev., 1929, 3, 35–49. Was there a suicide "wave" among college students in 1927? Sci. Mon., N.Y., 1932, 35, 66–67.

Beichl, H. Der Selbstmord in Baden in den Jahren 1927–1936. (Suicide in Baden in the years 1927–36). Beitr. gerichtl. Med., 1939, 15, 1–13.

Belbey, J. C. Aumento de los suicidios por cianuro de potasio en Buenos Aires. (Increase in suicides by potassium cyanide in Buenos Aires.) Sem. méd., B. Aires, 1928, 2, 286–288; Rev. Espec. Asoc. med. argent., 1928, 3, 472–478.

Bennewitz, C. Die Selbstmordsterblichkeit Deutscher Lebensversicherter. (Suicide mortality among German life insurance policy-holders.) Z. ges. VersichWiss., 1931, 31, 68–83.

Bingler. Statistische Betrachtungen über den Selbstmord im Reichsheere in den Jahren 1921–29. (Statistical accounts of suicide in the German army, 1921–29). Veröff. Heeressanitätsw., 1930, 84, 74–88.

Blondel, C. Le suicide. (Suicide.) Strasburg: Lib. Univ. D'Alsace, 1933.

Bond, H. Suicide from the sociological aspect. Brit. med. J., 1931, 2, 234–239.

Bonger, W. A. Zelfmoord als maatschappelijk verschijnsel. (Suicide as a social evil.) Mensch en Mattsch., 1929, 5, 281–303.

Boven, W. Considération sur le suicide en rapport avec la génétique. (Suicide in relation to genetics.) Schweiz. Arch. Neurol. Psychiat., 1942, 50, 158–159. Abstract. À propos du suicide en Suisse; considérations sur le suicide en rapport avec la génétique. (Suicide in Switzerland; considerations on suicide in relation to genetics.) Ann. med.-psychol., 1942, 100, (1), 83–84.

Brack, E. Statistisches und Kasuistisches über Selbsttötung in Hamburg. (Statistics and case reports of suicide in Hamburg.) Dtsch. Z. Nervenheilk., 1931, 123, 72–88.

Bratowska, Z. (Effect of atmospheric conditions on frequency of suicide.) Medycyna, 1939, 655–660.

Bratz. Increased incidence of suicide. J. Amer. med. Ass., 1923, 80, 1328.

Brokhansky, N. La frequenza e le cause del suicidio in Russia. (The frequency and causes of suicide in Russia.) Arch. Anthrop. crim., 1927, 47, 366–377.

Brown, H. A. Suicide in the registration area. N. Y. med. J., 1911, 94, 482. Our annual crop of suicides. Diet. Hyg. Gaz., 1912, 28, 283–287.

Brukhanski, N. P. (Suicides. A socio-psychiatric investigation of 359 cases of successful and attempted suicides from December 1, 1923, to May 31, 1924, in Moscow.) Leningrad: Priboi, 1927.

Cambor, C. G. Suicide and attempted suicide. Med. Bull. U. S. Army, Europe, 1957, 14, 103–105.

Candiotti, C., Dérobert, L., Moine, M., and Moine, C. Considérations statistiques sur le suicide en France et à l'étranger; ses répercussions sociales. (Statistical considerations on suicide in France and abroad; its social repercussions.) Ann. Méd. lég., 1948, 28, 1–53.

Casabianca. La suicide chez la femme chinoïse. (Suicide among Chinese women.) Ann. Méd. Pharm. colon., 1923, 21, 231.

The causes and prevention of suicide. J. Amer. med. Ass., 1931, 97, 1809.

Causes of suicide. Med. Rec., N.Y., 1900, 58, 777–778.

Cavan, Ruth S. Suicide. Chicago: Univ. of Chicago Press, 1928.

Cerezo Abad, T. El suicido en el ejército; estudio comparativo del suicidio en las edades de 19 a 25 años en el medio militar y en el civil; causas del suicidio en estas edades e influencia que puede tener la vida militar. (Suicide in the army; comparative study of suicide in the ages 19 to 25 in a military and a civil setting; causes of suicide in these ages and the influence of military life.) Bol. Med., Madrid, 1935, 3, No. 54, 2: No. 55, 5.

Chamberlain, B. H. Things Japanese. London: Murlay, 1898.

Child suicide in Germany. Med. Rec., N.Y., 1905, 68, 661.

Citrome, P. Conclusions d'une enquête sur le suicide dans les camps de concentration. (Conclusions of a study on suicide in concentration camps.) Cah. int. Sociol., 1952, 12, 147–149.

Clemmesen, C. (Statistics of suicides in Danish hospitals for the insane from 1922 to 1931.) Hospitalstidende, 1932, 75, 1421–1432.

Cohen, I. Suicide among Jews. New Statesman, 1929, 32, 693–694.

Corridore, F. Il suicidio al tramonte del secolo XIX. (Suicide in the latter half of the nineteenth century.) Torino: Clausen, 1903.

D., J. Le suicide en Chine. (Suicide in China.) J. Méd. Bordeaux, 1899, 29, 382–384.

Da Costa Doria, J. R. O suicidio (estudo médico-social). (Suicide [medico-social study].) Brasil-med., 1946, 60, 165–168.

Daumézon, G., Cor, J., and Rudrauf, J. Données statistiques sur les tentatives de suicide chez les alcooliques entrés à l'Admission de Sainte-Anne. (Statistical data on suicide by alcoholics in the St. Anne Asylum.) Ann. méd.-psychol., 1955, 113, 286–292.

Davezac. Du suicide à Bordeaux. (Suicide in Bordeaux.) Bull. Soc. Méd. Chir. Bordeaux, 1919, 93. Gaz. hebd. Sci. méd., 1919, 40, 177.

Delannoy, R. M. Selbstmorde und Selbstmordversuche in Wien 1926. (Suicide and attempted suicide in Vienna 1926.) Wien: Gerlach & Wiedling, 1927.

Delore, P., and Pommatau, E. Étude sur les facteurs écologiques du suicide. (Ecological factors in suicide.) Rev. lyon. Méd., 1957, 6, 849–860.

Department of Health, City of New York. Suicides in the City of New York. 1900–1925. Bost. med. surg. J., 1927, 196.

Dérobert, L. L'évolution du suicide et de l'homicide en France; étude statistique comparée de periodes 1925–1930 et 1945–1946. (Trend of suicide and homicide in France; statistical comparison of the periods 1925–1930 and 1945–1946.) Bull. Inst. nat. Hyg., 1948, 3, 12–23. L'évolution du suicide en France en 1947, 1948, et 1949. (Development of suicide frequency in France in 1947, 1948, and 1949.) Bull. Inst. nat. Hyg., 1950, 5, 643–650.

Derrick, E. H. Suicide and its prevention. Med. J. Aust., 1941, 1, 668–672.

Dieudonné. Zunahme des Selbstmordes Anfang des 19 Jahrhunderts. (Increase in suicide with beginning of Nineteenth Century.) Med. Welt., 1929, 3, 1233.

A discussion on suicide: its psychiatrical and social aspects. Brit. med. J., 1898, 2, 678–684.

Donalies, G. Statistische Erhebung im 3000 Fällen von vollendetem und versuchtem Selbstmord. (Statistical survey of 3000 cases of completed and attempted suicide.) Mschr. Psychiat. Neurol., 1928, 69, 380–396.

Donon, and Fribourg-Blanc. Suicides chez les militaires en campagne au Maroc (janvier-septembre 1933). (Military suicides in the Moroccan campaign [January-September 1933]) Bull. Soc. Méd. mil. fr., 1933, 27, 239–249.

Dornedden, H. Der Selbstmord in Deutschland. (Suicide in Germany.) Dtsch. med. Wschr., 1931, 57, 1750–1752.

Drastich, L. (Relation of suicide frequency to social status and to present-day economic situation.) Čas. Lék. čes., 1934, 73, 457–459.

Dreyfus-Sée, G. À propos de quelques statistiques de suicide. (Some suicide statistics.) Pr. méd., 1936, 44, 1573–1574.

Dublin, L. I., and Bunzel, Bessie. To be or not to be: A study of suicide. New York: Random House, 1933.

Duncan, C. Suicides in Tasmania. Med. J. Aust., 1954, 2, 166–168.

Durkheim, É. Le suicide; étude de sociologie. (Suicide; a study in sociology.) Paris: Alcan, 1897. (Trans. J. A. Spaulding and G. Simpson. Glencoe, Ill.: Free Press, 1951.) El suicidio, estudio de sociología por Emilio Duricheim... traducción y estudio preliminar sobre etiología del suicidio en España, por Mariano Ruiz-Funes... (Suicide, sociological study by Emile Durkheim... translation and preliminary study of the causes of suicide in Spain, by Mariano Ruiz-Funes...) Madrid: Editorial Reus (s.a.), 1928.

East, W. N. On attempted suicide, with an analysis of 1000 consecutive cases. J. ment. Sci., 1913, 59, 428–478.

Egger, N. L. An analysis of suicide in San Francisco from 1939 to 1950 with an educational program for prevention. Unpublished doctoral dissertation, Univ. of California, 1954.

Eisenstadt. Über die Ursachen des Selbstmords (unter Berücksichtigung der Sterbekarten des Verbandes mittlerer Reichs-Post-und Telegraphenbeamten). (Causes of suicide [from a review of the death register of the union of middle government postal and telegraph officials].) Med. Reform, Berl., 1909, 17, 565–569; 580–584.

Elo, O. Über Selbstmorde und Selbstmörder in Finnland. (On suicide and suicides in Finland.) Dtsch. Z. ges. gerichtl. Med., 1931, 17, 348–406.

Elwin, V. Maria murder and suicide. London: Oxford Univ. Press, 1943.

Erikson, E. V. O samoûbijstvakh na Kavkazie. (Suicide in the Caucasus.) Vopr. nerv.-psikh. Med., 1905, 10, 129–138. (Suicides in the Army.) Vo-Med. Zh., Spb., 1915, 242, med.-spec. pt., 336–348.

Erkkilä, S. (Suicide among children in Finland during the years 1885 to 1934.) Duodecim, 1937, 53, 536–547.

Fauré, M. Influence des taches solaires sur les suicides, les crimes et les accidents. (The influence of sun spots on cases of suicide, crime and accidents.) Gaz. Hôp., Paris, 1932, 104, No. 66.

Fedden, H. R. Suicide; a social and historical study. London: Peter Davies, 1938.

Fenton, W. N. Iroquois suicide: A study in the stability of a culture pattern. Anthrop. Papers, No. 14 (U.S. Bureau of American Ethnology, Bulletin No. 128) Washington: U.S. Government Printing Office, 1941, 79–137.

Fewer suicides in wartime. California's Health, 1944, 1, 939–994.

Francken, C. J. W. De zelfmoord. Een sociologische studie. (Suicide. A sociological study.) 's-Gravenhage, 1899.

Frenay, A .D. The suicide problem in the United States. Boston: Badger, 1927.

Freudenberg, K. Die Selbstmorde in Deutschland nach dem Kriege. (Suicide in Germany after the war.) Klin. Wschr., 1926, 5, 29–33.

Fribourg-Blanc, A. La réaction suicide dans l' Armée. (The suicide reaction in the army.) Paris Méd., 1932, 85, 422–427.

Frommett, B. Samoubiystva y politicheskikh tyurmakh i ssilkie. (Suicide in political prisons and exiled prisoners.) Vrach. Gaz., 1910, 17, 1606–1612.

Füllkrug, G. Der Selbstmord in den Kriegs- und Nachkriegszeit. (Suicide in war- and post-war time.) Schwerin: Bahn, 1927.

Gargas, S. Le suicide aux Pays-Bas. (Suicide in the Netherlands.) Arch Antrop. crim., 1930, 50, 673–688; Amer. J. Sociol., 1932, 37, 697–713.

Gibbs, J. P. A sociological study of suicide. Unpublished doctoral dissertation, Univ. of Oregon, 1957.

Gordon, J. E., Lindemann, E., Ipsen, J., and Vaughan, W. T. An epidemiologic analysis of suicide. *In* Epidemiology of Mental Disorder, 136–175. New York: Milbank Memorial Fund, 1950.

Gordon, J. E., O'Rourke, E., Richardson, F. L. W., Jr., and Lindemann, E. The biological and social sciences in an epidemiology of mental disorder. Amer. J. med. Sci., 1952, 223, 316–343.

Graf, R. Der Selbstmord in Beziehung zu Jahrezeit, Tagesstunde, und Wochentag. (Suicide in relation to the season, time of day, and day of the week.) Wien. Arch. Psychol. Psychiat. Neurol., 1952, 2, 15–24.

Grassl. Die Selbstmorde in Bayern, ein volkpsychologischer Beitrag. (Suicide in Bavaria, a folk-psychological contribution.) Friedreichs Bl. ger. Med., 1904, 55, 179, 259.

Grigoryeff, N. I. (Suicides and attempts at suicide in St. Petersburg during 1911.) Russk. Vrach., 1913, 12, 187–189.

Gruhle, H. W. Jugendselbstmord. (Juvenile suicide.) Z. Kinderforsch., 1936, 45, 157–203. Geographie des Selbstmordes. (Geography of suicide.) Nervenarzt, 1940, 13, 337–341.

Gruner, R. B. H. Der Selbstmord in der deutschen Armee. (Suicide in the German Army.) Inaug. Diss. Berlin: G. Schade (O. Francke), 1903.

Grzywo-Dabrowska, Marja. Samobójstwa modzieży szkolnejna podstawie ankiety. (Suicide in high schools.) Oświata i Wychowanie, 1932, 4, 38–75, 133–163.

Grzywo-Dabrowski, W. Suicide à deux, suicide en commun, etc ... à Varsovie. (Double and collective suicide ... in Warsaw.) Ann. Méd. lég., 1929, 9, 489–497. Suicides à Varsovie de 1921 à 1931 (d'après les données du Bureau statistique de la ville de Varsovie et les autopsies exécutées à l'Institut médico-légal de l'université). (Suicides in Warsaw from 1921 to 1931 [according to data from the statistical bureau of the city of Warsaw and from the autopsies executed at the medico-legal institute of the University].) Ann. Méd. lég., 1932, 12, 541–551.

Guilmain. Le suicide dans l'armée. (Suicide in the army.) J. Méd. Bordeaux, 1936, 113, 44–49.

Gunasekara, N. D. Some observations on suicide in Ceylon. J. Ceylon Br. Brit. med. Ass., 1951, 46, 138–148.

Gur-Gurewitsch, W. M. (Suicide among children and youth before and after the revolution period.) Pedologiya, 1930, 7, No. 1.

Guttman, M. J. (Der zelbst-mord ba Yidden un zeine sibos.) (Suicide among the Jews and its causes.) Yiddisher Viss. Instit. Ekon.-Statis. Sektzie. Shr. Ekon. Statis., 1928, 1, 117–121.

Halbwachs, M. Les causes du suicide. (The causes of suicide.) Paris: Alcan, 1930.

Hanäuer, W. Der Selbstmord bei den Frauen. (Suicide among women.) Dtsch. med. Wschr., 1927, 53, 1231.

Harpprecht, H. Beiträge zur Selbstmordstatistik des Oberamts Tübingen. (Notes on statistics of suicides from the official office in Tübingen.) Tübingen: Pietzcker, 1903.

Hart, B., and Nicole, J. E. Suicide and society. Ment. Hyg., Lond., 1934, April, 66–78.

Heddy, W. R. H. Methods of suicide. Practitioner, 1948, 160, 392–397.

Heiberg, P. (Suicides in Copenhagen, 1905–1925.) Ugeskr. Læg., 1926, 88, 626–627. (Suicide among Danish city population.) Nord. hyg. Tidskr., 1928, 9, 33–36.

Heindl, R. Der Selbstmord in Sowjet-Russland 1922–1925. (Suicide in Russia from 1922 to 1925.) Arch. Kriminol., 1927, 80, 252.

Helpap, K. Statistische Erhebungen über 485 versuchte und vollendete Selbstmorde, die auf der I. Inneren Abteilung des Horst Wessel-Krankenhauses, Berlin, in den Jahren 1935–1937 beobachtet wurden. (Statistical survey of 485 attempted and completed suicides observed at Horst Wessel Hospital, Berlin, 1935–1937.) Dtsch. Z. ges. gerichtl. Med., 1938, 30, 73–89.

Henry, A. F., and Short, J. F., Jr. Suicide and homicide. Some economic, sociological and psychological aspects of aggression. Glencoe, Ill: Free Press, 1954.

Heuyer, G., Desclaux, P., and Digo, R. Le suicide collectif. (Collective suicide.) Sem. Hôp. Paris, 1949, 25, 3625–3631.

Heyn, W. Der Selbstmord als soziales Phänomen. (Suicide as a social phenomenon.) Münch. med. Wschr., 1955, 97, 1389–1392.

Hiranuma, D. Der Selbstmord in Japon. (Suicide in Japan.) Arch. Kriminol., 1927, 80, 246–251.

Hoffman, F. L. Suicide problems. Newark: Prudential Press, 1928.

Holland, V. B. A glance at Wisconsin's suicides. Wis. Bd. Hlth Quart. Bull., 1942, 7, (3), 14–16.

Hopkins, F. Attempted suicide: an investigation. J. ment. Sci., 1937, 83, 71–94.

Hughes, C. H. Supposed favorite days for suicide in Prussia. Alien. & Neurol., 1909, 30, 634.

Hurlburt, W. C. Prosperity, depression, and the suicide rate. Amer. J. Sociol., 1931/32, 37, 714–719.

Ichok, G. Études sur la population française: le suicide. (Studies of the French population: suicide.) Biol. méd., Paris, 1935, 25, 49–78. La courbe des suicides en Allemagne. (The suicide curve in Germany.) Paris méd. (Annexe), 1936, 1, 11–13.

The increase in suicides. Med. Rec., N.Y., 1900, 58, 617–618.

Increase of suicide in New York. Med. Rec., N.Y., 1904, 66, 222.

Introna, F. Considerazioni sul significato antisociale del suicidio. (The antisocial significance of suicide.) Rev. int. Défense Soc., 1954, 8, 61–75.

Irwell, L. Racial deterioration; the increase of suicide. Med. News, 1897, 71, 421–424.

Kern, R. A. The growing problem of suicide. Calif. Med., 1953, 79, 6–10.

Khlopin, G. V. Samoûbiystva, pokusheniya na samoûbiystva i nestchastnîye sluchaï sredi uchastshikhsya russkikh uchebnîkh zavedeniv. (Suicide, attempts at suicide, and unfortunate accidents among Russian students.) S. Petersburg, 1906.

Kielberg, S. (Child suicide in Denmark.) Nord. med. Tidskr., 1936, 12, 1193–1199.

Knibbs, G. H. Studies in statistical representation. Statistical applications of the Fourier series. Illustrated by the analysis of rates of marriage, temperature, suicide, etc. J. roy. Soc. N.S.W., 1911, 45, 76–110. Suicide in Australia. A statistical analysis of the facts. J. roy. Soc. N.S.W., 1912, 45, 225–246.

Knopf, S. A. Suicide among American physicians—its causes and suggestions for prevention. N. Y. med. J., 1923, 117, 84–87.

Kollarits, J. Ein Erklärungsversuch für die Selbstmordhäufigkeit der Protestanten. (An attempted explanation of the suicide frequency of Protestants.) Z. ges. Neurol. Psychiat., 1919, 46, 357–372.

Kovács, N. (The first result of the new statistics of suicide.) Mag. statiszt. Szle, 1929, 7, 953–977. Öngyilkossági esetek Magyarországon. (Suicide cases in Hungary.) Mag. statiszt. Szle, 1943, 21, 407–420.

Kovalenko, I. Z. (Causes of suicide among townspeople in Russia; suicides in various nations and social groups.) Profilakt. med., 1926, 5, 47–60.

Krane, B. Om selvmordforsøk hos menn. (Suicide attempts of males.) Tidsskr. norske Lægeforen., 1949, 69, 480. Om selvmordforsøk hos kvinner. (Suicide attempts of women.) Tidsskr. norske Lægeforen., 1949, 69, 290–291.

Kress, D. H. The use of narcotics as related to the declining birth rate and race suicide. J. Inebr., 1911, 33, 62–71.

Kuzma, V. (Suicide in Lithuania.) Medicina, Kaunas, 1935, 16, 87–96.

Lattes, L. Il tentato suicidio nei militari. (Attempted suicide among the military.) Arch. Antrop. crim., 1917, 38, 381–396.

Laufer, L. G., and Casriel, D. H. Suicidal gestures in occupation personnel on Okinawa. U.S. Armed Forces med. J., 1952, 3, 1825–1830.

Lauterburg, F. Selbstmord und Trunksucht nach Jahreszeiten. (Suicide and dipsomania according to the seasons.) Gesundh. u. Wohlf., 1945, 25, 232–234.

Lavalée, G. Conditions sociales, économiques et morales du suicide. (Social, economic, and moral conditions of suicide.) Concours méd., 1948, 70, 1755.

Leighton, A. H., and Hughes, C. C. Notes on Eskimo patterns of suicide. Sthwest J. Anthrop., 1955, 11, 327–338.

Lendrum, F. C. A thousand cases of attempted suicide. Proc. Mayo Clin., 1933, 8, 179–180; Amer. J. Psychiat., 1933, 13, 479–500.

Leubuscher. Zur Selbstmordstatistik. (Suicide statistics.) KorrespBl. ärztl. Ver. Thüringen, 1899, 28, 374, 417–434.

Lewis, A. Statistical aspects of suicide. Canad. med. Ass. J., 1956, 74, 99–104.

Ligeiro declinio no indice de suicidios desta capital. (Slight decline in index of suicides at this capital.) Ann. paulist. Med. Cir., 1947, 53, 361.

Lindemann, E., Ipsen, J., Vaughan, W., Jr., and O'Rourke, E. Mental disorder as a mass phenomenon: A pattern for the study of minor and major disorders, as they affect populations of people, based on an epidemiologic analysis of suicide and other psychiatric disease. Arch. Neurol. Psychiat., Chicago, 1951, 66, 648–650.

Lindemulder, F. G., and Toomey, F. E. Suicide. Calif. West. Med., 1939, 50, 98–104.

Lindhardt, M. Selvmordshyppigheden i Danmark. (Frequency of suicide in Denmark.) Ugeskr. Læg., 1949, 111, 342–345.

Lo Cascio, G. I suicidi per veleno in Italia dal 1898 al 1923. (Suicides by poison in Italy from 1898 to 1923). Ann. Clin. med., Palermo, 1929, 19, 435–452.

Locket, S. Acute barbiturate poisoning and suicide. Med. ill., 1954, 8, 244–253.

Loewenberg, R. D. Über den Selbstmord in Hamburg in den letzten fünfzig Jahren. (Suicide in Hamburg in the last fifty years.) Berlin: Schoetz, 1932. Also Dtsch. med. Wschr., 1932, 58, 219–220; Veröff. MedVerw., 1932, 38, 517–595.

Lojander, W., Carpén, I., and Carpén, E. Drunkningsdöden viktig befolknings politisk. (Death by drowning, a serious population problem.) Nord. hyg. Tidskr., 1955, 36, 148–155.

Lomer, G. Über die Selbstmorde in Deutschland. (Suicide in Germany.) Pol.-anthrop. Rev., 1911/12, 10, 149–155.

Lumière, A. Variation de la mortalité par suicide à Paris de 1925 à 1949. (Variation of mortality by suicide in Paris from 1925 to 1949.) Avenir méd., Lyon, 1951, 48, 3–5.

Lunden, W. A. Suicides in France, 1910–1943. Amer. J. Sociol., 1946/47, 52, 321–334.

MacDonald, A. Statistics of child suicide. Amer. statist. Ass. Publ., 1906–07, 10, 260–264.

Manning, P. Stray notes on Oxfordshire folklore. IV. Traditions of Suicides, Folk-Lore, London, 1903, 14, 73–74.

Mapes, C. C. Suicide in children. Med. Age, 1903, 21, 289–295. Influence of the daily press as an incentive to suicide and other crimes. Med. Age, 1906, 24, 885–893.

Marchand, P. Caustic soda poisoning; the sociological aspect. S. Afr. med. J., 1954, 28, 415–419.

Marcuse, M. Geschlechterdifferenz bei den Selbstmordmethoden. (Sex differences in suicide methods.) Z. Sexualwiss., 1919/20, 6, 258–259.

Massarotti, V. Il suicidio nella vita e nella società moderna. (Suicide in life and modern society.) Rome: B. Lux, 1913.

Massias, C., and Vu-Cong-Hoe. Le suicide dans la société annamite. (Suicide in Annamese society.) Rev. méd. franç. Extr.-Or., 1938, 16, 78–93.

McGeorge, J. Attempted suicide. Med. J. Aust., 1942, 1, 67–74.

McKinley, P. L. Mortality from suicide in Scotland. Hlth Bull., Edinb., 1948, 6, 29–25.

Mead, F. H. The suicide-rate of San Diego. J. Amer. med. Ass., 1913, 61, 1999–2000.

Merton, R. K. Social structure and anomie. Amer. sociol. Rev., 1938, 672–682.

Mervyn Beech, W. H. Suicide amongst the A. Kikuyu of East Africa. Man, 1913, 13, 30, 56.

Michael, J. C., and Grimes, B. P. Attempted suicide. Investigation of one annual series in the Minneapolis General Hospital. Minn. Med., 1935, 18, 148–154.

Milorad, F. (Suicides in the Serbian army.) Voj.-sanit. Glasn., 1931, 2, 589–604.

Minogue, S. J. Suicide in Australia. Med. J. Aust., 1935, 1, 707–714. Suicides among returned soldiers of the 1914–1918 war. Med. J. Aust., 1945, 1, 195–200.

Modi, S.-ul-N. J. J. Suicides and old age. J. anthrop. Soc. Bombay, 1904–1907, 7, 577–590.

Moore, M. Cases of attempted suicide in a general hospital: A problem in social and psychologic medicine; report on local condition, including survey of 1147 records of attempted suicide cases admitted to Boston City Hospital. New England J. Med., 1937, 217, 291–303.

Morselli, E. Eutanasia e suicidio. (Euthanasia and suicide.) Ill. med. ital., 1923, 5, 69–72.

Morselli, H. Suicide: An essay on comparative moral statistics. New York: Appleton, 1882.

Mortality from suicide. Chron. World Hlth Org., 1956, 10, 170–171.

Mowrer, E. R. A study of personal disorganization. Amer. sociol. Rev., 1939, 4, 475–487.

Mulcock, D. Juvenile suicide. A study of suicide and attempted suicide over a 16-year period. Med. Offr., 1955, 94, 155–160.

Münster, A. Ursachen des Selbstmordes in Deutschland; eine zusamenfassende Darstellung. (Causes of suicide in Germany; an inclusive presentation.) Inaug. Diss., Berlin. Leipzig: Teubner, 1940.

Muraz, G. Comment et pourquoi se suicident les Annamites? (How and why do the Annamites commit suicide?) Pr. méd., 1939, 47, 213–214.

Murphy, H. B. M. The mental health of Singapore. I. Suicide. Med. J. Malaya, 1954, 9, 1–45.

Nelken, J. (Preliminary report on suicide in army in relation to season of year.) Roczn. Psychjat. (Psychiat. Annu., Warsaw), 1933, 403–408.

Oizumi, Y. (Studies on suicide.) Nagoya J. med. Sci., 1938, 48, 587–655.

Olbrycht, J., and Stanisz, J. Remarques sur le suicide. Les suicides à Cracovie entre 1899 et 1930. (Remarks on suicide. The suicides at Crakow between 1899 and 1930.) J. Méd. Lyon, 1937, 18, 633–636.

Ortiz Velasquez, J. Suicidio. (Suicide.) Rev. Med. legal Colom., 1947, 9, 45–70.

Ostrowsky, J. P. Zur Frage der Einführung einer einheitlichen Registrierung der Selbstmorde in Russland. (On the question of the introduction of the uniform recording of suicides in Russia.) Arch. KrimAnthrop., 1913, 51, 266–272.

Paraire, Velluz, J. Étude des tentatives de suicide observées au cours de l'anée 1948 dans le Service de neuropsychiatrie de Val-de-Grâce. (Study of attempted suicides observed in the course of the year 1948 at the Neuropsychiatric Service of Vol-de-Grâce.) Bull. Soc. Méd. mil. fr., 1949, 43, 86–89.

Parrish, H. M. Epidemiology of suicide among college students. Yale J. Biol. Med., 1957, 29, 585–595.

Peller, S. Zur Statistik der Selbstmordhandlung. (Statistics of suicidal behavior.) Allg. statist. Arch., 1932, 22, 343–364.

Pescor, M. J. Suicide among hospitalized drug addicts. J. nerv. ment. Dis., 1940, 91, 287–305.

Petráček, J. (Suicides in the Army during 1925/26—1932/33.) Voj. zdrav. listy, 1934, 10, 207–221.

Peyre, E. L. Le suicide et ses aspects dans les troups coloniales. (Suicide and its aspects among colonial troops.) Ann. Méd. Pharm. colon., 1936, 34, 939–966.

Phillips, W. F. R. Seasonal influence on suicide. Trans. Amer. climat. (clin.) Ass., 1909, 25, 156–166.

Pietrusky, F. Naturwissenschaftlich-kriminalistische und kriminal-psychologische Untersuchungen zur frage Selbstmord oder Unglücksfall. (Natural scientific, criminalistic, and criminal-psychological investigations on the question of suicide or accident.) Arch. Kriminol., 1936, 98, 193–212.

Piker, P. Eighteen hundred and seventeen cases of suicidal attempt. A preliminary statistical survey. Amer. J. Psychiat., 1938, 95, 97–115.

Pinero, H. M. El suicidio en la ciudad de Buenos Aires. (Suicide in Buenos Aires.) Sem. méd., B. Aires, 1939, 2, 840–847; Rev. Psiquiat. Crim., B. Aires, 1939, 4, 393–404.

Podio, G. Considerazioni statistiche sopra 6000 casi di tentato suicidio osservati nel ventennio di guardia 1914–1934, con particulare riguardo a quelli tentati con armi da fuoco. (Statistical considerations of 6000 cases of attempted suicide from 1914–1934, with particular reference to those attempted with firearms.) Osped. maggiore, 1934, 22, 494–498.

Pohlen, K. Di Morbidität und Letalität an Selbstmord. (Morbidity and mortality of suicide.) Dtsch. med. Wschr., 1, 1936, 777–779.

Pollack, B. Etiological factors in suicide. Med. Times, N.Y., 1938, 66, 421–425, 457.

Porterfield, A. L. Indices of suicide and homicide by states and cities: some southern-non-southern contrasts with implications for research. Amer. sociol. Rev., 1949, 14, 481–490. Suicide and crime in folk and in secular society. Amer. J. Sociol., 1952, 57, 331–338. Suicide and crime in the social structure of an urban setting: Fort Worth, 1930–1950. Amer. sociol. Rev., 1952, 17, 341–349.

Porterfield, A. L., and Talbert, R. H. Crime, suicide and social well-being in your state and city. Fort Worth: Leo Potisham Foundation, 1948.

Powers, D. Youthful suicide attempts. Part 1. Northw. Med., 1954, 53, 1001–1002; Part 2, 1213–1232.

Prozoroff, L. (Suicide of condemned prisoners.) Med. Obozr. Sprimona, 1911, 76, 76–84. (Suicides of the insane in hospitals.) Sovrem. Psikhiat., 1911, 5, 377, 425. (Suicide among military men.) Med. Obozr. Sprimona, 1914, 81, 865–883. (Suicides of the insane in hospitals: second article. Clinical data.) Sovrem. Psikhiat., 1915, 9, 117, 277.

Pur, K. (Suicides in Czechoslovakia) Spisy lék. fak. Masaryk. Univ., [Publ. Fac. Méd. Univ. Masaryk], 1947, 20, 113–151.

Ravicini, S. Omicidio e suicidio. (Homicide and suicide.) Difesa soc., 1934, 13, 367–374.

Ravn, E. (The health of some famous Romans. V. Suicide at the time of the birth of Christ.) Ugeskr. Læg., 1917, 79, 1307–1312.

Reck, J. Der Selbstmord in Bamberg im letzten Decennium. (Suicide in Bamberg in the last decennium.) Bamberg: Handelsdruckerei u. Verlagshandl., 1909.

Rehm, O. Arbeiten aus dem Gebiete der Kriminal- und Sozial-psychologie. (Contributions to the field of criminal and social psychology.) Z. Völkerpsychol. Soziol., 1929, 4, 446–463.

Reiter, R. Tagesbeispiele zur luftelektrisch-bioklimatischen Zusammenhängen, Wetterbeschwerden, Selbstmorde, Notsuchtverbrechen. (Everyday example illustrating atmospheric-electric-bioclimatic relationships, weather intolerance, suicide, criminal assault.) Med. Mschr., Stuttgart, 1952, 6, 45–48.

Révész, B. Der Selbstmord, eine sozialhygienische Skizze. (Suicide, a socio-hygienic sketch.) Arch. soz. Med. Hyg., 1905, 2, 240–248.

Richard, G. La pathologie sociale d'Émile Durkheim. (Durkheim's social pathology.) Rev. int. Sociol., 1930, 38, 113–126.

Romanelli, I. La mortalità per suicidio tra gli assicurati dell' Istituto Nazionale della Assicurazioni nel decennio 1920–1929. (Suicide mortality among the insured of the National Insurance Institute during 1920–1929.) G. Ist. ital. Attuari, 1931, 2, 177–184.

Rose, L. A modern review of the suicide problem. Med. Pr., 1952, 227, 40–43.

Rovinsky, A. Epidemic suicides. Bost. med. surg. J., 1898, 138, 238–239.

Rubenovitch, P. Les mobiles du suicide. (The fluctuations of suicide.) Proph. ment., 1931, 5, 385–388.

Russell, O. D. Suicide in Japan. Amer. Mercury, 1930, 20, 341–344.

Sainsbury, P. Suicide in London: an ecological study. London: Chapman and Hall, 1955; New York: Basic Books, 1956.

Saito, H. O suicidio entre os imigrantes Japoneses e seus descendentes no estado São Paulo. (Suicide among Japanese immigrants and their descendants in the state of São Paulo.) Sociologia, 1953, 15, 109–130.

Scherrer, P., Leclerc, J., Ariste-Le Bas, and Latouche, M. Note sur un mode peu connu de suicide: le suicide par ingestion massive d'alcool. (Description of a little-known method of suicide: drinking a large quantity of alcohol.) Ann. méd.-psychol., 1948, 1, 179–182.

Schmid, C. F. Suicides in Seattle, 1914 to 1925: an ecological and behavioristic study. Seattle, Washington: Univ. of Washington Publ., 1928, 5. Suicide in Seattle, Washington, and Pittsburgh, Pennsylvania: a comparative study. Univ. of Pittsburgh Bull., 1930, 27, 149–157. Suicide in Minneapolis, Minnesota: 1928–32. Amer. J. Sociol., 1933, 39, 30–48.

Schmid, C. F., and Van Arsdol, Jr., M.D. Completed and attempted suicides: a comparative analysis. Amer. sociol. Rev., 1955, 20, 273–283.

Schroeder, W. W. Suicide differentials in Michigan. Unpublished master's thesis, Michigan State Coll., 1951.

Schroeder, W. W., and Beegle, J. A. Suicide: an instance of high rural rates. Rur. Sociol., 1953, 18, 45–52. *In* A. M. Rose (Ed.), Mental health and mental disorder: a sociological approach. New York: Norton, 1955, Pp. 408–419.

Schwalbe, J. Zeitströmungen und Statistik. (Time trends and statistics.) Dtsch. med. Wschr., 1929, 55, 1007–1009.

Scouras, P. Le suicide dans l'Armée. (Suicide in the army.) Hyg. ment., 1931, 26, 153–182.

Die Selbstmorde in Preussen im Jahren 1924. (Suicides in Prussia in 1924.) Med.-statist. Nachr., 1927, 21, 195–200.

Self-destruction in Spain in 20 years. J. Amer. med. Ass., 1930, 95, 1276.

Sengupta, N. N. Studies in race-mind. III. Crime, suicide, and insanity as indices of the race-mind. Indian J. Psychol., 1944, 19, 54–57.

Serin, Suzanne. Une enquête médico-sociale sur le suicide à Paris. (Medico-social inquiry of suicide in Paris.) Proph. ment., 1926, 2, 230–235. Les causes du suicide d'après une enquête médico-sociale dans la ville de Paris. (Causes of suicide from a medico-social inquiry in the city of Paris.) Pr. méd., 1926, 34, 1404.

Shirotani, S. Statistical observation on suicide among patients with mental diseases. Far east. Sci. Bull., 1944, 4, 6–7. Abstract.

Sibbald, J. On suicide in Scotland. Brit. med. J., 1900, 1, 496–498.

Siebert, H. Selbstmorde durch Gift in Deutschland seit Kriegsende. (Suicide by poison in Germany since the end of the war.) Samml. Vergiftungsf., 1936, 7, C 73–74.

Sieveking, G. H., Koopman, H., and Boettiger, A. Die Selbstmorde in Hamburg wahrend der letzten drei Jahrfünfte 1909–1923. (Suicides in Hamburg during the last three five-year periods 1909–1923.) Dtsch. med. Wschr., 1925, 51, 694–698.

Simon, A. Bemerkungen zur badischen Selbstmordstatistik. (Remarks on suicide statistics in Baden.) Z. MedBeamte, 1932, 45, 60–67.

Simonetti, Nicola. Suicido e tentativo di suicidio. (Suicide and attempted suicide.) Difesa soc., 1957, 36, 66–111.

Simpson, G. Methodological problems in determining the etiology of suicide. Amer. sociol. Rev., 1950, 15, 658–663.

Smith, S. Suicide. Practitioner, 1938, 141, 41–52.

Sollaud. Le suicide en Annam. (Suicide in Annam.) Centre méd. pharm., 1904/05, 10, 25.

Speijer, N. Van den zelfmoord. (Suicide.) Rotterdam: de Voorpost, 1935. (Survey of suicide attempts with fatal outcomes in institutions for mental patients in the Netherlands during the period 1882–1932.) Ned. Tijdschr. Geneesk., 1938, 82, 2824–2827. Suicide in Jewish history. Folia psychiat. neerl., 1948, 51, 263–274.

St. Antonine, H. E. Suicide. U.S. Veterans' Bur. med. Bull., 1932, 8, 369–376.

Stchoukine, I. Le suicide collectif dans le Raskol russe. (Collective suicide among the Russian Raskol.) Paris: Floury, 1903.

Steinberg, M. Lezte Aufzeichnungen von Selbstmördern nebst kurzer Selbstmordstatistik der Stadt Bern von 1929 bis und mit 1935. (Last writings of suicides with brief statistics on suicide in the city of Bern, 1929–1935.) Ausz. Inaugr. Diss. Med. Fak. Univ. Bern, 1937–42.

Stephanescu-Goanga, F., Rosca, A., and Cupcea, S. Adaptarea sociala. (Social adaptation.) Cluj: Institutul de Psihologie al Universitatti, 1938.

Sternberg, A. Samoûbiystuo sredi russkikhvracheĭ. (Suicide among Russian physicians.) Ezhen. Zh. prakt. Med., (Ejened. J. "Prakt. Med.") 1897, 4, 197–202, 605–610.

Straus, Jacqueline H., and Straus, M. A. Suicide, homicide, and social structure in Ceylon. Amer. J. Sociol., 1953, 58, 461–469.

Strauss, E. B. Suicide. Brit. med. J., 1956, 2, 818–820.

Strauss, L. La importancia del suicidio en Panamá. (The importance of suicide in Panama.) Bol. Asoc. méd. nac. Panamá, 1949, 12, 1–15.

Styles, G. Suicide and its increase. Amer. J. Insan., 1900, 57, 97–102.

Suicide—a leading cause of death. J. Amer. med. Ass., 1952, 150, 696–697.

Suicide among physicians. Med. and surg. Reptr., 1897, 76, 271–273.

Suicide among soldiers. Brit. med. J., 1903, 1, 452.

Suicide and homicide in England as compared with America. J. Amer. med. Ass., 1923, 80, 1324.

Suicide by prisoners. Lancet, 1903, 2, 1308.

Suicide dans l'Armée. (Suicide in the army.) J. Méd. Bordeaux, 1935, 113, 44–49.

Suicide in California, births-deaths-marriages. California State Department of Public Health, 1955.

Suicide in cities. Amer. J. Sociol., 1905, 10, 562. (Abstract of Rost, H., Der selbstmord in den Stadten. Allg. statist. Arch., 1904, 6, 263–281.)

Suicide in Italy. Lancet, 1907, 1, 601.

Suicide in prisons. Lancet, 1911, 2, 1281–1282.

Suicide in Salford. Lancet, 1902, 1, 1501.

Suicide rarer in wartime. Sth. Med. Surg., 1942, 104, 683.

Suicide statistics. J. Amer. med. Ass., 1905, 45, 469.

Suicides drop in war. J. Amer. med. Ass., 1942, 120, 768.

Suicides in Budapest and in large European centers. J. Amer. med. Ass., 1929, 92, 999.

Suicides in the French Army. Med. Rec., N.Y., 1900, 58, 503.

Suicides in Italy. Brit. med. J., 1898, 1, 1424.

Suicides in United States during 1901. Med. Rec., N.Y., 1902, 61, 339–340.

Suicides of children. Lancet, 1907, 2, 328.

Suicides of physicians and the reasons. J. Amer. med. Ass., 1903, 41, 263–264.

Suicidios em Lisboa. (Suicides in Lisbon.) Med. contemp., 1904, 6, 190–192.

Suicidos no Parano. (Suicides in Parana.) Rev. méd. Paraná, 1940, 9, 209–211.

Swinscow, D. Some suicide statistics. Brit. med. J., 1951, 1, 1417–1423.

Tönnies, F. Der Selbstmord in Schleswig-Holstein. (Suicide in Schleswig-Holstein.) Breslau: Hirt, 1927. Der Selbstmord von Männern in Preussen, 1884–1914. (Suicide of men in Prussia, 1884–1914.) Mensch en Maatsch., 1933, 9, Nos. 1 and 2.

Tosti, G. Suicide in the light of recent studies. Amer. J. Sociol., 1898, 3, 464–478. Durkheim on suicide. The delusions of Durkheim's sociological objectivism: a reply. Amer. J. Sociol., 1899, 4, 171.

Total of suicides in the United States exceeds 300,000 for 1920–1938. J. Amer. med. Ass., 1940, 115, 326.

VandeGrift, W. B. Suicide and homicide by violence. Med. Clin. N. Amer., 1941, 25, 423–436.

Verkko, V. K. Om självmordsfrekvensen i Europa och speciellt i de nordiska. (Suicide rates in Europe, especially in the north.) Menneske og miljø, Kbh., 1946, 1, 215–224. Rusdrykernas inverkan på självmorden I Finland. (Influence of intoxicating beverages on the incidence of suicide in Finland.) Menneske og miljø, Kbh., 1948, 3, 243–253. Homicides and suicides in Finland and their dependence on national character with an additional chapter: The theories of Morselli and Ferri on homicides and suicides and the attitude to them of Tarde and Durkheim. København: G. E. C. Gad, 1951.

Vetere, C. Evoluzione della mortalità per suicidio in Italia ed in altri paesi. (The suicide mortality rate in Italy and other countries.) Ann. Sanità pubbl., 1956, 17, 367–460.

Vidoni, G. Contributo allo studio dei dati meteorological nel determinismo del suicidio, degli accesi epilettici e dell' alienazione mentale. (Contribution to the study of meteorologic data, epileptic attacks and mental derangement as determiners of suicide.) Manicomio, 1925, 38, 107–151. Note sulla diffusione della pazzia, del suicidio e del delitto fra gli Italiani. (Note on the spread of insanity, suicide, and crime among Italians.) Quad. Psichiat., 1926, 13, 221–229. Contributo allo studio del suicidio con speciale reguardo all 'eta e al sesso. (Contribution to the study of suicide with special regard to age and sex.) G. Psichiat. manic., 1927, 55, 1–34.

Voegelin, E. W. Suicide in northeastern California. Amer. Anthrop., 1937, 39, 445–456.

von Obermüller. Beitrag zum Jugendselbstmord in Baden. (Study of juvenile suicide in Baden.) Z. Kinderforsch., 1936, 45, 149–156.

von Ungern-Sternberg, R. Über die Ursachender Steigerung der Selbstmordhäufigkeit in Westeuropa. (Causes for the increase in the frequency of suicides in Western Europe.) Fortschr. Med., 1934, 52, 1124–1127. Die Ursachen der Steigerung der Selbstmordhäufigkeit in Westeuropa während der letzten hundert Jahre. (The causes of the increase in the frequency of suicide in Western Europe in the last hundred years.) Veröff. MedVerw., 1935, 44, 507–582. Die Bevölkerungsverhältnisse in Ungarn, mit besonderer Berücksichtigung des Selbstmordes. (The vital statistics of Hungary, with a special review of suicide.) Veröff. Geb. VolksgesundhDienst., 1942, 56, 317–359.

Vorwahl, H. Selbstmord und Rasse. (Suicide and race.) Münch. med. Wschr., 1936, 83, 767–768.

Vu-cong-hoe. Du suicide dans la société annamite. (Suicide in Annamite society.) Thèse Méd. (No. 84), Hanoi: Tonkinoise, 1937.

Wainer, A. Menor frecuencia en los suicidos; sus causas. (Decrease in incidence of suicides; its causes.) Día méd., 1955, 27, 1902–1903.

Waldstein, E. Der Selbstmord in der Schweiz. (Suicide in Switzerland.) Basle: Philogr. Verlag, 1934.

Wallinga, J. V. Attempted suicide: a ten year survey. Dis. nerv. Syst., 1949, 10, 15–20.

Walton, H. Attempted suicide in Cape Town. S. Afr. med. J., 1950, 24, 933–935.

Weiss, J. M. A. Suicide: An epidemiologic analysis. Psychiat. Quart., 1954, 28, 225–252.

Wendling, A. Suicide in the San Francisco Bay region: 1938–1942 and 1948–1952. Unpublished doctoral dissertation, Univ. of Washington, 1954.

Wessinger, J. D. Über den Selbstmord bei Frauen in den ersten zehn Jahren nach dem Kriege. (Suicide in women in the first ten years after the war.) Berlin: R. Schoetz, 1933; Veröff. MedVerw., 1933, 40, 241–274.

Westerland, F. W. Självmordern i Helsingfors. (Suicide in Helsingfors.) Finska LäkSällsk. Handl., 1914, 56, 749–804.

Williams, T. A. Suicide and civilization. J. sociol. Med., 1918, 19, 4–18.

Willoughby, R. R. A group of seven correlated social variables. J. genet. Psychol., 1928, 35, 331–334.

Wooley, J. M. Suicide among Indian convicts under transportation. J. ment. Sci., 1913, 59, 335–343.

Wright, M. B. Sociological factors which influence the suicide rate. Psyche, Lond., 1931, 12, 52–61.

Wyman, L. C., and Thorne, Betty. Notes on Navaho suicide. Amer. Anthrop. 278–288.

Wyss, R. Zur Psychopathologie zweier eigenständiger Befölkerungsgruppen des Berner Oberlandes. (Psychopathology of two autochthonous groups of population of the Berne Oberland.) Mschr. Psychiat. Neurol., 1953, 125, 756–768.

Zhbankoff, D. (Suicide statistics during 1905–1911.) Prakt. Vrach, 1912, 11, 520, 533, 543.

MEDICAL–LEGAL

Achard, C. Le médecin devant la suicide. (Duties of the doctor regarding suicide.) Strasbourg-méd., 1930, 90, 257–260; Bull. Acad. Méd., Paris, 1930, 103, 334, 428.

Adams, J. B. Suicide; from a general practitioner's point of view. Practitioner, 1915, 94, 470–478.

Andereggen, P. Àpropos de 273 tentatives de suicide par empoisonnement. Remarques statistiques et thérapeutiques. (273 cases of attempted suicide by poisoning. Statistical and therapeutic remarks.) Rev. méd. Suisse Rom., 1948, 68, 257–279.

Anderson, E. W. Psychiatric emergencies in general practice. Practitioner, 1952, 168, 363–367.

Anfimov, V. Y. (Prophylaxis of suicide; iatrogenic factor in suicide.) Trud. kubansk. med. Inst., 1941, 13, 285–294.

Attempted suicide. Brit. Med. J., 1952, 1, 339.

Attilio, A. Suicidio od omicidio per precipitazione; perizia medico-legale. (Suicide or homicide by falling from a height; forensic expertize.) Cesalpino, 1912, 8, 6, 97, 187, 389.

Baechi, W. Der Mordfall Näf-Zürich. (The Näf-Zurich murder case.) Arch. Kriminol., 1940, 107, 5, 93, 119.

Balázs, G. (Influence of menstruation on suicide among women.) Orv. Hétil., 1936, 80, 630–632.

Barbiturates in bulk. Lancet, 1952, 1, 879–880.

Bartel, J. Zur pathologischen Anatomie des Selbstmordes. (Pathological anatomy of suicides.) Wien. Klin. Wschr., 1910, 23, 495–504. Über Obduktionsbefunde bei Selbstmordfällen. (Post-mortem findings of suicide cases.) Dtsch. Z. ges. gerichtl. Med., 1922, 1, 389–400.

Bartmann, F. Dubiose Fälle: Grenzfälle von Mord, Selbstmord, Unglücksfall; zusammenstallung und Auswertung authentischen Materials von Fritz Bartmann. (Dubious cases: Borderline cases of homicide, suicide, accident; comparison and evaluation of authentic materials of Fritz Bartmann.) Lubeck: Polizeilische Faschschrifttum, 1954.

Beaudouin, H., and Joyeux, J. Intoxication voluntaire par un mélange d'atropine et de pilocarpine; considérations psychiatriques et toxicologiques. (Psychiatric and toxologic aspects of suicidal ingestion of a mixture of atropine and pilocarpine.) Ann. Méd. lég., 1949, 29, 228–232.

Beaussart, P. Tentative de suicide par coup de revolver, transfixiant, de la region frontale. Negation de l'acte et allégation fabulante. Dissimulation du amnésie avec myth morbide de compensation? (Attempt at suicide by revolver shot through the frontal region. Question of dissimulation or amnesia with morbid compensatory myth.) Ann. Méd. lég., 1937, 17, 553–558.

Beck, W. V. Auffällige Begleitumstände eines fraglichen Selbstmordes; typische Verwechslung von Ein- und Ausschuss. (Peculiar circumstances in questionable suicide; typical mistaking of entrance of bullet for exit.) Med. Welt, 1937, 11, 1178–1179. Die Beurteilung eigentümlicher Schussverletzungen. (Evaluation of peculiar bullet wounds.) Dtsch. Z. ges. gerichtl. Med., 1940, 32, 325–328.

Becker, W. Der Selbstmord, strafrechtlich gesehen. (Suicide, criminal jurisdiction examined.) Med. Welt, 1940, 14; 747.

Beitzke, H. Pathological-anatomisch Untersuchungen an Selbstmördern. (Pathological-anatomical researches on suicide.) Wien. klin. Wschr., 1938, 51, 625–628.

Belbey, J. Suicidio y accidente del trabajo. (Suicide and occupational accidents.) Arch. Med. leg., B. Aires., 1948, 18, 328–337.

Belser, R. Beitrag zur Frage des Frauenselbstmordes unter besonderer Berücksichtigung der ausserehelichen Schwangerschaft. (Contribution to the question of suicide by women by means of a review of cases of illegitimate pregnancy.) Inaug. Diss., Zürich. Innsbruck: Rauch, 1950, 35 p.

Bengtsson, L. Graviditet och självmord. (Pregnancy and suicide.) Svenska Läkartidn., 1947, 44, 1469—.

Berka, F. (Question of suicide or homicide in case of hanging.) Čas. Lék. čes., 1934, 73, 481–484.

Berner, O. (Question of murder or suicide in connection with a case.) Norsk Mag. Lægevidensk., 1936, 97, 289–294.

Billström, J. Läkarens ställning till självmord och självmordsfara. (Medical opinion on suicide and suicide risk.) Allm. svenska Läkartidn., 1920, 17, 305–316.

Bischoff, M. Un cas curieux de suicide avec mise en scène de meurtre. (Curious case of suicide, staged as a murder.) Ann. Méd. lég., 1948, 28, 140–142.

Blondel, A., Sollier, R., Dang-van-chung, and Nguyen-van-nho. Sur trente-neuf cas d'intoxication par le phosphorus; suicide per ingestion de pétards chinois: phao-cha. (Thirty-nine cases of phosphorus poisoning; suicide by ingestion of Chinese fire-crackers phaocha.) Pr. méd., 1953, 61, 1322–1323.

Boas, K. Über einen Mord- und Suicidversuch in der Menstruation. (Murder and suicide attempt in menstruation.) Arch. krimAnthrop., 1909, 35, 226–248. Ein weiterer Fall von Suicidium menstruale. (Further case of menstrual suicide.) Arch. krim-Anthrop., 1910/11, 40, 187–190.

Bodnar, J., and Nagy, V. L. Bestimmung des Nicotins in Leichenteilen von Selbstmördern. (Determination of nicotine in the organs of suicides.) Dtsch. Z. ges. gerichtl. Med., 1938, 30, 231–234.

Bohme, M. Selbstmord als Unfallfolge im versicherungsrechtlichen Sinne. (Suicide as sequel of accident in the insurance-law sense.) Veroff. MedVerw., 1934, 42, 261–336.

Bohne, G. Ist Selbstmord Unglücksfall? (Is suicide an accident?) Dtsch. med. Wschr., 1935, 61, 1407–1408.

Bommer, J. H. Selbstmord durch "Hammelstich"—Unfallfolge? (Suicide by stabbing—accident?) Dtsch. Z. ges gerichtl. Med., 1936, 26, 385–388.

Bond, E. D. Self-destructive tendencies and life insurance. J. Insur. Med., 1948, 3, 35–41.

Bonhoeffer, K., and Moeli, C. Verantwortlichkeit des Irrenarztes für den Selbstmord einer Geisteskranken. (Accountability of the alienist for the suicide of an insane person.) Vjschr. gerichtl. Med., 1915, 49, 177–193.

Bonjour, J. La guérison d'une idée impulsive par une action physique seule, ou la guérison de l'idée du suicide par abaissment de la minima arterielle. (Cure of impulsive idea by single physical action, or cure of suicide idea by reduction of diastolic pressure.) Schweiz. med. Wschr., 1930, 60, 919–922.

Bortolozzi, M. Sulla diagnosi differenziale tra omicidio e suicidio in caso di sgozzemento. (On the differential diagnosis of homicide and suicide in a case of cutting of the throat.) G. veneto Sci. med., 1937, 11, 681–693.

Boulin, R., Guéniot, M., and Lapresle, C. Le suicide chez les diabétiques. (Suicide of diabetics.) Hyg. ment., 1956, 45, 233–240.

Bramanti Jauregui, R. El suicidio en el ejército; aspectos médico-legales. (Suicide in the army, medico-legal aspects.) Rev. Sanid. milit., B. Aires, 1948, 47, 253–258.

Brandis, W. Selbstmord als mittelbare Folge eines Unfalls. (Suicide as indirect result of accident.) Med. Klinik, 1926, 22, 621–622.

Breyfogle, H. S., and Richardson, O. Medicolegal problems in distinguishing accident from suicide with special reference to Missouri cases. J. Mo. med. Ass., 1947, 44, 423–430.

Brooke, Eileen M. Too much barbiturate? Lancet, 1956, 1, 150–152.

Brosch, A. Die Selbstmörder. Mit besonderer Berucksichtigung der militarischen Selbstmorder und ihrer Obduktionsbefunde. (Suicides. With special regard to military suicides, and their postmortem findings.) Leipzig u. Wein: Deuticke, 1909.

Brosnan, L. J. Insurance—death by suicide. N. Y. St. J. Med., 1932, 32, 976–977.

Brunelli, A. M. Crímenes y suicidios. (Crimes and suicides.) Rev. Criminol., Santiago, 1949, 9, 55–57.

Brüning, and Weithold. Die Untersuchung und Beurteilung von Selbstmörderschusswaffen. (The investigation and determination of firearms used in suicides.) Dtsch. Z. ges. gerichtl. Med., 1934, 23, 71–82.

Buhtz, G. Schriftstücke (spez. Selbstmörderbriefe), ihre versicherungsrechtliche Bedeutung. (Documents [esp. suicide notes]; their significance for insurance claims.) Dtsch. Z. ges. gerichtl. Med., 1940, 33, 185–194.

Burkhardt, W. Sturz aus der Höhe. (Jumping from heights.) Dtsch. Z. ges. gerichtl. Med., 1939, 30, 334–341.

Busatto, S. Osservazioni e considerazioni sullo strangolamento suicidario. (Observations and considerations on suicide by strangulation.) Arch. Antrop. crim., 1942, 62, 272–310. Un nuovo criterio di diagnosi differenziale tra suicidio ed omicidio per colpo di arma da fuoco. (A new criterion for the differential diagnosis of suicide and homicide with gunshot.) Arch. Antrop. crim., 1935, 55, 903–906.

Buzzo, A., and Caratalá, R. E. Toxicología; estadistícas de intoxicaciones. (Toxicology; statistics on poisoning.) Sem. méd., B. Aires, 1933, 1, 980–984.

Calogera, E. Considerazioni medico-legali sul tentato suicidio in rapporto all'assicuriazione malattie. (Forsenic aspects of attempted suicide in relation to health insurance.) Minerva med.-leg., 1952, 72, Suppl. 7–9.

Camba, R., and Napoleone, F. Lobotomia involuntaria in un caso di tentato suicidio per arma da fuoco: considerazioni sulle modificazioni psichiche conseguite alesioni dei lobi prefronteli. (Involuntary lobotomy in a case of attempted suicide by firearm: psychic modifications following lesions of the prefrontal lobes.) Mass. med. Sarda, 1954, 56, 31–44.

Camps, F. E. Common household poisons. Med. Pr., 1952, 228, 414–418.

Canedy, F. J. A case of suspected homicide proved to be suicide by strychnia. Boston med. & surg. J., 1904, 151.

Cantieri, F. Casistica rara in tema di suicidio; due suicidio per annegamento atipico; con immersione della sola testa; in una vasca di scarsissima profondita. (Rare case studies on the theme of suicide; two suicides by burning; two by atypical drowning with immersion only of the head in a basin of very shallow depth.) Minerva med.-leg., 1952, 72, 94–102.

Canuto, G. Iconografiia medico-legale; omicidio e suicidio per ferite d'arma de fuoco. (Medicolegal iconography; homicide and suicide with automatic pistol.) Arch. Antrop. crim., 1938, 58, 340–343.

Carnuto, G. Sulla sede del foro d'ingresso nei suicidi per colpo d'arma da fuoco. (Court report on suicide by firearm.) Arch. Antrop. crim., 1923, 43, 38–48.

Carrara, M. Un caso di suicidio simulante un homicidio. (A case of suicide simulating homicide.) Arch. Antrop. crim., 1928, 48, 415–446.

Carrier, G. Contributions à l'étude des obsessions et des impulsions à l'homicide et au suicide chez les dégénérés au point de vue médico-legal. (Contribution to the study of obsessions and compulsions of suicide of degenerates from the medico-legal viewpoint.) Paris: Alcan, 1899.

Cattáneo, L. Diagnóstico retrospectivo de alienación mental en un suicida; consideraciones médico legales. (Retrospective diagnosis of mental alienation in a suiside: medico-legal study of case.) Rev. Med. leg. Jurisp. med., 1935, 1, 67–78.

Chavigny, M. Vom Eisenbahnzug überfahren: Mord, Selbstmord oder Unfall? (Homicide, suicide or accident after body is run over by train?) Arch. Kriminol., 1934, 94, 181–186.

Chiron, A. Gerichtlich-medizinische Studien über Selbstmörder in New York. (Forensic-medical studies on suicide in N.Y.) Dissertation, Bern: Switzerland, 1938.

Claps, A., and Giannini, A. Intossicazione massiva da digitale ad evoluzione begnina in un caso di malinconia. (Massive digitalis poisoning with benign evolution in a case of melancholia.) Rass. Neuropsich., 1953, 7, 366–376.

Cleghorn, C. Suicide by poison; a plea for restriction of the sale of carbolic acid. Long Is. med. J., 1911, 5, 7–9.

Clemmesen, C. (Phenobarbital preparations as means of suicide.) Ugeskr. Læg., 1932, 21, 299–302.)

Cox, A. N. Note on tuberculosis and suicide. Brit. J. Tuberc., 1931, 25, 173–174.

Crema, C. Infanticidio seguito da morte della madre per emorragia e tentativo di suicidio. (Infanticide followed by death of the mother by [uterine] hemorrhage and attempted suicide.) Arch. Antrop. crim., 1935, 55, 1034–1040.

Curatolo, L. Il pericolo dei barbiturici. (The danger of barbiturates.) G. Med. milit., 1950, 97, 46–54.

Dalchow. Zur Rechtsprechung des Reichsversorgungsgerichts bei Selbstmord. (Jurisdiction of the government compensation court in suicide.) Ärztl. SachverstZtg., 1932, 38, 11–13.

Damaye, H. (Suicidal forms of psychoses.) Progr. méd., Paris, 1918, 284.

Davis, O. C. M. Original papers; some aspects of suicide—1. Med. Pr., 1950, 222, 487–491; 2. Med. Pr., 1950, 222, 519–524.

De Acha, E. Pacto suicida y muerte del consenciente. (Suicide pacts and murder by consent.) Criminalia, México, 1943/44, 10, 187–192.

de Bellefeuille, G. L. Le suicide et la responsabilité. (Suicide and responsibility.) Un. méd. Can., 1929, 58, 729–739.

De Cerqueira Falcão, E. Sobre a accentuada preferencia dos suicidas pela ingestão de cyanêto de potassio, na cidade do Salvador (Bahia) e em Buenos Aires. (Great preference for suicide by ingestion of potassium cyanide in Salvador (Bahia) and in Buenos Aires.) Arch. Soc. Med. leg. Criminol. S. Paulo, 1935, 5, 97–111; Brazil-med., 1935, 49, 145–149.

Del piano, J., and Novaro, V. Un caso de filicidio y tentativa de suicidio. Intoxicación tuberculosa. In imputabilidad (informe médico-legal). (Filicide and attempted suicide. Tuberculous intoxication. Lack of responsibility [medico-legal study].) Sem. méd., B. Aires, 1939, 2, 1271–1273.

De Luna, A. Il suicidio nel diritto e nella vita sociale. (Suicide in the law and in social life.) Roma: Balbi, 1907.

de Negris Marella, F. Su un caso di morte per annegamento. (Contributo alla diagnosi differenziale tra suicidio ed omicidio.) (Case of death by drowning. [Differential diagnosis between suicide and homicide].) Arch. Antrop. crim., 1934, 54, 424–429.

Derome, W. Observation médico-légale; suicide par arme à feu. (Medico-legel observation; suicide by firearm.) Un. méd. Can., 1925, 54, 625–627.

Dewey, R. On the care of suicidal patients and the responsibility involved. Wis. med. J., 1909, 7, 475–477.

Díaz-Rivera, R. S., Collazo, P. J., Pons, E. R., and Torregrosa, Mercedes V. Acute phosphorus poisoning in man; study of 56 cases. Medicine, Baltimore, 1950, 29, 269–298.

Dingman, H. W. Why life insurance companies are interested in suicides and in the recognition of pre-suicides. Weekly Underwriter, 1930, 124, 923.

Doll, H. J. Suicide is unlawful. Mass. med. J., 1900, 20, 481–489.

Douglas, A. D. M., and Bates, T. J. N. Chlorpromazine as a suicidal agent. Brit. med. J., 1957, 1, 1514.

Drury, K. K., and Freer, C. E. J. Undecided compensation claim arising from suicide of voluntary patient. J. ment. Sci., 1937, 83, 461–471.

Dufour. Tentative de suicide simulant une tentative de meurtre. (Suicide attempt simulating an attempted murder.) Ann. Hyg. Publ., Paris, 1897, 38, 420–424.

East, W. N. Suicide from the medico-legal aspect. Brit. med. J., 1931, 2, 241–242.

Eastwood, J. Attempted suicide by head injury: report of a case, review of the literature. Med.-leg. J., Cambr., 1957, 25, 125–128.

Ehrnrooth, E. (Conditions of payment by our life-insurance companies in cases of suicide of insane persons.) Finska LäkSällsk. Handl., 1927, 69, 674–684.

Ekblad, M. Relation of the legal-abortion clientele to the illegal-abortion clientele and the risk of suicide. *In* M. Ekblad, Induced abortion on psychiatric grounds. A follow-up study of 479 women. (Trans. D. Burton.) Acta psychiat., Kbh., 1955, Suppl. 99. Pp. 93–98.

Epps, P. Women in prison on attempted suicide charges. Lancet, 1957, 2, 182–184.

Escande de Messières. Crime ou suicide? L'explication endocrinienne d'un drame mystére.

(Homicide or suicide? Endocrine explanation of a mysterious drama.) Clinique, Paris, 1935, 30, 42–44. Abstract.

Esser, A. Selbstmord nach Schädelverletzungen. (Suicide after cranial injuries.) Dtsch. Z. ges. gerichtl. Med., 1936, 25, 239–317.

Faenza, M. Note statistico-cliniche su 252 casi di assunzione di sostanze venefiche. (Statistico-clinical notes on 252 cases of ingestion of poisonous substances.) Rif. med., 1940, 56, 807–816.

Fallani, M. Il suicidio nel settorato medico-legale fiorentino dal 1896 al 1954. (Suicides in the Medico-Legal Department of Florence, 1896–1954.) Minerva med.-leg., 1956, 76, 97–113.

Fenton, Frances. The press and crimes against the person. Bull. Amer. Acad. Med., 1911, 12, 307–315.

Fongo, A. Considerazioni su 152 casi mortali per ferite da arma da punta e da taglio. (Study of 152 cases of death caused by stabbing and cutting weapons.) Minerva med.-leg., 1955, 75, 110–133.

Fourcade, J., Schneider, D., and Lévy, F. Le suicide à la hache; curieuse tentative avec mise en scène d'agression chez une schizophrène. (Suicide with the hatchet; a curious attempt on the part of a schizophrenic to give the appearance of murder.) Ann. Méd. lég., 1950, 30, 133–139.

Fournier, A. Syphilis and suicide. Int. Clin., 1904, 14, 73–83.

Franchini, A. Considerazioni statistiche e medico-legali sul suicidio a Genova. (Statistical and medico-legal considerations of suicide in Genoa.) Riv. sper. Freniat., 1939, 63, 125–159. Contributo allo studio dell' omicidio-suicidio. (Contribution to the study of homicide-suicide.) Arch. Antrop. crim., 1940, 60, 86–101.

Franck, E. Der physiologische Selbstmord. (Physiological suicide.) Ärztl. SachverstZtg., 1930, 36, 333–336.

Frank, M. S. If a patient attempts suicide. Mod. Hosp., 1941, 57, 57.

Freudenberg, K. Die Selbstmordhäufigkeit bei Tuberkulösen. (The suicide rate in tuberculotics.) Ärztl. Wschr., 1957, 12, 936–939.

Friedewald, V. E. Incidence and mortality of acute poisonings. J. Mo. med. Ass., 1939, 36, 411–413.

Friedman, G. A. Suicide, euthanasia, and the law. Med. Times, N.Y., 1957, 85, 681–689.

Fritz, E. Selbstmord oder Unfall? Ein ungewöhnlicher Fall von Erhängen durch den Halsausschnitt eines Anstaltskleides. (Suicide or accident? An unusual case of hanging by cutting out the neck of an institutional garment.) Arch. Kriminol., 1940, 107, 68–73.

Fryer, I. O. Deaths from poisoning. Manitoba med. Rev., 1951, 31, 669–670.

Gallo, D., and Berruezo, J. J. Psicoterapia hospitalaria del suicida; problemas que plantea. (Hospital psychotherapy for suicides; problems which arise.) Día méd., 1948, 20, 1189.

Gammage, E. A. Suicide and degeneracy. Physio-med. Rec. 1902, 5, 39, 62.

Gardner, E. Suicidal hanging. Med.-leg. Rev., 1942, 10, 129.

Garnier, P. Le suicide collectif au point de vue médico-légal. (Collective suicide from the medico-legal viewpoint.) Méd. mod., 1897, 8, 737–739, 745–747; Nice-méd., 1897/98, 22, 65–74.

Gerke, T. Morde und Selbstmorde mit Viehschussmasken. (Murder and suicide with slaughtering devices.) Arch. Kriminol., 1942, 111, 19–24.

Giese, E. Versicherungsbetrug? Naturwissenschaftlich-kriminalistische und kriminalpsychologische Untersuchungen zur Frage: Selbstmord oder Unglücksfall. Bemerkungen zu der Abhandlung von Prof. Pietrusky. (Insurance fraud? Criminalistic and criminal-psychological considerations in determining whether death is accidental or suicidal for sake of insurance. A comment on Pietrusky's article.) Arch. Kriminol., 1937, 100, 234–239. Zwei Gutachten als Beitrag zu der Frage Selbstmord oder Unfall? (Two reports as contributions to the question of suicide or accident.) Vjschr. gerichtl. Med., 1908, 35, 251–261.

Gil Fortun, R. Forma en que se hereda la corea crônica de Huntington y sus posibles relaciones con la demencia suicidal. (The form in which Huntington's chorea is inherited; possible relations to suicidal dementia.) Rev. clin. españ., 1947, 27, 104–111.

Goddard, C. Tod durch Gewehrschuss. Selbstmord, Unglücksfall oder Versicherungsbetrug? (Death from gunshot injury; suicide, accident, or insurance fraud?) Arch. Kriminol., 1932, 90, 141–144.

Goldsmid, J. A. Medico-legal note on cut-throat. Med. J. Aust., 1924, 1, 311.

Gorin, G., and Heger-Gilbert, F. Le diagnostic de l'homicide et du suicide. (The diagnosis of homicide and suicide.) Arch. int. Méd. lég., 1910, 1, 69–77.

Goroney, C. Der Selbstmord in Königsberg i. Pr. (Suicide in Königsberg, Prussia.) Vjschr. ges. gerichtl. Med., 1921, 62, 239–275.

Gorrell, J. Safety lock thwarts suicides. Mod. Hosp., 1944, 62, 110.

Graemiger, O. Beitrag zur Anzeigepflicht des Arztes bei Selbstmord und Selbstmordversuch. (Obligation of physician to report all cases of suicide and attempted suicide.) Schweiz. med. Wschr., 1933, 63, 1261–1264.

Grasso Biondi, I. Se gli accertamenti anatomo-patologici siano sufficienti a differenziare lo sgozzamento da suicidio dallo sgozzamento criminoso. (On whether the evidence is sufficient to differentiate suicidal from criminal cut-throat.) Arch. Antrop. crim., 1935, 55, 886–895.

Grossoni, A. Su un esperimento di assistenza medico-soziale a degenti per tentato suicidio nel Reparto Neuro Deliri dell' Ospedale Maggiore di Milano. (Experiment in medico-social assistance to patients attempting suicide at the neuro-psychiatric clinic of Ospedale Maggiore di Milano.) Minerva Med., 1954, 45, 1642–1643.

Gruhle, H. S. Selbstmord und Praktischer Arzt. (Suicide and the practicing physician.) Med. Klinik, 1933, 29, 379–381.

Grünewald, M. Über Selbstmordstatistik. (Suicide statistics.) Mschr. KrimPsychol., 1927, 18, 41–45.

Grzywo-Dabrowska, Marja. Samobójstwo wspólne oraz zabójstwo z samobójstwem złaczone. (Joint suicide and murder followed by suicide.) Hig. psychiczn., 1936, 2, 75–98.

Grzywo-Dabrowski, W. (Question of suicide or homicide by means of short firearm.) Warsz. Czas. lek., 1932, 9, 78, 100, 124.

Guareschi, G. Criteri diagnostici differenziali fra suicidio, omicidio ed accidente nelle lesioni da ordigni esplosivi. (Differential diagnostic criteria for suicide, homicide, and accidents by lesions from explosive contrivances.) Minerva med.-leg., 1951, 71, 89–96.

Guija Morales, E. Estudio médicolegal de la muerte por precipitación. (Medico-legal study of death by jumping from height.) Arch. Med. Cirug., 1932, 35, 281–287.

Gummersbach, H. Der Selbstmord. (Suicide.) Kriminalist. Mh., 1935, 9, 268–272.

Hájek, F. (Significance of gag found in mouth of suicide.) Čas. Lék. čes., 1937, 76, 989–991.

Hambourger, W. E. A study of the promiscuous use of the barbiturates. Their use in suicides. J. Amer. med. Ass., 1939, 112, 1340–1343.

Harbitz, F. Axthiebe-Mord oder Selbstmord. (Ax-murder or suicide.) Svenska LäkSällsk. Handl., 1934, 60, 266–268. Kasuistische gerichtlich-medizinische Erfahrungen bei der Beurteilung von Hiebwunden (Mord, Selbstmord, Unglücksfall). (Medicolegal study of injuries caused by severe blows [murder, suicide, accident].) Dtsch. Z. ges. gerichtl. Med., 1934, 22, 407–418.

Hart, R. N. The nervous phenomena following attempted suicide by hanging. Lancet, 1906, 1, 1821.

Hausbrandt, F. Selbstmord durch Erhängen in "geistiger Umnachtung," Versicherungsbetrug oder tödlicher Unfall bei sexueller Betätigung eines Transvestiten? (Beitrag zur Fehlbeurteilung sexualpathologischer Tatbestände und ihre versicherungsrechtliche Auswirkung.) (Suicide by hanging in "mental derangement," insurance fraud or fatal accident by the sexual practices of a transvestite? [Contribution on the misjudgement of the sexual-pathological facts of a case and their legal insurance consequences].) Dtsch. Z. ges. gerichtl. Med., 1941, 34, 412–422.

Head injuries and suicide. Med. Pr., 1903, 76, 149.

Heller. Un cas de tentative de suicide dans un état crepusculaire affectif. (Suicide attempt in a twilight affective state.) Strasbourg-méd., 1932, 92, 103.

Heller, A. Zur Lehre vom Selbstmorde nach 300 Sectionen. (Observations on suicide based on three hundred autopsies.) Münch. med. Wschr., 1900, 47, 1653–1658.

Hemenway, H. B. Report of the committee on publishing details of suicides in the public press. Bull. Amer. Acad. Med., 1911, 12, 253–263.

Hernet, M. N. (Criminality and suicide during and after the war.) Moscow: C.S.U., U.S.S.R., 1927.

Herrero, F. M. G., and de Echaben y Canino, F. J. La huelga del hambre. Su estudio médicolegal. (Hunger strike; medicolegal point of view.) Crón. méd., Valencia, 1932, 36, 463–473.

Heuyer, G., Desclaux, P., and Diatkine, R. Aspects particuliers médico-légaux du suicide collectif. (Particular medico-legal aspects of collective suicide.) Acta Med. leg. soc., 1948, 1, 259–265.

Hiller, K. Die Kriminalistische Bedeutung des Selbstmordes. (The criminological significance of suicide.) Heidelberg: 1908.

Hoff, H., and Ringel, E. Der Selbstmordversuch, seine Behandlung und Prophylaxe. (Treatment and prevention of suicide attempts.) Wien. Z. Nervenh., 1956, 12, 286–317.

Hoisholt, A. W. Suicide and alcohol. Calif. St. J. Md., 1909, 7, 61–64; J. Inebr., 1909, 31, 93–100.

Horáček, J. (Influence of menstruation on suicide among women.) Čas. Lek. čes., 1936, 75, 1173–1174.

Hossain, K. Suicidal poisoning in Calcutta. Indian med. Gas., 1946, 81, 418–422.

Hoyer, H. Über die Bedeutung des psychischen Traumas fur den Suicideversuch und die daraus resultierenden Konsequenzen für den Krankenhausarzt. (Importance of psychic trauma in attempted suicide from the viewpoint of the hospital physician.) Z. ges. inn. Med., 1956, 11, 951–953.

Hübner, H. Selbstmord oder "zufälliges Erhängen" aus sexuellen Motiven? (Suicide or "accidental hanging" from sexual motives?) Ärztl. SachverstZtg., 1927, 33, 134–136.

Huhtala, A. Kuolemaan johtaneista myrkytyksistä Suomessa 1936–49. (Mortality from poisoning in Finland 1936–49.) Duodecim, 1953, 27, 1–49.

Hulst, J. P. L. (Double murder and suicide.) Ned. Tijdschr. Geneesk., 1921, 2, 2688–2694; (Suicide or murder?) Ned. Tijdschr. Geneesk., 1925, 2, 698–709.

Hunter, R. C. A. General orientation toward the suicidal patient. McGill med. J., 1952, 21, 88–91.

Ichok, G. À propos du rôle des toxiques dans le suicide. (The role of poisons in suicides.) Biol. méd., Paris, 1935, 25, 79–92.

Im Obersteg, J. Das Selbstmord Problem in der gerichtlichen Medizin. (The suicide problem in legal medicine.) Schweiz. med. Wschr., 1955, 85, 1013–1016.

Inability to prove suicide creates a serious condition. Natl. Underwriter (Life Insurance Section), 1932, 36, (34), 8.

Inekaki, S., and Yamari, S. Decision whether murder or suicide. Gun Igaku Kwai Zasshi, Tokyo, 1902, 798–907.

Introna, F. Studio medico-legale della dinamico del suicidio in una coppia di amanti. (A medico-legal study on the dynamics of suicide in a pair of lovers.) Atti Ist. Med. leg. Assic., 1954, 2, 869–937.

Ipsen, J., Moore, M., and Alexander, L. Prevalence of alcoholism in the population and among suicides and accidents from poisoning, Massachusetts, 1938–1948. Quart. J. Stud. Alcohol., 1952, 13, 204–214.

Jefferson, F. A. The control of the sale of poisonous drugs purchased for the purpose of suicide. Chicago. med. Rec., 1913, 35, 649–653.

Jochmus. Unfall und Selbstmord. (Accident and suicide.) Wschr. Unfallheilk., 1942, 49, 311–315.

Johnsen, G., and Vogt, E. Selvmordforsøk med gift; 306 tilfelle hos 278 pasienter. (Suicide by poison; 306 cases in 278 patients.) Nord. Med., 1950, 43, 1013–1017.

Kaewel, R. Die Bedeutung der Selbsttötung in der Lebensversicherung. (The importance of the question of suicide in life insurance.) Mschr. Unfallheilk., 1938, 45, 137–141.

Kassai, A. (Alcohol content of blood of suicides.) Orv. Hétil., 1939, 83, 465–466.

Keferstein. Mord oder Selbstmord? (Murder or suicide?) Vjschr. gerichtl. Med., 1911, 42, 32–35.

Kersten, P. M. Suicide and the physician. Iowa med. J., 1955, 45, 610–614.

Kiernan, J. G. Forensic aspect of double suicide. Alien. & Neurol., 1904, 25, 273–291. Insane suicide, insane homicide, or murder, which? Alien. & Neurol., 1904, 25, 421.

Koopmann. Unfall bei abwegiger sexueller Betätigung oder Selbstmord? (Accident from sexual perversion or suicide?) Arch. Kriminol., 1942, 110, 60–61.

Köppen. Zur Frage der Beurteilung des Selbstmordes in Versicherungsangelegenheiten. (On the question of the estimation of suicide in insurance actuarial importance.) Charité-Ann., 1911, 35, 256–275.

Krauss, P. Selbsttötung und Kriegsbeschädigung. (Suicide and war disability.) Nervenarzt, 1957, 28, 516–518.

Krauss, W. Ein Selbstmord unter schwerem Verdacht des Muttermordes. (Suicide under heavy suspicion of matricide.) Arch. krimAnthrop., 1913, 51, 243–259.

Kuhr, Elfriede. Das Selbstmordproblem in der Lebensversicherung. (The suicide problem in life insurance.) Z. ges. VersichWiss., 1931, 31, 49–68.

Kurpjuweit, O. Ein Beitrag zur Frage de Selbsterdrosselung. (Contribution to the question of self-strangulation.) Vjschr. gerichtl. Med., 1908, 36, 81–87.

Lacassagne, A., and Martin, E. Tentative de decóllation à l'aide d'un couteau de cuisine, puis submersion; suicide double diagnostic differentiel du suicide et de l'homicide. (Attempt to behead with a kitchen knife, then submersion; double suicide—differential diagnosis between suicide and homicide.) Arch. Antrop. crim., 1903, 18, 571–577.

Laignel-Lavastine, and d'Heucqueville, G. Barbiturisme chronique d'asile, barbiturisme aigu d'hôpital et toxicomanie barbiturique. (Chronic barbiturism in an asylum, acute barbiturism in a hospital, and barbituric toxicomania.) Clinique, Paris, 1938, 33, 2–5.

Laignel-Lavastine, Gallot, H. M., and Feld, M. Section du médian et des artères du poignet gauche, par tentative de suicide liée a un choc emotif chez une neurosyphilitique. (Section of the median nerve and of arteries of the left wrist in attempted suicide after an emotional shock in a female neurosyphilitic.) Ann. méd.-psychol., 1939, 97(1), 791–794.

Larremore, W. Suicide and the law. Harvard Law Rev., 1904, 17, 331–341.

Lattes, L. La diagnosi medico-legale del suicidio doppio e dell' omicidio-suicidio. (The medico-legal diagnoses of double suicide and of homicide-suicide.) Riv. Med. leg., Pisa, 1916, 6, 201, 223. Le suicide masqué. (Disguised suicide.) Ann. Méd. lég., 1935, 15, 875–889. Der getarnte Selbsmord. (Disguised suicide.) Arch. Kriminol., 1940, 106, 1–15.

Laubenthal, F. Forman, Bedingungen, und Prophylaxe des Schlafmittelsmissbrauchs. (Forms, conditions, and prophylaxis of misuse of hypnotics.) Dtsch. med. J., 1955, 6, 303–309.

The law relating to attempted suicide. Brit. med. J., Suppl., 1947, 1, 103.

Legal medicine and suicides. Penn. Hlth. Bull., 1943, 4, 8.

Le Savoureux, H. Contribution à l'étude des perversions de l'instinct de conservation: le spleen. (Contributions to the study of perversions of the instinct.) Paris: Steinheil, 1913.

Leuw, K. Selbstrangulation, Selbstmord oder Zufalltod? (Self-strangulation, suicide, or accidental death?) Dtsch. Z. ges. gerichtl. Med., 1923, 2, 543–549.

Levontin, M. Epidemic of suicides. Harefuah, 1950, 38, 198.

Liebegott, G. Seltener kombinierter Selbstmord und seine versicherungsrechtlicher Auswirkung. (Rare combined suicide and its legal insurance aspects.) Dtsch. Z. ges. gerichtl. Med., 1949, 39, 351–355.

Littlejohn, H. On suicide. Edinb. med. J., 1899, 6, 222–233.

Lopes, C. Diagnóstico de enforcamento e da sua origem (suicídio, acidente ou homicídio). (Diagnosis of hanging and of its cause [suicide, accident or homicide].) Portug. méd., 1945, 29, 361–384.

Lorthiois, M. M. E. J. De l'automutilation; mutilations et suicides étranges. (Self-mutilation; strange mutilations and suicides.) Paris: Vigot, 1909.

Loudet, O. Alienación mental, suicidio y seguro de vida. (Mental disease, suicide and life insurance.) Rev. Asoc. méd. argent., 1933, 47, 2888–2892.

Loudet, O., and Martínez Dalke, L. Epilepsia y suicidio. (Epilepsy and suicide.) Rev.

Criminol., B. Aires, 1934, 21, 396–403; Sem. méd., B. Aires, 1934, 2, 394–397; Rev. Asoc. méd. argent., 1934, 48, 766–772.

Mackie, W. C. Are autopsies necessary in cases of suicide? Trans. Mass. med.-leg. soc., 1917, 5, 41–43.

Mackintosh, J. S. A problem in medico-legal psychology. Lancet, 1903, 2, 451.

Maigne. Le suicide barbiturique et les empoisonnements barbituriques. (Barbital suicide and barbital poisonings.) Ann. Méd.-lég., 1939, 19, 490–492.

Manes, A. Suicide as an insurance problem. J. Amer. Insur., 1932, 9, 23–24.

Manson, E. Suicide as a crime. J. Soc. Compar. Legis., 1899, 1, 311–319.

Marchand, L. and Ajuriaguerra, J. Du suicide chez les epileptiques. (Suicide among epileptics.) Pr. méd., 1941, 49, 407–411.

Marri, R. Dati statistici clinico-tossicologici raccolti in Firenze nel triennio 1935–1937. (Statistical, clinico-toxicological data on Florence in the years 1935–1937.) Riv. Clin. med., 1938, 39, 253–261.

Mauss, W. Unfall, Selbstmordversuch oder traumatischer Dämmerzustand. (Accident, suicide attempt, or traumatic twilight sleep?) Münch. med. Wschr., 1935, 82, 621–622.

Maync, H. Mord oder Selbstmord durch Erhängen. Ein Beitrag zu dieser Frage unter besonderer Berücksichtigung der Lage des Erhängten. (Homicide or suicide by hanging. A contribution to this question with particular regard to the position of those hanged.) Beitr. gerichtl. Med., 1942, 16, 80–99.

McGraw, R. B. Legal aspects of termination of pregnancy on psychiatric grounds. N. Y. St. J. med., 1956, 56, 1605–1609.

Mehl. Überfall und Mordversuch oder Selbstmordversuch? Meineid eines Schwerverletzten angesichts des todes. (Attack and murder attempt or suicide? Perjury of a severely wounded person facing death.) Arch. krimAnthrop., 1912, 47, 54–57.

Meixner, K. Selbstmord infolge körperlicher Schmerzen. (Suicide owing to physical pain.) Dtsch. Z. ges. gerichtl. Med., 1928, 12, 133–136.

Mikell, W. C. Is suicide murder? Columbia Law Rev., 1903, 3, 379–394.

Minty, L. M. Murder as a fine art. Med. leg. J., Cambr., 1957, 25, 11–22.

Mirto, D., and Nicoletti, F. Su di un caso di impiccamento simulante il suicidio e preceduto da morte per strangolamento. (Case of hanging simulating suicide and preceded by death by strangulation.) Arch. Antrop. crim., 1933, 53, 291–315.

Misliveček, Z. Sebevražda v pojišt'ovacím rízení. (Suicide in insurance proceedings.) Čas. Lék. čes., 1948, 87, 252–256.

Moloney, J. C. The biospheric aspects of Japanese death by suicide. Samīkṣā, 1949, 3, 104–124.

Morelli, A., and Preziosi, P. Considerazioni clinico-statistiche su l'ossicarbonismo accidentale, professionale e a scopo suicida. (Clinico-statistical considerations of carbon-monoxide poisoning; accidental, industrial and of suicidal intent.) Folia med., Napoli, 1953, 36, 640–657.

Morgenstern, Z. (Gunshot wounds in suicides.) Sudeb.-med. Ekspertiza, 1928, 8, 20–25.

Morgenthaler, W. Selbstmord und Zurechnungsfähigkeit. (Suicide and the subject's responsibility for his actions.) Schweiz. med. Wschr., 1940, 79, 865–866.

Mosdzien, K. Beitrag zur Lösung des Selbstmordproblems. Ein Vergleich von Motiv mit pathologisch-anatomischen Befunden. (Contribution to the solution of the suicide problem. A comparison of motive with pathological-anatomical findings.) Dtsch. Z. ges. gerichtl. Med., 1925, 6, 53–63.

Mouezy-Eon, A. Les medicaments du suicide. (The medicines of suicide.) Paris: Pharmacie Homéopathique Boiron, (n.d.) [195–?]

Mueller, B. Eigenartige Befunde an den Handen bei Selbstmord durch Erschiessen nebst Bermerkungen uber die kriminaltechnische Untersuchung der Patronenhulsen. (Peculiar findings on the hands after suicide by shooting and notes on the criminalistic technical examination of cartridge shells.) Dtsch. Z. ges. gerichtl. Med., 1933, *21*, 190–201. Schuss in die linke Schläfe. Mord oder Selbstmord? Beinflussung der Lokalisation der Einschussöffnung durch die gegenwärtige Frauenhutmode bei Selbstmord. (Gunshot in left temple. Murder or suicide? Influence, in suicide, of the localization of the bullet hole by current styles in women's hats.) Arch. Kriminol., 1933, *93*, 52–59.

Muller, M. Le diagnostic de l'homicide et du suicide par coup de revolver. (Diagnosis of murder or suicide with revolver shot.) Echo méd. Nord, 1934, *1*, 233–238.

Munck, W. Blutalkoholbestimmung bei Selbstmord. (Blood alcohol determination in suicides.) Dtsch. Z. ges. gerichtl. Med., 1940, *33*, 233–243.

Mysliveček, Z. (Suicide in insurance practice.) Čas. Lék. čes., 1948, *87*, 252–256.

Nannini, M. C. Considerazioni medico-legali sul reperto di aghi nell' organismo umano. (Medico-legal studies on the effect of needles on the human organism.) G. Clin. med., 1941, *22*, 147–154.

Neeser, J. À propos de cinquante-six cas d'intoxication barbiturique aiguë. (On fifty-six cases of acute barbituric intoxication.) Rev. méd. Suisse rom., 1939, *59*, 159–169.

Neste, E. Die Beziehungen des Status thymico-lymphaticus zum Selbstmord von Soldaten. (The relation of status thymicolymphaticus to suicide of soldiers.) Arch. Psychiat. Nervenkr., 1919, *60*, 43–71.

Neugebauer, W. Zur Frage Selbstmord oder Mord durch Erhängen. (The question of suicide or murder by hanging.) Dtsch. Z. ges. gerichtl. Med., 1937, *28*, 111–131. Selbstmord oder leichtfertig verschulder Tod durch den elektrischen Strom. (Suicide or accidental death from electric current.) Arch. Kriminol., 1938, *102*, 162–169.

Neuvicq, E. La responsabilité des établissements de soins en cas de suicide d'un malade atteint de maladie mentale. (Responsibility of sanitaria in cases of suicide of persons with mental illnesses.) Gaz. med. Fr., 1956, *63*, 1637.

Niedermeyer, A. Noch ein Wort zur "Selbstmordindikation für den künstlichen Abort." (Further word on "suicidal intent as indication for abortion.") Dtsch. med. Wschr., 1926, *52*, 714.

Niedermeyer, E. Untersuchungen bei suizidalem Erhängen. (EEG studies of suicidal hanging.) Wien. klin. Wschr., 1956, *68*, 555–556.

Numa Damonte, E. Importancia etiológica en el peritaje medicolegal por "suicidio a forma rara." (Etiological importance in a medico-legal expertise for a "suicide of a rare form.") Sem. méd., B. Aires, 1940, *2*, 546–550.

O'Dea, A. E. Medicolegal and pathological aspects of suicide. R. I. med. J., 1953, *36*, 245–247.

Olbrycht, J. (Murder, suicide or accident?) Polsk. Gaz. lek., 1936, *15*, 293, 317.

Oldfield, J. The suicide idea and capital punishment. Trans. med.-leg. Soc., Lond., 1921, *14*, 38–58.

Orth. Mord oder Selbstmord? Ein weiterer Betrag zu der besonders für die Aufklärung von Lebensverischerungs- und Einbruchversicherungsbetrug wichtigen Frage der Selbsfesselung. (Murder or suicide? A further contribution to the important question of tying self up, particularly in the clarification of life insurance and burglary insurance fraud cases.) Arch. Kriminol., 1935, 96, 203–208.

Palazzo, D. Il suicidio sotto l'aspetto fisiopatological. (The physiopathological aspect of suicide.) Napoli: E. Jovene, 1953.

Palmer, A. A. An interesting medico-legal case (double suicide?). Indian med. Rec., 1904, 25, No. 12, 18.

Palmerio, P. Il veleno della "morte bianca" e le recenti disposizioni legislative per la disciplina farmaceutica dei barbiturici. (The poison of the "white death" and the recent legislation for pharmaceutic control of barbiturics.) G. Med. milit., 1952, 102, 47–49.

Parabutschew, A. Status thymicus bei Selbstmördern als morphologischer Ausdruck der Störungen des inkretorischen Systems. (Status thymicus of suicides as morphologic expression of disturbances of the endocrine system.) Virchows Arch., 1929, 273, 134–139.

Parsons, R. W. Suicide; its considerations from a medical standpoint. Med. News, N.Y., 1905, 86, 1061–1067.

Pearson, C. B. Has there been an increase of suicide among the opium addicts since the passage of the Harrison Act, and if so why? Alien. Neurol., 1915, 36, 349–356.

Pedrazzini, A. L'omicidio del consenziente ed il suicidio nel diritto penale contemporaneo; con particolare riguardo al Codice penale svizzero. (Homicide by consent and suicide in contemporary penal law; with particular regard to the Swiss penal code.) Tesi, Locarno, 1949.

Pessler. Vorgestäuschte Selbstmorde; aus der Braunschweigischen Strafrechtspraxis. (Simulated suicide; from the practice of jurisprudence in Braunschweig.) Arch. KrimAnthrop., 1913, 55, 271–322.

Pfeiffer, H. Über den Selbstmord. (Suicide.) Jena: Fischer, 1912.

Phillips, W. F. R. Seasonal influence on suicide. Mon. Cyclop. med. Bull., 1909, 2, 522–528.

Piédlièvre, R., and Gaultier, M. Art et suicide; à propos d'une observation médico-légale. (Art and suicide; a medicolegal observation.) Paris méd., 1951, 41, 13–15.

Pietrusky, F. Versicherungsbetrug? Naturwissenschaftliche-kriminalistische und kriminalpsychologische Untersuchungen zur Frage Selbstmord oder Unfall. (Insurance fraud? Natural-scientific, criminalistic and criminal-psychological investigation of the question of suicide or accident.) Arch. Kriminol., 1936, 99, 21–27. Versicherungsbetrug? Bemerkungen zu der Äusserung von Prof. Giese. (The question of insurance fraud. Remarks to the comment of Professor Giese.) Arch. Kriminol., 1937, 100, 240–244.

Pinkham, J. G. Was it murder or suicide? The case of Edgar W. Meikle. Trans. Mass. med.-leg. Soc., 1917, 5, 44–53.

Plotner, E. Über die Rechtsprechung des RVA bei Selbstmord. (Jurisdiction of the government insurance lawyer in suicide.) Ärztl. SachverstZtg., 1923, 29, 181–186.

Prieur, A. Une enquête sur le suicide. (Inquiry into suicide.) Trib. méd., Paris, 1897, 30, 28–31.

Prokop, J. Zylástni lokalisace reznych ran pri sebevražedném pokusu duševne choré ženy. (The unusual location of self-inflicted cuts made by a mentally ill woman during an attempt at suicide.) Čas. Lék. čes., 1947, 86, 103–106.

Pronger, C. E. Insomnia and suicide. Amer. Med., 1914, 9, 648–654; Lancet, 1914, 2, 1356–1359.

Protigliatti-Barbos, M. Sulla frequenza degli omicidii e suicidii con arma blanca e con arma da punta e taglio in particolare. (Frequency of homicides and suicides with side-arms and with pointed and edged weapons in particular.) Acta Med. leg. soc., 1957, 10, 501–511.

Punzo, G. In tesi de diagnosi differenziale tra omicidio e suicidio. (On the differential diagnosis between homicide and suicide.) Rass. int. Clin. Terap., 1929, 10, 321–332.

Rehfeldt. Zum Selbstmordproblem. (On the problem of suicide.) Kriminalist. Mh., 1929, Sonderbeil. No. 3, 37–60.

Reichel, H. Dissimulierter Selbstmordversuch. (Simulated attempted suicide.) Arch. KrimAnthrop., 1910, 38, 153.

Reinsberg, J. Sebevražda utopenim aneb viazda? (Suicide by drowning or murder?) Soudné lék. Pos. čes. lék. Fak., 1909, 16–21.

Rennert, H. Über die versorgungsgutachtliche Beurteilung eines Falles von Selbsttötung bei Morphiumsucht nach Dienstbeschädigung. (Evaluation of compensation in a case of suicide in morphine addiction after military service.) Psychiat. Neurol. med. Psychol., 1952, 4, 246–248.

Reuter, F. Tötung durch Erwürgen mit nachträglichem Aufhängen der Leiche zur Vortäuschen eines Selbstmordes. (Killing by strangling with subsequent hanging up of the corpse, feigning a suicide.) Dtsch. Z. ges. gerichtl. Med., 1929, 14, 449–454. Aufdeckung eines Falles von vorgetäuschtem Selbstmord durch Ertrinken. (Discovery of a case of murder by drowning made to appear as suicide.) Arch. Kriminol., 1937, 100, 53–62.

Rezek, P. P. Suicide and insanity from the pathologist's viewpoint. Postgrad. Med., 1954, 16, A50, A52, A54, A56.

Ribeiro, E. B. Fractura fissuraria da extremidade inferior do; a proposito de um laudo medico-legal. (Fissural fracture of lower end of femur; medico-legal expertise.) Ann. paulist. Med. Cir., 1936, 32 (July), 23–53.

Ribeiro, L. Homicidio, suicidio ou acidente? Consulta medico-legal—resposta. (Homicide, suicide, or accident? A medico-legal opinion—reply.) Folha med., 1945, 26, 33–34.

Richardson, O., and Breyfogle, H. S. Medicolegal problems in distinguishing accident from suicide. Ann. intern. Med., 1946, 25, 22–65.

Ringel, E., and Wallentin, G. Zur Frage der Anerkennung des Selbstmordes als Dienstbeschädigung. (The problem of recognition of suicide as a military service injury.) Wien. med. Wschr., 1953, 103, 545–549.

Robinovitch, Louise G. Suicidal and homicidal acts. Their clinical aspects and medicolegal significance. J. ment. Path., 1903/04, 5, 7–36, 71–85, 137–147.

Rode, W. Die Grösse des Einschusses und des Ausschusses. Zur Klärung der Frage: Tötung durch eigene oder fremde Hand. (Size of the entrance and exit orifices of bullet wounds. On the clarification of the question of death by one's own or a strange hand.) Arch. Kriminol., 1937, 101, 77–80.

Rodiet, A. Tentative de suicide chez une alienée par déglutition voluntaire d'un fragment d'os de côtelette. (Suicide attempt by a psychotic by voluntarily swallowing a piece of cutlet bone.) Progr. méd., Paris, 1912, 465.

Rogari, E. Considerazioni medico-legali sui 1500 casi di suicidio osservati nell' Instituto di medicina legale di Roma a tutto l'anno 1939. (Medico-legal study of 1500 cases observed in the Institute of Legal Medicine of Rome in 1939.) Arch. Antrop. crim., 1940, 60, 937–949.

Roimiser, I. Intento de suicidio por intoxicación oxicarbonada en una psicosis paranoide. Curación immediata depués de prolongado coma. (Suicide attempt by carbon monoxide asphyxiation in a paranoid psychotic. Immediate cure after prolonged coma.) Rev. Asoc. méd. argent., 1945, 59, 76–78.

Rooks, G. Die Lage der Einschusswunde bei Selbstmord und Mord. (The position of gunshot wound in suicide and murder.) Arch. Kriminol., 1935, 96, 156–161.

Royer, P., and Broussolle, P. Prophylaxie du suicide par les barbituriques. (Prevention of suicide by barbiturates.) Rev. méd. Nancy, 1953, 78, 216–219.

Rudolf, W. Selbstmord, ein medizinisches Problem. (Suicide as a medical problem.) Med. Klinik, 1953, 48, 643–644.

Ruggeri, R. G. Il suicidio nell'encefalite letargica dei fanciulli ed adolescenti. (Suicide among children and adolescents with encephalitus lethargica.) Riv. sper. Freniat., 1943, 58, 1491–1498.

Säker, G. Ärztliches zum Selbstmordproblem. (Medical aspects of the suicide problem.) Münch. med. Wschr., 1938, 782–785.

Salomao, A. Ligeiras consideracôes acêrca de 3 casos de tentativa de suicidio em leprosos. (Legal considerations of 3 suicide attempts in lepers.) Arq. min. Leprol., 1947, 7, 27–29.

Schackwitz, A. Die Untersuchungen der Selbstmordfälle am Institut für gerichtliche Medizin. (Studies on suicide cases at the Institute for Legal Medicine.) Med. Klinik, 1920, 16, 1272; Münch. med. Wschr., 1921, 68, 91.

Schlegel. Mord oder Selbstmord! (Murder or suicide!) Arch. Kriminol., 1937, 100, 18–26.

Schneider, P. Mord durch Krebelung und Ertränken oder Selbstmord? (Question of murder or suicide by gagging and drowning.) Dtsch. Z. ges. gerichtl. Med., 1935, 25, 27–30.

Schneikert, H. Selbstmörderbriefe. (Suicide notes.) Arch. Kriminol., 1937, 101, 65–70.

Schottky, J. Über den Mordversuch eines Jugendlichen bei geplantem Selbstmord. Beitrag zur kriminalbiologischen Beurteilung asocialer Psychopathen. (An attempt at murder by an adolescent contemplating suicide. Contribution to the criminal-biological judgement of asocial psychopaths.) Mschr. KrimBiol., 1941, 32, 1–32.

Schou, H. I. (Phenobarbital preparations as means of suicide.) Ugeskr. Læg., 1932, 94, 492–493.

Schraepel, G. Die kriminalistische Bedeutung der kataleptischen Totenstarre. Selbstmord? Notwehr? Vatermord? (The criminal significance of cataleptic rigor mortis; question of suicide, self-defense, or parricide.) Arch. Kriminol., 1934, 94, 8–21.

Schultz, E. Der Kampf um die Rente und der Selbstmord in der Rechtsprechung des Reichservsicherungsamtes. (The struggle over compensation in suicide and the jurisdiction of the federal insurance court.) Samml. zwangl. Abh. Nervenkr., 1910, 10, 1–73.

Schwartz, F. Probleme des Selbstmordes. (Problems of suicide.) Berne: Huber, 1946.

Schwarz, H. Ein durch einen ungewöhnlichen Selbstmordversuch kompliziertes forensisch psychiatrisches Gutachten. (Forensic-psychiatric evaluation complicated by an unusual suicide attempt.) Psychiat. Neurol. med. Psychol., 1952, 4, 206–211.

Schwellnus. Unfall und Selbstmord. (Accidents and suicide.) Mschr. Unfallheilk., 1942, 49, 193–203. Erwiderung zu dem Artikel über "Unfall und Selbstmord" von Dr. Jochmus, Berlin. (Reply to the article on "Accidents and suicide" by Dr. Jochmus.) Mschr. Unfallheilk., 1942, 49, 316–317.

Selbstmord und Verbrechen infolge Hypnose? (Suicide and crime as results of hypnosis?) Arch. Kriminol., 1930, 87, 254–255.

Sen, A. N. Case of medico-legal interest. Indian med. Gaz., 1928, 63, 452.

Senff, A. Analyse von 1000 Selbstmordfällen unter besonderer Berücksichtigung bevolkerungspolitischer und versicherungstechnischer Belange. (Analysis of 1000 cases of suicide with special regard to the importance of the political population and the technical aspects of insurance.) Inaug. Diss., Berlin, 1936.

Shaw, T. C. Suicide and sanity. Trans. med.-leg. Soc., Lond., 1906/07, 6, 45–57; Lancet, 1907, 1, 1067–1069.

Sheppe, W. M. The emergency treatment of attempted suicide. Neuropsychiatry, 1951/52, 1, (4), 28–38.

Siéngalewicz, S. (Suicide from a pathological viewpoint.) Lwow. Tyg. lek., 1913, 8, 601, 613, 625.

Sieradzki, W. (Unusual medico-legal case of the genesis of suicide.) Lwow. Tyg. lek., 1912, 7, 356–360.

Simon, C. Suicide from a medical standpoint. Med.-leg. J., N.Y., 1900/01, 18, 204–206.

Sjövall, H. Om diagnosen självmord. (Diagnosis of suicide.) Svenska Läkartidn., 1953, 50, 1113–1140.

Slank. (Various methods of suicide.) Čas. Lék. čes., 1914, 53, 505–511.

Slavík, V. Die Mentstruationspsychose, ihre Beziehung zum Strafgesetz und zu der Zahl der Frauenselbstmorde. (Psychoses of menstruation, their relation to penal law and the enumeration of women suicides.) Rev. Méd. tchèque, (Suppl. to: Čas. Lék. čes.) 1909, 2, 112.

Smirnov. (Various signs of suicide by hanging.) Sudeb.-med. ekspertiza, 1928, 9, 41–44.

Soprana, C. Sulle impronte e stampo di parti mobili delle armi automatiche. Interpretazione del mechanismo di formazione. (Imprint of mobile parts of automatic weapons. Interpretation of mechanism of formation.) Zacchia, 1949, 12, 98–103.

Sorel, E. Suicide par submersion, procédé de tentative de suicide par arme à feu; discussion médico-legale. (Suicide by drowning, proceeding from a suicide attempt by a firearm. Medicolegal discussion.) Ann. Hyg. publ., Paris, 1921, 35, 13-17.

Spiegel, H. W. Der Fall Näf. Mord und Versicherungsbetrug, Selbstmord oder Unfall? (The Näf case. Determination of murder or suicide for insurance). Arch. Kriminol., 1937, 100, 98–122.

Spinner, J. R. Über das Vorwiegen der Frauen beim Giftselbstmorde. (On the predominance of women among poison-suicides.) Vjschr. gerichtl. Med., 1917, 54, 294–295. Der Giftselbstmord der Frauen. Zur Kritik der Theorie Überwiegen der Frauen im Giftselbstmord. (Poison suicide of women. Criticism of the theory of the predominance of women poison suicides.) Arch. Frauenk. Eugen., 1918, 4, 93–95.

Steidle, H. Thallium, das neue Mord-und Selbstmordgift. (Thallium, the new murder and suicide poison.) Med. Welt, 1939, 13, 1557–1560.

Steiner, M. Menstruation und Selbstmord. (Menstruation and suicide.) Dtsch. med. Wschr., 1926, 52, 2120–2121.

Steinklauber. Mord oder Selbstmord durch Halschnitt? Widerlegung der belastenden Zeugenaussage der eigenen Tochter durch den ärztlichen Sachverständigenbeweis. (Suicide or murder in a case of cut-throat; medical evidence refuting false witness of the daughter.) Dtsch. Z. ges. gerichtl. Med., 1940, 34, 342–345.

Stone, Margaret N. Αὐτοχειρία. Sixteenth century lawyer on suicide. Bull. Hist. Med., 1943, 14, 173–180.

Störring, G. E. Selbsttötung in versicherungs- und versorgungsärztlicher Hinsicht. (Insurance and socio-medical aspects of suicide.) Hefte z. Unfallheilk., 1956, 52, 27–36.

Suárez y Suárez, G. Envenenamientos frecuentes en Cuba desde el punto de vista médico-legal. (Frequent suicides by poisoning in Cuba from the medico-legal point of view.) Med. latina, Habana, 1954, 13, 1–16.

Suicide. Med.-leg. J. N.Y., 1889–90, 16, 251–256.

Suicide risk. West. J. Surg., 1951, 59, 658–659.

Tammenoms Bakker, S. P. Zelfmoord en zelfverminking in de huizen van bewaring te Amsterdam. (Suicide and self-mutilation in detention homes in Amsterdam.) Ned. Tijdschr. Geneesk., 1953, 97, 263–268.

Tansella, G. Il "suicidio-causa di servizio" in medicina legale militare. (Service-connected suicide in military legal medicine.) Rev. sper. Freniat., 1951, 75, 395–413; Minerva med.-leg., 1952, 72, Suppl., 102–103.

Tardif, F., and Sabatier, A. Mort par strangulation; simulacre de mort accidentelle ou volontaire par submersion—parricide. (Death by strangulation, simulating accidental or voluntary death by drowning; parricide.) Pr. méd., 1914, 22, (annex), 106–107.

Tarsitano, F. Suicidio ed assicurazione malattie. (Suicide and sickness insurance.) Folia med., Napoli, 1947, 30, 65–75.

Thomas, S. B. Suicide as a crime. Med.-leg. J., N.Y., 1900/1901, 18, 322–324.

Thurston, G. Suicide as a crime. Med.-leg. J., Cambr., 1957, 25, 152–154.

Tovo, S. Lo scannamento osservazioni su 39 casi di suicidio e 22 di omicidio. (Observations on cut-throat of 39 cases of suicide and 22 of homicide.) Arch. Anthrop. crim., 1946, 66, 159–184. Sul suicidio e sull'omicidio combinati. (Combined suicide and homicide.) Minerva med.-leg., 1952, 72, 1–26.

Trillot, J. Extériorisation d'une psychose mélancolique au réveil d'un coma barbiturique; tentative de suicide. (Emergence of melancholia on awakening from a barbituric coma; attempted suicide.) Ann. Méd. lég., 1952, 32, 363–364.

Triqueneaux. Auto-éviscération considérée a tort comme un crime. (Auto-evisceration wrongly considered a homicide.) Ann. Méd. lég., 1936, 16, 336–339.

Tubio Ovide, J. M. Consideraciones sobre el suicidio. (Considerations on suicide.) Crón. méd., Lima, 1947, 64, 14, 42.

Use of barbiturates. N. Y. Med., 1950, 6, 30–34.

Van Amberg, R. J. Prognosis of carbon monoxide poisoning in 15 patients, previously mentally ill. Psychiat. Quart., 1942, 16, 668–680.

The verdict of suicide while insane. Lancet, 1902, 2, 1478.

Villamizar Marquez, E. Contribución al estudio médico-legal del suicidio en Bogotá. (Contribution to the medico-legal study of suicide in Bogotá.) Rev. Fac. Med., Bogotá, 1946, 14, 465–480.

Vincent, J. P., Preyssas, J., and Naouri, G. Avortment ou suicide? (Abortion or suicide?) Ann. Méd. lég., 1954, 34, 251–252.

Vinnikoff, V. L. (Suicide by chemical poisons in Astrakhan for five years from 1907–1911, inclusive, according to data of the Astrakhan Municipal Hospital and the Receiving Chamber.) Izv. Obshch. astrakh. Vrach., 1913, 6, 79–84.

von Hentig, H. Gerichtliche Verurteilungen als Mittel des Selbstmordes und der Selbstverstümmelung. (Judicial sentences as means of suicide and of self-mutilation.) Arch. KrimAnthrop., 1913, 54, 54–55. Die jahr zeitliche Periodizität der weiblichen Selbstmöder. (The yearly periodicity of suicide among women.) Mchr. KrimPsychol., 1927, 18, 434.

von Weber. Selbstmord als Mordmotiv. (Suicide as a murder motive.) Mschr. KrimBiol., 1937, 28, 4.

Walcher, K. Enmittelung der Schusswaffe aus den Schussspuren an der Leiche. Mord oder Selbstmord? (Determination of the firearm from bullet marks on the corpse. Murder or suicide?) Arch. Kriminol., 1932, 90, 16–19.

Weatherby, F. E. The admission of violent or suicidal patients to a military hospital. Milit. Surg., 1939, 84, 486–491.

Weimann, W. Selbstmord oder Tötung auf Verlangen? (Suicide or death by request?) Arch. Kriminol., 1932, 90, 111–118. Der Schuss durch die Kleider als Unterscheidungs merkmal zwischen Mord und Selbstmord. (The gunshot wound through clothes as a means of differentiating between murder and suicide.) Arch. Kriminol., 1933, 93, 109–116.

Weinig, E. Die umfassende gerichtsmedizinische Untersuchung als Vorbedingung für die Klarstellung eines fraglichen Mordes. (Comprehensive medicolegal examination as preliminary to solution of suspected murder as case of suicide.) Dtsch. Z. ges. gerichtl. Med., 1940, 32, 494–500.

Weiss, M. O. Attempted suicide; then what? Amer. J. Nurs., 1949, 49, 290–293.

Weisser, G. Arztrechtliche Betrachtungen zum Selbstmord. (Medico-legal consideration of suicide.) Med. Welt, 1951, 20, 226–228.

Wellington, R. H. The verdict of suicide whilst temporarily insane; a legal contradiction. Trans. med.-leg. Soc., Lond., 1902–04, 1, 78–91.

Werther, K. H. Tuberkulose und Selbstmord. (Tuberculosis and suicide.) Inaug. Diss., München, 1953.

Weyrich, G. Blutgruppen, Körperbau und Selbstmord. (Blood groups, body build and suicide.) Dtsch. Z. ges. gerichtl. Med., 1934, 23, 387–390. Körperbau und Selbstmord. (Bodily structure and suicide.) Dtsch. Z. ges. gerichtl. Med., 1935, 24, 284–300.

White, S. E. Suicide in borderland cases. Brit. med. J., 1922, 1, 79–80

Wiingaard, P. Sovemidlerne i søgelyset. (Narcotics and suicide.) Ugeskr. Læg., 1949, 111, 335–337.

Wilder, B. G. Revised interpretation of the central fissures of the educated suicide's brain exhibited to the Association in 1894. J. nerv. ment. Dis., 1900, 27, 537–541.

Williams, G. L. The prohibition of suicide. *In* G. L. Williams, The sanctity of life and the criminal law. New York: Knopf, 1957. Pp. 248–310.

Wuth, O. Selbstmord und Diestbeschädigung. (Suicide and military service injuries.) *In* C. Heinemann-Gruder and E. Rühe (Eds.), Der Arzt in der Wehrmachtversorgung. (The physician in the Wehrmacht supply, (2d ed.) Dresden: Steinkopf, 1942. Pp. 302–313.

zur Redden, J. Das Problem des Selbstmordes unter den Krüppeln. (The problem of suicide among cripples.) Z. Krüppelfürs., 1931, 24, 152–155.

RELIGIOUS—PHILOSOPHICAL

Bayet, A. Le suicide et la morale. (Suicide and morality.) Paris: Alcan, 1922.

Boehm, G. The right to commit suicide. Bull. med.-Leg. Cong., 1895, N.Y., 1898, 462–464.

D'Agostino, V. Plinio il giovane e il problema del suicidio. (Pliny the younger and the problem of suicide.) Arch. ital. Psicol., 1930, 8, 95–126.

Gibbons, J. The moral aspects of suicide. Century Mag., N.Y., 1960/07, 73, 401–407.

Greither, A. Selbstmord und Erziehung. Eine kulturphilosophische, psychologische, und pädagogische Studie. (Suicide and education. A cultural-philosophical, psychological and pedagogical study.) Leipzig: Meiner, 1939.

Gurnhill, J. Morals of suicide. New York: Longmans, 1900.

Holmes, J. H. Is suicide justifiable? New York: John Day, 1934; Toronto: McLeod, 1934.

Hook, S. The ethics of suicide. Int. J. Ethics, 1926/27, 37, 173–188.

Ingersoll, R. G. Is suicide a sin? New York: Eckler, 1899.

Kempf, E. J. The meaning of suicide. New Republic, 1927, 50, 324–327.

Landsberg, P. L. Essai sur l'experience da la mort, suivi de le problème du suicide. (The experience of death. The problem of suicide.) Paris: Editions de Seuil, 1951. The moral problem of suicide. *In* P. L. Landsberg, The experience of death. The moral problem of suicide. (Trans. Cynthia Rowland.) New York: Philosophical Library, 1953. Pp. 65–102.

Lodge, O. The ethics of suicide. Fortnight. Rev., 1921, 110, 594–600.

Meynard, L. Le suicide, étude morale et métaphysique. (Suicide; moral and metaphysical study.) Paris: Pr. Universitaires de France, 1954.

Morgenthaler, W. Selbstmord und Zurechnungsfähigkeit. (Suicide and the subject's responsibility for his actions.) Schweiz. med. Wschr., 1949, 79, 865-866.

Perls, A. Der Selbstmord nach der Halacha. (Suicide according to the Halakah.) Mschr. Gesch. Wiss. Judentums, 1911, 55, 287–295.

Right to die. Brit. med. J., 1911, 2, 1215–1217.

Roberts, H. The ethics of suicide. *In* H. Roberts, Euthanasia, and other aspects of life and death. London: Constable, 1938. Pp. 27–32.

Schnyder, B. Der Selbstmord in katholischer Sicht; zur ärztlichen Beurteilung von römischkatholischen Selbstmördern hinsichtliche eines kirchlichen Begräbnisses. (Suicide from the Catholic point of view; on the physician's evaluation of Roman Catholic suicides regarding a church burial.) Schweiz. med. Wschr., 1946, 76, 393–395.

Schuwer, Camille. La signification métaphysique du suicide. (The metaphysical significance of suicide.) Paris: Aubier, 1949.

Tapie, J. Le suicide et la doctrine chrétienne. (Suicide and the Christian doctrine.) Bull. Soc. Méd. St Luc, 1936, 42, 163–167.

Tong, H. K. Where suicide is a virtue. Independent, N.Y., 1912, 73, 899–901.

von Andics, Margarethe. Über Sinn und Sinnlosigkeit des Lebens. (The meaning and meaningless of life.) Wien: Gerold, 1938. Suicide and the meaning of life. London: Hodge, 1947.

von Olshausen. Das Recht auf den Tod. (The right to die.) Med. Klinik, 1913, 9, 1918.

von Surg, K. Beitrag zur Kasuistik des Selbstmordes während der Geburt. (A contribution to the question of right and wrong of suicide at time of birth.) Münch. med. Wschr., 1908, 55, 1534–1536.

Westermarck, E. Suicide. A chapter in social ethics. Social. Rev., 1908, 1, 12–33.

Name Index

Subject Index